Developments in British Politics 10

10th edition

Edited by

Richard Heffernan

Colin Hay

Meg Russell

Philip Cowley

 macmillan
education   palgrave

© Selection and editorial matter © Richard Heffernan,
Colin Hay, Meg Russell and Philip Cowley 2016

Individual chapters (in order): © Andrew Gamble; Ben Yong and Tim Bale; Alan Renwick;
Paul Webb; Michael Kenny; Meg Russell; Philip Cowley; Maria T. Grasso; Catherine Haddon;
Richard Heffernan; Deborah Mabbett; Maria Sobolewska and Robert Ford; Charlie Jeffrey;
Andrew Geddes; Colin Hay 2016

First published 2016 by
PALGRAVE

Palgrave in the UK is an imprint of Macmillan Publishers Limited,
registered in England, company number 785998, of 4 Crinan Street,
London, N1 9XW.

Palgrave Macmillan in the US is a division of St Martin's Press LLC,
175 Fifth Avenue, New York, NY 10010.

Palgrave is a global imprint of the above companies and is represented
throughout the world.

Palgrave® and Macmillan® are registered trademarks in the United States,
the United Kingdom, Europe and other countries.

ISBN 978–1–137–49473–3 hardback
ISBN 978–1–137–49474–0 paperback

This book is printed on paper suitable for recycling and made from fully
managed and sustained forest sources. Logging, pulping and manufacturing
processes are expected to conform to the environmental regulations of the
country of origin.

A catalogue record for this book is available from the British Library.

A catalog record for this book is available from the Library of Congress.

Printed and bound by CPI Group (UK) Ltd, Croydon, CR0 4YY

To Steven Kennedy, to mark his retirement from Palgrave

Contents

List of Boxes, Figures and Tables

Boxes

Figures

Tables

Preface and Acknowledgements

There are far harder professional tasks in life, but events and happenings which unsettle the present, prompting change, naturally vex editors and writers of chapters in a book such as this. Capturing events in motion is always a challenge, but studying developments in British politics is even more problematic, when developments keep developing. It has always been thus, but this reality was brought home to us editors by Britain's referendum on remaining in or leaving the European Union (EU). In this vote, held on the 23 June 2016, just as this book was going to press, the British people voted on a 72 percent turnout to leave the EU by 52 percent to 48.

This vote to leave, however narrow, prompted the resignation of the Prime Minister, David Cameron, on the morrow of the ballot. Cameron, returned to No 10 at the last election, heading up the first Conservative majority since 1992, fell on his sword because the British people rejected his strongly argued advice to vote remain. It now falls to his successor, the former Home Secretary Theresa May, to lead the government and the country through Brexit, the British exit from the EU. This will now be negotiated between Britain and the EU over the next two or so years. As a result Britain's future relationship with Europe, and with it Britain's place in the world, enters a period of considerable flux. Britain's established political arrangements have become uncertain, with Brexit calling into question the future of the United Kingdom as Scotland, ever pressed to exit the union by a resurgent nationalism, could be seemingly prepared to prioritise being in the EU over remaining part of the UK.

Such unfolding momentous events prove, as scholars of the contemporary world have long known, that study of the present can easily find itself recast as history. Nothing is certain. Events and happenings, prompting change, make the new old quickly. Cameron's premiership, being very much present as this book was prepared, is now past. May's is beginning. But we hope that the chapters in this book will help its readers to explore and explain what has been happening in British politics. They provide a guide – especially in terms of background and context – to contemporary events.

This is the tenth edition of Developments in British Politics and it is published some 33 years after the first. A third of a century is a long time in politics. We editors used many earlier editions as students. For this edition Meg Russell has joined the editorial team. As always, the list of authors is completely new. We are entirely in their debt, not only for their expertise and insights, but for their forbearance in the face of the numerous exacting demands made of them. Not least in their happy willingness to recast settled chapters in light of unfolding and significant events. Our grateful thanks to them all. Steven Kennedy, our redoubtable Palgrave publisher, shepherded all past editions to press, but has now retired, so we have found ourselves in the very capable hands of his successor, Stephen Wenham. Our thanks to Stephen W. And our best wishes in his retirement to Steven K., to whom we dedicate this edition.

Richard Heffernan
Colin Hay
Meg Russell
Philip Cowley

Notes on Contributors

Tim Bale is Professor of Politics at Queen Mary University of London where he specialises in British and European Politics. He is the author of, among other books, *The Conservative Party: From Thatcher to Cameron* and *European Politics: A Comparative Introduction*, both of which are published in new editions in 2016.

Philip Cowley is Professor of Politics at Queen Mary University of London.

Robert Ford is Professor of Political Science at the University of Manchester.

Andrew Gamble is Professor of Politics at the University of Sheffield and Emeritus Professor of Politics at the University of Cambridge. His most recent books include *Crisis Without End? The Unravelling of Western Prosperity* (2014) and *Can the Welfare State Survive?* (2016).

Andrew Geddes is Professor of Politics at the University of Sheffield and holds, for the period 2014–2019, an Advanced Investigator Grant from the European Research Council for a project on the drivers of global migration governance.

Maria Grasso is Lecturer in Politics and Quantitative Methods at the University of Sheffield and Deputy European Editor of *Mobilization*. She is the author of *Generations, Political Participation and Social Change in Western Europe* (Routledge, 2016) and co-editor of *Austerity and Protest: Popular Contention in Times of Economic Crisis* (Routledge, 2015). She is Principal Investigator on two European collaborative projects on citizens in times of crisis (LIVEWHAT, FP7, 2013–16) and transnational solidarity (TransSOL, H2020, 2015–18).

Catherine Haddon is resident historian at the Institute for Government. She joined the Institute in November 2008 from academia. She leads the Institute's work on the history of Whitehall and reform, the constitution and the civil service, and on managing changes of government. She is currently leading an AHRC-funded joint project with King's College London, on the history of Whitehall 1979–2010.

Colin Hay is Professor of Political Science at Sciences Po, Paris, and an Affiliate Professor of Political Analysis at the University of Sheffield where he co-founded the Sheffield Political Economy Research Institute. He is the author of many books including, most recently, *Civic Capitalism* (Polity, 2015, with Anthony Payne), *The Legacy of Thatcherism* (Oxford University Press, 2014, with Stephen Farrall), *The Failure of Anglo-Liberal Capitalism* (Palgrave, 2013) and *The Political Economy of European Welfare Capitalism* (Palgrave, 2012, with Daniel Wincott). He is lead editor of *New Political Economy* and founding co-editor of *Comparative European Politics* and *British Politics*. He is a Fellow of the UK Academy of Social Science.

Richard Heffernan is a Reader in Government at the Open University and a Visiting Professor at the University of Notre Dame.

Charlie Jeffery is Professor of Politics and Senior Vice Principal at the University of Edinburgh. He directed the Economic and Social Research Councils Future of the UK and Scotland Programme in 2013–2015, focused on the Scottish independence referendum.

Michael Kenny is Director of the Mile End Institute and Professor of Politics at Queen Mary University of London. He is the author of *The Politics of English Nationhood* (2014), *The Politics of Identity* (2004) and co-editor of *Rethinking British Decline* (1999).

Deborah Mabbett is Professor of Public Policy in the Department of Politics, Birkbeck, University of London. She has published widely on political economy and social policy in journals such as *Politics and Society*, *Review of International Political Economy* and *Regulation and Governance*. She is co-editor of the journal *Political Quarterly*.

Alan Renwick is Deputy Director of the Constitution Unit at University College London. His research analyses electoral systems, electoral reforms, and referendums in the UK and around the world. He is most recently the author, with Jean-Benoit Pilet, of *Faces on the Ballot: The Personalization of Electoral Systems in Europe* (Oxford University Press, 2016).

Meg Russell is Professor of British and Comparative Politics in the School of Public Policy, University College London (UCL), where she is also Director of the Constitution Unit. She has written extensively on parliament and parliamentary reform, her most recent book being *The Contemporary House of Lords: Westminster Bicameralism Revived*

(Oxford University Press, 2013). She is a former specialist adviser to the Leader of the House of Commons and to the Select Committee on Reform of the House of Commons, among others.

Maria Sobolewska is a Senior Lecturer in Politics (Quantitative Methods) at the University of Manchester.

Paul Webb is Professor of Politics at the University of Sussex and co-editor of the journal *Party Politics*. He is author of numerous publications on party and electoral politics in the UK and abroad, and is an elected Fellow of the Academy of Social Sciences.

Ben Yong is a Lecturer in Law at Hull University. He has co-authored two books with Robert Hazell: *Politics of Coalition: How the Conservative-Liberal Democrat Government Works* (2011) and *Special Advisers: Who They Are, What They Do and Why They Matter* (2014).

Chapter 1

What's British about British Politics?

ANDREW GAMBLE

Britain is a settled polity. It has been a full democracy for almost 100 years, and it has representative institutions and a continuous political tradition stretching back to the seventeenth century. During that time its external fortunes have risen and fallen but it has not experienced either internal revolution or external invasion and occupation. Many have argued that it is this experience that has made Britain special, the essential context for understanding its politics, and its success in managing orderly and peaceful change.

Britain is also a troubled polity. The unity of the UK was first broken when Ireland separated in 1921, and in recent decades it has been threatened again by the conflict in Northern Ireland and by the rise of the Scottish National Party (SNP) to dominate the politics of Scotland. The SNP only narrowly lost the referendum on independence in September 2014, and the issue has not been closed. Britain held another referendum, on its future within the European Union (EU), in June 2016, with public opinion divided on the merits of leaving or remaining. Britain's external standing and global reach has declined sharply in the last hundred years as its empire collapsed and its industrial pre-eminence receded. Trust in the integrity and competence of its political class has weakened too, because of the 2008 financial crash and its aftermath, inconclusive military interventions such as Iraq and Libya, and political scandals and anxieties about immigration. The mismatch between representative institutions and grassroots democracy has steadily grown, with anti-system and anti-politics insurgencies challenging established elites (Ford and Goodwin 2014).

Does any of this make British politics distinctive? Does Britain's experience stand out from the experience of any other European state of similar population and resources in the last 70 years?

Every nation state in the modern world claims that its own experience is special, and has developed its own national myth. That makes states different, but does it make them distinctive? Or are all modern states just variations on a common theme? If we look closely, are not all states that have reached a certain stage of economic and political development pretty similar, and the way they conduct their everyday politics essentially the same? The evidence from Eurobarometer indicates that while there is considerable variation of attitudes within member states, it is much less than might be expected.

This chapter explores these issues by examining some of the main features of the British state which are said to make British politics distinctive – its multinational character, its highly centralised institutions, its uncodified constitution, its imperial legacy, its Anglo-liberal political economy and its liberal political culture. Each of these is examined to see whether or not these features truly mark out Britain as distinctive or whether they are merely variations on patterns found in many other countries.

Long-term social and economic trends – industrialisation, secularisation, rationalisation, globalisation and regionalisation – shape the contexts and constraints within which all politicians have to operate and reduce their autonomy. They are often seen as inexorable forces which lead states to become increasingly alike, ironing out national differences and idiosyncrasies, and obliging governments to behave in very similar ways. Because modern states share many of the same problems, they often gravitate to similar solutions. They learn from one another, they compete with one another, and they imitate one another. In this way they become more like one another.

If politics is a universal and necessary aspect of human experience, an activity which arises whenever human beings form associations, managing the conflicts of interest which arise among them, then we might expect politics to be much the same everywhere, with the same patterns and underlying logic. If this were so, there would be nothing particularly distinctive about British politics, nothing especially 'British'. Politics in Britain would be fundamentally the same as politics in France, politics in the US or politics in Egypt.

What makes politics distinctive in different places and different times, such as Britain in the twenty-first century, is that politics arises to manage the clash not just of different interests but different beliefs and different perspectives, and in doing so helps create and sustain a common world of values, institutions, rules and discourses, making it possible for human beings to cooperate with one another. These common worlds are more than just a matter of common interests; they also involve common identities and common institutions (Gamble 2000). Understanding politics through identity focuses on who we are and where we belong, distinguishing between friends and enemies, those who are included and those who are excluded from a political community. Understanding politics through institutions focuses on the rules and discourses which create an order, establishing a set of assumptions and prescriptions which define the context in which political activity takes place. Both these understandings of politics anchor politics in a specific time and space. In the modern era the most common site for politics has been the nation state, defined by notions of sovereignty and territory, and supplying a framework for a common world, a community of fate. Such a community is formed when all its members are inescapably bound together because they share a common identity. They belong to an *order* which is distinctive and exceptional. The peculiarities of each nation state shape its politics.

A multinational state

From this perspective, Britain (like all other bounded national political systems) is a specific configuration of identity and interest, which creates an order which is distinctive but not unique. There are differences, but also many commonalities. One of the most distinctive aspects of British politics has always been the notion of Britishness, rooted in the territorial politics of its multinational state.

Several other European states have territorial politics as complicated as the UK, among them Belgium, Spain and Italy. In all these states, significant minorities claim a separate national identity and assert the right to self-determination and the establishment of their own state. The desire of many Scots to secede from the UK is not so different from the desire of many Catalans to secede from Spain. The norm in Europe has been for states to express a single national identity, but a number of European states like the UK remain multinational. Where Britain's multinational state is different from others is that it came into existence before the modern era of national self-determination and popular sovereignty. Scotland's accession to the union in 1707 was the result of agreement rather than annexation, and so created a union state (Mitchell 2009), which was different from either a unitary state or a federal state, the two main forms of European state in the modern era, because it was founded on the union of two independent nations. One of the things that makes British politics distinctively British has been the internal dynamics of Britain's union state, which include the asymmetry of the governing arrangements of its different territories, nationalist insurgencies against Westminster rule, and the way the party system has been shaped by territorial as well as class cleavages in the modern era. The trumping of the Labour Party's class appeal by the new identity politics of the SNP in 2015 and at the Scottish Parliament elections of 2016, depriving Labour of one of its most important electoral strongholds, is the most recent example of this.

Table 1.1   *The four nations of the UK*

	Population (million) Census 2011	Population %	MPs at Westminster (2015)	Devolved Powers
England	53	84	533	No English Parliament. Greater London Authority, established in 1999. Proposed powers for Northern cities 2016–present.
Scotland	5	8	59	Scottish Parliament, established in 1998.
Wales	3	5	40	Welsh Assembly, established in 1998.
Northern Ireland	2	3	18	Northern Ireland Assembly, established in 1998.

Most other European states made determined efforts to weld their citizens into a single nation, actively suppressing regional institutions, languages and cultures, making the nation the focus of loyalty and identity, the primary imagined community within a territorial space, and the state its expression. In many parts of Europe, the nation was deemed to exist before a state had been created to represent it, and often that meant altering boundaries to bring the two into alignment. In the Kingdom of Great Britain and then, after 1801, in the *United Kingdom* of Great Britain and Ireland, the position was rather different. The state had been created first, and although some effort was put initially into creating a unified British nation to underpin it, the separate cultural identities of the four nations did not disappear but flourished alongside one another within the same state (Davies 1999). The UK became (accidentally) an early experiment in multiculturalism and multinationalism. There were other much larger multinational states in Europe, notably the Austro-Hungarian Empire and the Russian Empire, but the British multinational state is unusual for surviving into the democratic era.

The establishment of the British state as a union between more than one nation was the key fact in the emergence of Britishness. It exists

Table 1.2 *The formation of the UK*

1284	Statute of Rhuddlan; Incorporation of Wales into England
1541	Henry VIII proclaimed King of Ireland
1603	Union of the Crowns of England and Scotland
1707	Act of Union; Establishment of one Parliament for England and Scotland, and one Kingdom, the Kingdom of Great Britain
1800	Act of Union; Creation of the United Kingdom of Great Britain and Ireland
1927	Royal and Parliamentary Titles Act, 1927; UK renamed the United Kingdom of Great Britain and Northern Ireland, following the creation of the Irish Free State in 1921

because a British state exists. There was no prior British nation which could give it legitimacy. Instead, a British national identity had to be created alongside separate Scottish, Irish, Welsh and English national identities. British national identity was originally a product of the union of Scotland and England. This new union state contained within it the annexed territories of Wales and Ireland. It took them much longer to be accorded the privileges Scotland enjoyed from the beginning. Ireland did not even appear in the name of this new state – Great Britain. A new British identity and British institutions gradually emerged in the course of the eighteenth century (Colley 1992). The monarchy had been British since the union of the Crowns in 1603; now it was joined by Parliament and the army. The British (Scots, English and Welsh) were also united by being predominantly Protestants against the Catholic monarchies of Europe, although Protestantism itself was internally divided, and the Scottish Kirk remained very different from the Church of England. The pursuit of colonies and commerce also came to unify the new nation, but many things remained separate. The Bank of England, for example, which had been established in 1694 just before the union, was never renamed the Bank of Britain, although in time it came to preside over a UK-wide currency union.

Over the next 250 years, the new state was adorned by new British institutions from the British Museum and the Royal Mail to the BBC and the National Health Service. The British built the richest and most powerful state in the world and set international standards in many different fields. Their soft power, the cultural appeal of the British way of doing things and the spread of the English language, went alongside the hard power of their gold and guns. The inventions which poured from Britain were not only technological and industrial but also included new sports and games and a remarkable range of social and cultural organisations which came to be copied in many other countries, as well as dress, manners, hobbies and much else which came to define the modern world (Veliz 1994).

World leadership after 1815 for a time made Britain seem more exceptional among other European states than it really was (Bell 2007). In the democratic era, Britain was unable to defend its Empire or even its union against the claims of national self-determination. The loss of Ireland from the union in 1922 foreshadowed the much larger dismemberment that was to come after 1945 with the withdrawal from the great majority of Britain's overseas possessions. It compelled Britain to readjust its position in the world, becoming in the process a normal European state again. Empire, along with the creation of a welfare state, had helped define Britishness and keep the union together. But with the empire no more, apart from a few scattered outposts, and with the push to devolution fragmenting the sense of a common citizenship with the same social and economic rights, defining Britishness had become much harder by the beginning of the twenty-first century. Since the 1970s in particular, the identities associated with the four nations which make up the UK (Kenny 2014) have become more salient. At one time, most English people thought of themselves interchangeably as English and as British. The Unionists in Northern Ireland gave their primary identity as British. The Scots and the Welsh were more equivocal, but large numbers still embraced both identities. That position has changed in recent years, particularly since the big push to devolution began in the 1990s. Now a majority of Scots identify themselves as more Scottish than British and, within that majority, around 25 per cent refuse the label of British altogether. In England, too, attitudes have begun to change, although less dramatically. There is now a significant number of the English who give their primary identity as English (17 per cent) and another 12 per cent who consider themselves more English than British. While 44 per cent still think of themselves as equally English and British, it is noteworthy that this is no longer a majority position.

The nature of Britishness is changing, and as a result, British politics is becoming more fragmented. The UK is less united by the activities of its state than it was in the past, whether through the promotion of empire or the welfare state, and with the weakening of these bonds of unity the identity which this state promoted is weakening too. British politics is still distinctively British because the British state and its core institutions continue to exist, but it is distinctively British in a new way. It is the increasing exclusiveness of the separate national identities rather than the way they are integrated into a harmonious whole in which they complement Britishness rather than compete with it, which has come to characterise British territorial politics (Jones et al. 2013).

A centralised state

Britain is often seen as more centralised than other states, partly because its constitution concentrates rather than disperses power and is unitary rather than federal (as discussed in the next section), and partly because of London, which is much more dominant than capital cities in comparable states. Only Paris comes close. London's dominance can be measured by many indicators including the concentration of wealth, finance, media, the arts, politics, sport, tourism, transport links, infrastructure spending, employment and government agencies in the capital and its immediate hinterland. As a global city London has its own distinct political economy, and has become noted for its high levels of immigration, its cosmopolitan culture and the spiralling cost of its housing. It tends to suck talent and resources from the rest of the country, and although the imbalance has long been recognised, rectifying it has proved difficult.

The centralisation of decision-making in London can be observed in the way the British state manages public spending. In many respects, the British state operates as other European states do. The size of the state falls within the European range, towards the middle or low end. Public spending was below 10 per cent of national income before 1914, stabilised at around 20–25 per cent in the 1920s and 1930s, following the big increase in the First World War, before rising sharply again in the Second World War and stabilising at around 38–42 per cent in the post-war period. It has occasionally risen higher than this, as a result of the severe recessions in 1974 and 2009, prompting fiscal squeezes to bring public spending back into line with the shrunken economy. Politically it seems very difficult to push the percentage of public spending higher or lower than the post-war average. The Thatcher Government talked about rolling back the state, but the size of the state did not alter very much. The composition of public spending was changed, but not the overall amount. It proved much harder than expected to make significant inroads into the state, except for short periods.

The reasons for this can be found in the functions which modern states carry out. The original functions of the state were preserving external defence, internal law and order, maintaining sound money and protecting property rights. In the twentieth century, the state gradually assumed major roles in stabilising and regulating market economies to prevent slumps and promote growth and prosperity; in providing social protection and social investment through welfare, education and health programmes; and in investing to promote technological innovation, provide better infrastructure and foster faster growth. States have as a result become multi-purpose, multi-agency and multi-layered, with highly complex systems of governance and coordination.

These features are true of all states and have been made necessary by the way modern economies and societies and democracies work. All advanced economies, for example, have developed welfare states. They vary in their generosity, and this is reflected in the proportion of national resources devoted to them and therefore in the fiscal regime which underpins them. As Esping-Andersen (1990) observed, by the end of the 1980s three distinct worlds of welfare capitalism had emerged based on the strength of the different class coalitions in different countries. The British welfare state had become distinctly less generous than either the Nordic social democratic welfare states or the conservative welfare states of central Europe. Britain belonged to a cluster of liberal residual welfare states, although even within this group there were important differences. While income support in Britain has over time become much less generous than many other welfare states, Britain has retained some universal services free at the point of use, most notably its National Health Service (NHS). All three models of welfare capitalism in Esping-Andersen's schema are recognisably welfare states. The politics of the welfare state in Britain, as in other residual welfare states in the Anglo-American world, has come to discriminate between the deserving and the undeserving poor ('strivers' and 'shirkers') by focusing on squeezing the benefits of those deemed capable of working, while protecting those of groups deemed deserving, such as pensioners, and also protecting the universal services. Difficult though this is to do in practice (many of the working poor receive tax credits), this is a distinctive pattern when compared with many European welfare states, but it is not a unique pattern. Britain shares it with several other liberal market economies (Hay and Wincott 2012).

While the core functions of the state do not differ very much from what is found elsewhere, the degree of centralisation of the British state and some key public services like the NHS is distinctive. Most taxes are collected centrally, the Treasury has control of all budgets, there is very little hypothecation of taxes (tying taxes to particular programmes), and very little autonomy for local bodies. Many taxes are spent locally, but the priorities are established centrally. More than two thirds of the resources available to local government are collected and allocated centrally. Only around 15 per cent of local government revenue is raised through the council tax, and even this is subject to government control. The pattern is very different in most other European countries, where local autonomy is buttressed by a much greater degree of fiscal autonomy. This used to be the case in Britain, but successive governments have found it useful to control spending priorities from the centre and not allow any real devolution of powers. Even in the case of Scotland and Wales one of the most contentious issues has been the extent of fiscal devolution they should be given by Westminster. The UK has long been one of the most centralised states in Europe, but devolution has begun to change this, and more decentralisation is expected. How far this will challenge the dominance of Whitehall and London is unclear. Up to now this dominance has been a distinctive feature of British politics. The British political tradition being that all parts of the UK were subordinated to London, controlling the levers in Whitehall has been the main focus of political competition, and much less energy has gone into local politics.

An uncodified constitution

A second distinctive feature of British politics is the particular combination of representative and responsible government that Britain developed over three centuries and which became known as the Westminster model (King 2015). In the twentieth century, even after the transition to democracy, the aristocratic and monarchical elements in the British constitution were still pronounced, in part because in contrast with almost all other democracies, Britain never adopted a formal codified constitution. Several important aspects of its state were adopted in premodern and pre-democratic times, particularly the prerogative powers retained by the monarch as Head of State, but exercised by the Prime Minister; the unelected second chamber, the House of Lords; the doctrine of Parliamentary sovereignty, Crown-in-Parliament, and the first-past-the-post electoral system. The gradual evolution of this aristocratic polity into a democratic one left many features of the old British state intact. In comparative terms this has placed Britain among Western democracies as concentrating power rather than dispersing it, majoritarian rather than pluralist, and centralised rather than decentralised (Lijphart 1999). Despite the devolution of some powers to Wales and Scotland since 1997 and changes to the voting systems for many subordinate bodies in the UK, this characterisation still holds good for Westminster itself.

The doctrine of Parliamentary sovereignty, for example, implies that there is no higher authority than Parliament. Its sovereignty is potentially unlimited. Popular sovereignty, although a de facto reality since universal suffrage, is not formally acknowledged in Britain, as it is in all other democracies. It is recognised indirectly in the supremacy of the elected chamber of Parliament, the House of Commons, over the unelected chamber, the House of Lords, since the Parliament Act of 1911. Perhaps surprisingly for the country that gave birth to Magna Carta, constitutional doctrine still maintains that there is in principle no law which a Parliament cannot change, because no Parliament can bind its successors. In practice there are a host of conventions, procedures and organised interests in the state and outside of it which prevent Parliament acting despotically. But the principle of unfettered sovereignty remained the cornerstone of the legal authority of the British state.

This has begun to change, in ways that may ultimately make British politics less distinctive but during the process of transition emphasise just how different British political institutions are from other democracies. These changes include current membership of the EU, devolution to the Scottish Parliament and the Welsh Assembly, and the passage of the Human Rights Act. There are now things which a British Parliament is in practice unable to change, and legal parameters it has to work within. In theory the British Parliament could still dissolve the Scottish Parliament and the Welsh Assembly and rescind the devolution settlement. It could also in theory repeal by a simple majority vote the acts which established universal suffrage. In practice there are some changes which once made become politically irreversible. There is no prospect, for example, of devolution being overturned, except in response to an extreme emergency. That means the sovereignty of the Westminster Parliament is now qualified. It has to acknowledge the sovereignty of the other representative assemblies in the UK. There may not yet be a constitution in the way the rest of Europe understands it, but as Vernon Bogdanor has argued (2009), a new constitution has gradually emerged, which marks a break from the traditional Westminster model. In this sense British politics is becoming less idiosyncratic and more European, but there is still a considerable way to go. House of Lords reform has taken a hundred years already and is still not complete. With 813 unelected members in 2016, it has become by a considerable margin the largest second chamber anywhere in the democratic world and is playing an increasingly important part in policymaking (Russell 2013).

Britain used to be celebrated for its success in combining representative and responsible government in contrast to less happy lands (Beer 1965). What is now distinctive about British politics is that its traditional constitution is increasingly a source of instability rather than stability, whether it is the asymmetry of its devolution arrangements, the lack of a body to oversee the arrangements between the different parts of the UK and adjudicate conflicts, or the mismatch between votes and seats delivered by the first-past-the-post electoral system.

Britain has long enjoyed a greater degree of institutional continuity than most other European states. There has never been an occasion in the recent past for a wholesale rewriting of the British constitution, starting again from a blank slate and a constitutional convention. The British disposition is to muddle through, seeking only incremental change, and dealing with the unforeseen consequences of piecemeal change as they arise. The untidiness of British constitutional arrangements does not bother most of the British who accept the often complex, arcane and convoluted practices by which Britain is governed as natural.

Traditionalists bemoan the loss of the old uncodified constitution, and its dense patchwork of laws, conventions and precedents (Johnson 2004). Reformers are in despair at the slow pace of change. There is endless tinkering, and adjustments to the present arrangements, but little sense of direction or what a desirable constitutional order for the UK should now be. Key constitutional arrangements, such as whether there should be two classes of MP in the Westminster Parliament, are in flux and open to question. Legitimacy has drained away from Parliament and the political class, in part because of scandals like the parliamentary expenses scandal in 2009. Yet although some argue that the amount of corruption in the UK has increased (Whyte 2015), it remains lower than in many other states, and far below the levels of the early nineteenth century. A greater cause of declining legitimacy is the way in which Parliament no longer represents the current multinational and multiparty reality of British politics. British politicians were once distinctive for the ability to manage the orderly evolution of its political institutions. But with so many unresolved constitutional questions and anomalies which recent reforms have created, that ability is now in question.

A post-imperial state

A third distinctive aspect of British politics arises from the role Britain plays in the international state system, and in particular Britain's continuing ambivalence between Europe and America (Gamble 2003). Britain's capacity and global reach may have declined in the last 70 years, but British politics is still shaped by Britain's experience as an empire and a leading great power for more than 200 years. It is responsible for many policies which are characteristic of the British polity, such as the debates on whether Britain should or should not retain a nuclear deterrent, whether it should continue to spend a larger proportion of its national income on its armed forces than other European states and whether as a permanent member of the UN Security Council or as an ally of the US it should be willing to deploy its troops abroad.

Britain became the closest ally of the US in forming the Western alliance and reconstructing the post-war international market order, and has been willing on several recent occasions to support US military interventions and also to conduct military interventions of its own (see Table 1.3).

Table 1.3   *British overseas military inventions since 1990*

1990–1991	Kuwait, Iraq – Operation Desert Storm
1991–2003	Iraq – Enforcement of no-fly zone
1992–1995, 1995–2002	Bosnia – peacekeeping (UNPROFOR, IFOR)
1999	Kosovo
2000	Sierra Leone
2001–2014	Afghanistan
2003–2009	Iraq
2011	Libya
2014–	Iraq – bombing of ISIL targets
2015–	Syria – bombing of ISIL targets

Source: RUSI

British political culture since the Second World War has been notice-ably more willing to celebrate its military and favour military action than has been the case in most other European states. The European country Britain most resembles in this respect is France, another former European imperial power. Britain spends the same proportion of its national income (2 per cent) on defence as France, which is double that spent by Germany, Italy or Japan. But in Britain there is something else as well. Its experience in the Second World War of successfully resisting invasion and occupation and then being part of the victorious coalition against the Axis powers has become the most important single compo-nent of a reworked national story, Britain standing alone against impos-sible odds. As a result, 70 years since it ended, British culture at all levels is still saturated with references to the Second World War. This is not the case anywhere else in Europe apart from Russia. The British politi-cal elite from right to left is still deeply preoccupied with geopolitics and Britain's international status and international influence. British politics is constantly convulsed with arguments not on whether Britain should intervene but on how it should intervene, militarily or in some other way.

Britain's past history and inherited commitments are used to justify a continuing role in the international state system which is often in danger of outrunning the capacities of the British state to fulfil. Although it had to accept the absolute decline in its power, the British political class still had great difficulty in adjusting to it and finding an appropriate role to play. This was captured by Dean Acheson, one of the key architects of US foreign policy after 1945, who observed in 1962 that Britain had lost an empire and not yet found a role. He argued that Britain could no longer expect to play a role apart from in Europe, maintaining 'a special relationship' with the US and aspiring to be a broker between them and Russia, based primarily on being the head of a commonwealth which had 'no political structure, or unity, or strength'. British policy, he argued, had become as weak as its military power (Dimbleby and Reynolds 1989).

The British political class came to accept this criticism. After the failed Suez intervention in 1956, British governments were already aware that a special relationship with the US was no longer available on the old terms, and that it was increasingly impossible to stand apart from Europe. Britain therefore attempted to join the new Common Market which was emerging in Europe, which it finally achieved in 1973. The special relationship entered a new and relatively troubled phase, but then was reinvigorated in a new form, particularly under the premierships of Margaret Thatcher and Tony Blair.

The attempt to combine these two roles has meant Britain never fully committed to its membership of the EU, the Common Market of yesteryear. Despite a referendum held in 1975 which confirmed Britain's membership, and the general election defeat of the Labour Party in 1983 when its manifesto pledged to withdraw from the EU, Britain's relationship with Europe was never settled. It has remained contentious in British politics and has frequently divided both major parties. There is Euroscepticism in many European countries, and many populist anti-system parties which like the United Kingdom Independence Party (UKIP) want to sever ties with the EU, but nowhere else is the mainstream political class and the mainstream media as divided over their country's membership of the EU as has been the case in Britain.

British ambivalence towards Europe has made Britain an awkward partner. Britain has shown itself reluctant to participate as a full member of the EU, seeking opt-outs from key European initiatives such as the Schengen Treaty on open borders and the European single currency. Yet Britain only voted narrowly to disengage completely, and British governments have been unwilling to accept relegation to a second tier of European states within the EU. At the heart of this problem is the unresolved tension between Europe and the US as the main focus of Britain's identity and loyalty following the end of Empire. Churchill's vision of Britain as the intersection of three circles, Empire, Anglo-America and Europe, contained the assumption that the Empire, with the British union at its core, was the fundamental one. Britain had strong ties with the US and the rest of the English-speaking world, and equally strong ties with Europe, but Britain because of its empire and global reach had no need to be absorbed by either. It could deal with both as an independent power.

When the withdrawal from Empire began, some seized on Europe as a surrogate, but the attraction of Europe was always counterbalanced by the special relationship which British political leaders aspired to enjoy with the US (Dumbrell 2001; Hitchens 2004). British leaders, with the exception of Edward Heath, when forced to choose between Europe and the US have always chosen the US. French leaders, by contrast, have always given priority to Europe. The nature of Britain's special relationship with the US has been distinctive and sets Britain apart from the rest of Europe, as was shown clearly in the 2003 invasion of Iraq. Other European states, such as Spain, supported the invasion, but many others did not, even though they were members of NATO and the Western alliance.

The unwillingness to contemplate a European future is not primarily a yearning for isolationism. The supporters of disengagement from Europe often desire not less but more involvement with the outside world. They argue that Britain has a different political economy from the rest of Europe, which is criticised for being too inward-looking, too protectionist, too bureaucratic and too regulated. Britain, by contrast, is said to thrive on having access to markets and cultures around the world. It is a global power not a regional power. By disengaging from Europe, Britain can open itself once again to the fastest growing markets around the world, such as China, India and Brazil, as well as renewing its links with Australia, New Zealand, Canada and the US, creating a new kind of network commonwealth (Bennett 2004). This would certainly make Britain distinctive at least in comparison with the rest of Europe. But the enthusiasm of the other proposed members is limited. The US in particular is keen that Britain remains with the EU, since a Britain detached from the EU would be less valuable as an ally to the US.

In its post-imperial phase, the British political class has not wanted Britain to abandon its global reach and global status. Britain remains committed to its membership of the UN Security Council, and the maintenance of worldwide interests and responsibilities. Political leaders across all parties believe Britain should provide leadership, if not military then moral, to sort out conflicts around the world. To sustain such a role presumes either a very close relationship with the US or a much closer union with Europe. The first has occurred whenever a particular national security emergency has meant that the US needs to hug Britain close. This has happened less often than sometimes supposed. Only two British Prime Ministers have received the Presidential Medal of Freedom since it was inaugurated in 1963, Margaret Thatcher and Tony Blair, and only two have received the Congressional Gold Medal, Winston Churchill and Tony Blair. Many British Prime Ministers have not formed a close relationship with US Presidents, yet most of them have wanted it. British politicians of both parties have found it easier to identify with the US than with Europe, and this Atlanticist orientation continues to mark Britain out from its European partners. In 40 years of

EU membership, the British economy has become increasingly integrated with the European economy, in terms of flows of goods, capital and labour, but this has not led to a shared European identity and solidarity. The British have gone back to imagining themselves as *in* Europe but not *of* Europe, and certainly not run *by* Europe. Most British people continue to think of Britain not as part of Europe but standing outside it.

An Anglo-liberal political economy

A fourth distinctive aspect of British politics arises from its political economy. This has been shaped by the particular role Britain has played in the global economy since the seventeenth century. Britain emerged as an entrepreneurial commercial society and then the first industrial society, using naval power to protect its trade and expand its colonies. Some of the things that used to be most distinctive about Britain's political economy, such as its status as the first industrial nation, have become less marked or disappeared altogether. Whatever their initial starting points, modern capitalist economies have steadily converged. Little now separates the performance of the French and British economies. Similarly, Britain was once very distinctive for the size of its working class, the extent of its urbanisation and the small proportion of its population engaged on the land, and British politics was dominated for a hundred years by the struggle to contain the rising labour movement; this struggle produced, especially after the exit of the Irish Republic from the UK, a more polarised class politics than in any other comparable modern state. But with the transition from an industrial to a service economy, the salience of class as a basis for political allegiance and party politics has declined markedly in Britain in recent decades as it has elsewhere.

What makes British political economy distinctive today is not its former status as the workshop of the world but the importance of its financial and commercial sectors. One million people now work in financial services in the UK, as many as once used to work in the mines. The City of London and the role it plays in British politics, is greater than any in of equivalent size. The financial sectors of some other countries such as Switzerland are even larger in relation to their host economies, but the populations are much smaller. The importance of the City in the UK stems from the rise of London in the nineteenth century to become the leading centre for financial, shipping and insurance services for the rest of the international economy. This cluster of expertise survived long after the disappearance of the economic and military power which made it possible, and has revived in spectacular fashion since the development of the Eurodollar market in the 1960s. Successive British governments were willing to allow the City of London to act as though it were an offshore financial centre, free of many of the regulations which other jurisdictions, including the US, imposed on their financial centres. One of the main reasons why the 2008 crash hit the UK economy so hard was because London had become such a key international financial centre, and its banks were leading players in the practices which burst the boom and Western prosperity and almost caused the collapse of the international financial system (Bell and Hindmoor 2015).

The policy of giving the City of London free rein and ensuring that it remained ahead of other financial centres was established under Labour and Conservative governments in the 1960s and 1970s, and received a major boost with the Big Bang in 1986, which removed many restrictions on the entry of foreign banks into London. The encouragement given to the development of financial services was a bipartisan policy, and during the long boom between 1993 and 2008 the major parties competed with one another in supporting light-touch regulation and removing obstacles to London's success. The crash forced revaluation and some reforms, but the British political class remains very wary of hobbling the City of London and UK financial services, since this is such an important part of the UK economy, and one of the main areas where the UK is competitive internationally. So despite popular anger at bankers, there have been few moves to change fundamentally how the banking system operates. Protecting the City of London was one red line in the renegotiation of the terms of the UK's membership of the EU ahead of the referendum.

Britain's variety of capitalism, the Anglo-liberal model (Hay 2013), places it in the liberal market rather than the coordinated market group (Hall and Soskice 2013). The importance of finance in the UK is a key component of the British model. All actual political economies are hybrids, including elements from several models rather than just one, but there remain important ways in which the political economy of the UK is distinct from most other members of the EU (Ireland is closest to it), and this has important political effects, not least the reluctance of the UK to participate in further European integration. Distinctive aspects of the British political economy include flexible labour markets and weak trade unions; a system of corporate governance which treats the company as a private association rather than a public corporation; a hybrid welfare state which while retaining some universal features such as the NHS has steadily moved to a residual conception of welfare; and since the 1980s a sharply widening gap in both income and wealth inequality, highlighted in particular by the pay and bonuses of CEOs and bankers.

Many of these trends date in particular from the 1980s and the changes introduced by the Thatcher Government, but the broad pattern, with some variations, has continued since. The UK economy shed its image of relative decline in the 1990s, overcame its long-running sterling problem and embarked on the longest period of continuous expansion in its history. It became one of the most successful economies in the neo-liberal era, partly because successive governments were willing to embrace the logic of the changes in the rules governing the international economy which the US promoted after the structural crisis of the 1970s. One of the consequences was to make London and the south-east of England the main beneficiaries of this policy, and by the time of the 2008 crash the economy had become very unbalanced, with the dominance of London over all other regions ever more pronounced. The 2008 crisis initially hit Britain much more severely than most other European countries because Britain was one of the two leading centres of the financialised open liberal market economy which had been so dominant for 30 years, and London was one of its two leading financial centres. The economy began finally to recover in 2013, after relaxation of the austerity programme pursued by the government. It was helped by a further rise in house prices and household debt, but investment, productivity and wages remained low, and the balance of payments deficit continued to increase. It had reached 5 per cent of national income by 2015. Despite plans to rebalance the economy and create new export-led growth, the distinctive patterns of the British political economy in 2015 were very familiar from the past.

A liberal political culture

Ideology and culture are often the most idiosyncratic features of a state, but also the hardest to pin down. Is there anything distinctive about British ideological traditions and political culture which mark them out as especially British? Britain's ideological traditions are part of wider families of ideas which shape the discourses and institutions in many countries. Trying to disentangle Britain from broader European currents of thought is no easy task, but there are some important aspects of ideological discourse in Britain that are distinctive.

The first of these is the strength of the Anglo-American community of ideas and political discourse. This has been a predominantly liberal tradition, which has influenced all other ideological doctrines, and helps explain the liberal forms which both conservatism and socialism have assumed in Britain, in contrast to many other countries. This liberal tradition is Anglo-American, and often the terms of ideological debate on both right and left in the UK are Anglo-American rather than European. This is partly the result of the common language, but it also reflects the way that English political traditions and ideas shaped the American experience, and made debates in Britain part of transatlantic debates rather than merely British debates. This has been true ever since the War of American Independence, the French Revolution and, closer in time, the New Deal and social democracy which resulted from the Great Depression and the neo-liberalism which arose in the 1970s and influenced the Thatcher Government and the Reagan Administration.

A second important context shaping British ideological discourse has been the nature of the party system. The first-past-the-post electoral system has forced parties seeking to form governments to form broad ideological and interest coalitions. Partly as a result of this, the two main British parties in the last hundred years (Conservative and Labour) have been unlike Centre-Right and Centre-Left parties in the rest of Europe. The Conservative Party was obliged to become a party which had to draw support from the urban industrial working class rather than rely on the votes of those working on the land. Conservative ideology tended to be pragmatic and not doctrinaire, organised around the defence of key institutions – Crown, Church, Union, Empire, Property – rather than a set of abstract ideas. The priority given to the pursuit of power and being in government meant that the party was usually able to sideline its diehards and became throughout the twentieth century Britain's default party of government, the most successful Centre-Right party in any Western democracy. The Labour Party was also distinctive from social democratic parties elsewhere, particularly because the party was created by the trade unions and they retained the dominant say until relatively recently in the governance of the party. This meant that one of the strongest influences on the ideology of the party was Labourism, the defence and protection of the interests of the trade unions, and this contented with various currents of socialism, but the party even under Tony Blair never fully became a social democratic party on the European model, based on individual membership.

The liberalism of British political culture is bolstered by certain institutions, notably the universities and the BBC. Such liberalism has suffered sustained attack by some tabloid newspapers, which are noted for their stridency and their partisanship, which reflects the structure of their ownership. The particular character and ideological leanings of the British media have always been a distinctive part of British politics, but there are doubts as to how long this media can survive in the internet age.

In terms of its broader political culture, Britain has been subject to the same trends towards the secularisation and individualisation of politics which can be observed across Western Europe. On some specific issues such as capital punishment and gun laws, Britain appears much more European than American. The same is true of secularisation which has advanced much further in Europe, with declining church attendances, than in the US. In Britain the trend has been particularly marked, but it has been a common European experience. The Protestant–Catholic divides in Europe and within Britain itself have become less important. Britain, like many other European countries, has also experienced a decline in solidarity and, since the onset of the economic crisis engendered by the post 2008 crash, in the emergence of more punitive attitudes to the poor.

In recent decades, Britain has become a much more multicultural country, as a result of high levels of immigration, and also a much more socially liberal country with legislation to extend equal rights to minorities which suffer discrimination. The acceptance of same-sex marriage in 2014 (although not yet in Northern Ireland because it is a devolved matter) was a notable milestone. These, too, are common trends across Europe. In Britain they have been particularly marked.

Where British political culture is different from that of most European countries is the large numbers of British people, particularly English people, who do not identify themselves as European. This is not the same as xenophobia, which, while it undoubtedly exists in Britain, is not noticeably out of line with attitudes in other countries. Being anti-European is more of a distinguishing aspect of British politics. There is a paradox. Britain is in many ways becoming much more European. But this has not quenched the strong urge of many in Britain to define themselves against Europe. The narrow vote for Brexit in the June 2016 Referendum showed how strong that feeling remained in England, outside London. But the Scots and the Northern Irish voted to Remain by a larger margin than the English and the Welsh voted to Leave. Support for an independent Scotland rose sharply after the result was announced, and England's decision makes another Independence Referendum in Scotland almost certain in the next few years. Scots suffer from many of the same consequences of globalisation and austerity but still find it easier than do many of the English to reconcile their national identity with a European identity. The consequences of Brexit are far-reaching and will shape British politics for a long time to come. The breakup of the UK has become even more likely, if not yet certain, than it was before. British politics may not be British for much longer.

Chapter 2

Britain's Experience of Coalition Government: Continuity and Change

BEN YONG AND TIM BALE

Traditionally 'British government', or at least that part of it which is conventionally known as 'Whitehall', has been seen as centralised, power-hoarding, majoritarian and hierarchical – characteristics reinforced by a long line of single-party majority administrations. So when David Cameron, leader of the Conservatives, issued his 'big, open and comprehensive offer' of coalition government to the Liberal Democrats (henceforth Lib Dems) following the May 2010 general election, it could be seen as much of a challenge to Whitehall's way of doing things as it was to Westminster's. With power shared between two parties, could things really work – should they really work – the way they had for decades? Would coalition lead to more consultation and perhaps, therefore, to policy based more on evidence than ideology? Or would it be one long tale of disruption, dither and instability?

In practice, both the positive and the negative possibilities brought about by coalition turned out to be exaggerated. The 2010–2015 experience has demonstrated that it is perfectly possible to run a coalition at the national level without decisions being unduly delayed or contested. In spite of persistent media reports of 'crisis' and 'splits', the coalition was in fact remarkably stable both in Westminster and Whitehall. But coalition government did not remedy the purported weaknesses of the latter. Indeed, what the 2010–2015 experience shows is that the underlying structure and political culture of British government – very strong departments and a weak centre, coupled with an insistence on efficiency and clear lines of control – remains highly resistant to change.

The Whitehall model in theory and practice

In the traditional understanding of British executive government – sometimes known as 'the Whitehall model' – relationships within the executive are fairly fixed. The key decision-making body in the executive is the Cabinet, which consists of key ministers (usually Secretaries of State) and the Prime Minister. The latter is seen as *primus inter pares*: he or she is first among equals – with the emphasis on 'equals'. Collectively, Cabinet, and Cabinet Committees, determine the direction of government through deliberation; individually, each Secretary of State is responsible for a department and, in that respect, accountable to Parliament. Ministers are also supported in their duties by civil servants, permanent staff who are employed to provide advice and implement policy in a politically impartial way.

The executive in theory and practice

The traditional model is one to which political actors and the media continue to cleave. It remains a standard against which changes in the executive are measured. For political scientists, however, this traditional understanding of British government is too normative and lacks descriptive power: it ignores shifting power relationships and disparities within the executive, and takes little account of changes that have taken place outside the executive. It has now been supplanted by the core executive model (Dunleavy and Rhodes 1990; Elgie 2011). In this model, key actors in the executive work in a context of resource scarcity and dependency. This means that they must act in cooperation with others in order to achieve their goals: power is relational, a mix of fixtures and fluidities.

This framework better describes an executive which is pluralistic, rather than unitary, and asymmetrical rather than uniform in the distribution of power. Whitehall is more a federation of several centres (mostly departments) rather than a pyramid on which the Prime Minister and Cabinet sit at the apex. In the core executive model, key decisions are made by 'the core executive': 'all those organizations and structures which primarily serve to pull together and integrate central government policies, or act as final arbiters within the executive of conflicts between different elements of the government machine' (Dunleavy and Rhodes 1990:4). In short, key decisions in government are not necessarily made by Cabinet at all; it can depend very much on the subject matter, on the actors and the resources to which they have access. Thus while Tony Blair has often been portrayed as a powerful Prime Minister – charismatic, popular (at least in the earlier years) and endowed with large majorities in the Commons – he was in practice often hampered in his time in government (1997–2007) by his querulous Chancellor, Gordon Brown. And while Blair attempted to strengthen the centre by creating units, employing more advisers and bypassing Cabinet and its committees in favour of bilateral relationships, that centre remained relatively weak (Kavanagh 2007).

Coalitions in theory and practice

In the post-war period, coalitions at Westminster and Whitehall have been non-existent. Single-party government has been the norm. It is hardly surprising, then, that so many British observers were worried about the twin threats of instability and ineffectiveness. Yet about 70 per cent of all European governments in the same period have been coalitions. Thus there is a large academic literature on coalitions, although it tends to focus on formation and termination, and rather less on governance – that is, how coalitions actually operate once they are formed (Strom, Muller and Bergman 2010). That said, it remains obvious that at the heart of coalition governance is the problem of ensuring cooperation and avoiding conflict. How can two or more parties work together to provide stable and coherent government, given that they have different and sometimes opposing histories, policies and objectives – and that their ultimate goal, re-election, may be a zero-sum game?

There are, as that literature shows, a number of means which coalition governments have employed to respond to this dilemma:

- coalition agreements which set out shared policies and conflict resolution processes;
- formal and informal coordinating and oversight mechanisms in the executive and in the legislature; and
- the sharing of executive posts and committees, usually in proportion to seats won in the legislature.

Much of this was novel to those who focused on Westminster and Whitehall politics. But even though there was 'a sense of the provisional rather than the permanent' (Riddell 2015: 119) much of what was established by the Conservative–Lib Dem government appeared to students of coalition, for the most part, to be a very typical coalition indeed.

In fact, those looking for lessons from other jurisdictions for Westminster and Whitehall didn't have to go as far many assumed. In England itself there had long been coalitions at the local government level. In Scotland, two of five Holyrood administrations since devolution in 1998 have been majority coalitions: the Labour–Lib Dem coalitions of 1999–2003 and 2003–2007. In Wales, there have been also been two majority coalitions in Cardiff since devolution: the Labour–Lib Dem coalition of 2000–2003 and the Labour–Plaid Cymru coalition of 2007–2011. Meanwhile in Northern Ireland, parties are constitutionally obliged to share power. Moreover, while the Conservative–Lib Dem coalition may have been the first at Westminster in over 60 years, there having been only four coalitions between 1900 and 2010, it is unlikely to be the last, notwithstanding the Tories winning a surprise overall majority in May 2015.

There are a number of lessons to take away from the experience of Scotland and Wales. The first is that majority coalitions tend to be powerful relative to the legislature. Coalitions in both nations have rarely, if ever, lost votes of confidence, and their majority in the legislature means they are able to enact policies broadly acceptable to both coalition parties (Hazell and Paun 2009). The second is that thanks to Scotland and Wales having a fixed term, coalitions are generally more stable than commonly thought. The threat to coalition stability is not so much from inter-party tension but rather intraparty tension (Cairney 2011): backbenchers often feel excluded from the executive decision-making process. The third lesson is that smaller parties in coalitions tend to gain little or do poorly at the second election – something clearly demonstrated in the case of the Lib Dems at the 2015 general election. That is because the smaller party (or parties) tend to be overshadowed by the larger partner; they find it difficult to have a visible impact. The fourth and final lesson perhaps follows from the third: coalitions do not necessarily lead to further coalitions – again, as can be seen from the 2015 election. Coalition government in Scotland after devolution was eventually followed by single-party minority government (2007–2011) and majority government (2011–2016). In Wales there have been single-party minority governments after coalition government, too.

The impact of the 2010–2015 coalition

In response to coalition, changes were made to the way in which the executive worked, but often long-term practices and structures in Whitehall persisted. This could be seen, for instance, in the establishment of the coalition itself, which was formed within five days of the 2010 general election. This was unusually slow by British standards, where single-party government are invariably formed the day following the election, but improbably fast by the standard of countries which commonly have coalition governments. The persistence of long-familiar practices, structures and problems within the executive is a common theme of the 2010–2015 coalition.

The two coalition parties recognised that working together in government would require inter-party cooperation, information sharing and the peaceful resolution of conflict – and an established means for this to happen. These were set out in a number of documents, including the *Programme for Government* and the *Agreement for Stability and Reform* (HM Government 2010a; 2010b). A 'principle of balance' was seen as key to the working of the coalition, although in practice, as we shall see, this was applied unevenly.

Following the formation of the coalition, ministerial portfolios were allocated by David Cameron in consultation with Nick Clegg. The Conservatives took the bulk of the posts, some 18 Cabinet ministers and 59 junior ministers, with the Lib Dems allocated five Cabinet ministers and 12 junior ministers. The number of posts allocated to the Lib Dems was slightly disproportionate to the number of seats they had gained in the Commons, but any marginal advantage thus gained was more than offset by their foregoing traditionally high-profile portfolios in return for a number of 'centre' (Deputy Prime Minister, Chief Secretary to the Treasury) and departmental posts, including Secretary of State for the Departments for Business, Innovation and Skills (BIS) and Energy and Climate Change (DECC). The Lib Dems' thinking was that this approach would allow them to influence the work of the coalition as a whole. But the decision meant that the Conservatives were gifted the great offices of state (the Home and Foreign Offices), and the two of the biggest-spending departments (Work and Pensions, and Education). This was a crucial mistake. As we have already noted, governing takes place in Britain primarily on a day-to-day basis through departments, not through the centre. It is Secretaries of State in departments who hold the levers of power in the British state. The Lib Dems had little power at the centre, and they spread themselves thinly through departments. As a result, they had to settle for the essentially negative power of veto.

The Prime Minister and the Deputy Prime Minister, Cameron and Clegg, shared a number of key prime ministerial prerogatives: ministerial posts, as we have seen, were to be determined between the two, and removals could only take place with the consent of both; they also determined the composition of Cabinet Committees. More generally, both were to have a 'full and contemporaneous overview of the business of government'. As the Lib Dems quickly discovered, the formal equality implied by the Agreement did not extend to resources, or in departments. The Prime Minister had No 10, which, while small, had fixed institutional status, dedicated staff and attracted high-quality talent. The post of Deputy Prime Minister, on the other hand, is historically titular. Being a departmental head would have given Clegg clout within Whitehall and a serious number of staff. Instead, he was situated in the Cabinet Office, a small department by Whitehall standards, and initially given very few resources in terms of civil servants and special advisers in comparison to No 10. Only over time was this imbalance redressed, but this was precious time lost.

Collective Cabinet responsibility – the idea that ministers toe the government's line in public whatever their arguments in private – was qualified. The *Programme for Government* explicitly set out exceptions where Cabinet ministers and their respective parties could 'agree to disagree': renewing Trident; the referendum on electoral reform; nuclear power stations; transferable tax allowances for married couples; and the Browne review on university tuition fees. In practice, adherence to this political convention was patchy, particularly in the latter half of the 2010–2015 Parliamentary term.

Under the coalition, Cabinet Committees were revived as a means to ensure that both coalition parties were kept informed of, and engaged in, developments across government. As such, they were often jointly chaired. A number of formal coalition dispute mechanisms were also established, but in practice these rarely met. This elaborate coalition machinery promised extensive information-sharing processes and greater consensual policymaking. Most of these mechanisms were supplanted over time by informal groupings which emerged in the early months of the coalition. These included the 'Quad' (comprising two key principles from each party: Prime Minister Cameron, Deputy Prime Minister Clegg, the Chancellor George Osborne and the Chief Secretary to the Treasury Danny Alexander), bilaterals and multilaterals between select ministers. All these groups made key decisions affecting the coalition and often resolved disputes. This was unsurprising: in practice, formal machinery for decision-making within the core executive has regularly been accompanied by, and more often than not supplanted by, informal mechanisms – in plainer English, personality and practice can often trump attempts to formalise authority.

The most momentous attempt to ensure coalition stability, one which had both constitutional significance and the potential to be the lasting political (as opposed to policy) legacy of the coalition, was the Fixed-term Parliaments Act 2011. This ended the prerogative power – in practice an institutional advantage of incumbency exercised by the Prime Minister – to dissolve Parliament and call for a general election. The Act was passed to prevent either coalition party from engineering a split to maximise electoral success. But the effect was to create a five-year Parliamentary term in which governments (single party or coalition) could hold power with relative stability – unusually long by domestic historical practice and international standards.

The coalition and the civil service

Initially, the civil service appeared slightly unsure how to deal with two parties in government. Sir Gus O'Donnell, the then Cabinet Secretary, sent around a circular reminding civil servants to 'coalitionise' their work – for instance, signalling in ministerial submissions how particular policies stemmed from or met the objectives of the respective coalition parties. Application of this was, however, uneven at best. Sometimes the frameworks set in place by ministerial teams in the different departments made that unnecessary; in other cases Whitehall simply reverted to old practice – treating the Secretary of State as the primary political head (Riddell 2015). The junior minister from the other party was treated as a 'normal' junior minister, only given the information that he or she required in his or her specific portfolio – rather than as the representative of one of the two coalition parties. As a result, it was, on the whole, 'business as usual' for civil servants. To a large extent, the problems officials dealt with and faced were not unique to coalition government. They were used to dealing with a divided executive – the 'TBGBs' (the Tony Blair–Gordon Brown split) were still fresh in the minds of many officials – and interdepartmental conflict was normal, as were squabbles between Secretaries of State and junior ministers. By the end of the parliamentary term, however, there were specific tensions related to the coalition. Leaving aside the matter of civil service reform, there were reports that civil servants were being asked by ministers of one coalition party to develop policy, but being told to keep this secret from ministers from the other coalition party (Riddell 2015).

Governing in a coalition

In spite of the media being hungry for stories of coalition splits, and even the smallest of differences liable to be declared to be a 'coalition crisis', for the most part ministers from both coalition parties worked together in relative harmony, particularly in the first half of the parliamentary term. Explicit breaches of Cabinet responsibility – or agreements to disagree – were actually quite rare, and none of these seriously threatened the coalition. Bust-ups within the executive were just as likely – if not more so – to originate within one of the parties (e.g. between No 10 and Theresa May in the Home Office; between Theresa May and Michael Gove in Education; and between virtually all departments headed by Tories and the Treasury) as between the junior and senior partners.

Relationships did, however, change, and to some extent deteriorate, over the course of the Parliamentary term. At the beginning of the coalition, both parties – in particular, the Lib Dems – were keen to stress unity in government and so downplayed differences where possible. By the mid-term, following a series of failures over constitutional reform (the Alternative Vote referendum in 2011 and Lords reform in 2012) the Lib Dems shifted towards more explicit 'differentiation' – that is, stressing the differences between themselves and the Conservatives. Sometimes this differentiation was deliberately choreographed, and other times it arose from necessity. From time to time, the coalition parties had to indicate to the party outside government and to the wider public that, although they were working with another party, they remained true to their policy goals. One example of explicit differentiation was the decision in 2012 that Prime Minister Cameron and Deputy Prime Minister Clegg would deliver separate parliamentary statements on their views of the recommendations of the Leveson report on practices and ethics of the press.

By 2014, differentiation – choreographed or not – had become more overt, with Lib Dem ministers (primarily Clegg, Alexander, Business Secretary Vince Cable and Education/Cabinet Office minister David Laws) pointing to the various ways in which the Lib Dems differed on policy from their Tory colleagues. Relationships became transactional. In the case of Vince Cable, a self-styled social democrat, this was par for the course. For Clegg, Alexander and Laws, all of them 'Orange Book' liberals, it was something of a departure, although far from a bolt from the blue. In early 2011, for example, they had witnessed Cameron switch from supposed neutrality to hostility to the Alternative Vote (Seldon and Snowden 2015; D'Ancona 2014) and then had to watch when, towards the end of the year, he vetoed a set of proposed changes to the Lisbon Treaty which would have imposed stringent budget constraints on all European Union members including the UK. Clegg was apparently not consulted about this, and was reportedly furious.

Lower down, within departments, the picture was far more variable. Most major spending departments were run by Conservative Secretaries of State, usually with the Lib Dem junior minister having his or her own portfolio. Relationships between ministers from the two coalition parties in departments ran from the warm to the indifferent – the latter being more common (Hazell and Yong 2012). So, for instance, one Lib Dem, Norman Baker, quit his job as junior minister in the Home Office in late 2014, citing the Home Secretary Theresa May's inability to share information. But such public breaks were rare; and in any case, conflicts between junior ministers and Secretaries of State are by no means unique to coalition government. Likewise, many Lib Dem ministers found themselves overextended and under-resourced as junior ministers. Their lack of resource was and remains a problem for most junior ministers, regardless of whether the government is a single-party majority or otherwise.

The Prime Minister

Some of the Prime Minister's traditional institutional powers – ministerial selection and deselection, determining the composition of Cabinet Committees and so on – were modified by the fact of coalition. That presented Cameron with some problems, but these were often blessings in disguise. The Fixed-term Parliaments Act is one example. The power of reshuffling ministers is another. Key posts could not be reshuffled regularly, because this would complicate coalition relations. This meant that Cameron could not fully use the power of patronage to reward ambitious and useful MPs. As a consequence, there were only three set-piece reshuffles over the 2010–2015 period, with most 'big beasts' remaining in their departments for the entire Parliamentary term. Moreover, a 'one in, one out' principle was adopted: if one Conservative minister left a department, he or she was replaced with another Conservative minister, with the same going for the Lib Dems. But such a constraint was also beneficial: both Tony Blair (1997–2007) and Gordon Brown (2007–2010) were criticised for reshuffling ministers and departments too often, leading to disruption and a lack of focus in government. By contrast, the coalition enjoyed relatively high ministerial tenures, which arguably meant greater stability and continuity.

Politically, Cameron was hampered in what could be implemented by the executive. But, in practice, having another party onside also meant that he could rely less on the more extreme wing of his own party in Parliament. Coalition, in this sense, strengthened Cameron as head of the executive rather than making him weaker. Moreover, while it is true that initially Cameron had chosen to have a pared-down operation in No 10, that was not caused by the coalition; and when he realised the need to strengthen his operation, this was accomplished with relative ease – suggesting the powers and resources of the office are still there for a Prime Minister who wants to call on them. Clegg, on the other hand, always had a fairly ad hoc arrangement of staff pulled together from various sources. Similarly, it was David Cameron who was the recognised head of government in foreign affairs, whereas Clegg was 'merely' a Deputy Prime Minister. And it was Cameron who received greater media coverage while much of Clegg's work was undertaken behind the scenes and he struggled to have an impact (Bennister and Heffernan 2012; 2015).

Within his own party, however, the picture was more mixed. Cameron, unlike Blair, did have a good relationship with his Chancellor, George Osborne. Indeed, it was the fundamental solidity of this relationship which ensured Conservative dominance within the executive and the coalition as a whole. Many Conservative MPs and ordinary party members, however, seemed determined to hold on to the illusion that Cameron, having failed to win the majority they believed was there for the taking in 2010, should have formed a minority government, despite the fact that, once the Lib Dems decided they wanted to join a government, such an arrangement was never a realistic option. This, plus the fact that coalition necessarily reduced the number of jobs that Cameron could dispense, ensured that many Conservatives, whose ideological concerns might otherwise have been assuaged, remained hostile to the whole enterprise – so hostile, indeed, that they seemed unable to appreciate what was obvious to any objective observer, namely that Cameron had negotiated a deal that, both in terms of policy and portfolios, was far better than any party with more coalition experience than the Lib Dems would ever have let him get away with. Cameron's inability to persuade them otherwise saw him forced, first, into withdrawing support for Lords reform (initially a Lib Dem manifesto pledge to replace the House of Lords with a smaller, elected chamber) and therefore abandoning Parliamentary boundary changes (which would have advantaged the Conservatives by equalising constituency sizes and reducing Labour's electoral advantage in terms of seat share) and, second, allowing himself to be pushed to the right on issues such as migration and asylum.

Coalition policymaking: Case studies

In an ideal world, coalition would lead to better policymaking, because any measure, since it requires the consent of both partners, would be subject to more rigorous testing. Three case studies, which encompass areas generating differing degrees of success and disagreement between the governing parties, suggest that this is not necessarily the case. Indeed, coalition is just as likely to produce lowest-common-denominator deals and policy that is suboptimal for some or all of those involved and for the country as a whole.

Austerity

George Osborne and David Cameron committed themselves to eliminating the UK government's deficit and making a start on repaying its debt before the election – a policy which, given their reluctance to raise taxes too much, clearly implied large spending cuts. The Lib Dems, like Labour, acknowledged the need for deficit reduction. Indeed, beneath the rhetoric, the differences in the plans published by all three parties were not as wide as many assumed. But they also cautioned against overdoing austerity, lest it choke off economic growth. After the election, and especially following Osborne's first emergency budget in the summer of 2010, it was patently obvious that it was the Conservatives rather than the Lib Dems who were driving the nation's economic and, in particular, fiscal policy. The ease with which this was allowed to happen surprised many, but perhaps it should not have. The Lib Dem's main economic spokesman in opposition, Vince Cable, had been kept out of coalition negotiations and then the Treasury. But even he appears to have been persuaded by the argument that a combination of a dire international situation and the sheer scale of the deficit demanded tougher and swifter action than originally envisaged. Lib Dem concerns about what amounted to cuts of nearly a quarter in the spending of non-protected departments over five years were also assuaged by the fact that the NHS, overseas aid, and schools' budgets were to be exempted from savings – and by the fact that the Conservatives (not least for electoral reasons) agreed to Lib Dem proposals to effectively gold-plate pension increases and introduce a new state-backed occupational pension scheme.

Osborne appeared to get what he wanted on the economy because of an early, crucial political decision taken by the Lib Dem leadership – in particular by Clegg and his confidantes David Laws and Danny Alexander – that there was no point in trying to distance the Lib Dems from what the coalition was doing in this respect, even if they had little or no influence on it. Better, they reasoned, to own it by declaring ad nauseam that it was being done in 'the national interest' and in the hope that this would ultimately deliver results, by which time they would have put their own runs on the board in the shape of electoral and Lords reform, the pupil premium (extra money going to schools which admitted poorer children) and rises to the threshold at which people paid income tax. As a result, with the exception of occasional rogue, off-message comments by Cable and some of those working for him, the Lib Dems continued to treat Osborne's budgets and statements (which were in part prepared by Danny Alexander as Chief Secretary) as if they were their own. This meant that they acquiesced in the Chancellor's denials that there had been any easing up on austerity when Plan A's 'expansionary fiscal contraction' had patently failed to deliver and his boasting about 'a long-term economic plan' which seemed mainly designed to deliver a debt-fuelled boost for the Conservatives campaign strategy just in time for the election (Lee 2015). This continued almost to the very end of the Parliament, when Alexander suddenly made a risibly ineffective effort (revolving around an excruciatingly embarrassing photo-op with a yellow budget box) to suggest the Lib Dems would be doing things differently. In short, despite there being two parties in the coalition, then, a degree of groupthink on the economy occurred which, if we are to take the majority of macroeconomists seriously, did the finances of the nation and most households little good and maybe even some unnecessary harm, at least in the short term. Whether the coalition's patent failure to eliminate the deficit in the 2010 Parliament had much, if anything, to do with the presence of the Lib Dems in a Conservative-led government is a moot point – and one that in some senses may only be answered by seeing how (and how well) the Conservative majority government elected in 2015 tackles the challenge.

University tuition fees

The Browne review into the funding of higher education, which reported in October 2010, was always going to prove problematic for the Lib

Dems. It was widely predicted that, as a way of reducing the Treasury's contribution to the sector, it would suggest raising loan-based university tuition fees, which the Lib Dems (despite the misgivings of some in the leadership) had made very public pledges they would scrap if elected to government. The fact that the universities minister, the Conservative David Willetts, who had been consulted by the last Labour government about the setting up of the Browne review, swiftly announced that the government would only allow fees to be raised to a maximum of £9,000 did little or nothing to help his coalition partners. Nor, it turned out, did the get-out clause in the coalition agreement which allowed the Lib Dems to abstain on the issue. Unfortunately for Nick Clegg (who had tried and failed to privately persuade his party to drop its promise to abolish fees before the election), it quickly became clear that a fair few of his Parliamentary colleagues were determined to try and escape responsibility for the measure by going further and actually voting against it, thereby forcing the leadership (and those Lib Dem MPs it could persuade not to vote against or abstain) to support the measure in Parliament. The alternative would have been to risk the measure being defeated in the House and as a result do possibly irreparable damage to the idea that the coalition was a workable arrangement only months into its operation. As a result, the Lib Dems split three ways, although the overriding impression among voters was not one of chaos but of betrayal of a solemn promise – one that accelerated the erosion of support for the party among left-leaning and younger voters which was already underway since the election.

It is possible to argue that the destruction of the Lib Dems was a price well worth paying for a policy that some say not only protected higher education funding but, as the evidence seems to suggest, did not result in any long-term decrease in the number of young adults applying for full-time, degree-level study. But it is clear that the Lib Dems ultimate 'hard choice' did not necessarily result in good policy. For one thing, part-time study by mature students seems to have declined precipitously – so much for 'life-long learning'. For another, the very generous repayment terms which were put in place so as not to disincentivise potential students, as well as the fact that it is so easy for overseas students to escape repaying, means that getting on for half of the money loaned to those taking them will never be repaid, creating a bigger and bigger black hole worth hundreds of billions in the government's accounts. Meanwhile, very few universities – and certainly none of the most selective – decided to charge less than the maximum, meaning that the envisaged competition fees would inject into the system never came about. Nor, of course, did the even-greater competition that Browne's original proposal – to uncap fees altogether – would have ushered in. In short, the fact that one coalition partner had major reservations about the new system proved insufficient, notwithstanding the fact that the department responsible for it (BIS) was headed by a Lib Dem (Vince Cable), to get the government to think twice about introducing it. Meanwhile, the lack of attention paid to the issue by Cameron and Osborne (whose main interest was in all but doing away with the teaching grant the Treasury used to give the universities) speaks volumes about continued lack of central oversight and ongoing short-termism at the heart of Whitehall.

NHS reform

The reform of the NHS (in England) under the coalition illustrates the power of a determined Secretary of State, and the practical limits on the power of other political actors to constrain him. The NHS has an iconic status in the UK, and all political parties were careful in the run-up to the 2010 election to avoid any suggestion that they might interfere with it. Andrew Lansley, responsible for Conservative Party health policy since 2004, had formulated big plans for change if elected, but these were deliberately downplayed in the 2010 Conservative manifesto. The manifesto did, however, promise structural reform of a vague nature. The Lib Dems' manifesto similarly promised structural reform, but it focused on localising and democratising health services.

The initial coalition agreement on 12 May stated in a single sentence that NHS funding would increase in real terms every year – a remarkably short statement of intent for Britain's largest public service, and one which accounts for almost a third of all public spending (Timmins 2012: 45). The more detailed *Programme for Government* followed ten days later. The section on the NHS had been worked up at speed, with little consultation outside of the centre (including Lansley himself and Paul Burstow, the Lib Dem minister in the Department of Health). The two parties' health policies were shoehorned together into an incoherent whole. The Programme stated that there would be no further 'top-down reorganisations of the NHS', but then went on to promise the introduction of more competition while at the same time introducing elected elements at the local level of management.

This initial messy melding of policy, and the need to make large savings, provided the impetus for Lansley to revisit health policy and introduce radical new reform through legislation. In a July 2010 White Paper, Lansley announced his intention to reform the NHS, by stripping the Secretary of State and the Department of Health of any capacity to interfere with the running of the NHS and place control in an internal market, regulated by arms-length bodies (Glennister 2015). But it was the publication in early 2011 of the Health and Social Care Bill, which set out the details of this vision, that rang alarm bells. Power and accountability for the management of the NHS was to be devolved from the Secretary of State and Department of Health to a set of central agencies, including what eventually became NHS England (the national commissioning body), the Care Quality Commission (responsible for quality control) and Monitor (an economic regulator). At the same time, the middle levels of the NHS – Strategic Health Authorities and Primary Care Trusts – were to be abolished and replaced by GP-led Clinical Commissioning Groups (CCGs). The organisational change being proposed was so big that then Chief Executive Sir David Nicholson stated that 'you could actually see it from space' (quoted in Glennister 2015: 291).

Lansley's Bill had gone through the machinery of government: departmental discussions, Cabinet committees and Cameron's policy unit – but it was only during the Bill's passage through Parliament that the centre became aware of the tremendous political ramifications of the proposed reform. Publication of the Bill focused opposition: there was dissent at the 2011 Lib Dem Spring Conference, coupled with increasing public criticisms from various interest groups as Royal Colleges of General Practitioners and Nursing as the Bill passed through Parliament. The centre had been slow to intervene because it was underpowered and lacked the expertise to challenge Lansley (Timmins 2012). Moreover, Cameron himself in the early stages of the coalition had a slimmed-down centre, taking a hands-off approach to departments, and Clegg and his advisers were spread too thinly.

In an unusual move, Cameron – by now certain that unless he did something he would be unable to count on the Lib Dems to get it through – ordered a 'pause' of the Bill's progress through Parliament, and a 'listening exercise' was held. The point of the 'pause' and the exercise was not to reverse the direction of the Bill, but rather to quell the political firestorm and allay the fears of the public. Lansley himself became subject to greater oversight from the centre. Minor reforms were made to make the Bill politically palatable to the various interest groups, but the overall shape of the proposed legislation was left intact. The Health and Social Care Act received royal assent in early 2012, but Lansley was reshuffled to another post shortly after.

The Lansley reforms have been broadly regarded as disastrous (Glennister 2015; Jarman and Greer 2015). It was not at all clear that the NHS required such extensive restructuring, and it had required the expenditure of an extraordinary amount of money, and political time and management on the part of the executive, which might have been better spent on other matters; it reinforced the idea that the Conservatives were not to be trusted with the NHS; and for yet others it signalled the intensification of the health system's privatisation. But as an example of coalition policymaking and implementation, the NHS reforms suggest the Lib

Dems only had very incidental influence. Perhaps more importantly, the reforms illustrate the extraordinary power of a departmental Secretary of State determined to implement his own policy, and the weakness of the core executive as then organised under the coalition. None of the other players – the other coalition partner, the Cameron and Osborne centre, the civil service or Parliament – appeared able to reverse Lansley's reforms (Jarman and Greer 2015).

The political consequences of coalition

Most governing parties, irrespective of the electoral systems in which they operate, lose support between general elections. And there is a small but significant tendency for junior partners in coalition governments to lose more support than senior partners. Clearly both the Conservatives and the Lib Dems hoped to buck these trends, but only the former managed to. Cameron's decision to do a deal with the Lib Dems in 2010 made him Prime Minister for five years, but utterly failed to reconcile large numbers of his own MPs and party members to the idea of coalition: many saw it as an unjustified constraint from which they could not wait to escape and had no intention of repeating if they could possibly help it. However, for the Conservatives the coalition provided several pluses:

- its electoral consequences were nowhere near as damaging as some had feared; and
- it provided the stability and time needed for the Tories to build the reputation for economic competence and relatively strong leadership which stood them in such good stead in 2015.

For the Lib Dems, however, coalition proved to be a near unmitigated disaster from start to finish. They achieved none of their big constitutional ambitions, precious few of their other policies were enacted or, if they were, were not recognised as achievements distinct from those of their Conservative partners. Perhaps the most painful examples of such policies being the pupil premium and the raising of income tax thresholds. Having spent years positioning themselves to the populist left of Labour, particularly in the wake of the Iraq war, they went into government with the Conservative Party, making it look as if they had sacrificed their principles for ministerial cars and seats at the top table that saw them do 'politics as usual' rather than 'break the mould'.

In spite of all this, however, the Lib Dems did not fall apart organisationally. They may well have lost members – estimates suggest that membership declined from around 65,000 in 2010 to just over 40,000 by 2015 – but the Parliamentary party stayed together and there was no attempt to unseat Clegg. This unity is one of the least remarked upon but actually one of the most striking aspects of the coalition. In most other countries, not least those with long experience of coalition, loss of support on the scale suffered by the Lib Dems would have triggered increasingly urgent and widespread calls for the party in question to leave the government and to replace its leader (Bale 2012). Yet none of this – unless one counts a laughably disorganised and abortive coup against Clegg in late spring 2014 – ever happened. Explanations as to why must be tentative but may include the following:

- the lingering belief that, eventually, the public would give the party credit for its role in providing stable government for five years;
- the equally misplaced conviction among many of its MPs that their personal vote, along with the party's traditional strength in on-the-ground campaigning, would allow them, as individuals, to survive a swing that would see many of their colleagues swept away;
- the fact that, because they were such a small party, many MPs got to serve in government; and
- the fact that the Lib Dems' years in the wilderness had created a long-suffering togetherness that meant members were better able than their counterparts in other parties to discount disastrous polling and election results without becoming disheartened or mutinous.

The political impact on the electorate's preference for single-party government over coalitions seems to have been minimal. Although a few early polls suggested that voters were attracted to the idea of parties putting aside squabbles to work in the national interest, surveys throughout the period suggested that they regarded coalition as an aberration or even a necessary evil that in the end would and should give way to the much more familiar single-party majority government (Walker 2015). That said, and although there is no survey research to test this, the experiment probably wasn't so disastrous as to make people think it should never be tried again if, in the future, needs must. On the other hand, it is clear that there are deals and there are deals. Evidence emerging from studies of the 2015 election seems to show that one of the reasons the Conservatives were able to win an overall majority (albeit a slim one) had something to do with widespread concerns about a possible agreement (however loose and implicit) between Labour and the Scottish National Party (SNP). Had an arrangement between the Tories and the United Kingdom Independence Party (UKIP) looked likely, which it never did, it too may have caused just as much disquiet. What we do not know is whether there would have been anything like the same level of concern had the deal most talked about during the campaign been between, say, Labour and the Lib Dems – but it seems doubtful.

Ultimately, of course, because the Lib Dems were routed, then such a deal would not have helped Labour, even if it had managed to do what many forecasters suggested it might do and come close to the Conservatives on seats. That the rout occurred was mainly down to Clegg's decision to go into coalition in the first place and the way that the party played its hand thereafter. But it was also down to the fact that, certainly by the latter half of the Parliament and probably from its very beginning, the Tories felt no compunction at all about winning as many (if not more) seats from their coalition partners than from the opposition. And that, of course, was exactly what happened. By carefully, if stealthily, targeting resources in Lib Dem constituencies, the Conservatives won 27 of them, as opposed to the eight they took from Labour in May 2015. Early talk by some 'liberal' Tories – notably junior minister Nick Boles – about the two parties coming to some sort of electoral arrangement had by then become a distant and, for the Lib Dems at least, hollow memory. Whether one wants to talk about a black widow effect – the Tories mating and then cannibalising their erstwhile partner – or instead see the relationship as one between carnivores and vegetarians (Bale 2012), coalition was never a marriage of equals between two parties with perfectly matched intentions.

Conclusion

When the coalition first formed in May 2010, there were many observers who found it hard to believe that it would last a full term. Even the passing of the Fixed-term Parliament Act failed to convince the sceptics, who argued that if and when the government fell apart, a way could and would be found to engineer a dissolution. In the event, there was no need to do so. The two parties involved grew further apart over time, and there were one or two occasions where their mutual antipathy, or at least frustration, boiled over into very public disagreement, most obviously over constitutional reform and boundary changes to parliamentary constituencies. Yet the coalition remained intact. Moreover, it was able to provide not just five years of stable government, but also a reasonably coherent, if not necessarily successful or well-thought-through, programme aimed primarily at reducing the UK's deficit by cutting spending to benefits and services judged non-essential and electorally less sensitive. In this policy sphere and in others – the NHS, welfare, immigration and Europe, for example – the coalition also illustrated how much the government's programme was shaped by the Conservatives rather than the Lib Dems.

That the coalition was never in any danger of falling apart despite the very different prospectuses that the two parties in it had offered to the electorate was due less to the formal institutions of coalition management established and more to the good working relationships established between those at the top: both at an interparty (the so-called Quad) and at an intra-party level, best exemplified by the good relationship between Cameron and Osborne, with the latter playing the role not just of closest political friend and Chancellor but also the Conservatives' strategist-in-chief. It also owed much to the fact that the leadership of the Lib Dems had passed – to an extent that many commentators had failed sufficiently to appreciate before the election – to politicians whose views were nowhere near as far away from those of their Conservative counterparts as their party's official positions led many of its supporters to assume. The downside of this convergence, at least for the Lib Dems, was that it alienated large numbers of people who had voted for them in 2010. Add to this the fact that, like most junior partners in a coalition, the Lib Dems found it difficult to claim credit for their achievements, and the fact that they inevitably ceded their place as populist outsiders to parties like UKIP and the Greens, and their potentially catastrophic drop in support was all too predictable.

The practices and machinery of government were modified to take account of having two parties within the executive. Various means were used:

- coalition agreements;
- supervision by the centre and the relationship of Cameron and Clegg, and of Osborne and Alexander (Bennister and Heffernan 2012; 2015);
- loosening of collective responsibility;
- a principle of 'balance';
- sharing of departments; and
- additional resources.

But what is striking is that, in practice, the 'deep structure' of Whitehall – in particular, the importance of personality, party and 'informal' relationships, the inherent power of departments – remained, and was often key to understanding the coalition's operation. Where things worked, it was often due to the close working relationships between particular ministers. Where things failed to work, it was often because of the way that resources remain distributed through the executive. With a single-party Conservative government now 'returned' to Whitehall – something that only happened, note, because the Tory campaign was so ruthless and so successful in targeting Lib Dem seats – what is noticeable is how few signs there are that there a coalition ever existed: it has sunk almost without trace and the waters have closed over it. Once more there is now no Deputy Prime Minister.

Still, if one remembers some of the dire predictions about the dangers of a hung parliament and the 'stitch-ups' that would inevitably follow – most of them made, ironically, by the party which eventually ended up leading the coalition – then one cannot but be struck by the success of the experiment rather than its flaws and failures. This should not be surprising, given the experience of coalition at the subnational level; but it was not enough to convince sufficient numbers of voters at the 2015 general election to vote for the Lib Dems, the party which had, in effect, bet the house on proving that governing arrangements that are seen as par for the course in many other European countries could work perfectly well in Britain too. Notwithstanding the Lib Dems' electoral collapse, it is obvious that – in this respect at least – they were right. Whatever it might like to think, Britain is not so *sui generis* that the mechanisms used to make coalition work in other polities were irrelevant; rather, they were all there: running all the way from ministers of state placed in the 'other party's' departments, through increasingly tetchy agreements to disagree, to intensive relationship management at the very apex of government. But, as is so often the case in those other polities, those mechanisms could do nothing to prevent the junior partner paying a bigger incumbency penalty than the senior partner; nor could they compensate for the fact that that penalty was all the more serious in the Lib Dems' case because they did a deal that was not only a poor one, but ran counter to what so many of those who had voted for them wanted. Partly as a result, and unless we see another hung parliament in, say, the next ten to fifteen years, the 2010–2015 coalition is likely to be remembered as at best a testament to the resilience of the institutions that preceded it, if not as a once-in-a-lifetime aberration.

Chapter 3

Voting Behaviour and Electoral Outcomes

ALAN RENWICK

The general election of 7 May 2015 was seen in advance as the most unpredictable for decades. The polls put the two main parties – Conservative and Labour – almost neck and neck. A second consecutive hung Parliament seemed very likely. It appeared that the traditional pattern of British electoral politics, where two dominant parties competed to form single-party-majority governments, might finally – having been weakened in 2010 – be consigned to history.

In fact, the election delivered no such result (see Table 3.1). The Conservatives increased their share of the vote compared with 2010 and secured a slim majority of seats in the House of Commons. The British electoral system appeared to have reverted to type, delivering majority power to one party on the basis of a plurality of votes. Indeed, in a sense, the election was exceptional in the degree to which change did *not* happen. For the first time in any post–Second World War election, the vote shares of both main parties moved by less than 2 percentage points. Those parties' seat totals changed by fewer than 30 seats each. The Prime Minister remained in office. The composition of government changed only because the Conservatives moved from just under to just over the majority threshold.

Beneath this surface calm, however, the 2015 election saw two dramatic shifts. First, the combined vote share of the three traditional parties – Conservatives, Labour and Liberal Democrats – dropped precipitously. Their vote share in Great Britain (that is, excluding Northern Ireland, which has its own party system), having never before dropped below 90 per cent, fell to just 76.9 per cent. This reflected a collapse in support for the Liberal Democrats. The vote share of the United Kingdom Independence Party (UKIP), meanwhile, quadrupled. Second, the election in Scotland delivered a political earthquake. The Scottish National Party (SNP) rose from six of Scotland's 59 seats to 56, reducing the three traditional parties to just one apiece. For the first time, four different parties won the election in the UK's four constituent nations.

Table 3.1   *General election results: 2010 and 2015 compared*

	Votes			Seats (out of 650)		
	2010 (%)	2015 (%)	Change (%-age points)	2010	2015	Change
Conservative	36.0	36.8	+0.8	306	330	+24
Labour	29.0	30.4	+1.5	258	232	–26
Lib Dem	23.0	7.9	–15.1	57	8	–49
UKIP	3.1	12.6	+9.5	0	1	+1
Green	1.0	3.8	+2.8	1	1	–
SNP	1.7	4.7	+3.1	6	56	+50
Plaid Cymru	0.6	0.6	+0.0	3	3	–
DUP	0.6	0.6	+0.0	8	8	–
Sinn Féin	0.6	0.6	–0.0	5	4	–1
SDLP	0.4	0.3	–0.0	3	3	–
UUP	0.3	0.4	+0.0	0	2	+2
Alliance	0.1	0.2	+0.1	1	0	–1
Others	4.2	1.7	–2.5	2	2	–

Source: Author's calculations based on results at BBC News (2015b).

In important ways, these patterns were products of short-term political events and realities: Ed Miliband's failure to connect with voters; the hit on the Liberal Democrats from entering government and compromising on many policies; the charisma of UKIP's Nigel Farage in appealing to voters who felt disconnected from the political elite; the rise of Scottish nationalism around the 2014 referendum on independence; and the corresponding fear among many voters in England and Wales of government in Westminster wagged by an independence-focused Scottish tail.

But we can understand the roles of such factors best by seeing how they fitted into deeper shifts in the nature of elections in the UK. The 2015 election did not spring from nowhere: it reflected trends that have been apparent for 40 years.

Two broad shifts deserve attention: change in the voting behaviour of citizens; and change in the institutions of elections themselves. Voters have become much more detached than they were in the early post-war decades from the traditional political parties and much more inclined either to turn to a different party or not to vote at all. And though the electoral rules for Westminster elections have remained largely unaltered – a bid to replace the traditional single-member plurality

(SMP – or 'first-past-the-post') voting system with the alternative vote (AV) system in a referendum in May 2011 was defeated by a large margin – a range of electoral systems have proliferated at other elections. Indeed, Westminster elections and local elections in England and Wales are now the only public elections in the UK where plurality rule survives.

This chapter begins by outlining changes in citizens' approach to voting, the deeper societal trends that underlie this shift, and the manifestations of these patterns in 2015. It then examines how these changes have been reflected in electoral trends over recent years. Finally, it considers the impact of electoral systems, looking at patterns across a range of elections across the UK.

Citizens' changing approaches to voting and politics

It is often said that democracy in the UK – as in much of the industrialised world – is in crisis: that voters are disengaged and dissatisfied as never before and that the traditional institutions of democratic politics are failing to respond (e.g. Lent 2014). Whether this is accurate or not is debated: Norris (2011: 102–115), for example, points out that there is no clear long-term decline in satisfaction with democracy or trust in politicians, as revealed by surveys. What does appear clear, however, is that today's voters are no longer bound into politics and electoral democracy by ties to political parties to the degree that they were in the past. In the early 1950s, the three main UK parties – Conservative, Labour and the Liberals – claimed around 4 million members; by 2013, their combined membership was less than a tenth of that (Keen 2014). Though the final months of 2014 saw surging membership for the SNP and Greens, and the months after the 2015 election saw membership growth for Labour and the Liberal Democrats too, there is little reason to think these changes are more than the latest blip in a general downward trend. Opinion surveys show steady decline since around 1970 in willingness to identify with a political party among the electorate as a whole (Denver, Carman and Johns 2012: 71).

This reflects a profound shift in how voters relate to politics. Whereas in the early post-war decades, voters were typically content to throw in their lot with one party and stick with it through successive elections, today more people are willing to 'float' from one party to another. Whereas, once, voting behaviour was strongly shaped by stable class identities (Butler and Stokes 1974: 77; Pulzer 1967: 89), today, those identities have weakened and fragmented (Denver, Carman and Johns 2012: 66–70). Instead, the dominant interpretation of how voters decide whom to vote for today is the so-called 'valence model'. According to this, parties and voters agree on most things: the economy should grow;

unemployment should be low; healthcare and education should be good. Elections are fought as contests not among alternative conceptions of the future, but among alternative teams of leaders seeking to show themselves competent to deliver what people want. The key to electoral success is thus a reputation for competence, not a set of novel ideas (Clarke et al. 2004; Denver, Carman and Johns 2012: 90–122).

Equally, we should not simplify such trends too far. Class was never the only determinant of voting (Clarke et al. 2004: 73), and it still matters today: as Denver (2015: 17–19) points out, the Conservatives do best where large numbers of managers and professionals live, while Labour do so in constituencies with most manual workers. Ethnicity has an effect too (Heath et al. 2011). Furthermore, those who vote for smaller parties often do so precisely because they dislike valence-style politics, in which politicians, seeking the broadest possible support, say little of substance to avoid putting anyone off.

These patterns were visible in the 2015 general election. The most reliable evidence will come in the reports of the British Election Study, which were unavailable at the time of writing. It appears clear, however, that valence politics dominated the battle between the Conservatives and Labour: David Cameron consistently outpolled Ed Miliband by a wide margin when voters were asked who would make the best Prime Minister, and the Conservatives scored better in terms of perceived economic competence (Denver 2015: 23). At the same time, those who turned to UKIP or the Greens clearly wanted very different kinds of politics.

The result in Scotland challenges the valence model, but starkly illustrates the degree to which voters have freed themselves of traditional party ties. Scottish electoral politics had, until 2014, elegantly illustrated the rise of valence politics. Voters had increasingly differentiated their votes in Holyrood elections from those in Westminster in pursuit of the team who looked most likely to deliver competent governance at each level. Thus, though the SNP won the Scottish Parliament election in 2007, Labour returned to an easy victory in Scotland in the UK general election of 2010 (Mitchell and van der Zwet 2010). But the nationalist wave that grew through the 2014 independence referendum swept that pattern away. It unleashed polarisation around a policy question that appears destined to dominate Scotland's electoral politics for some time.

Symptoms of electoral change at Westminster

If voters are no longer as attached as they were to specific political parties, we can expect three principal changes in their voting habits over time. First, if one of the reasons citizens voted in past elections was a desire to express their partisan identities, a weakening of those identities should reduce *electoral turnout*. Second, voting should be more *volatile*:

we should expect voters to change whom they vote for more readily from election to election. Third, given the breakdown of class-based politics, we should expect a rise in the *number of parties* that voters are willing to support. This section investigates each of these possible patterns in turn in relation to UK general elections.

Figure 3.1 confirms that *turnout* has indeed fallen, the great bulk of the change having occurred with remarkable speed between 1992 (when turnout was probably pushed above trend by a close race) and 2001 (when it was below trend, at least in part because the outcome was a foregone conclusion).

The 2015 election – in which 66.2 per cent of those registered to vote turned out – continued a slow turnout recovery that began in 2005. But participation in 2015 was probably boosted by the exceptionally tight pre-election polls. And it remained lower than at any other modern general election before 2001.

Electoral volatility refers to the degree of change in whom voters support from one election to the next. Figure 3.1 charts it since 1950 (1945 is not included because of the long gap since the preceding election, in 1935). Specifically, it shows *net volatility*, which is based on changes in

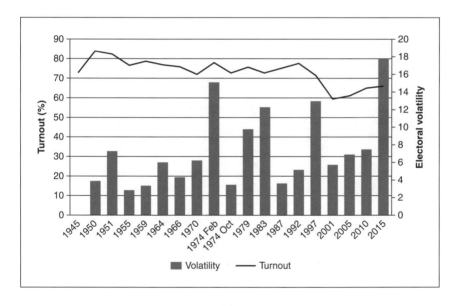

Figure 3.1   *Turnout and net volatility at UK general elections since 1945*

Note: Net volatility is measured by Pedersen's index, which takes the value of 0 if all parties win vote shares identical to those in the previous election and 100 if all votes are cast for parties that received no votes in the preceding election. It is calculated by adding up the changes in the vote percentages of all parties (ignoring whether they are increases or decreases) and then dividing by 2.

Sources: Turnout: Kavanagh and Cowley (2010: 350–351); Hawkins, Keen and Nakatudde (2015: 7). Volatility: Calculated by the author from data in Mackie and Rose (1991), Nohlen and Stöver (2010) and BBC News (2010; 2015b).

the total vote shares for each party. In reality, even where all the parties' vote shares are unchanged, there is some movement among voters: in 2015, for example, though Labour's vote share changed only slightly, it gained many votes from former Liberal Democrats while losing others to UKIP. We normally focus on net volatility because it is impossible to see such interparty 'churn' from the official election results.

As Figure 3.1 shows, volatility in 2015 was the highest since 1950. The change in the Liberal Democrats' vote share (15 percentage points) was the largest experienced by any party (up or down) during this period. The rise in UKIP's share (10 percentage points) exceeded all other post-war changes but one (the fall in Conservative support in 1997). This extended a pattern that has been apparent since 1974. Before that year, volatility was always limited: in no election did it reach the average for the period as a whole. Since 1974, however, volatility has been much higher at many – though not all – elections.

Figure 3.2 presents information on the *number of parties* that matter and confirms the intuition that British elections are no longer simple

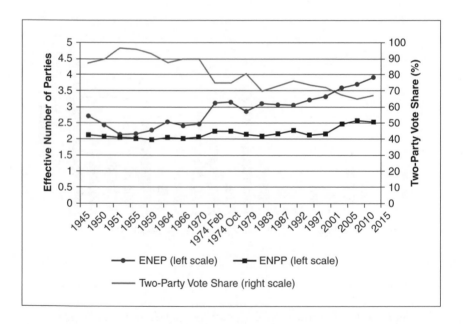

Figure 3.2   *Effective number of parties and two-party vote share at UK general elections since 1945*

Notes: ENEP is the Effective Number of Electoral Parties, calculated in terms of the parties' shares of the votes cast in the election. ENPP is the Effective Number of Parliamentary Parties, based on the seats won in Parliament. Two-Party Vote Share is the combined vote share of the Conservative and Labour parties.

Sources: Gallagher (2015) and author's calculations.

two-party affairs. The grey top line (which plots to the right-hand axis) shows the combined vote share of the Conservative and Labour parties at each election since 1945. Since peaking in 1951 at 96.7 per cent, this has fallen steadily, and in 2010 hit a low of 65.0 per cent. It recovered slightly (to 67.3 per cent) in 2015.

The two lower lines in Figure 3.2 offer a more sophisticated indicator of the number of parties, taking into account the strength of all the parties, not just the big two. The effective number of parties in terms of the votes cast at each election (the effective number of electoral parties (ENEP)) has been rising steadily since the 1950s and reached a new high in 2015 of 3.93. The effective number of parties calculated by the parties' shares of the seats in Parliament (the effective number of parliamentary parties (ENPP)) has taken longer to respond – we discuss this difference shortly, when we turn to electoral systems. But it, too, has been higher in the last three elections than at any other time since the Second World War.

The analysis in this section shows that 2015 was indeed an exceptional election: both the dispersion of votes across multiple parties and the change in voting patterns since the previous election were higher than at any other time in the post-war era. But this result did not come out of the blue: rather, it reflected an intensification of trends that have been ongoing since at least the 1970s. Voters' disengagement from the traditional parties has created an environment in which – given such short-term circumstantial factors as were mentioned in the chapter introduction – an election quite unlike any other in the UK could occur.

Before we consider the impact of electoral systems, it is worthwhile to consider how these patterns in the UK relate to those experienced in other democracies. Figure 3.3 compares the UK trends with those across the 16 European countries that have been continuously democratic since at least 1950 (the 'E16'). The upper panel shows average turnout decade-by-decade; the lower panel does the same for electoral volatility and the effective number of parties (in terms of votes cast). The trend towards rising volatility is even more consistent across democratic Europe than it is in the UK: volatility across the E16 has risen in every decade since the 1950s, most rapidly in the first half of the 2010s. The rise in the number of parties has been broadly parallel to that found in the UK (though the average number of parties is higher, reflecting, at least in part, different electoral systems). The general fall in turnout has been somewhat smaller than that in the UK, but this masks considerable variation between countries.

These patterns again point to the importance of looking at deep underlying factors to understand electoral outcomes in the UK. If the particular personalities or tactics at play in any single election were all that mattered, we would not find such consistent trends across such long periods and so many countries. This suggests that we cannot expect a 'return to normal' – to traditional two-party politics – any time soon.

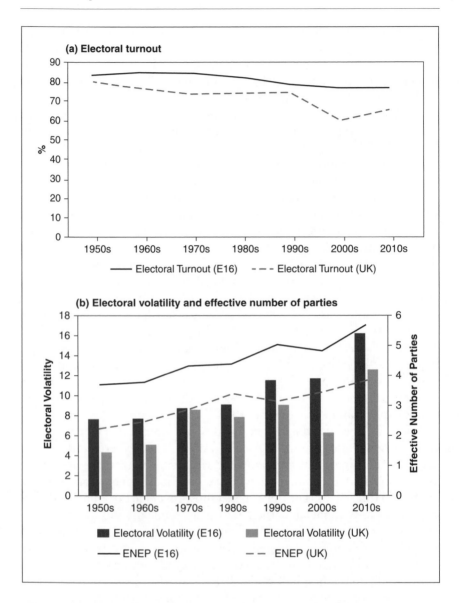

Figure 3.3   *Electoral trends in the UK and Europe compared*

Sources: Author's calculations from data in Dassonneville (2015), Gallagher (2015) and IDEA (2015).

The impact of electoral systems

So far this chapter has examined voting behaviour and its social under-pinnings. But electoral outcomes are also shaped by the rules governing the sorts of vote that voters can cast and how those votes are translated into seats – that is, by electoral systems. The previous section focused on Westminster elections, where the electoral system has been unchanging: since 1950, all Commons seats have been filled through single member plurality (SMP). The country is divided into constituencies that each elect one MP; whichever candidate secures most votes wins the seat. Beyond Westminster, however, the rules vary widely. In fact, voters in parts of the UK face a greater diversity of electoral systems than anywhere else on Earth, with an array of systems having been introduced over the last 20 years for elections to the European Parliament and devolved assemblies, as well as elections for local councils, mayors, and police and crime commissioners.

This section starts by surveying the electoral systems now used around the UK. It then analyses the impact of those systems upon election results. Finally, it considers how different systems might have affected the 2015 outcome.

Electoral systems in the UK today

Figure 3.4 sets out the electoral systems in use in public elections around the UK today. These systems belong to two broad families: majoritarian and proportional. Majoritarian systems generally involve competition for one position: either a single executive post such as a mayor or a seat in a single-member constituency. The candidate with most support wins that position. In proportional systems, by contrast, multiple positions are available in each competition and are allocated to contestants in proportion to the votes they win.

Each of these families contains multiple siblings. While all majoritarian systems give the position to the candidate with most votes, they differ in how they work out which candidate that is. Under SMP, voters choose one candidate, and whoever wins most votes is elected. That candidate can be elected with less than 50 per cent of the vote provided they win more votes than any other (i.e. they are 'first past the post'). Under supplementary vote (SV), by contrast, voters express their first and second preferences, while under AV they can rank as many candidates as they wish. Under SV and AV, candidates can only be elected having secured 50 per cent of the vote, with second preferences (or others) being taken into account if need be. Lower preferences come into play if no candidate gets an absolute majority of first preferences. SV is currently used to choose local mayors wherever they are directly elected (most notably in London) and for police and crime commissioners throughout England and Wales outside London and Manchester. AV was proposed for Westminster elections in the referendum of May 2011 (see below), but its defeat in that referendum means it has only very limited usage in the UK: for local council by-elections in Scotland.

System family	Majoritarian			Proportional		
Specific system	Single-Member Plurality (SMP)	Supplementary Vote (SV)	Alternative Vote (AV)	Closed-List PR	Mixed-Member PR (MMP)	Single Transferable Vote (STV)
Units of competition	single-member constituencies or single offices	single-member constituencies or single offices	single-member constituencies or single offices	multi-member constituencies	mix of single and multi-member constituencies	multi-member constituencies
Votes that voters can cast	single vote for one candidate	first and second preferences among candidates	ranking of all candidates	single vote for one party list	one vote for a candidate and one for a party list	ranking of all candidates
How votes translate into outcomes	the candidate with most votes wins	preferences are counted in sequence until a candidate has an absolute majority	preferences are counted in sequence until a candidate has an absolute majority	seats are distributed among parties in proportion to votes	constituency seats go to candidates with most votes; other seats are distributed to give proportionality across parties	preferences are counted until sufficient candidates meet a quota
Bodies and offices elected by this system in the UK	House of Commons; local councils in England and Wales	elected mayors; police and crime commissioners	local councils in Scotland (by-elections only)	European Parliament seats in Great Britain	Scottish Parliament; Welsh Assembly; London Assembly	local councils in Scotland and NI; NI Assembly; European Parliament seats in NI

Figure 3.4 *Electoral systems in the United Kingdom today*

Until the late 1990s, proportional representation (PR) electoral systems were confined in the UK to Northern Ireland: the single transferable vote (STV) form of PR has been used for Northern Ireland's local elections since 1973 and its European Parliament elections since 1979. Proportional systems became much more widespread, however, through the Blair government's reforms between 1997 and 2001: closed-list PR was adopted for European Parliament elections in Great Britain, the mixed-member proportional (MMP) system for the devolved assemblies in Scotland, Wales and London, and STV for elections to the Northern Ireland Assembly. STV has also subsequently been introduced and for Scottish local elections. (For details of these systems, see Farrell 2011; Renwick 2011.)

Electoral systems and the party system

Electoral systems can be expected to have two main effects upon the distribution of power across parties. First, the degree of proportionality in the electoral rules should influence the proportionality also of outcomes: the more electoral systems are designed to distribute power proportionally across parties, the more likely they are in fact to do so. Second, electoral systems affect the number of parties: majoritarian systems tend to concentrate power in the hands of a few parties, while proportional systems often spread it out across many.

These effects are illustrated for the 2015 election in the upper panel of Figure 3.5. As almost always occurs under SMP, the large parties won greater shares of the seats than of the votes, while the reverse was true for the smaller parties. Indeed, this was dramatically so. The Conservatives won a 14-percentage-point bonus in their seat share (51 per cent) over their vote share (37 per cent). Even Labour, though it lost the election badly, did better on seats (36 per cent) than votes (30 per cent). By contrast, UKIP, with 12 per cent of the votes, secured just one seat (0.15 per cent), while the Liberal Democrats won 1.2 per cent of the seats from 7.9 per cent of the votes. The performance of the SNP and, on a smaller scale, Northern Ireland's Democratic Unionist Party (DUP), might appear anomalous: they are small parties that scored better on seats than on votes. The reason is that, within their particular areas, they are large parties, able to reap the benefits of SMP. (For further analysis of the electoral system in 2015, see Curtice 2015.)

The lower panel of Figure 3.5 compares this with the result of the most recent European Parliament elections (in Great Britain only, because Northern Ireland uses a different system). Here too, the larger parties (including, this time, UKIP) tended to do better in terms of seats than votes, at the expense of smaller parties – the electoral system used does not achieve perfect proportionality. But the differences were generally smaller than in the general election.

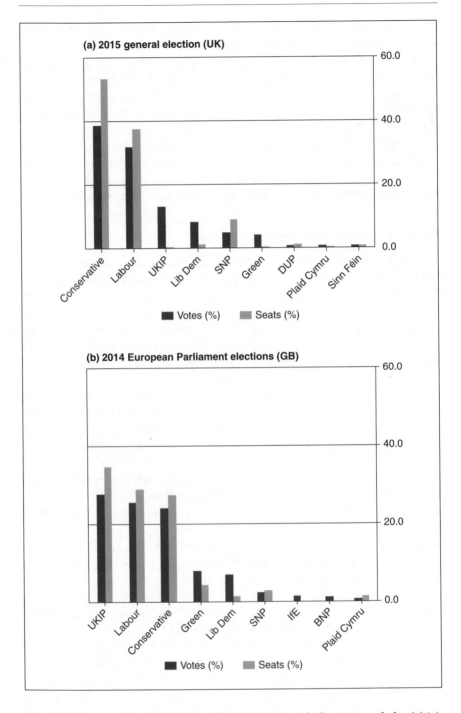

Figure 3.5   *Proportionality in the 2015 general election and the 2014 European elections*

Sources: BBC News (2014; 2015b).

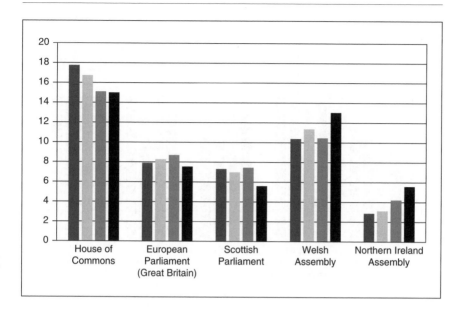

Figure 3.6 *Gallagher's index of disproportionality in the last four elections to each law-making body in the UK*

Note: House of Commons elections: 2001, 2005, 2010, 2015; European Parliament elections: 1999, 2004, 2009, 2014; Scottish Parliament, Welsh Assembly and Northern Ireland Assembly elections: 2003, 2007, 2011, 2016.

Sources: Gallagher (2015); author's calculations from BBC News (2014, 2016).

Gallagher has developed an index for comparing overall levels of proportionality in different elections (see Gallagher and Mitchell 2005: 602–605). Figure 3.6 shows the values of this index for the last four elections to various bodies. Higher numbers indicate higher levels of *dis*proportionality. Thus, as expected, disproportionality is higher in general elections – using SMP – than in any of the elections under PR. Still, there is significant disproportionality even in the supposedly proportional systems. It is highest in Wales, where there are just four PR seats per region – too few to compensate for all the disproportionalities in the constituency results.

We can repeat this analysis for the number of parties. Figure 3.7 charts the effective number of parties – calculated in terms of the votes cast (ENEP) – for the four most recent elections to a range of bodies. It shows that the number of parties has generally been lower in Westminster elections than under the various proportional systems. But the differences are not large. Indeed, going beyond the data shown, the effective number of parties in both Scotland and Northern Ireland in the general election in 2010 was higher than in the corresponding devolved assembly elections a year later – though this pattern was not repeated in 2015/16.

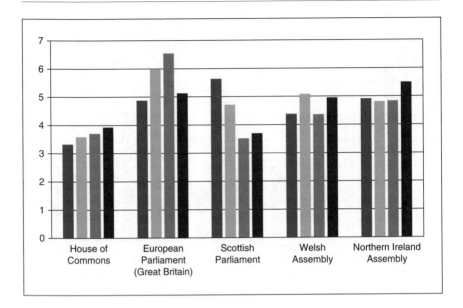

Figure 3.7   *The effective number of parties in votes (ENEP) in the last four elections to each law-making body in the UK*

Note: Election dates as in Figure 3.6.

Sources: Gallagher (2015); author's calculations from BBC News (2014, 2016).

To understand what is going on here, it is useful to consider why majoritarian systems might lead to fewer parties. The French political scientist Maurice Duverger (1954) famously argued that electoral systems have two effects – mechanical and psychological – upon the number of parties. The mechanical effect comes from how the system translates votes into seats. In majoritarian systems, small parties can win seats only if they have local pockets of strong support; otherwise, the large parties win everywhere. In more proportional systems, however, the same votes give smaller parties more seats. The psychological effect, meanwhile, comes from the fact that voters and politicians know about the mechanical effect and adjust their behaviour accordingly: voters might avoid casting a 'wasted vote' for a candidate with little prospect of victory; politicians might avoid creating a new party that faces a high barrier to success.

Because Figure 3.7 shows the effective number of parties in terms of votes (ENEP), it takes account only of the psychological effect. To capture the mechanical effect as well, we need to look at the effective number of parties in terms of parliamentary seats (ENPP). Indeed, when we looked at both measures in Figure 3.2, we saw that, while ENPP has increased somewhat in recent Westminster elections, it has risen much less than ENEP. And if we repeated the analysis of Figure 3.7 for ENPP, we would find a larger gap between the plurality elections for Westminster and the proportional elections elsewhere. The mechanical effect, therefore, continues to function.

But the trend shown in Figure 3.2 suggests that the psychological effect has weakened: voters seem readier to vote for smaller parties today than in the past. Part of the explanation for this is that Duverger's argument really applies to individual constituencies, not the nationwide result: voters, he predicts, will choose between the serious contenders; but the contest in each constituency is separate; so what matters is who has a chance of winning locally. If different parties are strong in different parts of the country, that could lead to high ENEP even when Duverger's mechanisms are working fully. Indeed, the rise of nationalist parties in Scotland and Wales and the tendency of Conservative and Labour votes to concentrate in, respectively, the south and the north do indicate a regional differentiation of voting patterns.

Even if this is the case, however, the dispersion of votes *within* constituencies has increased too. The combined vote share of the top two candidates in each constituency peaked in 1951 at an average of 97.8 per cent (author's calculations from data kindly supplied by Jennifer Hudson). By 1997, however, it had fallen to 80.7 per cent, and by 2015 to 75.5 per cent. So voters today are apparently more willing to vote for candidates with little chance of winning than in the past. The power of the electoral system to shape the election result has weakened.

There are several possible explanations for this pattern. One could be that, now that many voters are less engaged with politics, they have less understanding of who the main contenders in their area are. Such understanding is also harder when more parties are in contention nationally. But many voters clearly do understand what they are doing. As voters see less difference between the main parties, they may think there is more value in sending the political establishment a message by supporting an outsider than in influencing which of the mainstream parties wins. They might also hope that a gradual build-up of support for a small party could foster long-term change in electoral dynamics. Thus, for many voters, the characterisation of a vote for a hopeless candidate as a 'wasted vote' is no longer valid.

A further explanation is that the proliferation of proportional electoral systems away from Westminster may influence how people vote in general elections too. It is difficult for new parties to break into Westminster politics in part because, under SMP, such parties struggle to overcome the initial hurdle of looking like credible contenders: so long as they are viewed as also-rans, they attract little attention or support. If they overcome the credibility gap in proportional elections, however, that can seep into their subsequent performance under SMP. UKIP's success in winning the 2014 European Parliament elections, for example, raised its profile and credibility and fuelled its entry to Westminster politics. Similarly, while the SNP has long held some seats in Westminster, it broke out of its traditional bastions only after developing its support base and network of activists through elections to Holyrood.

Thus, even if SMP constrains the party system less today than in the past, electoral systems still matter. That fact was cruelly apparent to UKIP and Liberal Democrat supporters in the wake of the 2015 election, while Conservative and SNP supporters were its beneficiaries.

Would the Alternative Vote (AV) have made a difference?

Under the Conservative–Liberal Democrat coalition deal, a referendum was held in May 2011 on whether to change the system for electing the House of Commons from SMP to AV. The Conservatives are long-standing supporters of SMP, the Liberal Democrats of PR. The AV referendum was a compromise between them. As noted above, AV is not a proportional, but a majoritarian, system. The Liberal Democrats hoped it would provide a stepping stone to more fundamental reform. They expected – and previous projections predicted (e.g., Sanders et al. 2011) – that they would gather many second preferences from other parties' supporters, thereby gaining extra seats. The Conservatives, meanwhile, hoped to defeat the measure, and could reassure themselves that, even if adopted, AV would likely change the distribution of seats only marginally. (On the processes leading to the referendum, see Curtice 2013a.)

In the end, the Conservatives' calculations proved correct: AV was heavily defeated, by 68 per cent to 32 per cent. The idea of electoral reform did not capture the public imagination, and many voters opted for the familiarity of the status quo (Laycock et al. 2013).

Nevertheless, we can ask how AV – or, indeed, more fundamental electoral reform – would have affected the election outcome in 2015. There was some pre-election speculation that the Conservatives might come to rue their decision to oppose AV: the rise of UKIP might split the right-of-centre vote under SMP, allowing Labour or the Liberal Democrats to secure extra seats (Hanretty 2015). Following the Conservatives' unexpected victory, such possibilities were forgotten. But it is useful to examine the evidence.

Table 3.2 compares the actual election result with projected seat distributions under four alternative systems: a very pure version of PR

Table 3.2   *The 2015 election result under alternative electoral systems (Great Britain only)*

	Actual	*Pure PR**	*Regional PR***	*STV****	*AV*****
Conservative	330	239	252	276	336
Labour	232	198	211	236	227
UKIP	1	82	81	54	1
Lib Dem	8	51	49	26	9
SNP	56	31	30	34	54
Green	1	25	6	3	1
Plaid Cymru	3	4	4	3	3
TUSC	0	1	0	0	0
Speaker	1	1	0	0	1

*Author's calculations, using the Sainte-Laguë formula in a single district covering the whole of Great Britain.

**From Curtice (2015: 38), dividing Great Britain into the eleven European Parliament regions and applying the d'Hondt formula with a 5 per cent regional threshold.

***From Garland and Terry (2015: 27–28, 33–35), applying STV in small multi-member districts of 2–5 seats, drawing on polling evidence on second and lower preferences.

****From Garland and Terry (2015: 27–28, 33–35), applying AV to existing constituencies, drawing on polling evidence on second and lower preferences.

where all seats (in Great Britain) are distributed in a single district with no electoral threshold; a more realistic form of PR, where seats are distributed in the regions used for European Parliament elections with a 5 per cent threshold; STV applied in small multi-member constituencies; and AV itself.

Such projections should be treated with caution. Those for pure and regional PR are calculated simply by applying the specified electoral system to the votes that were actually cast. They therefore show mechanical effects, but take no account of any psychological effect. The STV and AV estimates draw on information from a large-scale survey for the Electoral Reform Society in which respondents were asked to rank parties in order of preference (Garland and Terry 2015: 33–35). This allows psychological as well as mechanical effects to be explored. But it still asks voters who experienced the election under SMP to imagine their hypothetical preferences under a different system. Had STV or AV actually been used, the campaign might have unfolded differently, leading to different final preferences.

Still, accepting the projections for what they are, we can first see the degree to which the actual result deviated from a purely proportional result, reflecting the considerable disproportionalities already discussed. Regional PR with a 5 per cent threshold would have secured high proportionality in most respects, but would still have underrepresented the Green Party, who passed 5 per cent in only two regions. The small constituencies used for the STV projection lead to greater deviation from pure proportionality, but still no party would have approached an overall majority. Finally, two features of the AV projection are notable. First, it is very similar to the actual result, confirming AV's limited differences from SMP. Second, the Conservatives would, as predicted, have done better under AV – but only marginally.

Conclusion

The 2015 general election restored single-party majority government to the UK. Beyond that apparent return to 'normal' politics, however, the result was exceptional in many ways. Electoral volatility and support for non-traditional parties both hit record highs. The Liberal Democrats suffered losses unseen by any party in the post-war period. UKIP and the SNP (in very different ways) experienced record gains. These changes did not spring from nowhere. Rather, they were the latest manifestations of long-term trends that have been building since the 1970s. Voters have become increasingly disengaged from their traditional parties and increasingly willing to experiment with new alternatives. In recent years, these trends have been strengthened by the introduction of a range of innovative electoral systems, whose effects have seeped back to Westminster. Despite the surface calm, the 2015 election confirmed that UK electoral politics has changed profoundly.

Chapter 4

The Party System: Turbulent Multipartyism or Duopolistic Competition?

PAUL WEBB

How should we best characterise the British party system in the wake of the 2015 general election? Has it undergone a significant and enduring realignment, or merely experienced a moment of passing turbulence, after which things have returned to the seemingly eternal verities of stable two-party competition? The notion of party system realignment was pioneered by US political scientists (Key 1955; Burnham 1970) and essentially refers to the process by which blocs of electoral support which have habitually been associated with particular parties shift towards their rivals; such a process also generally entails a change in the ideological or programmatic nature of party competition. The closely related concept of a 'critical election' refers to an election in which the process of changing links between social groups and parties is catalysed by the impact of particular issues, candidates or events. These are the moments when a long-term process of realignment becomes manifest. While realignment may be something that only occurs once every few generations, and is therefore likely to be driven by gradual forces of underlying change, it may take one or sometimes two consecutive elections for these forces to achieve a critical mass that will effect the realignment. In the United States, such critical elections are widely held to have occurred in 1800, 1828, 1860, 1896, 1932 and 1964. In Britain these were the elections of:

- 1924 (when the Liberals were surpassed by Labour as one of the major two parties);
- 1945 (when Labour first achieved a parliamentary majority as millions of working-class voters previously loyal to the Conservatives flocked to its banner); and perhaps
- 1979 or 1983 (when Margaret Thatcher's Conservatives wrested back the support of a large chunk of working-class support and changed the terrain of policy debate in an enduring way).

How then to regard the period surrounding the general elections of 2010 and 2015? Might they jointly constitute a moment of critical realignment? Or a relatively prolonged transition from a period of Labour Party domination to one of Conservative Party ascendancy based on a regular swing of the electoral pendulum? In other words, a simple affirmation of the age-old dynamics of the two-party system? Having reviewed the long-term context of change in the party system from 1970 to 2010, the chapter considers the key developments of the past few years, noting in particular the effects of the coalition experience on Conservative and Liberal Democrat support, the strategic travails of Labour and the surge in popularity enjoyed by the United Kingdom Independence Party (UKIP), the Scottish National Party (SNP) and the Greens. How have these things affected the dynamics of the party system? It is simplistic to conclude that the UK remains a case of unalloyed two-partyism in its fundamentals: it is too fragmented inside Parliament and (especially) within the electorate for this to be convincing. The sheer volatility of electoral behaviour has seen an extraordinary amount of individual level churn as voters switch from one party to another (or to and from abstention). But, for all that, one of the defining features of two-party politics – the ability of parties to form governments on their own – has returned, and may be here for the foreseeable future. The electoral system used for House of Commons elections remains key to understanding why this is so, and means that the pattern of a multiparty system and coalition or minority governments that eventuated in 2010 has not yet been institutionalised as a norm of Westminster politics. The picture remains unclear: at the level of the electorate, multipartyism combined with significant electoral volatility are clearly present, but this has not yet translated fully into a realigned system of multiparty politics in Parliament.

The transformation of two-party unitary politics in terms of vote share, seat share and party membership, 1970–2010

Since 1970 the party system has become significantly more fragmented as the major parties have haemorrhaged support to the smaller parties, and the politics of coalition has become increasingly normal across Britain's multiple levels of government. In essence, these developments are important features of the ongoing transformation of Britain from a centralised unitary state with a simple two-party system into a decentralised multilevel state with a complex multiparty system. Developments during the period 2010–2015 have to be set in the context of the longer-term processes of secular transformation that characterised the erosion of the old two-party duopoly after 1970.

Changing vote and seat share

Explicit in much of the literature on British electoral behaviour and party competition is the notion that something started to change from the general election of February 1974. From 1945 to 1970 it is perfectly appropriate to speak of party interactions in Britain in terms of the classic two-party system which is inherent to majoritarian democracy; thereafter, matters are not so clear-cut (Denver, Carman and Johns 2012). A number of key features characterised the period up to 1974, including: the high proportion of votes absorbed by Labour and the Conservatives; the degree of electoral balance between them; a centripetal pattern of competition usually targeted on trying to command the electoral centre-ground; the ability of one or the other of the major parties to govern alone; and a regular alternation in power of the major parties. Since 1974, much in this picture of simple two-party competition has changed:

- the average share of the vote absorbed by the major parties, which stood at 90.3 per cent for the period 1945–1970, has remained below 75 per cent since 1974, and reached a new low of 65 per cent in 2010;
- the degree of electoral imbalance between the major parties has grown perceptibly, from a mean difference of 3.9 per cent in their levels of national support up to and including 1970, to 9.0 per cent in 2010; and
- as a corollary of major-party decline, we have witnessed the emergence of significant 'minor' parties since 1970; most notably, of course, the Liberal Democrats (and their predecessors) achieved an average vote of around 20 per cent in the elections from 1974–2010 (compared to just 7.1 per cent previously), while the Scottish and Welsh nationalists emerged as significant electoral forces in their respective regions.

The advent of devolution has only served to enhance the importance of the nationalist parties to the British political system, as the devolved parts of the UK have continued to gain more powers at the expense of Westminster. Moreover, the continuing fragmentation of the party system has handed the minor parties an increasing significance at Westminster as well, given their potential for coalition-building.

The simplest way of measuring this growing party system fragmentation which threatens the norm of single-party government at Westminster is by referring to the changing 'effective number of parties' (Laakso and Taagepera 1979). This well-known indicator takes account of both the number of parties in the system and their relative strength, and tells us, for instance, that in any system comprising just two equally strong parties, the effective number will indeed be 2.0, while a system consisting of three equally strong parties will generate an effective number of 3.0, and so on. However, a system consisting of two large parties and one small party would have an effective number far closer to 2.0 than to 3.0.

This measure can be calculated either on the basis of party shares of the popular vote (the effective number of *electoral* parties (ENEP)), or on the basis of shares of seats won in Parliament (the effective number of *parliamentary* parties (ENPP)). Table 4.1 reports general election results since 1945, and clearly shows a growth in the effective number of parties after 1970. Given the distorting effect of 'first-past-the-post' single-member plurality (SMP), this is less pronounced in respect of parliamentary parties than electoral parties, though it is still apparent.

The average ENPP from 1945 to 1970 was 2.05, but it increased to 2.24 for the period from 1974 to 2010; the ENEP average shows a more marked increase, from 2.36 (up to 1970) to 3.25 (post-1970). By 2010, the ENPP stood at 2.56, and the ENEP at 3.56. These trends neatly summarise the emergence of a multiparty system in both electoral and legislative arenas at central government level.

Underpinning the loosening grip of the traditional two-party system has been a general loss of partisan attachment among voters. Although British Election Study data suggests that the average number of voters claiming a habitual partisan identification only dropped moderately, from 92 per cent in the 1960s to 86 per cent in the 1980s (at which level it has broadly stabilised ever since), the number admitting to a 'very strong' partisan identification has dropped sharply – from 44 per cent in the 1960s, to 30 per cent in the 1970s, and just 13 per cent by the 2000s.

Declining party membership

Even more notable has been the precipitous decline in the proportion of Britons who join political parties (see Table 4.2). Although in purely numerical terms the Conservative Party was probably for many a year the closest thing to a mass-membership party in Britain, it is evident that it has suffered greatly from membership decline:

- in 1953, the Conservatives claimed some 2,800,000 members nationally;
- in 1974, the Royal Commission on party finance (the Houghton Commission) estimated that this had fallen to 1,500,000;
- in 1992, Whiteley, Seyd and Richardson (1994: 25) put the national figure at approximately 750,000;
- by the time of the 1997 general election, this had collapsed to 400,000; and
- by 2010 to 177,000 (whereafter it continued to fall). Thus, it seems that Conservative Party membership fell by approximately 95 per cent over the course of little more than half a century.

Table 4.1   *UK general election results since 1945*

| | Conservative | | Labour | | Liberal Democrat | | Others | | | | |
	Vote	Seats	Vote	Seats	Vote	Seats	Vote	Seats	ENEP	ENPP	Turnout
1945	39.8	213	48.3	393	9.1	12	2.7	22	2.52	2.07	72.8
1950	43.5	299	46.1	315	9.1	9	1.3	2	2.40	2.07	83.9
1951	48.0	321	48.8	295	2.5	6	0.7	3	2.13	2.05	82.6
1955	49.7	345	46.4	277	2.7	6	1.1	2	2.16	2.03	76.8
1959	49.4	365	43.8	258	5.9	6	0.9	1	2.28	1.99	78.7
1964	43.4	304	44.1	317	11.2	9	1.3	0	2.53	2.06	77.1
1966	41.9	253	47.9	363	8.5	12	1.7	2	2.42	2.03	75.8
1970	46.4	330	43.0	287	7.5	6	3.1	7	2.46	2.08	72.0
1974F	37.8	297	37.1	301	19.3	14	5.8	23	3.13	2.25	78.8
1974O	35.8	277	39.2	319	18.3	13	6.7	26	3.16	2.25	72.8
1979	43.9	339	37.0	269	13.8	11	5.3	16	2.87	2.14	76.0
1983	42.4	397	27.6	209	25.4	23	4.6	21	3.45	2.09	72.7
1987	42.3	376	30.8	229	22.6	22	4.4	23	3.33	2.17	75.3
1992	41.9	336	34.4	271	17.8	20	5.8	24	3.03	2.26	77.7
1997	30.7	165	43.3	419	16.8	46	9.3	29	3.21	2.11	71.5
2001	31.7	166	40.7	413	18.3	52	9.3	28	3.25	2.10	59.5
2005	32.3	197	35.2	355	22.0	62	10.5	32	3.48	2.46	60.9
2010	36.1	307	29.0	258	23.0	57	11.9	28	3.56	2.56	65.1
2015	36.9	331	30.4	232	7.9	8	24.8	79	3.95	2.54	66.1

Note: 'Liberal Democrat' refers to the Liberal Party for the period 1974-1979, and the SDP–Liberal alliance in 1983 and 1987. 'ENEP' refers to Laakso and Taagepera's index of the effective number of electoral parties in a system; 'ENPP' refers to the effective number of parliamentary parties (Laakso and Taagepera 1979).

Sources: Nuffield election studies; British Governments and elections website (http://www.psr.keele.ac.uk/area/uk/uktable.htm).

Table 4.2   *Major party individual membership in the UK since 1964*
(selected years)

Year	Labour	Conservative	Lib/Lib. Dem.
1964	830,116	2,150,000	278,690
1966	775,693	2,150,000	234,345
1970	680,191	2,150,000	234,345
1974	691,889	1,500,000	190,000
1979	666,091	1350000	145,000
1983	295,344	1,200,000	145,258*
1987	288,829	1000000	137,500*
1992	279,530	500,000	100,000
1997	405,000	400,000	100,000
2005–10	177,000**	177,000***	65,000***
2015a	190,000	149,800	44,576
2015b	370,658	149,800	60,844

Note: 2015a = reported figures at time of general election in May; 2015b = post-election figures reported in various sources. * Includes SDP membership figures; ** (2007); *** (2010).

Sources: Labour Party NEC Annual Reports; National Union of Conservative & Unionist Associations; Liberal Democrats Information Office; Berrington and Hague 1997: 48; LibDem Voice; *Daily Telegraph*; Conservativehome.com; http://www.conservativehome.com/thetorydiary/2014/09/conference-survey-and-membership-figures.html; http://www.libdemvoice.org/lib-dem-membership-up-for-15th-consecutive-month-43221.html; Richard Keen 'Membership of UK political parties', Standard Note SN05125, House of Commons Library, August 2015; Jon Stone 'More people have joined Labour since the election than are in the entire Conservative Party', *The Independent*, 8 October 2015; http://eastlibdems.org.uk/en/article/2015/1111728/record-number-of-members-head-to-liberal-democrat-conference.

Labour, too, has suffered a dramatic loss of individual members during this period, although this derives in part from a change in party rules in 1980 (Webb 2000: 220), and has occurred notwithstanding moments of resurgence, such as the early years of Tony Blair's leadership in the mid-1990s, and indeed, in the aftermath of the general election of 2015:

- it claimed 830,000 individual members in the 1960;
- it boasted 405,000 members at the height of the 'Blair bounce' in 1997;
- it fell to 177,000 members by the time that Ed Miliband was elected leader in the autumn of 2010;
- but recovered slightly to 190,000 by the end of 2014 (Nardelli 2014), even if still representing a drop of 77 per cent over the period as a whole.

In proportionate terms, this is almost identical to the decline that the Liberals/Liberal Democrats suffered in the same span of time – from 278,690 to 65,000. By the end of the 2010–2015 Parliament, Liberal Democrat membership had further fallen to just 44,576 members (Keen 2015). That said, both Labour and the Liberal Democrats enjoyed remarkable and unexpected surges in membership following their respectively disappointing results in the 2015 election (see below).

The only counterpoint to this generalised picture of membership decline prior to the election was offered by the growth that some of the smaller parties enjoyed – most obviously, the SNP, the Greens and UKIP. One of the corollaries of the electoral progress forged by the minor parties since 2010 has been the recent rise in membership numbers they have enjoyed. In the wake of the Scottish independence referendum of September 2014, there was a surge in SNP popularity which enabled the party to draw in many new members; indeed, by January 2015, the party was claiming 92,000, making it Britain's third-largest party by this indicator. At the same time, the Green Party totalled approximately 50,000 members, while UKIP matched them closely at 41,514. Plaid Cymru had around 8,000 members (Ramsay 2015). In all, approximately 1 per cent of registered UK voters were signed-up party members by the time of the 2015 election.

Party politics 2010–2015

The changes that have affected the British party system since 1970 have mainly been gradual, as if the tectonic plates of the country's politics have been slowly shifting. But when the movement of tectonic plates reaches a certain point, the cumulative pressure of change can become critical and lead to structural realignment. There was a palpable sense in which the election of 2010 might have proved to be a moment of critical realignment, in so far as it signalled the final death-knell of the old two-party duopoly and the undeniable emergence of fully fledged multiparty politics. This change implied that the era of single-party majorities at Westminster was behind us, which is not to suggest that they would henceforward be entirely unimaginable, but rather that for the foreseeable future they would be less likely to be the norm. Minority governments and coalitions would instead become a not uncommon state of affairs, in as much as which Britain would become a country more, rather than less, like most of its continental European counterparts. However, the outcome of the 2015 election casts this interpretation in considerable doubt, for the surprising emergence of a majority Conservative government would seem to take us back to the future of classic two-partyism.

The Tories: Once more the natural party of government?

The unexpected victory of the Conservatives in 2015, based on stability of support rather than a significant surge forward, meant that the party was now guaranteed an unbroken minimum run of 10 years in national office. This marks a welcome return for the Conservatives to the often-claimed role of Britain's 'natural party of government' after a lengthy hiatus in which it had failed to win a majority since the (also unexpected) victory of John Major's party at the 1992 general election. This is indeed a blessed position for the party to be in after five years of sharing power with the Liberal Democrats, even if their more recalcitrant backbenchers were wont to complain about the constraints imposed by the compromises necessitated by coalition.

Yet there are reasons for the Conservatives to be cautious about their position after the triumph of 2015. First, there is little to suggest that affinity for the party runs deep among British voters. The British Election Study post-election survey suggests that just 29.5 per cent of voters were willing to define themselves as people who generally identify with the party; remarkably, given the result, this is actually fewer than the number (30.8 per cent) identifying with the defeated Labour Party. Moreover, only 8 per cent of voters saw themselves as 'very strong' Conservative partisans. Similarly, the Tories earned a lower average mark (4.29) than Labour (4.53) on a scale running from 0 ('dislike') to 10 ('like'). Perhaps most extraordinarily of all, the Conservatives are generally perceived to be more remote from the average voter in general ideological terms than any of the main parties. The mean self-location of electors on a scale running from 0 (left) to 10 (right) is 5.08; these voters regard the Liberal Democrats as the nearest on them on the whole, with an average score just −0.33 to their left, while they see the SNP (−1.72), Plaid Cymru (−1.83), Labour (−2.00) and the Greens (−2.26) further left. Only two of the main parties are seen as being to their right: UKIP (+2.64) and the Conservatives (+2.71) (British Election Study 2015). Even so, the Tories won, and they did so largely because of the impact of two highly salient considerations in voters' minds:

- they were perceived to have the best candidate for the Prime Minister's job in David Cameron (whose evaluations far outstripped those of Labour leader Ed Miliband, just as they had done in respect of Gordon Brown in 2010); and
- they were trusted as the safer option in managing the economy (Bale and Webb 2015: 50–51).

Furthermore, there is no doubt that the quirks of the electoral system assisted them in achieving an overall majority in the Commons. Perhaps the central paradox of the 2015 result is that the chief beneficiary of

Labour's progress at the expense of the Liberal Democrats was the Conservative Party. That is, while disgruntled ex–Liberal Democrat voters were more likely to defect to Labour than to any other party in 2015, this actually helped the Tories most in terms of overall seat gains. Of those who voted Liberal Democrat in 2010, some 30.4 per cent opted for Labour in 2015, compared to 11.2 per cent for the Conservatives (and 29.2 per cent for the Liberal Democrats again) (British Election Study 2015). However, this profited Labour little and the Tories greatly, given that in 33 of the 57 seats that the Liberal Democrats were defending, their nearest challengers were the Conservatives, compared with only 17 in which Labour were the main rivals. Thus, Labour took Liberal Democrat votes and let in Tory winners. In the event, the Conservatives gained 27 seats from the Liberal Democrats, while Labour took just 12 seats from them. Under any kind of reasonably proportional electoral system, such an outcome would not have been possible.

The electoral system benefited the Conservatives in Scotland – not in the sense that the party made any direct gains there, but rather in the way that it benefited from Labour's electoral mauling at the hands of the SNP. Labour lost hugely north of the border in 2015, with its 2010 vote share of 42 per cent dropping to just 24.3 per cent, while the SNP surged from 20 per cent to 50 per cent. Dramatic as this shift in public opinion undoubtedly was, however, it could not have resulted in a situation in which the nationalists took 56 out of 59 Scottish seats (95 per cent) had the disproportional SMP not been the electoral system. Despite having the support of a quarter of the Scottish electorate, Labour returned just one MP, which was less than 2 per cent of Scottish seats.

Almost serendipitously, then, the Conservatives regained their once habitual status of the single and 'natural' party of government. How would they respond? At the time of writing, the answer appears to be by adopting a strategy that is in many ways the mirror image of that which new Labour adopted during its heyday, which is to say, by adopting the rhetoric and tone of moderation and centrism, while acting rather more radically in practice. While Blair and Brown had plainly sought to reassure middle England through creating a carefully constructed image of moderate centrism (Heffernan 2001; Hindmoor 2004), they were able to act radically in a number of significant ways (unprecedented levels of expenditure on health and education, the introduction of the minimum wage and new trade union recognition rights, a one-off 'windfall tax' on privatised utilities, and a raft of major constitutional reforms such as devolution and the adoption of a Human Rights Act). Early in the new Parliament, David Cameron, chancellor George Osborne and their team showed signs of attempting the mirror image of this strategy: at the party conference in 2015, there was prominent talk of One-Nation Toryism, the Tories as the party of working people, an 'attack on poverty', and even reform of the prison system with a new emphasis on rehabilitation and social justice (from Justice Minister Michael Gove no less, hitherto a bête noire of the left). They have been assisted in this apparent manoeuvre by Labour's shift to the left (of which more below), which opens up the centre-ground. At the same time, however, much of the new government resonated rather more with the right-wing politics of the Thatcher era – council house sell-offs, welfare cuts, curtailment of local government financial cross-subsidies, and of course the prospect of further widespread financial austerity across the public sector (Milne 2015). It remains to be seen how this will play out under Cameron's successor as Prime Minister, Theresa May. But given the enfeebled position of the opposition, this may prove an effective strategy for long-term success by the Tories. The risks to the party stem from the slimness of its Commons majority (just 12) and, as ever, the potential disruption of unexpected or unmanageable events: the most obvious challenges are the need to steer the UK successfully through Brexit referendum, without dividing the party, and the impact on economy and electorate of further austerity.

Labour's travails

Labour's response to the electoral defeat of 2010 was to choose Ed Miliband as leader and seemingly settle on what some said was a '35 per cent strategy'. This was the idea of adding a few percentage points onto the 2010 score of 29 per cent, largely by absorbing disgruntled progressives from the Liberal Democrats. This reflected the assumptions that:

- the electorate might have shifted to the left in the wake of the financial crisis of 2008; and
- the bias in the electoral system which had helped Labour at general elections since the 1980s would continue to operate.

It was hoped this would be enough to deliver the party an overall majority in the Commons in 2015. In order to achieve this, the party simply had to distance itself from the now tarnished legacy of new Labour, in the process reasserting an image that was more distinctively (if not necessarily radically) left-wing. Thus, little attempt was made to defend the policies of the Blair and Brown years (even in the face of the frequent and, in principle, contestable attacks by the coalition parties, especially on Labour's record of economic management), while promises were made to reintroduce a 50 per cent top rate of income tax, impose price freezes on the energy companies, introduce a 'living wage' as part of a 'pre-distribution' strategy, and criticising 'predatory' (as opposed to 'productive') capitalism (Fielding 2015). While this hardly amounted to a brand of socialism that was red in tooth and claw, it was still portrayed by opponents as lurch to the left by 'Red Ed' and did not serve to convince the electorate as a whole that the party could be trusted with the direction of the economy; and neither did Ed Miliband ever manage to persuade enough of his personal credentials to be Prime Minister. Thus, while the party made modest progress at the 2015, it was nowhere near enough to muster the 35 per cent that had been deemed necessary and sufficient to reclaim the keys of Downing Street.

The response of the party to defeat in 2015 was even more unexpected than that of 2010. While the victory of Ed over David Miliband in the party leadership election of 2010 was a surprise to most observers, the extraordinary campaign of Jeremy Corbyn in 2015 was truly astonishing. Several Labour' MPs who did not actually support him nominated Corbyn merely in order to allow a candidate of the radical left to stand and thereby broaden the debate. None of them expected what followed. His downbeat, unspun style lent him an air of authenticity, while he was able to set out a position that was more distinctly left-wing than those of any his established frontbench rivals (Yvette Cooper, Andy Burnham and Liz Kendall). This played well with many disillusioned party members and trade unionists. The new rules for the leadership election also gave the right to participate to anyone willing to declare themselves party 'supporters' and pay £3 for the privilege. Over the course of the summer of 2015, a remarkable surge in grass-roots enthusiasm swept Corbyn to an emphatic victory as the party membership swelled from 190,000 in May to 370,000 in the autumn. An additional 112,000 signed on as 'registered supporters', and there were also 148,000 'affiliated members' from the trade unions (Stone 2015). Some 60 per cent of the 420,000 eligible voters who cast a ballot chose Corbyn, the 66-year-old backbench veteran of the left and MP for Islington North since 1983. During this time, he had developed a reputation as an implacable critic of Labour's frontbench and by rebelling against the party line in Commons divisions more than any other serving parliamentarian.

As leader, Corbyn and his left-wing ally, shadow chancellor John McDonnell, rapidly set out positions as anti-austerity politicians, open to renationalisation of the railways, a higher minimum wage, new trade union rights and reversing Conservative welfare payment caps. Most controversially, being a life-long unilateral nuclear disarmer, Corbyn declared he would never under any circumstances use Britain's nuclear capability were he Prime Minister. Hence, Labour's response to two successive general election defeats seemed to be to move further leftwards on each occasion. But Corbyn, if popular with Labour members, lacked any significant base of support among Labour MPs, something reflecting the huge disparity in attitude towards his leadership between its grass-roots members on the one hand, and its MPs and the wider public, on the other. This pointed to a unique dilemma for Labour: it had an unpopular leadership that was apparently doing it no favours in terms of the party's electoral standing (which was lagging 15 points behind the Tories at the end of 2015) – but with little prospect of the leadership being changed given its popularity among those who elect it (the membership). The unpromising position of Labour under Corbyn was underlined in the first major electoral test the party faced after the general election, the local and devolved elections of May 2016. Labour was pushed down into third place in the Scottish parliamentary elections, being superseded by the Tories as the new official opposition at Holyrood, while Labour lost local councils seats across England and Wales – the first time in more than half a century that a new Leader of the Opposition did so in his first electoral test.

The eclipse of the Liberal Democrats

The continued fragmentation of the party system since 2010 owes much to the participation of the Liberal Democrats in government. For so many years since 1970, the Liberal Democrats and their predecessor parties (the Liberals and Social Democrats) had established themselves as a significant presence in British party politics precisely because they were the major option for expressing protest against the Conservative–Labour duopoly. While considering themselves a party with serious policies and qualities, far more than a mere 'protest party', there can be little doubt that their availability as a means of expressing dissatisfaction with the major governing options formed part of their enduring appeal. With their participation in the governing coalition of 2010, that option was removed. Voters dissatisfied with the performance of the Conservative–Liberal Democrat coalition, but unconvinced by Ed Miliband's Labour opposition, would henceforward have to look further afield – or simply to abstain – if they were to find acceptable alternatives at the ballot box. This explains why British Election Survey data reveals that of those who voted Liberal Democrat in 2010, more than 40 per cent defected to Labour or the Conservatives in the 2015 election. It should, however, be noted that many others opted for minor party alternatives. The principal beneficiaries would be UKIP and the Greens, who each absorbed about 9 per cent of former Liberal Democrat voters. Nick Clegg's party ended up with just 8 per cent of the votes cast (down from 23 per cent in 2010) and eight seats (down from 57).

Plainly, the experience of becoming a governing party wrought immense electoral damage upon the Liberal Democrats. Struggling to show their specific contribution to government policy, they became associated with unpopular austerity economics and – worse – with a notorious U-turn on university tuition fees that the party agreed to perform as part of the coalition deal in 2010. Leader Nick Clegg's personal ratings with the public never recovered from that episode, while the party's opinion polls scores dropped precipitously. In the aftermath of the election, former party president (and one of its few remaining MPs) Tim Farron comfortably defeated Norman Lamb for the party leadership, Clegg having stood down immediately after the general election. Farron, a backbencher, came with a reputation as someone from the progressive social liberal wing of the party, and was not tainted by the experience of having been a member of the coalition government. Time will tell if Labour's move to the left under Corbyn presents an opportunity for the Liberal Democrats to attract voters on the progressive but non-socialist centre-left of British politics – the sort who might have been attracted by new Labour administrations previously but were dismayed by Corbyn's Labour.

The nationalist parties in Scotland and Wales

In many ways the most remarkable performance in the 2015 election was achieved by the Scottish nationalists. Founded as far back as 1934, the SNP's political fortunes began to surf on a developing wave of popular nationalist sentiment from the late 1960s. A famous by-election victory at Hamilton in 1967 is often cited as the turning point in the party's history, and in 1974 it enjoyed an unparalleled surge in electoral support, first to 21.9 per cent of the vote in Scotland and seven seats at Westminster (February), and then to 30.4 per cent and 11 seats (October). Having endured a slump in support and a period of factionalism in the 1980s, Scottish devolution proved a huge advantage to the SNP, particularly once new Labour began to lose popularity from around 2005. By 2007, the SNP had overtaken Labour as the biggest party in the Scottish Parliament and could form a minority government on its own, with leader Alex Salmond becoming first minister. In 2011 it won a majority at Holyrood, taking 69 of the 129 seats there. Having won 6 seats at Westminster and 20 per cent of the vote in Scotland in 2010 (compared to Labour's 41 seats and 42 per cent of the vote), but just one year later, the SNP took 44 per cent of the regional list vote in the elections for seats at Holyrood, compared to Labour's 27 per cent, marking a remarkable surge in fortunes, which the party has maintained since. This was a clear harbinger of what was to happen in 2015. Hitherto, the unique dynamic of party competition that had developed in Scotland seemed to work out differently in Westminster and Holyrood elections, with the SNP generally faring far more impressively in the latter. However, as previously noted, it swept to a remarkable victory north of the border in 2015, taking 50 per cent of the vote and 56 out of 59 seats. This owed much to the fact that the SNP could demonstrate its being a safe pair of hands as the governing party in Edinburgh under the stewardship of Salmond and his successor, Nicola Sturgeon.

The SNP surge also reflected the very positive response of many voters to the particular qualities of Sturgeon, who was thought to have had a good election. It also seems clear, however, that the Scottish independence referendum of September 2014 played a role in changing the dynamic of Scottish party politics, boosting the SNP's fortunes and eclipsing Labour's and those of other parties. Notwithstanding the fact that the referendum produced a comfortable victory for the 'no' side – by 55 per cent to 45 per cent – the process and outcome were in many ways political triumphs for the SNP. For many years prior to 2014 a stable proportion of the Scottish electorate – approximately one third – had indicated a preference for Scottish independence, but once the referendum campaign began in earnest following the publication of the Scottish government's Green Paper *Scotland's Future* in November 2013, the yes campaign made inroads into public opinion. From February 2014 it was notable that support for independence began to swell once the unionist parties at Westminster indicated their opposition to continuing currency union between England and Scotland in the event of a 'yes' vote. This was portrayed as untenable by the 'yes' campaign, and bullying behaviour to boot. Polls increasingly indicated a narrowing of the gap between the two sides as the campaign wore on, and ultimately the proportion of pro-independence Scots grew considerably. In the aftermath, the SNP enjoyed a remarkable surge in fortunes as their membership swelled (see above) and their popularity took them to the position where they could claim the support of an absolute majority of voters north of the border. This was an astonishing and rare achievement in party politics anywhere in the democratic world. While such SNP success brought little damage to the Conservatives, who had failed to win many MPs north of the border since the 1980s, it came at a devastating cost for Labour. While the SNP lost lost its overall majority at Holyrood in the Scottish parliamentary election of May 2016, it nevertheless remained much the strongest protagonist in the system and retained its status as incumbent government in Edinburgh for the third successive time. Its position as the new dominant actor in the Scottish party system has unquestionably been cemented then.

In many ways, the Welsh party system bears a striking resemblance to the Scottish system, with Plaid Cymru substituting for the SNP – albeit with a far-lower level of support. Founded in 1925, Plaid has traditionally articulated the grievances of those Welsh voters who have sought to protect the Welsh language and identity, and who have aspired to a degree of home rule for their country. In terms of its political economy, it shares with the SNP a position that is broadly Keynesian–social democratic, and under the leadership of Leanne Wood displayed a similar opposition to the coalition's austerity policies in the 2015 election campaign. As with Scottish nationalism, the electoral growth of Welsh nationalism had become evident from the mid-1960s. After by-election success at Carmarthen in 1966, an electoral breakthrough occurred in February 1974, with Plaid securing over 10 per cent of the vote in Wales and returning two MPs to Westminster. This level of electoral support has been broadly maintained for elections to Westminster, with the party winning 12 per cent of the vote and three MPs in 2015. This support is largely though not exclusively concentrated in North Wales.

What does all this mean for the nature of the party system in Wales? Labour has long enjoyed a degree of electoral dominance in the country, but while it has remained the largest party in Wales since devolution, it has not always been able to govern alone in Cardiff. Labour has enjoyed periods of single-party rule, but has also been obliged to form coalitions, first with the Liberal Democrats (2000–2003), and later with Plaid Cymru (2007–2011). In short, Wales has long had a dominant party system, in which the primary opposition to Labour has often been on the centre-left (that is, Plaid Cymru in parts of the North, and the Liberal Democrats elsewhere) rather than the right. However, Labour's long-standing dominance within Wales has shown signs of eroding over the past few years. From a zenith in 1997 when Labour won 55 per cent of the vote and 34 out of 40 parliamentary seats, by 2015 Labour only accounted for 37 per cent of the vote and 25 seats in Wales. Moreover, at the Welsh Assembly elections of 2016, the party won just 34.7% of the constituency vote, a reduction of 7.6% on the previous election in 2011. Though still the largest party in Wales, it lost its overall majority in Cardiff.

Overall, the parallel between Scotland and Wales is striking, albeit developments have started from different baselines and varied in degree. But in both cases, Labour appears to have been the primary loser from devolution. In each instance, the party was used to being the primary actor (indeed, the dominant actor in the case of Wales), but the experience of devolved power has placed the nationalist parties front and centre of politics in their respective parts of Britain, lending them greater authority and legitimacy in the eyes of many voters as they have found themselves participating in government in Edinburgh and Cardiff. They have often been able to enjoy the benefit of being parties of government in this way, while still having the luxury of critical 'outsiders' in respect of government in London (especially in the case of the SNP). Moreover, the dynamics of politics in Wales and Scotland have pushed the agendas there in their direction; devolution has proved popular with voters, and successive pieces of legislation issuing from Westminster have bestowed greater powers on Cardiff and Edinburgh since the birth of devolved government in the late 1990s. If devolution was, among other things, intended to sustain the union by dampening down the separatist instincts of voters in Wales and Scotland, and in so doing to shore up the traditional positions of strength enjoyed there by the Labour Party, it seems to have failed singularly in these objectives. In so doing, it has contributed to the continuing fragmentation of the British party system.

The UKIP surge

Undoubtedly one of the most recent striking features of British party system developments has been the rise of UKIP. Founded in 1993 as a successor to the Anti-Federalist League, it campaigned for British withdrawal from the EU. Overshadowed by James Goldsmith's short-lived Referendum Party, UKIP benefited from an influx of support from the latter after Goldsmith's death. In 1999 UKIP won 7 per cent of the vote and three seats in Britain's European parliamentary elections, a feat surpassed five years later when this was increased to an impressive 16.1 per cent of the vote and 12 members of the European Parliament (MEPs). It also picked up a handful of local council seats and two places in the Greater London Assembly. In 2001 it ran 420 candidates at the general election, and won 1.5 per cent of the vote nationwide. This was undoubtedly rapid progress for a minor party in Britain, and the party's hopes were high going into the general election of 2005, at which UKIP ran 495 candidates and won 2.3 per cent (2.5 per cent in seats contested) of the vote. By now it was able to win between 5 and 10 per cent of the vote in a few constituencies (for example Boston and Skegness, Thanet South, Totnes).

The pattern of moderate progress continued at the 2010 general election, when the party achieved 3 per cent of the popular vote across the UK. Since then, however, it has enjoyed unprecedented levels of electoral support. By the end of 2012 it consistently rated around 10 per cent in the opinion polls, and achieved by-election support as high as 22 per cent in Rotherham in November of that year, and 28 per cent in Eastleigh in February 2013 (in both of which its candidates placed second). In the local elections of May 2013, UKIP averaged 23 per cent where it stood, returning 147 councillors, and it topped the European parliamentary elections of 2014 in the UK, gaining 27.5 per cent of the nationwide vote and 24 MEPs. To cap off a beatific year for the party, it won its first MPs at Westminster and Tory backbenchers Douglas Carswell and

Mark Reckless defected to UKIP. Each immediately resigned as an MP, but stood successfully as UKIP candidates in their respective by-elections at Clacton and Rochester in late 2014. As the general election campaign opened in the first quarter of 2015, UKIP was performing consistently strongly in the opinion polls, averaging around 15 per cent, which placed it third behind Labour and the Conservatives, and comfortably ahead of the Liberal Democrats.

One of the features of UKIP's post-2010 surge in popularity is that the party started to attract support from a more diverse array of voters than had hitherto been the case. Its leader, Nigel Farage, contended that whereas UKIP had generally tended to run candidates mainly in Conservative territory, as the party grew it targeted more and more Labour-held seats, rendering the breadth of UKIP's appeal increasingly apparent. There is something to this claim. The party's stated *raison d'être* has been to exploit the failings of a liberal metropolitan elite that fails to connect with or represent the concerns of tradition working-class voters. These concerns relate primarily to immigration and secondarily to the European Union, of course. This might help explain why opinion research consistently suggests that UKIP fares relatively well among older, less well-educated, white working-class voters (especially males). These are the 'left-behinds' who have failed to reap the benefits of social and economic change in contemporary Britain (Ford and Goodwin 2014). They tend to feel disillusioned with the major parties, embittered by immigration, and Eurosceptic. In view of this, it is not surprising that UKIP's popularity was clearly evident in some of Labour's traditional heartland in northern England. In the event, Labour probably lost a handful of seats in 2015 because of the impact of UKIP, most notably in Morley and Outwood (where shadow chancellor Ed Balls lost his seat). Equally, UKIP probably stole enough of votes to deny Labour some of the target seats that it had hoped to win. In net terms, then, Labour may have been damaged to the tune of around a dozen seats by the UKIP surge.

In truth, UKIP's expansion now meant that it offered a threat to both major parties (and even to the Liberal Democrats). For the Conservatives, the most tangible risks from UKIP were seen off. Nonetheless, behavioural and attitudinal evidence suggested a greater overall proximity between UKIP supporters and the Conservatives. Prior to the European parliamentary elections of 2014, estimates suggested that between 45 per cent and 60 per cent of UKIP supporters were ex-Tory voters, compared to around 10 per cent who were ex-Labour (Kellner 2013; 2014). But by the 2015 election, as the ranks of UKIP voters swelled, the dependency on former Tories appeared to have shrunk, with 38.0 per cent claiming to have voted Conservative in the 2010 general election, 13.5 per cent for Labour,

19.0 per cent for Liberal Democrats – and 11.3 per cent to have abstained in 2010 (British Election Study 2015). Even so, this still represented a preponderance of 2:1 in favour of former Conservatives over former Liberal Democrat supporters, and nearly 3:1 over ex-Labour voters. Moreover, we have already noted that UKIP supporters appear to see themselves as significantly closer to the Tories in terms of general left-right ideology. A similar pattern holds across a range of political issues. Ten-point scales on how far the state should intervene in running the economy, how much it should tax and spend on public services, how far it should seek to pursue greater equality through redistribution of income and wealth, and how far European integration should go, all reveal that the average UKIP supporter is significantly closer to the Conservatives than to Labour. Interestingly, UKIP supporters proved most right-wing on the vexed issue of same-sex marriage which had caused the Conservatives so much trouble when Cameron's government decided to push the relevant legislation through Parliament in 2013. Once again, they found themselves closer to the Tories than to any other party, but they still saw themselves as further from Cameron's party on this than on any other issue, which perhaps underlines the capacity of the liberty–authority dimension of politics to generate the kind of angst that inspires some people to defect from the Conservatives to UKIP (Webb and Bale 2014).

While UKIP seemed to make adjustments to its programme in the year preceding the 2015 general election in order to broaden its appeal (for instance, through promises to increase state pensions, and to remove of the coalition government's controversial 'bedroom tax'), a careful examination of its policies confirms that the majority still conformed with what Farage once described as a 'traditional conservative and libertarian' profile. These included

- withdrawal from the European Union;
- economic deregulation and reduced bureaucracy, especially for small businesses;
- a review of sentencing, and more prisons;
- a 'points system' for immigration that would be introduced for evaluating work permit applications;
- border controls reinstated;
- 'Britishness' tests introduced to encourage those settling in the country to assimilate into society;
- new migrants to be compelled to buy private health insurance for five years until they became eligible for free NHS care; and
- repeal of the Human Rights Act.

In the election, UKIP maintained the growth in popularity that it had built since 2010, winning 3.8 million votes or 12.9 per cent of the vote overall (a share of the vote that it came close to repeating in the local elections of 2016). Outside of Scotland (where its support barely shifted), UKIP gained significantly across all regions of the British mainland, especially in a swathe of seats running from the north-east to the East Midlands (Denver 2015). But, having came third across the UK as a whole in terms of the number of votes, finishing in the top two places in more than a hundred constituencies, it only gained one seat in the Commons, holding onto Clacton in Essex. For the first time in the post-war era, a major vote-winning party other than the Liberal Democrats (or their predecessors) suffered egregiously at the hands of the electoral system.

A Green wave?

A further beneficiary (and cause) of the ongoing fragmentation of the party system in recent year has been the Green Party. Its most striking electoral achievement in its early years was to win 15 per cent of the UK-wide vote in the 1989 European Parliamentary election (although this earned them no representation in the European Parliament, given the operation of SMP in such elections at that time). The Greens have never again won such a high proportion of the vote across the UK, but have maintained a stable level of support, gaining 6.3 per cent and two MEPs in the European Parliamentary elections of 1999 (the first held under list-PR in the UK), 6.1 per cent and two MEPs in 2004, 8.7 per cent and two MEPs in 2009, and 7.9 per cent and three MEPs in 2014. Under SMP, they have fared less strongly in British general elections, gaining 0.7 per cent of the UK-wide vote (2.8 per cent in seats contested) in 2001, 1.07 per cent (3.4 per cent in seats contested) in 2005, and 0.96 per cent (1.81 per cent in seats contested) in 2010. However, in 2010 they returned an MP to the House of Commons for the first time, as Caroline Lucas wrested Brighton Pavilion from Labour. In addition, they had two seats on the Greater London Assembly, numerous local councillors across the country, and won control of Brighton & Hove Unitary Authority in 2011. In the run-up to the 2015 election, opinion polls consistently placed Green support in a range of 4–11 per cent, averaging approximately 6 per cent. Despite concentrations of relative strength in a few seats such as Norwich South, the only real prospect of representation in the Commons in 2015 was for Lucas to retain Brighton Pavilion, something which she did achieve. However, the party enjoyed a remarkable surge in membership recruitment in the latter part of the 2010 Parliament. Some of this seems to have been fed by a public row about whether the Green party leader Natalie Bennett should be allowed to take part in a televised leaders' debate in the election campaign. Following initial proposals (later withdrawn) by the broadcasters which would have included UKIP's Nigel Farage but excluded Bennett, a rush of sympathisers flocked to join the Greens. However, the party's membership had already been climbing prior to this time. At the end of 2010, Green membership had amounted to 12,768, and it remained broadly stable at just 13,809 in 2013. However, by the end of 2014 it had already risen to 30,809, before surging rapidly to 50,000 by the time of the general election.

The Green Party's post-materialist and socially liberal stance emphasises policies such as opposition to economic austerity, opposition to use of the Private Finance Initiative to fund public services, higher marginal rates of income tax for the wealthy, a 'living wage' for all, the replacement of VAT with 'eco-taxes' such as aviation fuel tax and plastic bag tax, the substitution of council tax by land-value tax, extra funding for the NHS and public transport, the scrapping of road-building schemes, massive investment in renewable energy, a radical and rapid reduction in carbon dioxide emissions, and opposition to genetically modified crop initiatives and fracking. Such a radical left-liberal stance is most likely to attract votes from dissatisfied Labour and Liberal Democrat supporters. Analysis of the party's support in 2015 seems to confirm this: fully 53.4 per cent of Green voters claimed to have supported Liberal Democrat candidates in the 2010 General Election, 14.5 per cent to have voted Labour, and further 9.5 per cent to have voted Conservative. Some 11.2 per cent declared that they had not voted at all in 2010. In short, the advance of the Greens, albeit less spectacular than that of the SNP and UKIP in recent years, has almost certainly impacted more on Labour and especially the Liberal Democrats than on the Tories.

Party politics following the EU referendum

The extraordinary impact of the referendum on membership of the EU in June 2016 should not go unremarked. Cameron's gamble on calling the referendum – that he would be able to win a majority for remaining within the EU and thus close down the debate that had caused his party so many divisions over the years – backfired spectacularly. Immediately following the shock of the outcome of the referendum of 23 June, Cameron announced his resignation as party leader and Prime Minister, thereby setting in train a new election to choose his replacement. While Boris Johnson had long been recognised as the darling of the Tory grassroots, his ambition failed when his erstwhile colleague on the Brexit campaign, Michael Gove, announced that he would stand himself. Five candidates emerged, but after the elimination of Gove, Liam Fox and Stephen Crabb in votes by Conservative MPs, the final run-off was between long-standing Home Secretary Theresa May and the less experienced and less well-known Energy Minister Andrea Leadsom. Leadsom abruptly withdrew from this contest, leaving Theresa May to go on to become Britain's second female Prime Minister.

At first blush, the contest seemed to capture a new faultline in British politics, in that it pitted Leavers against Remainers. This fault-line runs deeper than the question of Britain's relationship itself, however. Rather, the EU is a key signifier of a division between those of a cosmopolitan, outward looking world view, the beneficiaries of globalisation, confronted by others who react against what they regard as an elite-driven project which threatens their national identities and material well-being. In terms of social constituencies, this sets younger generations (meaning those under 50) and better educated, middle-class citizens against older, less well-educated and often (though not always) less prosperous voters. The potential for this to impact further on party politics is undeniable now.

Whatever the disruption this episode has caused for the Conservative party, it seems to have been devastating for Labour. Labour's traditional voters outside London deserted the party in large numbers to vote for Brexit. Following the referendum, Shadow Foreign Secretary Hilary Benn's rebellion prompted a mass resignation of most members of the Shadow Cabinet, all of whom demanded the resignation of Jeremy Corbyn, deemed by many a lacklustre leader and to have been an unconvincing campaigner for the Remain side. Eighty per cent of Labour MPs subsequently supported a vote of no confidence in him and a formal challenge to his leadership from the MP Owen Smith followed. At the same time there was a further remarkable influx of 100,000 new members into the party, most of whom indicated on their application forms the intention of supporting Corbyn. Theresa May, now Prime Minister, if ruthless enough, could well consider an early general election for autumn 2016 to capitalise on Labour's dysfunction.

This degree of division within the Labour party raised the possibility that many of the 172 MPs who supported the no confidence motion in him would resign the Labour whip to form an independent group in Parliament – and perhaps a completely new party on the centre-left, in a re-run of the SDP breakaway of 1981. In any event, Labour's public image and standing has taken such a beating that the possibility of further defections of its voters to other parties – especially, perhaps, UKIP – must be considered strong. This depends in part on UKIP re-defining its *raison d'etre* now its key objective of a British withdrawal from the EU has seemingly been achieved. One can readily imagine that this will prove possible, even without the leadership of Nigel Farage, who announced his own resignation shortly after the referendum. There will be plenty of scope for dispute about the precise terms of British exit from the EU, a political battlefield for which UKIP is amply suited. In any case, the

party's remit has long since stretched beyond the confines of EU membership, with particular reference to the vexed question of immigration and
a populist critique of the established parties. In such a role, UKIP could
well continue to drain further support away from both Labour and the
Conservatives.

Conclusion: Multiparty realignment or return to stable two-party politics?

So what do these events imply for the British party system – realignment
or a return to the status quo *ex ante* of two-partyism? The case for the
latter is fairly obvious: the major two parties' combined share of the vote
in the 2015 general election stabilised at around two thirds of the ballot,
and one of them succeeded in winning an overall majority so that it could
govern alone again. As Table 4.3 shows, the disproportional effects of the
electoral system continue to favour the major two parties in Parliament,
as well as the SNP now.

Clearly, however, while the effective number of parties in Parliament
has been held in check by the limiting impact of the electoral system,
the fragmentation of the party system in the electorate has continued

Table 4.3   *Vote shares and parliamentary seat shares, 2015*

	Conservative	Labour	Liberal Democrat	UKIP	Green	SNP	Plaid Cymru	Other
Vote %	36.9	30.4	7.9	12.6	3.8	4.7	0.6	3.1
Seat %	50.8	35.7	1.2	0.2	0.2	8.6	0.5	2.8
Seat % – Vote %	13.9	5.3	–6.7	–12.4	–3.6	3.9	–0.1	–0.3

Note: 2015a = reported figures at time of general election in May; 2015b = post-election
figures reported in various sources. * Includes SDP membership figures; ** (2007); ***
(2010).

Sources: Labour Party NEC Annual Reports; National Union of Conservative & Unionist Associations; Liberal Democrats Information Office; Berrington and Hague 1997: 48;
LibDem Voice; *Daily Telegraph*; Conservativehome.com; http://www.conservativehome.
com/thetorydiary/2014/09/conference-survey-and-membership-figures.html; http://www.
libdemvoice.org/lib-dem-membership-up-for-15th-consecutive-month-43221.html;
Richard Keen 'Membership of UK political parties', Standard Note SN05125, House of
Commons Library, August 2015; Jon Stone 'More people have joined Labour since the
election than are in the entire Conservative Party', *The Independent*, 8 October 2015;
http://eastlibdems.org.uk/en/article/2015/1111728/record-number-of-members-head-to-
liberal-democrat-conference.

to grow; Table 4.1 shows that the effective number of electoral parties now stands at 4, the highest yet. This of course reflects the progress of the minor parties, especially the SNP, UKIP and the Greens. Thus the evidence of underlying electoral volatility is unmistakeable; there is a powerful sense, only made clearer in the aftermath of the EU referendum, that below a veneer of two-party stability in terms of which parties can form a government, there lies an extraordinary degree of electoral churn. Employing the widely used Pedersen Index as a simple measure, we can see that 2015 was by some distance the most volatile election since 1945. This index simply equals the cumulative gains in votes of all winning parties (or cumulative losses of all losing parties) from one election to the next. The index can run from zero to 100, with any score over 10 representing a high level of electoral volatility (Pedersen 1979). In post-war Britain, high-volatility elections have tended to occur in the context of changes of government and/or landslide victories – 1983 and 1997 being good examples. In 1983 the Labour Party achieved its worst share of support since 1918, handing Margaret Thatcher's Conservatives a landslide. In 1997, Tony Blair's new Labour was swept into power by an even more overwhelming margin. However, a rather different kind of high-volatility election was that of February 1974, when neither major party was able to earn a majority from a disillusioned electorate, and each started to leak support to the minor parties. The general election of 2015 has something in common with this, but at an even higher level electoral instability. While the volatility index stood as 14.5 in February 1974 – previously the highest since 1945 (Webb 2000: 47) – in 2015 it reached 15.1. This reflects an extraordinarily high level of switching by voters as the Liberal Democrats haemorrhaged support to Labour, the Greens and UKIP, while Labour lost heavily to the SNP and less spectacularly to UKIP – and even the Conservatives shed a significant amount of support to UKIP.

It is not yet possible to be certain whether any of this volatility constitutes enduring realignment, but it is certainly conceivable that at least some of it might do so. The strongest likelihood is that some of the huge movement of Scottish voters from Labour to the SNP will be sustained enough for us to designate this an authentic realignment in terms of the Scottish party system. Neither can we rule out the possibility that some of the gains made by UKIP or the losses made by the Liberal Democrats will persist over time or if Labour implodes under the leadership of Jeremy Corbyn. The local elections of May 2016 suggested that these might be enduring features. Twelve months after the general election, Labour's collapse at the hands of the SNP in Scotland, UKIP's significant presence in England and Wales, and the Liberal Democrats' continuing weakness were all confirmed. It is, however, equally likely that much of the volatility should be better understood as part and parcel of a more dealigned electorate, in which fewer and fewer voters are anchored by habitual loyalties to particular parties. Furthermore, it would be unwise to regard the Conservative majority as a sign that the 2010 election was a quirk rarely to be repeated in future: for one thing, governments with larger majorities than the Conservatives' have been known to lose them before the full parliamentary term is out; for another, the fragmented nature of the party system is now such that the capacity of the electoral system to generate single-party majorities in closer contests than 2015 seems much diminished. Fragmentation, volatility, realignment and dealignment are all elements in a complex array of British party system features that are likely to make governing outcomes increasingly unpredictable in the future.

Chapter 5

Ideological Politics and the Party System

MICHAEL KENNY

This chapter provides an assessment of some of the most important streams of political thinking in the UK between 2010 and 2015. Most political commentary tends to home in on the personalities, factions and tactics that figure in the daily political battle. But this makes it harder to see the broader ideological patterns which shape perceptions of, and thinking within, politics, and that ultimately provide essential resources which enable political behaviour. In order to bring these into view, we need to take several steps backwards to get a better sight of the language, concepts and ideas that actors – be they politicians, parties, campaigning groups, think tanks or citizens – employ when they are formulating plans, justifying their actions and arguing with opponents.

Political ideologies are best seen as fluid webs of belief that offer flexible, but familiar, maps of the political world, and furnish the conceptual language that make possible the many 'speech acts' that lie at the heart of politics (Freeden 1998). Academic specialists disagree profoundly about whether traditional ideologies, like conservatism and socialism, have disappeared as a source of ideas and allegiance in British politics, with some viewing the current era as a post-ideological one, and others stressing the ubiquitous and shifting character of ideological patterns in political life. In supplying an overview of the major trends in political ideology and thought which had a bearing upon politics in the UK from 2010 to 2015, this chapter is more rooted in the second of these two views.

The chapter begins by exploring the growing appetite for a more salient ideological politics in Britain, and links this to some fundamental changes in the character of its economy and society. These have generated demands and anxieties that are not easily recognised by the party system, and which all the main parties have found difficult to process. There has been a contrast between a growing proliferation of doctrines and ideologically rooted arguments in public life, on the one hand, and a party system that, in key respects, has been surprisingly durable at the UK level. Elsewhere, however, the picture is different, and in Scotland a new pattern of political discourse has accompanied the ascendancy of the Scottish National Party (SNP). The chapter proceeds to anatomise a range of debates and developments associated with different parts of the ideological spectrum in these years, and demonstrates their integral importance to questions of strategy and policy. It focuses upon ideas associated with the political right, the centre-left and a newly ascendant socialism, and also discusses those ideological streams that do not fit with, and indeed tend to undermine, a left–right analytical focus – including feminism, environmentalism and faith-based perspectives. It includes an exploration of the emergence in political discourse of arguments and divisions associated with questions of culture, sovereignty and nationhood.

Within a context of broader political and economic change, this chapter hence offers a map of the major ideological currents that ran through politics during these years. A systematic focus upon ideas, doctrines and ideologies is important for students of recent British politics for two particular reasons. First, this was a period coloured by the growing desire, from different quarters, for the terms of political debate to be altered, and by a growing appetite for political arguments that were anchored in ideological paradigms. And, second, attention to the ideational dimension of politics reveals the degree to which issues, allegiances and arguments associated with the themes of culture, belonging and identity began to make themselves central to politics, confounding the expectations of most of those who practice and comment upon it.

The return of ideology?

There has in recent years been a notable tendency to depict mainstream party politics as devoid of ideologically shaped ideas, and dominated by self-interested and remote political actors whose apparent disagreements obscure their shared values. A growing chorus of voices has called for a politics more clearly rooted in moral principle and political narrative. Indeed, this aspiration has been central to the emergence of some of the most striking ideological phenomena of recent times, including the sudden rise of the United Kingdom Independence Party (UKIP) on the political right after 2012, and the extraordinary tide of enthusiasm that swept veteran left-winger Jeremy Corbyn to victory in the Labour leadership election of 2015. This widely held view reflects the conviction that British politics suffers from a tacit consensus – especially on sensitive topics such as immigration – which is the result of the prevalence of an increasingly professional group of politicians who travel lighter in ideological terms than their predecessors (Oborne 2008). Such arguments were vigorously aired in the course of tributes to two of the most iconic political figures of the late twentieth century – Tony Benn (who died in 2014) and Baroness Margaret Thatcher (who died in 2013).

This position also reflects a marked recoil against former Prime Minister Tony Blair's depiction of the 'new Labour' party of the 1990s as a political force that would solve problems in a pragmatic, rather than doctrinal, manner – a stance that both denied the legitimacy of political doctrines and rested upon a tacit ideological blend of social democratic and pro-market beliefs. The notion that politicians are more effective when they travel with little or no ideational baggage was an important, and increasingly contested, legacy of the new Labour era. It informed an approach to policymaking which relied heavily upon expert advice and was often technocratic in nature. It combined, somewhat awkwardly, with the popularisation of the notion of the politician-as-celebrity, rather than ideologist. Both of these trends were encapsulated in the person of Labour leader and Prime Minister Blair. Since his early years in office, no figure has come near to uniting these different ideas of political leadership.

For some time, Blair presented himself with considerable success as a charismatic technocrat, aspiring to float above the partisan fray of party politics, at a time when one party was utterly ascendant and was able to set the terms of political debate. But as these conditions disappeared in the early 2000s, the traits he embodied became increasingly suspect among publics dealing with the more anxious, fearful times associated with the banking and financial crises of 2007–2008. A demand for a less technocratic, more principled and responsive politics, which would speak openly to issues that mainstream politicians were seen as avoiding or marginalising, has grown apace. And, in a situation where few mainstream politicians appear able to meet these expectations, figures from the political margins have benefited from this gathering mood. In the period in question here – 2010–2015 – it was the SNP's Alex Salmond and Nicola Sturgeon, and UKIP's Nigel Farage, who prospered most notably. And their success prefaced the extraordinary victory of Corbyn, a self-styled outsider who became the most unlikely possible heir to Blair – his victory in the Labour leadership contest of 2015 placing him at the helm of one of the two largest parties in British politics.

The context and drivers of change, 2010–2015

In order to understand the shifting ideological map of British politics in this period, it is important to bring into focus some of the long-range transformations in the economic and institutional contexts that have shaped people's sense of political allegiance in this country and in many other parts of Europe. The first of these involves changes associated with the emergence of what many social scientists call 'post-industrial' society. This term denotes significant alterations to the structure and culture of Western society, from the late 1970s onwards. Like other countries, the UK ceased being a predominantly manufacturing economy and instead began to rely upon different sorts of services, notably in the financial sector. This shift resulted in a more stratified, and less clear-cut, pattern of class relationships, but also engendered new, deeper divisions of wealth and income across society as a whole. Identities and loyalties other than those which related to the class divisions of mass industrial society also loomed larger – with gender, sexuality, religion, ethnicity and locality all gaining in importance. Social scientists have observed, and argued about, the nature, speed and consequences of this new paradigm, and the way in which its effects have been shaped and interpreted by political ideas which have their roots in different national experiences and cultures. In the UK, an important debate has developed about whether the extant party system would be reshaped as a more diverse set of political ideas and identities emerged due to these social and cultural changes. But, despite the new political demands and pressures associated with them, the institutional structures of British politics have remained pretty resilient even as demands for reform of some of its key features – for instance the voting system – have gained ground.

The emergence of post-industrial society has been associated with and shaped by the development of a more open, globalised economic system. This has brought profound changes to the nature and experience of work, community and family for many. This shift was presented positively by mainstream politicians, with Labour in the 1990s becoming the champions of globalisation and arguing that those at the bottom of society needed to be equipped to flourish in this emerging world. For a majority in Britain, the long economic boom of 1995 to 2003 delivered increasing prosperity, rising wages and new opportunities. But for those at the bottom, this was a period of growing insecurity, longer hours and shrinking chances. From the early 2000s, wages began to fall, productivity slowed and new divisions in British society became apparent. These were accentuated by the economic downturn brought about by the banking collapse of 2007 and the financial crisis that followed. This laid bare the fragile and risky nature of a growth model predicated on high levels of household debt, an uncontrolled property bubble and the country's economic dependency upon the financial services industry. The fall-out from such a major shock continued to be felt in the years under consideration here. It engendered a powerful, culturally rooted recoil against a globalised economic system, rising concerns about immigration, and a deepening attachment to forms of communal identity beneath the level of the state. Right across Europe this was a period when a chasm opened up between working-class voters and social democratic parties. As a result, new issues – for instance economic security and the effects of migration – moved to the heart of the political agenda in different countries, creating openings for populist politicians from both right and left (Mudde 2007).

These developments helped to shape a period of ideological innovation and growth. Older ideological patterns continued to figure, but become more fragmented, and some of their core elements were recombined in new, quite unexpected, ways. Populist ideas in particular added a Kryptonite ingredient to political doctrines that had long been cast to the margins of British politics – including Euroscepticism and militant socialism.

A separate set of changes also began to exercise considerable effects upon political discourse in this period. These concerned the unpredictable consequences of the introduction of devolved government in Scotland, Wales and – by rather different processes – Northern Ireland and London from the late 1990s. Devolution has turned out to be a continuing process, not a one-off event, as demands for more powers to be passed from the centre have grown over time and have been vigorously debated in each of these different territories. One consequence of this process has been the development of a much more differentiated set of political cultures and debates across the UK. And this became palpable in the period 2010–2015 in the two largest territories within it – England and Scotland – as political parties promoting populist and nationalist ideas began to set much of the political weather, and changed the terms of debate on constitutional and national questions.

In Scotland, this proved to be a momentous and contentious period in political and constitutional terms, as a result of the referendum of September 2014 which determined whether the country should remain part of the UK. Such a dramatic, transparent exercise of national sovereignty happens rarely in the lives of nations, and invariably generates extended soul-searching and acrimony. This was certainly true in the Scottish case, although some commentators were struck by the democratic qualities of the discourse that ensued, and by the departure from the mood of political disenchantment which had appeared pervasive in preceding years. The referendum campaign was also notable as it gave rise to an increasingly potent ideological nexus in Scotland – between populist, nationalist and loosely social democratic sentiments.

The right and centre-right

Within the Westminster Parliament, the advent of a coalition government involving two parties – the Conservatives and Liberal Democrats – ushered in a more conflictual tone, and injected a stronger ideological caste, to interparty debate. The main reason for this was the major programme of reduction in public spending – 'austerity' as its opponents called it – which was pursued by the coalition. This resulted in the redrawing of some of the established lines of political argument in British politics, and the erosion of a broad, unspoken consensus among the main parties about questions of state expenditure and fiscal management which had prevailed since the early 2000s.

The Conservatives were the primary architects of austerity, and also reaped most political benefit from the recovery of the UK economy during the latter half of the Parliament, although the question of whether their cuts were hindering or helping recovery was a difficult issue for them until 2012. They also faced a political challenge as a result of the growing gap between the incomes of those at the very top and the vast majority of working- and middle-class people in these years. The introduction of austerity, and the party's commitment to make major changes to the organisation and delivery of some of the core public services delivered in England, gave a distinctly ideological flavour to the otherwise pragmatic style of governing which Prime Minister David Cameron projected. The promotion of austerity represented the most significant response to the financial crisis which the UK had experienced, and was to a considerable degree rooted in conservative arguments for a smaller state and for a recovery driven by growth in the private sector. Several leading Conservatives argued that reducing the proportion of GDP spent on state-provided services ought to be seen not just as a contingent necessity but as an intrinsically valuable goal (Kwarteng et al. 2012). Along with its reforms to welfare benefits, which included setting a limit upon what any single family could receive, and tightening rules of access, the government attempted significant reforms in education, health, prisons and criminal justice (Seldon and Snowdon 2015).

The pro-market dispensation that informed the coalition's approach to policymaking was offset by the political imperative to develop a sense of shared mission for the government as a whole, and to allow some latitude for the sensibilities and priorities of the junior coalition partner. The economically liberal orientation that had emerged under Nick Clegg's leadership of the Liberal Democrats initially underpinned cooperation between the parties. Nonetheless, some of Clegg's ministers, notably Vince Cable and Chris Huhne, framed their social democratic liberalism as the source of an alternative governing agenda to their coalition partners. But while there were real differences of ideology and policy between the two partners, there were also points of connection, not least because of the socially liberal outlook which prevailed in the highest parts of the Conservative Party, and which underpinned major reforms such as the introduction of same-sex marriage. Clegg did his utmost to promote close working relations with his Conservative counterparts until party rivalries burst into the open over the campaign for the introduction of a new voting system for Westminster elections – which resulted in a heavy defeat for the Alternative Vote method in the referendum of 2011. In the later years of the Parliament, as the supporters of both governing parties grew disenchanted with coalition, and as the Liberal Democrats struggled to win back lost supporters, the party leaderships began to pull further apart and a period of open, mutual criticism ensued.

For Cameron, the harsh notes which austerity required were partially offset by his circle's social liberalism, and by his commitment to a different strand of the Conservative lineage – the idealisation of voluntary activity and the 'little platoons' of civil society. These themes, which were strongly redolent of the thinking of eighteenth-century writer Edmund Burke (regarded by many as the 'father' of British Conservatism), had long been integral to the English Conservative tradition (Norman 2014). Cameron accented them in the run-up to the election of 2010 to underscore a potent critique of the inefficiency and ineffectiveness of the bureaucratic state. These ideas, encapsulated in his celebration of the 'Big Society', were presented as the basis of the approach which the new government would pursue. But, despite receiving many plaudits for this thinking, the Prime Minister found it impossible to develop and promote a substantive policy agenda to back up the slogan. The accusation of hypocrisy arising from sharp cuts to the funding of many third-sector and voluntary organisations helped ensure its quiet disappearance from government discourse.

In the last two years of the Parliament, the tenor and focus of the party's leadership shifted quite markedly. This was partly in response to the unpopularity of the coalition among large sections of the party, the meteoric rise of UKIP as a vehicle appealing to a broad coalition of disillusioned voters over the right shoulder of the Tory party, coupled with the rising prominence of a succession of political issues. These included the European Union (EU), Scotland and the future of the UK, as well as ongoing debates over immigration. All of them reflected the growing prominence in political life of the themes of sovereignty and belonging.

Following their success at the 2015 general election – which, against the predictions of commentators – resulted in the return of government by a single party, the Conservatives were able to pursue policy goals that reflected their core ideological preferences, without the hindrance of a coalition partner. They embarked on a major further programme of reducing public expenditure, seeking to make £12 billion of further cuts to the welfare bill. But, as well as seeking to shrink the state, they set out to represent themselves to working-class voters, proposing to raise the level of the minimum wage.

The centre-left and a socialist alternative

Labour performed poorly in the election of 2010, experiencing its second-worst result since 1928, and losing a swathe of seats in England outside its northern industrial heartlands. This experience led to intense debate in some parts of the party, but left some convinced that it would reap sufficient advantage from the Liberal Democrats' participation in government and profit from the damage that UKIP might do to the Conservatives, to march straight back into power. But there was, from 2010, a strong expectation of a clear shift of direction away from the new Labour years following the surprise election to the leadership of Ed Miliband, who defeated his brother David in a 'Cain and Abel' contest that had the media enthralled. The successful Miliband distinguished himself by campaigning on the idea of a shift away from 'new Labour' both in terms of economic and foreign policy.

In a series of set-piece speeches after 2010, the new leader targeted the pro-market thinking which had informed British economic policy for two decades, and sketched the outlines of a second, distinct ideological response in British politics to the financial crisis of 2007–2008. His enthusiasm for radical-sounding rhetoric in part reflected a shift in public attitudes, as a growing hostility to the position and behaviour of bankers, and questions about the tax avoidance strategies of global corporations and wealthy individuals, became the focus of public concern. And yet Labour reaped little political benefit from these issues and was unable to forge a stable ideological framework that might draw voters towards it. This was, in part, the result of the Miliband team's inability to address the most obvious challenge which Labour faced following its election defeat – the need to re-establish its credentials as a competent economic manager (Bale 2015). The party's immediate instinct, following its loss in 2010, was to signal its opposition to the coalition's efforts to reduce public spending. This helped create the impression that Labour subscribed to an entirely different approach to fiscal management to the government.

But, over the course of the next few years, this leftist rhetoric gave way, under the influence of Shadow Chancellor Ed Balls, to the adoption of a slightly more modest deficit reduction plan to that developed by the coalition.

Miliband made some headway by focusing upon the sharp rise in the cost of living affecting many families early in the Parliament. His discourse on the economy was typically couched in moralistic terms as he criticised those companies that pursued a 'predatory' rather than 'productive' approach to profit maximisation. He did not, however, clarify what this distinction meant, in either legal or policy terms, and gradually fostered a largely anti-business reputation for his party. This leftwards tilt in Labour's thinking on questions of political economy was an important precursor to the more wholehearted socialist prospectus offered by Corbyn in the leadership contest of 2015. Miliband called repeatedly for reform to the system of bankers' bonuses, argued against 'zero hour' contracts, and made some eye-catching announcements designed to identify Labour as the party standing up for consumers against powerful corporate interests – for instance his call for a cap on energy bills. In part, these moves reflected a desire to open an ideologically rooted divide between Labour and the government, and gestured towards the resumption of a more wholeheartedly social democratic pathway for Labour after the centrism characteristic of the new Labour period.

Miliband was also influenced by academic arguments for 'predistribution' (Diamond and Chwalisz 2015) – a term which signalled the need for 'upstream' reforms designed to make the economy fairer from the outset. For instance this meant improving levels of pay and skills, in contrast to the kinds of 'downstream' intervention which Labour had favoured in power, through its heavy reliance upon tax credits. But a lack of policy groundwork and strategic understanding left Miliband and his party increasingly prone to fall back upon the default positions associated with Labour's time in office. Miliband's unassured performances on those mainstream media outlets where popular impressions are formed did not help his cause. The lack of clarity about where Labour stood on a raft of different issues, allied to the disparate character of the ideological signals that emanated from its leadership, left the party unable to reach out beyond its core voters, at a time when many of the latter were increasingly open to populist and nationalist arguments. Miliband's championing of the traditional Conservative slogan of 'one nation', which was hailed as a tactically astute move in 2012, tended to contribute to the general impression of vagueness rather than offering clarity and direction to the party's thinking. On the two most salient economic questions of this period – the party's record of fiscal management, and whether austerity was avoidable – Labour appeared evasive. A significant current of opinion on the political left became increasingly sceptical of its 'austerity-lite' positioning, on which Labour was openly criticised by other parties – notably the Greens, the SNP and Plaid Cymru. And Corbyn's election as leader in 2015 enabled a further leftwards turn in the party's political economy. It followed the example of 'new left' parties, like Podemos in Spain, and presented itself as straightforwardly anti-austerity. Corbyn also opted to project Labour as the party that would defend, rather than reform, the public sector and promote the interests and values of the trade unions.

Working-class alienation and the left

The ideas associated with the short-lived 'Blue Labour' grouping, which rose to prominence in 2011 and 2012, represented a rare attempt to think more deeply about some of the challenges facing Labour, and to examine its increasingly troubled relationship with working-class voters. What began as an academic seminar turned into a ginger group promoting new ideas for the party (Geary and Pabst 2015). Blue Labour articulated a powerful and resonant critique of some aspects of new Labour, and argued that Labour should respect and engage some of the (small-c) conservative aspects of working-class culture, and speak more directly to the virtues of family, community and country. Although the group disbanded almost as soon as it had begun, it exerted considerable influence on leadership circles up to the election of 2015. Thematically, it identified one of main political challenges facing the party which others were reluctant or unable to address – its growing distance from working-class voters. Its leading political exponent, MP Jon Cruddas, was appointed head of the party's policy review process in the run-up to the general election.

Miliband's unease, and that of some of his advisers, with much of this agenda prevented the incorporation of these ideas into the party's thinking. Labour lacked a compelling narrative about the UK's future, and seemed to duck some of the major challenges of the period. Despite his penchant for defining himself as an ideological politician in the Thatcher mould, Miliband remained vulnerable to the criticism that he lacked the strategic will to carry ideas forward and the communicative ability to impress himself upon the public consciousness.

But while this was a troubling period for social democratic politics throughout Europe, further to the left there were signs of a renewed sense of energy and vigour, and a readiness to open up to the powerful winds of populism that were blowing through British politics. From early in this period there was a lively debate about the possibility of a populist party of the socialist left – a left-wing UKIP, as some put it. The spectacular victory of George Galloway, leader of the left-wing Respect Party, in a by-election held in Bradford West in 2012, proved a false dawn for this idea, and indeed for his own party which was subsequently racked by internal feuds. But his victory signalled the growing potential of a more populist left-wing politics.

Indeed, a wider culture of left-wing dissent was rekindled in this period. This was given vivid embodiment by the 'Occupy' movement which set up camp outside St Paul's Cathedral in January 2012, and by groups, like UK Uncut, which employed creative forms of direct action to bring tax avoidance onto the political agenda. These, and various other online communities, offered spaces and vehicles for a cohort of younger idealists, most of whom viewed Labour in increasingly jaundiced terms. This trend was reflected by the emergence of a younger generation of talented commentators – for instance Owen Jones and Laurie Penny – who combined activist authenticity with a polemical style of writing tailored to the era of the blog. In the case of comedian Russell Brand (2014), this culture was rather awkwardly joined to the pervasive cult of celebrity. The latter's argument against voting for a Labour Party that was deemed insufficiently distinct from its Tory opponents resonated widely on the radical left, and was an important harbinger of the party's decisive leftward turn after Corbyn's election in 2015.

Territory, identity and political ideology

One further cause of the diminution of mainstream political progressivism needs emphasis. This concerns the growing salience of issues and questions associated with the interwoven themes of culture, territory and sovereignty, which have been generating an increasingly loud pulse – in the UK and elsewhere. For the mainstream parties and their leaders, there has been little option but to turn – usually reluctantly – to face these challenges, but little sign of a willingness or ability to grasp their deeper significance. Leading a Parliamentary party which was preponderantly Eurosceptic and increasingly under pressure from UKIP's rise, Cameron responded with some bold and eye-catching policy initiatives. His dramatic announcement in January 2013 that a future Tory government would hold a referendum on the UK's membership of the EU by 2017 sought to take the steam out of the European issue. But, instead of lancing this boil, it had the effect of giving renewed hope to anti-EU campaigners within his own party. It also changed the political weather significantly, producing the referendum on Britain's EU membership in June 2016, so reopening Conservative debates about the European question. On immigration, too, Cameron attempted to be decisively proactive, but failed to renegotiate the principle of the free movement of labour within the EU and could not secure the radically reduced – and unrealistic – target for reducing the numbers of incomers hailing from beyond the EU. And, following the announcement of the result of the Scottish referendum, he had made perhaps his most bold and ideologically transformative attempt to harness new currents of territorial sentiment – as he turned his party into the vehicle for a burgeoning sense of English national consciousness.

This move came hot on the heels of the unexpectedly narrow defeat of the argument for independence in Scotland, and was interpreted by many as an attempt to respond to a growing sense of English nationalism, carrying risks for the future of the domestic union. The debate leading up to the result in Scotland was long and intense, stimulating extended democratic deliberation throughout Scottish society and engendering some deep divisions. In political terms, it helped to make the nexus of nationalist and leftist thought associated with the SNP an ascendant force in its politics. By the end of the campaign – despite the defeat of the 'Yes' campaign – an important shift in the character of political argument had taken place in Scotland, with the SNP established as the vehicle for a powerful and insurgent political outlook, as it gave voice to a broadly social democratic set of sentiments, identifying itself as the defender of the welfare state and an opponent of the 'austerity' associated with the Westminster government. The wide-ranging national rhetoric of the SNP allowed different sections of Scottish society to connect their own frustrations and aspirations with the idea of independence. And so, while social democracy as an ideological template receded elsewhere in the UK, in Scotland it remained a popular frame of reference.

But it was not just in Scotland that questions of territory and sovereignty began to carry a greater ideological load. The campaign, and the growing popularity of support for independence, were viewed with considerable interest, and some concern, in other parts of the UK. The Scottish referendum resulted in an intensifying debate about the constitutional position of both Wales and Northern Ireland. It also helped trigger the politicisation of the English question, and this became an additional source of territorially rooted argument and debate from 2014. While the imminent award of additional powers to the Scots provided additional fuel, English national identity had been shifting in character for some while, and had become the focus of growing political interest and policy debate (Kenny 2014). This long-range trend provided the backdrop to the nationalism evoked by UKIP, which – despite the party's name – appealed most powerfully in England during this period.

Since 2010 there has been a significant growth of interest in the question of the relationships between those English regions, cities and towns outside London and the capital itself. This concern has been animated by growing economic disparities between different regions. The conventional dismissal of arguments for a more decentralised system of governance in England was, in these years, displaced by a growing consensus among politicians about the need to tackle widening geographical imbalances and to address the highly centralised character of the way in which England is governed. Towards the end of the Parliament, Chancellor George Osborne unveiled an audacious plan to devolve major new powers – including over health budgets and corporation tax – to the Greater Manchester region, in conjunction with a plan to introduce a new directly elected mayor.

Cameron also tried to make his party the beneficiary of growing English disquiet at the further devolution 'offer' that was hastily made to the Scottish people in the final days of the referendum campaign in September 2014. He announced the formation of a Cabinet committee to report on the main different options relating to the West Lothian Question – the anomaly whereby MPs from devolved territories can vote on issues that affect England only, while English MPs cannot vote on equivalent issues in the devolved areas. The Cabinet committee reported quickly, recommending the introduction of a version of the principle of 'English votes for English Laws' in the House of Commons. This relatively modest proposal reflected a political desire to identity the Conservatives as the expression of (rising) English grievance and also offered a powerful example of the intrusion of populism into high politics in these years.

Nationhood and territory were by no means the only pulse in the developing politics of identity which helped to redraw the familiar ideological landscape during this period. In fact, there has been a growing tendency for political thinking and argument to derive from traditions and sources outside the party system, and a simultaneous diminution in the creativity and appeal of political thinking associated with the major parties. In the face of these complex cross-currents of opinion, Cameron sought to respond firmly and decisively, hence his dramatic interventions on both the EU referendum and the English questions. And, in this respect, he drew a stark contrast between his activism and the indecision and uncertainty exhibited by Labour. But, in a deeper sense, all of the mainstream parties were discomforted by some of the major ideological trends of this period, not least the emergence of waves of populist sentiment which broke over British party politics in powerful and unexpected ways, and generated new dynamics on the right and left of the political spectrum.

Right-populism ascendant?

Populism represents a powerful set of countercultural, and sometimes insurgent, ideas, which have been harnessed in modern politics by figures and forces from both right and left. Populists typically claim to speak for the will of the people, and often present the national interest in its most traditional guise. They regularly counterpose the common sense and popular culture of the people to the self-interested nature and metropolitan character of elites (Taggart 2000).

The hegemony of the two main parties in British politics, and the social deference upon which they called, exercised a significant restraint upon populism, until recently. But in the early twenty-first century, as the two-party duopoly continued to weaken, and new concerns about territory and sovereignty were prominent, populism broke through. This occurred most dramatically in the form of UKIP's successes in the local and European elections of 2014, and victories in two by-elections to the Westminster Parliament in the same year. These results signalled the party's emergence as a vehicle for disaffected voters from different parts of the political spectrum (Ford and Goodwin 2014). While commentators have drawn attention to the demographic characteristics of UKIP supporters – who are most likely to be white, working-class and older – less attention has been paid to the disparate ideas and anti-political rhetoric that the party employs. The mixture of socially conservative and nationalist sentiments which UKIP projects had a major impact upon political thinking and public debate in this period.

At the core of the party's ideological appeal has been the harnessing of two distinct currents – a rising sense of disenchantment with mainstream party politics, on the one hand, and the growing appeal of the burgeoning ethos of self-government on the other. A deepening sense of alienation from politics has created a fertile breeding ground for the argument that there is little distinction between the beliefs of the mainstream parties. UKIP's leader Nigel Farage – despite his own background in the financial services sector – was able to reinvent himself as a prophet in his own land, speaking unpalatable truths to those holding political power, and arguing that, on iconic questions such as immigration and membership of the EU, politicians of left and right were unwilling to listen to the will of the people. This right-populist reflex, and its associated ideas and motifs, have become a familiar part of the ideological landscape in Europe (Mudde 2007). For Labour's Corbyn and his followers, on the other hand, it is the alleged hold of neo-liberal orthodoxies over the main parties that is the target of their neo-socialist politics.

Populism – as both a political style and a substantive body of ideas – poses significant threats to the values and culture upon which representative democracy rests, and also to the ideological diversity that the party system in the UK has permitted. The exponents of populist arguments, be they right- or left-wing in their orientation, seek to efface meaningful differences between their political opponents, and identify an abiding, overriding cleavage between how the elite thinks and what the people want.

The dream of an Anglosphere

The interweaving of populism with nationalism has been an important source of ideological development in these years. Formerly prominent ways of thinking have been reanimated in a context where established ideas about the national interest and the UK's position within the world have come to appear far less secure, leading some to wonder whether the British political tradition itself faces mortal threat. On the political right there has re-emerged the dream of an entirely different geopolitical and economic future for the UK, one that claims to relocate it in the historical trajectory and distinctive values that once made Britain great. In a context where scepticism about the UK's position within the EU has promoted Brexit, a growing number of Conservatives have revived the notion of an alliance made up of some of the leading English-speaking countries spread across the world. The idea of the 'Anglosphere', and a deep interest in the policies and strategies pursued by some of the political leaders of its constituent countries, has become a source of increasing, almost magnetic, appeal to many British Conservatives.

This concept reflects the long-held belief that the UK's interests lie in forging closer relationships, and perhaps even some kind of institutionalised alliance, with those countries with broadly similar political structures and systems, and which also tend to cherish the values of Parliamentary government, individual liberty, the rule of law and the free market. What gives the concept of the Anglosphere striking contemporary resonance is that it frames an account of how the UK could prosper in a global economy dominated by the rise of Asia. Liberated from the EU, it has been suggested, Britain could reinvent its open trading heritage, harnessing its colonial history to integrate itself into the new global economy of the Asian century. Importantly, this position resists the perceived retreat to the hinterland of economic and cultural nationalism associated with UKIP and conservative thinkers like Roger Scruton (2014) in this period, and instead offers a vision of a wider geopolitical alliance. In the title of an influential Conservative Free Enterprise Group pamphlet published in 2012, it is 'Britannia Unchained' (Kwarteng et al. 2012).

What was once a fairly marginal idea in Conservative circles has, since 2010, forced its way into the political limelight. Various leading Tories have, in different ways, identified themselves with this idea, among them former senior ministers such as David Willetts, John Redwood, Liam Fox and Michael Howard. During a trip to Australia in 2013, Boris Johnson spoke of the 'historic and strategic decision that this country took in 1973' in which 'we betrayed our relationships with Commonwealth countries such as Australia and New Zealand' (Baxendale and Wellings 2014: 124). This trend has been stimulated by the emergence of a new generation of politicians for whom Euroscepticism is a political given, and it provided considerable ballast for the arguments of leading Brexiteers, like Boris Johnson, Michael Gove and Daniel Hannan, during the EU Referendum campaign of 2016.

Other ideological sources

Identities and attachments formed outside the political realm have become even more important as sources of political thinking and activism, as the ideological traditions that have nurtured the major political parties have weakened. Religious conviction has remained an important source of political thinking and activism, and framed the manner in which different communities have responded to various policy decisions and political trends. It was on the basis of Christian sentiments that public opposition to some of the welfare policies pursued by government was at times expressed by leading figures in the Church of England – notably Archbishop of Canterbury Justin Welby – and the Catholic Church. And religious actors were prominent in expressing reservations to the legalisation of same-sex marriage, though some faith voices, for instance the Quakers, were on the other side of this argument. More generally, a continuing debate about the position and standing of Muslim communities was a feature of this period, and a small, but notable, number of Muslim politicians broke into the highest echelons of politics, for instance Baroness Sayeeda Warsi and Sajid Javid, who both served as Conservative Cabinet ministers. And it was in the name of a highly doctrinaire and fundamentalist understanding of Islam that a small, but growing, number of young people became involved in, or identified with, extremist and terrorist groups in this period, or journeyed to Syria to join the radical jihadist group Islamic State.

Other forms of collective identity also sustained radical and challenging perspectives on political issues, and contributed to an increasingly variegated public discourse. Feminism continued to develop and diversify, finding a younger generation of exponents and advocates, and becoming a major presence on many university campuses. Its arguments were accompanied by deep disagreements about its direction and most authentic commitments (Moran 2012). But while some commentators lamented a lack of internal diversity, the appearance of a new set of campaigns and activities launched in the name of feminism suggest an ideological paradigm that is continuing to develop and gain momentum among younger people (Bates 2014). Its development was affected too by the dispersal of new digital technologies and social media, although these also provided visceral evidence of the depth and extent of the hostility and prejudice that feminists were seeking to challenge.

This proved to be an auspicious period more generally for a number of the new social movements that had their origins in the radicalism of the 1960s and 1970s, both because of the steady liberalisation of social attitudes, and as new technologies offered opportunities for cheaper campaigns and the rapid development of online communities. Campaigners for a range of different environmentalist goals were especially prominent in the online world, as well as in the campaigning and NGO sectors. The disparate elements of the diverse green ideology that had slowly and unsteadily come together in previous decades were expressed in powerful and accessible terms (Jackson 2011), although conflicts around the different shades of light and dark green remained a feature of this period. More generally, arguments over political strategies and tactics continued to divide these communities. But new points of unity also emerged, not least in the shape of widespread opposition to the increasingly contentious practice of 'fracking'.

Environmentalist thinking was supplemented by a growing discourse of patriotic conservationism, which had been developing since the early 2000s, and which has been influenced by a diverse band of campaigners and writers. It was articulated by public figures such as former poet laureate Andrew Motion, and was mobilised to considerable political effect on various occasions – for instance in response to the government's proposal to sell off parts of the national forest in England, in 2011, and against the Planning Bill of 2012. These decisions brought together a disparate oppositional alliance made up of conservationists, green radicals, shire Tories and Nimbys (Not In My Back Yard), and ensured a continuing market for both conservationist and environmentalist ideas.

Conclusion

Some of the most divisive and significant issues in British politics in this period have been triggered by conflicts and claims rooted in debates over territory, tradition and identity, and these do not align easily with a party system rooted in a binary sense of left–right polarisation. In each of the main UK parties, there emerged important areas of disagreement between social liberals and those adopting a more conservative moral and cultural outlook. Depictions of the aloof, cosmopolitan values of the leadership grouping around Cameron and Osborne, among some Conservative supporters, were echoed by a growing chorus of complaints about the preponderance of metropolitan perspectives and voices on Labour's front bench, and its lack of feel for the experiences and values of working-class citizens living outside London.

Overall, this period witnessed a major shift in the contours and tenor of ideological politics in Britain as political thinking was buffeted by disputes over culture and territory, and was animated by distributional questions that had been less prominent in the period 1997–2007. Both of these shifts presented significant challenges for the mainstream parties, forcing issues onto the political agenda which the Tories, Labour and the Liberal Democrats would have preferred to keep at the margins. The growing power of the language of nation and culture engendered a shift away from the broadly liberal heritage which had been central to British party politics since the nineteenth century. In these years, an important disjuncture began to open between the language and ideologies associated with the extant party system, on the one hand, and the emergence of powerful new arguments and ideas which emerged from outside it.

In response, while the Conservatives have made bold efforts to respond to some of these forms of thinking and the demands that they spawn, Labour struggled to articulate a coherent, ideologically rooted response to these challenges. Instead, it opted to rehearse some familiar, comforting tunes. The vacuous nature of party discourse was thrown into stark relief by the three 'mainstream' candidates, Andy Burnham, Yvette Cooper and Liz Kendall, who competed in the leadership campaign of 2015 and whose platitudinous pitches were easily trumped by Corbyn's straight-talking socialism (Richards 2016).

As mainstream, professional politicians are increasingly depicted as lacking doctrinal roots and serious moral principles, the call for political leaders who are willing and able to present themselves in more vivid ideological colours has become ever louder. At the end of this turbulent period, there is a palpable appetite for political discourse that speaks to the kind of existential questions which have, for some considerable while, lived in the shadows of British party politics.

Chapter 6

Parliament: A Significant Constraint on Government

MEG RUSSELL

Parliament sits very visibly at the heart of British politics. Worldwide, the Palace of Westminster is an emblem not just of parliamentary institutions but of democracy itself. Yet at home the Westminster Parliament has often been dismissed – as out of touch, old-fashioned or, perhaps most damningly, peripheral to the policy process. The classic twentieth-century view saw British politics instead as executive (i.e. government) dominated.

In recent years, Parliament has undergone important changes. Shortly before the 2010 general election, the MPs' expenses crisis risked further undermining public confidence in the institution. But the crisis also opened up opportunities for reform, and for the Commons to become more assertive. The general election then resulted in the formation of the first coalition government at Westminster since 1945, bringing further opportunities to reshape Parliament's relationship with the executive. In 2015, the election of a Conservative government with a narrow majority might be seen partly as a return to the status quo ante. But its closest recent comparator was the delicate Conservative majority of John Major's 1992 government, whose relationship with Parliament was extremely rocky. Plus, some fundamentals had changed. Aside from the tenfold increase in Scottish National Party (SNP) representation in 2015, reforms implemented in 2010 had strengthened backbench independence in the Commons. In the Lords, the Conservatives faced – for the first time ever – a potential centre-left majority that could block their policies. These changes suggested increasing tensions, and possibly further reforms, ahead.

This chapter reviews developments in Parliament during the 2010–2015 coalition and in the first year following the 2015 general election. It does so from the viewpoint of Parliament's power to constrain and influence government. Even before 2010, academics were charting moves away from the old stereotype, and towards a more assertive and effective Parliament. As Philip Cowley (2006) put it in a previous edition of this volume, Parliament had already begun to 'matter' significantly more. This chapter argues that subsequent developments further augmented such power and influence, but that the picture is complex, and future reversals are possible.

The chapter begins by briefly summarising traditional views of Westminster's relative weakness, and developments pre-2010. It then considers, in turn, the 2010 coalition Parliament and the new Parliament following the 2015 election. In each case, it reflects on the challenges for government of managing relations with both chambers, the evidence of parliamentary power, and debates about parliamentary reform. A central argument is that parliamentary power is complex and multifaceted. It is most visible in terms of forcing governmental policy changes; but Parliament's agenda-setting power is also crucial. Yet Parliament's greatest power may be that which is least visible: in terms of affecting the policies that government chooses to bring forward for approval.

Traditional views of the Westminster Parliament

'Westminster' is synonymous with Parliament in Britain. But, perhaps counter-intuitively, the term 'Westminster model' (frequently used in the literature in a loose way, to describe systems based on British traditions) is more synonymous with executive than parliamentary power. In the nineteenth century, Walter Bagehot famously suggested that the 'efficient secret' of the British constitution was the effective fusion of executive and parliamentary power in the House of Commons. Such fusion is not uniquely British – the hallmark of a 'parliamentary' system of government (compared for example to a 'presidential' one) is the executive's need to maintain the confidence of parliament. These systems are common throughout Europe and beyond. But another British hallmark was traditionally single-party majority government – allowing the winning party to reliably win votes in the House of Commons. The unelected House of Lords (which has no equivalent confidence relationship with government) was meanwhile generally seen as weak. Coupled with other factors, such as the lack of a written constitution or a regional tier of government, this left the UK executive fairly unconstrained.

Since the nineteenth century there has hence been almost constant lamentation about Westminster's relative powerlessness, particularly in the face of cohesive political parties. Flinders and Kelso (2011) trace this 'parliamentary decline thesis' back over more than a century. By the 1970s, some academics even claimed that Britain had become a 'post-parliamentary democracy', where Parliament was sidelined by ministers, civil servants and pressure groups, who conducted policy negotiations privately in Whitehall (Richardson and Jordan 1979). Journalists, and indeed some politicians (particularly when in opposition), have often been happy to propagate such views, which have percolated deep into the British consciousness, despite the visibility and ostensible centrality of Parliament.

The description of Britain by comparative scholars has tended to reinforce this picture. Early legislative studies scholars placed the UK Parliament at the weak end of an international spectrum of legislative power, with the US Congress at the opposing end. Westminster was presented as a 'reactive' legislature, and Congress as an 'active' one (Mezey 1979); Westminster as an 'arena' legislature, and Congress a 'transformative' one (Polsby 1975). Some obvious differences stem from the United States being a presidential democracy – where the same kind of interdependence or 'fusion' of executive and legislative power simply doesn't apply, allowing relations between the two branches to be more combative. But Westminster has also been presented as weak in comparison to its continental European neighbours (e.g. Martin and Vanberg 2011), thanks to other structural factors. Important among these is that minority and coalition government is the norm in many other European democracies. Additionally, countries such as Germany and Italy have powerful second chambers.

Recent changes in the UK, including those summarised below, mean that such differences are shrinking. Yet, popular perceptions have a tendency to crystallise, and not be updated in light of new evidence. One of the functions of objective academic study is to assess the evidence available, and dispel lazy assumptions where they persist. But such analysis is undoubtedly challenging. It is far from straightforward to assess Westminster's policy influence, and it is sometimes only long after the event that the importance of past change really becomes clear.

Parliament before 2010

Parliament is subject to frequent change, of both a structural and a political kind. Examples of the former include the addition of life peers to the House of Lords in 1958 (before which it was an almost wholly hereditary institution), and the establishment of the House of Commons departmental select committee system in 1979. Examples of the latter include Labour's landslide 1945 majority, its later narrow-to-vanishing majority in the 1970s (when third and minor parties gained a foothold in the House of Commons), and the abrupt switch to a Conservative government in 1979. These two types of change often feed each other.

Box 6.1   The Wright committee reforms

The Select Committee on Reform of the House of Commons was created in 2009, and chaired by Labour backbencher Tony Wright. It was asked to consider three main topics: how members and chairs of select committees were chosen, how the Commons could gain greater control of its own agenda, and how the public could better influence what the Commons discussed.

The Commons departmental select committees shadow government departments, scrutinising their work, holding ministers and officials to account and conducting policy investigations. But while the committees were respected, and generally published unanimous cross-party reports, pre-2010 their members were effectively selected by party whips (Kelso 2009). Committees then elected their own chairs, again with input from the whips. The Wright committee recommended that chairs should instead be elected by all MPs in a cross-party secret ballot, and committee members in a secret ballot within their parties.

The House of Commons agenda has long been seen as strongly controlled by the government. Standing Order 14 states that '[s]ave as provided in this order, government business shall have precedence at every sitting', then lists key exceptions, including opposition day debates and private members' bills. In contrast, in many other parliaments time belongs by default to Parliament itself. The Wright committee proposed an important new exception for 'backbench business', to collectively belong to backbenchers and be programmed by a new Backbench Business Committee. This proposal faced significant resistance from the whips, but was – like the select committee changes – nonetheless implemented in 2010 (Russell 2011).

In the third area, the Wright committee supported new mechanisms for citizens to petition Parliament and spark debates. This was slower to take full effect. Initially the Backbench Business Committee filtered such proposals, but a new Petitions Committee was established in 2015.

In 1997, Tony Blair's large Commons majority meant that Labour could easily prevail in the division lobbies, reinforcing traditional assumptions of executive dominance. Some important structural changes ensued. A new House of Commons Modernisation Committee proposed various reforms, such as ending late-night sittings and introducing 'programming' of legislation. These were characterised by critics as 'efficiency' rather than 'effectiveness' reforms (Kelso 2009) – that is, changes which would make the government's life easier. But Blair's large Commons majority also allowed increasing numbers of backbench Labour MPs to feel that they could defy the whip – safe in the knowledge that this was unlikely to result in government defeat – and backbench rebellions became more common (Cowley 2002; 2005). Restive backbenchers helped drive further 'effectiveness' reforms, such as greater resources for the select committees and new evidence-taking power for public bill committees. Blair's concession of a Commons vote in 2003 on the decision to go to war in Iraq sparked a new convention that Parliament should be consulted on deployment of British troops.

In the Lords the key change was structural, with crucial political effects. The House of Lords Act 1999 removed the great majority of hereditary peers from the chamber, which ended Conservative dominance and left a far more politically balanced body. Despite some expectations to the contrary, this made life more difficult for Labour – as peers became more confident to challenge government policy. To avoid defeat, ministers often had to negotiate with the Lords. Bicameralism in Britain – long seen as being in decline – was significantly 'revived' (Russell 2013).

The end of Labour's period in office coincided with the 2009 MPs' expenses scandal (Van Heerde-Hudson 2014). This forced the resignation of the Commons Speaker, and election in his place of John Bercow. To help defuse the expenses row, Prime Minister Gordon Brown announced a new Select Committee on Reform of the House of Commons – generally referred to as the 'Wright committee' – which recommended further reforms (see Box 6.1).

The post-2010 Parliament: The numbers

The new Parliament that gathered after the 2010 general election was very different to its predecessor, in two important ways. First, obviously, the Commons was 'hung' – with no single party holding a majority (see Table 6.1). Second, there had been a major turnover of personnel. Labour lost a net 91 seats and the Liberal Democrats lost five, while the Conservatives gained 97. In addition, there were numerous retirements (some of them following expenses allegations). In total, more than a third of MPs were replaced.

In 2015, turnover was again relatively high, with 177 first-time MPs elected. The Conservatives made a net gain of just 24 seats, and Labour a net loss of 26. But this masked other seismic changes. The Liberal Democrats lost 49 of their 57 seats, while the SNP increased their number from just six to 56, mostly at the cost of Labour. Hence almost the entire SNP contingent comprised first-time MPs.

Table 6.1   *Composition of both chambers of Parliament 2010 and 2015*

	Commons May 2010		Lords April 2010		Commons May 2015		Lords April 2015	
	N	%	N	%	N	%	N	%
Conservative	306	47.2	186	26.3	330	50.9	225	28.7
Labour	258	39.7	211	29.8	232	35.7	215	27.4
Liberal Democrat	57	8.8	72	10.1	8	1.2	103	13.1
SNP	6	0.9	0	0.0	56	8.6	0	0.0
Plaid Cymru	3	0.5	0	0.0	3	0.5	2	0.3
NI parties	17	2.6	6	0.8	17	2.6	6	0.8
Green	1	0.2	0	0.0	1	0.2	1	0.1
UKIP	0	0.0	2	0.3	1	0.2	3	0.4
Crossbench	-	-	186	26.3	-	-	179	22.8
Bishops	-	-	26	3.7	-	-	26	3.3
Other	2	0.3	18	2.5	2	0.2	24	3.1
Total	650	100.0	707	100.0	650	100.0	784	100.0

Note: Lords figures exclude those temporarily absent due to leave of absence, disqualification, etc.: 29 members in January 2010; 54 in April 2015.

Of course, The House of Lords' membership does not change at general elections. Instead, it undergoes gradual renewal – with occasional batches of new appointments, and a steady trickle of deaths and (since 2014) retirements. In 2010 the Conservatives and Liberal Democrats already jointly held more Lords seats than did Labour, alongside large numbers of other peers (particularly Crossbench independents). By the end of that Parliament, the situation was broadly similar, though the coalition parties had gained strength. David Cameron made large numbers of appointments to the Lords, both before and after 2015, causing the chamber to grow significantly (as discussed below). Nonetheless, once the Conservatives formed a single-party government in May 2015, they were significantly outnumbered by the other parties in the Lords. This remained the case a year later.

The 2010 coalition Parliament

An obvious question is whether and how Parliament changed under the 2010 Conservative–Liberal Democrat coalition. The switch to two government parties rather than just one, and consequently from two main opposition parties to one, could be expected to have significant effects – given that single-party majority government was the post-1945 Westminster norm. But as just indicated, these changes coincided with the Wright committee reforms, and with the arrival of large numbers of new members. It is thus difficult to disentangle the effects of these various potentially important factors.

The effect of coalition government on parliaments is somewhat disputed among academics. For example, the respected comparativist Arend Lijphart (1999: 12) claims that '[i]n multi-party parliamentary systems, cabinets – which are often coalition cabinets – tend to be much less dominant'. Yet this need not necessarily strengthen Parliament. If the executive knows that it will have difficulty holding together the component parts of the coalition, there may be far more behind-the-scenes negotiation in government, resulting in greater reluctance to concede to backbench or opposition pressure in Parliament. Other comparative studies suggest that where there is a dominant coalition partner (such as the Conservatives in the UK), it generally falls to the smaller partner (e.g. Liberal Democrats) in Parliament to 'police the bargain', and hold the government to its coalition agreements (Martin and Vanberg 2011). Recent British experience is hence an interesting case study to test such theories.

Adjustment to coalition might have been expected to be difficult. In fact, the immediate transition in both chambers proved surprisingly smooth. Westminster standing orders recognise the rights of government, and political parties to some extent, but compared to other parliaments, much depends on convention, leaving flexibility for change. There was some initial wrangling over speaking rights, with the Liberal Democrats losing their previously assumed right to contribute from the frontbench at the start of most debates. They also faced a major financial loss, as their entitlement to opposition party funding (previously worth around £2 million per year) ended. The two governing parties notably retained their separate organisation, and separate whipping arrangements.

Party management in Parliament

As detailed by Yong and Bale in this volume, the coalition agreements of 2010 set out policy compromises in detail. Where tensions occurred – both on issues in the agreements, and others not included – these were often manifested in Parliament.

The Commons. Commons management post-2010, from the government's point of view, was almost certainly more difficult than previously. This was partly as a result of coalition dynamics, but also of the high turnover of members, bringing many newcomers not socialised in pro-cedures and traditions, and of the new opportunities ushered in by the Wright committee. Despite much behind-the-scenes negotiation between the coalition partners, and much of the government's legislation actu-ally passing relatively harmoniously and unscathed, tempers were often frayed.

As a relatively small parliamentary party, the Liberal Democrats had tended to be highly cohesive, with a fairly blurred boundary between front and backbench. Entry into government necessitated a more formal separation, with the establishment of new backbench policy committees (Yong 2012). Their co-chairs (one from the Commons and one from the Lords) adopted a new position as party 'spokespeople' in debate, articulating collective backbench views – sometimes critical of the gov-ernment. In general, the party faced a dilemma in responding to policy. From the outset of the coalition, there were careful attempts to resolve disputes behind the scenes in government, rather than allowing these to emerge openly in Parliament. But any influence by the junior coalition partner in these forums clearly occurred out of the public eye. On some matters there were high-profile rows. Clear divisions occurred for exam-ple on the Health and Social Care Bill, which was 'paused' following vocal Liberal Democrat concerns. Controversial measures in the Welfare Reform Bill (2010–2012) such as introduction of the so-called 'bedroom tax' (whereby housing benefit was cut for those considered to have one or more 'spare' rooms), and the overall cap on household benefits, led to backbench anxiety and public criticism of the party. But its worst embar-rassment occurred over university tuition fees. The coalition agreement had explicitly allowed the parties to 'agree to disagree' on the matter, with the expectation that Liberal Democrat members would abstain on raising the cap on annual fees to £9,000. But it became clear that many instead planned to vote against the rise. To head off a government defeat, the party leadership changed its position to one of support. Ultimately, 21 Liberal Democrats voted against the policy, five abstained and the rest voted for it (Cowley 2015). This resulted in a government victory, but grave reputational damage for the party.

It was not only the junior coalition partner that proved difficult to manage. At the outset of the Parliament, David Cameron sought to gain control of the Conservative Party's 1922 Committee, by ending its historic status as a forum solely for backbench MPs, and instead giving voting rights to frontbenchers. But backbenchers firmly rebuffed this and asserted their independence, forcing Cameron to back down. Where such independence was exerted in the division lobbies, it was focused above all else on European matters. A rebellion in October 2011 by 81 Conservative MPs on a backbench motion calling for a referendum on

Britain's EU membership kicked off a chain of events that led to a formal change in party (though not coalition) policy. By 2013 the government only avoided a defeat on the Queen's Speech via the unusual step of allowing Conservative MPs a free vote on an amendment 'regretting' the lack of a pledge to hold an EU referendum, and promised Conservative leadership support for a private member's bill on this matter. But the biggest Conservative rebellion of the Parliament came in July 2012 over House of Lords reform (discussed below), where 91 Tory MPs defied the whip to vote against second reading of a government bill promoted by Liberal Democrat leader Nick Clegg.

The obvious differences between the parties over policy matters contributed to the 2010 House of Commons being the most rebellious on record, as Cowley (2015) documents. Levels of backbench Commons dissent have risen gradually since the 1970s, with the previous high point being the 2005 Parliament, when 28 per cent of divisions included some rebel votes. During 2010–2015, this figure reached 35 per cent, including 20 per cent among Liberal Democrats and 25 per cent among Conservatives.

The Lords. Some similar dynamics existed in the Lords, but there were also crucial differences between the chambers. While the outcome of the 2010 general election made Liberal Democrat votes matter far more in the Commons – with the party becoming the key 'swing' or 'pivotal' group – something close to the reverse happened in the Lords. After 1999, the Liberal Democrats had become primarily responsible for deciding the outcome of Lords votes. Because Crossbenchers voted in relatively low numbers, and never as a cohesive block, if the Liberal Democrats backed the government, it almost invariably won, whereas if they supported the Conservatives, the government was often defeated (Russell 2013).

But in the 2010 Parliament, this group was clearly expected to vote routinely with the government. The coalition was consequently in a far stronger position in the Lords than the Labour governments that preceded it, making defeats less likely and changing the chamber's dynamics very substantially. To win a vote against the coalition, the Labour opposition needed to enlist sufficient independent Crossbenchers, plus, ideally, government rebels. The Crossbenchers, most of whom are chosen by the House of Lords Appointments Commission on the basis of achievements outside politics, thus gained pivotal status. In 2005–2010, an absence of Crossbench votes would have prevented only 19 per cent of government defeats in the Lords; in 2010–2015, this figure reached 71 per cent. But because such members are not elected, and have no connections to political parties, they are largely invisible to the public. They also tend to be cautious in pushing their objections to government policy too far.

Crossbenchers played a key role in some of the most major conflicts between the coalition government and the Lords. For example, the Health and Social Care Bill faced a challenge on the NHS constitution, fronted by well-known historian Lord (Peter) Hennessy. The Welfare Reform Bill was subjected to seven defeats during its initial passage, six of which were led by Crossbenchers and one (on the benefit cap) by a bishop. Hence the new political dynamic demanded that the opposition worked partly in the background, in support of initiatives led by non-party peers. This made arguments look less partisan, and helped to encourage government backbenchers to rebel on controversial measures, or at least to abstain. Coalition was uncomfortable for Liberal Democrat backbench peers, if anything more so than for the party's MPs, as many represented a different generation of the party – some of whom had split from Labour in the 1980s to form the Social Democratic Party (SDP).

As in the Commons, the level of rebellion in both government parties was high. No fewer than 53 per cent of divisions included some rebel votes, with a 30 per cent rebellion rate among Conservatives and 42 per cent among Liberal Democrats. However, this downplays the true extent of disagreement, as peers unhappy with their party line more often simply stay away. Overall, while the government suffered 48 Lords defeats in the initial 2010–2012 session, relations subsequently calmed down, with only 51 more by the end of the Parliament. In contrast, Labour suffered 175 defeats during 2005–2010, and 245 during 2001–2005. Due to their narrowness, and the Crossbenchers' caution, it was also relatively easier for the coalition government to overturn Lords defeats.

The power of Parliament

Backbench rebellions and Lords defeats are indicative of parliamentary conflict, but do not necessarily demonstrate actual parliamentary power. Commons rebellions don't usually lead to defeat; Lords defeats can potentially be overturned in the Commons. So what can be said about the power of Parliament in the 2010–2015 period? This is not a straightforward question. The most obvious place to look is for government policy reversals, of which there were clear examples. But the power of Parliament goes far beyond that. Parliament helps to determine which policies are discussed in the first place, through 'agenda setting'. It may also persuade government to change its policy ahead of public discussion, to avoid visible dissent and possible defeat.

Parliament forcing policy change. **Despite** difficulties in both chambers, the government largely prevailed in most public disputes. For example, following the 'pause' triggered by Liberal Democrat unease, the Health and Social Care Bill proceeded with most of its content intact. Likewise, the Lords defeats on the Welfare Reform Bill were mostly overturned, with fairly limited concessions. In contrast, the Conservative rebellion on the Lords reform bill, which did not in itself defeat the second reading (thanks to Labour support), signalled such serious trouble ahead that the government dropped the bill. In explicit retaliation, Liberal Democrat peers then engineered a defeat on the government's proposals for revising parliamentary boundaries – which would have shrunk the House of Commons from 650 to 600 MPs and primarily benefited the Conservatives. This went on to be repeated in the Commons, and was the biggest policy reversal driven by the junior coalition partner. Here, uniquely, the two coalition parties walked cohesively through two different division lobbies in opposition to each other – on a policy which had appeared in the coalition agreement. The effect was that the changes were put on hold.

On some matters there was parliamentary resistance from both sides of the coalition. A significant example of impact in the Lords was the government's Public Bodies Bill (2010–2012), which sought to deliver the so-called bonfire of the quangos. Because the bill was introduced via the Lords, the Commons (under the Parliament Acts) had no ultimate override power in the event of a dispute. The government faced fierce resistance from both Conservative and Liberal Democrat backbench peers, as well as the Labour opposition and many Crossbenchers. Substantial parts of the bill were abandoned, including those allowing for the privatisation of public forests and for numerous bodies to face future abolition with little parliamentary scrutiny via secondary legislation. Although the bill was radically amended, most changes were wrought without the need for defeat, through far-reaching government concessions. This illustrates how it is not necessarily the most adversarial conflicts that have the largest effects. As occurred on Lords reform, the government often retreats in the face of danger.

A particularly spectacular policy reversal occurred in the Commons in August 2013, when David Cameron recalled Parliament during the summer recess to seek MPs' endorsement for military action in Syria. With MPs away from Westminster, it was more difficult than usual for the whips to check that there was adequate support for the government's position. Labour chose not to support the government, while 30 Conservative MPs and nine Liberal Democrats also voted against. This resulted in a Commons defeat, bringing an abrupt end to the government's military plans.

Thus there are clear examples of parliamentary resistance driving large-scale policy reversals under the coalition. But despite common assumptions to the contrary, reversals of this kind have occurred under most recent governments (see Russell and Cowley 2015). Hence, whether those under coalition were greater is hard to say without far more detailed analysis. There was relatively little outward sign of the Liberal Democrats 'policing the bargain', as the academic literature might suggest. For example, the minor party seemed powerless to hold the Conservatives to Lords reform. Instead, it was often outspoken Conservative backbenchers who dragged the coalition away from its commitments, and from what the Liberal Democrats wanted. As Eunice Goes (2014) has argued, this was maybe a peculiarity of UK coalition, played out particularly over the issue of Europe. But these policy changes also crucially depended on Parliament's agenda-setting power.

Parliament's agenda-setting power. As well as making decisions on government policies presented to it, Parliament has important powers – of various kinds – to help determine what gets discussed. Routes such as opposition day debates, private members' bills and parliamentary questions have long been available to place items on the parliamentary agenda which are awkward for government. The Wright committee reforms significantly extended this power. The new Commons Speaker John Bercow also played his part. He ran for election (under revised procedures used for the first time in 2009) on a clear prospectus of reform, and subsequently sought to be an independent-minded 'voice for the Commons' – meaning primarily backbenchers. He took particular pride in granting more 'urgent questions' – which force ministers to attend and answer at short notice – than his predecessors. Just two such questions were granted in the 2008–2009 parliamentary session; in the six years to 2015, Bercow allowed well over 200.

Established agenda-setting mechanisms played a part in some of the policy reversals mentioned above. For example, the potential privatisation of public forests (which was also the subject of a noisy external campaign), was raised at Prime Minister's Questions in the Commons, and in a Labour opposition day debate. This very visible parliamentary pressure, alongside amendments supported by government backbenchers in the Lords, helped force the government to change its position.

On other matters, the new agenda-setting powers proved important – not just in constraining the government on existing policy, but also pushing it further. The new Commons Backbench Business Committee invited proposals which demonstrated cross-party support, on matters unlikely to be debated in government time, for backbench debates which could end with a decision by vote. By the end of the 2010–2015 Parliament, more than 300 such debates had been programmed by the committee, including some provoked by public petitions. Topics included prisoners' voting rights, the Hillsborough football disaster and the recognition of Palestine. Crucially, the government's 2013 defeat on Syria was preceded by agreement of a backbench motion to insist that any military action must be subject to prior parliamentary approval. Yet, the most influential backbench debate was almost certainly that of October 2011 demanding an EU referendum, which was sparked by a public petition. This debate enabled Conservative Eurosceptics to push the party leadership into a change of policy. Their campaign subsequently used other conventional agenda-setting tools, including the private member's bill and Queen's Speech vote.

In addition to what is discussed on the floor of the two chambers comes the work of select committees, which decide their own agendas. The committees seemed to gain greater independence and confidence as a result of the Wright committee changes. Immediately after the 2010 general election, some chair elections were hotly contested. For example, independent-minded Conservative Andrew Tyrie won the chair of the Treasury Select Committee, while Margaret Hodge won a contest among six Labour candidates to chair the prestigious Public Accounts Committee (PAC). Tyrie went on to lead the high-profile Parliamentary Commission on Banking Standards, while Hodge used the PAC to call representatives of Google, Amazon and Starbucks to public hearings on tax avoidance. The Culture, Media and Sport Committee likewise questioned well-known media executives over the phone-hacking scandal. Such private sector figures would otherwise have avoided public questioning. These developments helped drive both the media and political agenda. Before 2010, the committees already enjoyed considerable policy impact (Benton and Russell 2012) and media profile (Kubala 2011), and both have almost certainly now grown. Committee independence was further demonstrated in 2014 when Conservative Sarah Wollaston – a former GP, who had previously been blocked by the whips from membership of the public bill committee on the Health and Social Care Bill – was elected as chair of the Health Committee. The whips still control public bill committee membership, but in the reformed environment of the select committees Wollaston became not only a member of the committee covering her field, but its chair.

At the end of the Parliament, Speaker Bercow became embroiled in controversy over his attempt to reshape the role of the most senior Commons official, and to bring in an outsider. A backbench debate triggered the establishment of a committee on Commons Governance, which devised an alternative plan. But a clumsy attempt by government whips to unseat Bercow on Parliament's final sitting day before the 2015 election was rejected, with senior Conservative backbenchers speaking and voting against. This felt like the final defiant act of an independent Parliament.

Parliament and anticipated reactions. Agenda-setting is a subtle power, hard to quantify but clearly visible when you look. Even more difficult to assess is Parliament's 'power of anticipated reactions'. Legislative studies scholars have long noted that the most important power of Parliament may be keeping certain policy proposals off the agenda altogether (e.g. Mezey 1979). When Labour was in government 1997–2010, explicit internal mechanisms were developed to anticipate the response of the Lords, and to minimise conflict (Russell 2010; 2013), which helps to explain the decline in government defeats in the chamber between 2001–2005 and 2005–2010. Ministers must of course also anticipate the responses of the Commons; but this may come more naturally, as most senior ministers are drawn from there and know the mood of their own backbenchers – on whose support they crucially depend.

It is possible to find occasional evidence of anticipated reactions in action. For example, while the Liberal Democrats achieved only fairly small policy reversals to the published Welfare Reform Bill, the government's original plan to restrict housing benefit for the long-term unemployed (as announced in George Osborne's 2010 budget) was omitted from the bill, apparently as a result of Liberal Democrat backbench pressure. But most such reversals leave little to no trace on the public record. Generally, though this may be Parliament's greatest power, it is also mostly hidden.

An important question is how these dynamics may have changed under coalition. In summary, the Commons became relatively less predictable, given ministers' dependence on two parties, while the Lords became relatively more so, due to the weakened opposition. The Commons – particularly thanks to its new procedures – was fairly clearly strengthened, while the Lords was muzzled to some extent. Hence the effect on Parliament as a whole is debatable.

The coalition and parliamentary reform

As is already clear, the coalition had significant plans for parliamentary reform, key parts of which were abandoned. The boundary review was blocked by the Liberal Democrats. Lords reform was, in effect, blocked by the Conservatives (see Box 6.2). In addition (as indicated in Alan Renwick's chapter), the proposal to move to the Alternative Vote (AV) for House of Commons elections was rejected by referendum in 2011.

An outstanding proposal from the Wright committee, to adopt a cross-party 'House Business Committee', with responsibility for scheduling government business, appeared in the coalition agreement but was quietly shelved.

The one major change during 2010–2015 was the Fixed-term Parliaments Act 2011, which limited the Prime Minister's discretion over when a general election could be called, fixing the length of each Parliament instead at five years. Such a change had long been called for by some reformers, who argued that the governing party could unfairly manipulate election timings (see Blick 2016). The reform nonetheless had critics, who argued that the average length of post-war parliaments was less than four years, while a fixed four-year term applied in the devolved legislatures. But the passage of the Act was largely pragmatic – to tie the two coalition partners into a five-year deal. In this it fulfilled its purpose.

Box 6.2 House of Lords reform bills 2010–2015

The coalition's House of Lords Reform Bill, published in draft in 2011, proposed to leave the chamber's powers unchanged, but to replace the system of life peerages with a chamber where 80 per cent of members were elected, and 20 per cent appointed as independents. It was sponsored by Nick Clegg, as Deputy Prime Minister. The draft bill faced criticism from a specially established joint parliamentary committee of MPs and peers, and from Conservative backbenchers. Ironically, since it was almost identical to proposals published by the Brown government in 2008, it also faced fierce criticism from the Labour frontbench. Lords reform had been a long and painful saga under Labour (Russell 2013), and both main parties were split on the question. For years there had been pressure for a largely elected chamber, to bring democratic legitimacy to the Lords. But critics of the new proposals feared that such a chamber would become too powerful, and be far more partisan and less 'expert' than the present body.

As indicated above, the government's bill was ultimately withdrawn in 2012 following Commons opposition. Subsequently, some more minor changes were agreed via private members' bills. The House of Lords Reform Act 2014 (originally sponsored by Dan Byles MP and Lord (David) Steel) allowed peers voluntarily to retire from the chamber. An even smaller measure in 2015 (sponsored by Baroness Hayman) allowed the Lords to expel members permanently for bad behaviour. But neither bill tackled the chamber's most glaring problem: its ballooning upward size.

The first year of the 2015 Parliament

Being freed from coalition in 2015 and able to govern alone, the Conservatives might have hoped to implement their desired policies with relative ease, far less constrained by Parliament. If they did, it would have been partly a product of their unexpected arrival in office. Few people predicted a single-party Conservative government. Had there been serious planning for this eventuality, some early problems that occurred in the government's relationship with Parliament might have been better anticipated.

Party management in Parliament

The new political dynamics of the Commons were relatively familiar for a government with a narrow majority. If as few as eight Conservative MPs voted against the whip (given that Sinn Fein MPs do not take their seats) the government could potentially face defeat. Ministers therefore needed to be particularly sensitive to the concerns of their own backbench MPs. Since many Conservatives had developed a habit of rebellion in the previous Parliament, this situation was delicate. But small groups of rebels can only inflict defeat if there is a united opposition. In this respect, Jeremy Corbyn's election as Labour Party leader provided an unexpected gift for the government. On some sensitive issues (as discussed below), Corbyn's own benches were at least as likely to be split as Cameron's. The new Labour leader had the dubious pedigree of having been the most persistent rebel against his own party's government 1997–2010 (closely followed by his Shadow Chancellor, John McDonnell). In addition, even if Labour was united, the most rebellious Conservative MPs were to Cameron's right rather than his left, creating further obstacles to forming a majority against the government.

The new wildcard in Commons management was the SNP. The party was from the start a very cohesive bloc and, despite some natural disdain for Westminster, maintained high attendance in the chamber. SNP members seemed determined to challenge some Commons conventions, and pushed the boundaries of what Speaker Bercow would allow. But they were not simply outsiders. Following the Liberal Democrat collapse, the SNP gained the position of second-largest opposition party, with rights to speak in most debates from the frontbench, control some opposition day debates and also chair two select committees. The party quickly sought to flex its muscles – for example, signalling that it would vote against the government's proposed relaxation of the hunting ban, despite this having no direct effect on the law in Scotland.

Managing the Lords was a bigger and less familiar challenge for all concerned. Previous Conservative governments had always enjoyed a preponderance of members in the chamber, if not an actual majority, due to the hereditary peers. For example, in the 1996–1997 session the Lords had 477 Conservative members and just 116 Labour – with the balance held by 322 Crossbenchers, 57 Liberal Democrats and various others (Vollmer 2012). In contrast, the 2015 Conservative government found itself heavily outnumbered in the chamber, and in a substantially weaker position than the coalition. With the Liberal Democrats now in opposition, the dynamic reverted to one similar to that faced by previous Labour governments. Labour and the Liberal Democrats together could potentially form a centre-left bloc and defeat the government.

This situation was novel not just for the Conservatives, but also for Labour, and a big question was the extent to which the opposition would use its new power. The Conservatives in opposition had tended to exercise restraint in the Lords, to avoid challenges of illegitimacy when confronting an elected Labour government. They were mindful of their role as 'government in waiting'. Conventions established in the twentieth century (most famously the 'Salisbury convention', on manifesto commitments) suggested that major government policies should not be blocked by the Lords. But the Liberal Democrats had always been disdainful of such conventions. Now in opposition, and bruised by its recent electoral collapse, the party had potential to wreak revenge on its former coalition partners via the Lords. But it could only do so in cooperation with Labour.

The early months of the government saw regular Lords defeats – 23 by the end of 2015, compared to eight during the equivalent period of coalition. This caused significant ministerial aggravation, which peaked over the tax credit vote in October 2015 (described below). It was the Liberal Democrats who made the key difference to most of these defeats. This was plainly frustrating for ministers, given that Liberal Democrat seats in the Lords significantly outstripped the party's share of both Commons seats and general election votes. But, ironically, almost half of Liberal Democrat peers had been appointed to the chamber by David Cameron.

The power of Parliament

The potential hence existed for both chambers of the 2015 Parliament to force significant policy reversals on the government. Of course the Commons retained its ability, as enhanced in 2010, to influence the policy agenda, while the Lords could not only debate matters itself, but throw them back to the Commons to consider. Consequently, ministers needed to think very carefully in terms of anticipating how Parliament would react before proceeding with policy.

Three very clear examples can be seen of the interplay between these forces in the government's early months. The first, already mentioned above, came when ministers planned a Commons vote before the 2015 summer recess to relax the terms of Labour's Hunting Act 2004 in England and Wales. As the Scottish Parliament controls its own system of regulation north of the border, the SNP was not initially expected to participate in any such vote. The party had long indicated its respect for a broad principle of 'English votes for English laws' at Westminster. But as the decision approached, SNP leader Nicola Sturgeon announced that her MPs would oppose the change. As some Conservatives would also vote against (the party having promised a free vote), while Labour MPs almost universally opposed hunting, the government cancelled the vote to avoid a seemingly inevitable Commons defeat.

Two other Commons decisions were quite publicly delayed until ministers were satisfied that they could prevail in the division lobbies. The first was adoption of new standing orders to enforce 'English votes for English laws' – further discussed below. With united Labour and SNP opposition, ministerial concerns about possible Conservative rebels meant that a promised vote in July was postponed until October. By then, any rebellion had dissipated. Another key matter on which ministers took careful soundings was a revived proposal for military action in Syria. Following the embarrassment of the 2013 defeat, government sources quite openly admitted that the parliamentary vote was awaiting clarity that there was adequate Commons support. When the vote finally took place in late November 2015, there were just seven Conservative rebels, and ministers also gained substantial support from the Labour benches. The more serious split, indeed, occurred on the Labour side, where a free vote was conceded due to the shadow cabinet's inability to agree a collective line. Shadow Foreign Secretary Hilary Benn spoke passionately in favour of action from the frontbench, while his leader spoke and voted against.

The politics of the Lords required careful ministerial handling, negotiation and concessions, but on some issues ministers tried to stand firm. This succeeded when the Lords demanded that the franchise in the EU referendum should be extended to 16- and 17-year-olds. Ministers persuaded the Commons to overturn a Lords defeat, and peers backed down. The EU referendum was a key Conservative manifesto commitment, and for the Lords to derail it (or at least delay it while an extended electoral register was prepared) would have been controversial. Nonetheless, Liberal Democrat leader Tim Farron characterised

Labour peers' refusal to fight on as 'pathetic' (*Guardian*, 13 January 2016) – demonstrating the tensions between the two opposition parties in the Lords.

The biggest flashpoint by far between the government and the Lords came in October 2015 over the vote on the Tax Credits (Income Thresholds and Determination of Rates) (Amendment) Regulations. This seemingly obscure measure, enacted through 'secondary legislation' which is generally used for small policy adjustments, promised to save over £4 billion in public expenditure by greatly limiting eligibility for tax credits among low income households. The Lords has a veto over secondary legislation, though this has historically only been used a handful of times. When ministers learned of trouble brewing in the Lords, there were loud protests (particularly from Chancellor George Osborne) on the basis that the Commons had approved the measure and its financial implications were very great. But although the rhetoric reached fever pitch (including threats to 'flood' the Lords with Conservative peers), the measure was defeated. This sparked a review of the Lords' powers, as discussed below, but also led Osborne to drop the policy. Though he could have asked the Commons to vote again, it was clear that there was widespread dissent on the Conservative backbenches – which, indeed, was a key reason why peers had held their nerve.

This was a major victory for Parliament, and illustrates two important points. First, the Lords normally achieves policy change only with implicit or explicit Commons support – this was as much a victory for Conservative backbenchers as for opposition peers. Second, the government had not adequately anticipated Parliament's response. Had Osborne been more attuned to the mood in the Lords, and among his own backbenchers, the policy would have been withdrawn or amended before the vote. This example again demonstrates the potential for the power of anticipated reactions, as well as the Lords' power to put awkward issues onto the Commons agenda. All three forms of parliamentary power were therefore visible during the Conservative government's early months.

The Conservative government and parliamentary reform

The Conservative government, unlike its predecessor, had few ambitions for parliamentary reform. Changes implemented by the coalition – the Fixed-term Parliaments Act, and a change to allow public 'recall' of miscreant MPs, passed late in the coalition's term – were to be adhered to. The boundary changes delayed by the Liberal Democrats were to be revived. Lords reform was explicitly described in the Conservative manifesto as 'not a priority in the next Parliament', though there was a pledge

Box 6.3   English votes for English laws

The parliamentary change which most Conservatives wanted was enforcement of 'English votes for English laws'. Ever since Labour's devolution to the Scottish Parliament (and parallel bodies in Wales and Northern Ireland) in 1998–1999, awkward questions had remained about the ability of Scottish (and potentially Welsh and Northern Irish) MPs to vote on English matters that were now devolved in their home area – that is, the so-called West Lothian Question. The principle of 'English votes for English laws' (EVEL) was supported by the Conservatives from the 2001 manifesto onwards. The coalition couldn't agree on the matter, but established a Commission chaired by former Commons Clerk Bill McKay to review it.

The 2015 government was determined to act, and proposed changes to the Commons standing orders which differed from McKay's recommendations. The Speaker would be required to certify bills, or parts of bills, that applied only to one part of the UK. They would pass through the normal process, but also be subject to potential veto by a 'legislative grand committee' comprising MPs drawn only from that area. Scottish MPs would hence not be prevented from voting on English matters, but English MPs could potentially override them. The Commons agreed this system in October 2015 in a wholly partisan vote – with Conservatives in favour, Labour, Liberal Democrats and SNP against. Its effects, in terms of procedural complexity and possible game playing, were unpredictable. But its bigger political effect was likely to be felt only in the future. While the Conservatives enjoy a majority both in the UK and in England, a future Labour government might be more dependent on Scottish and Welsh votes. That such a policy was adopted indicated growing tensions in British territorial politics (as described in the chapter by Charlie Jeffery).

to 'address ... the size of the chamber'. The main manifesto promise was to implement 'English votes for English laws' (see Box 6.3).

Despite challenges of governing with a small Commons majority, it was difficulties with the Lords that seemed particularly likely to dog Cameron's second term, fuelling demands for reform. Large-scale change to Lords membership (e.g. to introduce elected members) was clearly off the agenda, but there was no immediate indication of how the ballooning size of the chamber was to be 'addressed'. This was largely a problem of Cameron's making: by late 2015 he had attained a record of appointing to the chamber at a faster rate than any other Prime Minister since life peerages began in 1958. He had made over 250 appointments, and the size of the chamber (after deaths and retirements) had consequently increased by roughly 130. Partly this reflected Cameron's attempts to strengthen his own Lords benches, but (ill-defined) conventions demand that appointments are made from across the party spectrum, and even in late 2015 he created further Labour and Liberal Democrat peers. There were increasingly urgent discussions on means to boost retirements, and (further spurred by the threats of 'flooding') to regulate prime ministerial appointments.

But while the Lords' composition has long been debated, the tax credits row suddenly put its powers onto the agenda. In October 2015, ministers tasked the senior Conservative Lord Strathclyde with reviewing the chamber's power over secondary legislation, and his report proposed that the veto power should be ended. But the review – and indeed the whole tax credits affair – raised more questions than it answered. A bill to curb the Lords' powers looked difficult, and, on balance, unlikely. Meanwhile, the whole question of the extent of secondary legislation, and the adequacy of its scrutiny in Parliament, became a surprise hot topic. Use of this route for other controversial changes – for example, to licence fracking and cut student grants – caused some to claim that ministers were seeking to avoid scrutiny by two potentially awkward parliamentary chambers, not just one.

Conclusion: An ever more independent Parliament?

This chapter has charted key developments in Parliament throughout the whole of one government, and through the first year of the next. It has charted considerable constraints placed on ministers by Parliament. Far from being an acquiescent, or peripheral, institution, Westminster appears vibrant and increasingly independent. This results from both political and structural changes.

The most obvious and historic shift in the 2010 Parliament was the arrival of coalition government. The two governing parties, albeit bound together by a coalition agreement, had different political priorities and interests. There were attempts to contain differences behind the scenes; but there were also electoral incentives for both parties to engage in public disagreements, most of which played out in Parliament. Some of the key casualties in policy terms were changes to Parliament itself: Nick Clegg's House of Lords reform proposals, and the attempts to reform Commons boundaries (while the AV referendum also failed). But these were only some of the policy reversals forced on the government or – in the case of pressure for an EU referendum – on the Conservative leadership.

Such reversals might appear to support academic claims that parliaments are stronger under coalition government. But important structural changes occurred in the same period as well. The Wright committee reforms gave MPs greater control over the Commons agenda, encouraging cross-party groups of backbenchers to coalesce and force debates on matters uncomfortable for ministers. The full force of the new convention on votes for military action was felt by the government in 2013. The new Commons speaker, John Bercow, also played his part. The Commons select committees became more independent, adding to an environment where power was slipping away from the whips. While whips continued to control seats on bill committees, they could no longer promise members seats on select committees, and their agenda control was also eroded by the Backbench Business Committee and introduction of public petitions. For all of the reasons above, party cohesion in the coalition Parliament reached an all-time low – in continuation of a trend which started in the 1970s, and accelerated under Blair and Brown.

Structural change to the House of Lords is also central to explaining government's changing relationship with Parliament, and in this area the political change brought by coalition was a weakening. The chamber found a new confidence post-1999; but in 2010, when the Commons likewise became a 'hung' chamber, the Lords' contribution became less unique. Negotiations with the Liberal Democrats were essential to carrying government policy, but if this was acceptable to the party in the Commons, the same would generally apply in the Lords. Any majority that the Labour opposition could garner against the coalition was necessarily small and fragile. In 2015, however, this situation radically changed again, with a centre-left majority in the Lords able to defeat a Conservative government for the first time. A crucial function of the Lords is to throw difficult issues back to the Commons for decision, which proved tricky for government in both the 2010 and 2015 Parliaments.

Far from the old stereotypes, we therefore see that Westminster has a central role in determining, and constraining, government policy. This operates through at least three mechanisms: forcing policy reversals, helping set the policy agenda and getting ministers to trim their ambitions in anticipation of what Parliament will accept. The first of these is fuelled by more independence on the government backbenches, and a more assertive 'no overall control' House of Lords. The second has been enhanced by new mechanisms in the Commons. As a consequence of both, the third kind of policy power – anticipated reactions – has almost certainly grown as well. The fact is that in a parliamentary system such as Britain's, ministers ultimately depend on the confidence of Parliament in order to survive. The relationship may be less conflictual than in a presidential system, but lack of visible conflict does not necessarily indicate an absence of parliamentary power – indeed, sometimes the reverse is true.

Looking ahead, it cannot be assumed that Parliament's strength will necessarily keep increasing. In the past, a dialectic has existed between structural and political change, with each to an extent driving the other. There is also a pattern of reaction and counterreaction: when Parliament is weak, there are pressures for reform to strengthen it; if it becomes too strong, this pressure (particularly from government) will go into reverse. In the early months after the 2015 election, concerns of various kinds were expressed about government's relationship with Parliament. Ministers were keen to constrain the House of Lords' powers, and were accused of bypassing both chambers by overuse of secondary legislation. Excessive appointments to the Lords threatened both that chamber's effectiveness and its reputation. The opposition in the Commons, meanwhile, was unusually weak. The remains of the 2015 Parliament looked set to be fractious, with unpredictable results.

Chapter 7

Political Recruitment and the Political Class

PHILIP COWLEY

The House of Commons elected in May 2015 was a disproportionately white, male, middle-class and middle-aged institution. Just 29 per cent of MPs were women – making the UK one of the worst countries in Western Europe for female representation – and just 6 per cent of MPs were from ethnic minorities. A full third had been educated at fee-paying schools in a county where the figure for the population as a whole is just 7 per cent, and a mere 2 per cent were under the age of 30. The Commons was, in the words of that hackneyed phrase, 'male, pale and stale'.

The House of Commons elected in May 2015 contained more women MPs than ever before, putting the UK in the best 20 per cent of countries in the world for female representation; it contained more MPs from ethnic minorities than ever before; and it contained not only more out lesbian, gay, and bisexual MPs than ever before, but more than in any other parliament in the world. The Commons was, to quote one study of its composition, 'the most diverse in 100 years' (Criddle 2015).

Both of the above paragraphs are accurate – and the tension between them is one of the themes of this chapter. British political institutions, and not just the House of Commons, remain unrepresentative of the British population in a descriptive sense. That is, in almost every case, those doing the representing do not resemble those they are representing. 'They' are not like 'us'. But they never have been, and the composition of Parliament and other political bodies is changing, with previously excluded groups becoming represented in ever greater numbers. The record-breaking numbers of women, ethnic minorities and lesbian, gay and bisexual (LGB) MPs in 2015 in every case replaced previous records set in 2010. The pace of change may be slower than some would like, but the general direction of travel is clear.

Perhaps the most interesting aspect of contemporary discussions of political representation, though, is not the numbers themselves, but that it is now widely accepted that the numbers are important. It used to be commonplace to be told that it did not matter who MPs were, as long as they were 'the best person for the job'. Those days are now largely over. What Anne Phillips, who was one of the pioneers of this work in the UK, termed 'the politics of presence' (1995) has become a widely, if not wholly, accepted part of political discourse. David Cameron's very first speech as party leader in 2005 had contained the claim that 'We will change the way we look. Nine out of ten Conservative MPs, like me, are white men.' As Labour leader, Ed Miliband repeatedly argued for the need to change the composition of Parliament, so that it better reflected the nation. 'We need', he said in July 2012, 'a politics where politicians look like the constituents they represent. That's not what Westminster looks like today.' All the major parties have signed up to the principle that politicians should (broadly) resemble the wider population – even if they vary in the seriousness with which they take this commitment.

Moreover, this concern now encompasses a much wider range of social characteristics than it used to. In recent decades, politicians discussing this subject would talk about the sex and then more recently the ethnicity of politicians – occasionally along with a vague reference to (rarely specified) 'other groups' – but discussion of representation has now begun explicitly to include a wider range of characteristics, including class, sexuality and disability. The scope of the politics of presence is thus broader now than at any point for the last 100 years. This broadening makes the debate more interesting, perhaps, but more complicated too. It also draws attention to some of the groups previously included in representative institutions, but now increasingly marginalised – most obviously the decline of working-class representation.

And entwined with this debate is another about the rise of the 'political class' or 'career politicians', who do not share the aims, experiences and aspirations of 'normal' people. This debate is theoretically and intellectually distinct from the debate about the socio-demographic composition of political elites, but in practice, the two have become connected, as part of a more general discussion about whether Britain has the right sort of people as its politicians, and what, if anything, can be done about it. Who do we want to govern us? And who do we get?

This chapter starts by discussing the extent to which British political bodies are representative – or not. Any analysis of political representation involves comparisons, most obviously between the represented and those doing the representing. But doing the exercise properly also involves other comparisons: with the past, with other professions, with other countries and between parties. The chapter then discusses the broadening nature of the debate in the UK and the possible effects that group representation can have, and ends by discussing the rise of the career politician.

Who's there, and who's not

Most of those who write on this topic seriously do not argue for any form of 'pure' microcosmic representation – in which parliaments or other bodies are required to have the precise percentages of every social characteristic seen in the wider population. The saloon bar criticism that we should not want a parliament with the absolutely direct proportionate number of idiots, for example, is easily batted away, on the grounds that there are very good reasons why we would not want or expect lots of idiots in our representative assemblies. Instead, writers on this subject (mostly) argue for the inclusion of groups that have previously been excluded or are otherwise marginalised, focussing on three reasons to justify their presence: 1) on grounds of justice; 2) because of the symbolic benefits that might result from their presence; and 3) because of the substantive changes that might result from their presence.

Table 7.1 (below) focuses on the two groups still most commonly referred to in discussions of political representation in Britain, showing the percentage of women and members of ethnic minorities in a variety of UK political institutions.

The precise figure for the level of female representation varies, from the 25 per cent in the House of Lords up to the 42 per cent for the National Assembly for Wales – but all are below 51 per cent, the percentage of women in the population. The figure for the percentage of non-white politicians also varies, from 0 per cent in the Northern Ireland Assembly up to 32 per cent in the London Assembly; but again, all are below the relevant

Table 7.1   *Proportion of women and ethnic minority members in UK political institutions*

	Women	Non-white
European Parliament (UK members)	41%	10%
National Assembly for Wales	42%	5%
Scottish Parliament	35%	2%
London Assembly	40%	32%
House of Commons	29%	6%
Councillors (England, Wales & Scotland combined)	28%	4%
House of Lords	25%	6%
Northern Ireland Assembly	28%	0%

figure for the wider population: the figures for the various UK-wide institutions are all below the 13 per cent non-white figure in the 2011 census, and those for parts of the UK are also all below the equivalent census figure for that area. The 32 per cent of ethnic minority representation in the London Assembly, for example, looks sizeable until you remember that 40 per cent of Londoners gave their ethnic identity as something other than white in 2011.

Data on other socio-demographic groups are harder to find, do not exist for every institution and are often less reliable where they do exist. But to take education, which is often used as a proxy for wealth and privilege, a third of the House of Commons went to a private (fee-paying) school, along with half of the members of the House of Lords, way above the 7 per cent for the wider population. The figure for the Scottish Parliament in 2016 was lower, at 20 per cent, but still above the approximately 4 per cent of Scots who go to private schools.

Or take sexuality: the percentage of out LGB MPs in the House of Commons stands at just below 5 per cent (a total of 32 MPs), lower than most estimates for the population as a whole (variously estimated as somewhere between 5 and 9 per cent); the equivalent figure for the Welsh Assembly is also 5 per cent. The figure for the Scottish Parliament is 8 per cent (including three Scottish party leaders in the Parliament, and, outside the Parliament, the leader of UKIP Scotland); that for the London Assembly stands at 12 per cent.

Politics is not exceptional in any of this. Table 7.2 shows equivalent figures to Table 7.1, but for seven senior professional roles in the UK, along with an equivalent figure for politics (calculated as the mean of the four UK and GB-wide figures in Table 7.1). Women make up more than half of all head teachers and around half of GPs, but they are under half of those in the senor civil service, the directors of FTSE 100 companies, judges, senior police officers and, worst of all, professors (boo!) – and in the last four of these professions, women are less well represented than in politics. With the exception of GPs, ethnic minorities fare even worse, being under-represented in all but one of the professions, and with the figure for politics being equal or higher than all but one.

The 32 per cent of MPs educated at private schools is clearly high, but it looks somehow less shocking when we realise that the figures for senior police officers is 22 per cent, that for FTSE 100 CEOs is 34 per cent, that for the senior civil service is 48 per cent, that for what one report called 'top doctors' is 61 per cent and that for senior judges is 74 per cent (Social Mobility and Child Poverty Commission 2014; Kirby 2016). To note this is not to dismiss or downplay the issue in representative bodies (not least because we might care more about the issue in explicitly *representative* bodies than in those that make no such claims), but it does indicate that

Table 7.2   *Proportion of women and ethnic minority members in comparable professions*

	Women	Non-white
Head Teachers	65%	3%
GPs	51%	22%
Senior Civil Service	39%	7%
Politics [UK/GB wide]	31%	7%
FTSE 100 Directors	26%	5%
Judges	25%	6%
Senior Police Officers (Chief Inspector and above)	21%	3%
Professors	20%	7%

the reasons politics is so unrepresentative in a descriptive sense are not all specific to politics. A lot of ink is spilt on how various political institutions (Westminster, in particular) are somehow off-putting to underrepresented groups, and that things would change if only we changed the environment – the sitting hours, say, or if MPs stopped shouting at each other at Prime Minister's Questions and instead sat around in a circle, holding hands, and singing 'Kumbaya'. The data just discussed make these sort of claims look pretty implausible.

Data on cross-national comparisons are also harder to come by, but what there is does not show the UK doing massively worse than many other political systems. Data on female representation is the easiest to analyse, not least because it is routinely collected by the Inter-Parliamentary Union (IPU). The IPU's figures for lower chambers – including the House of Commons – placed Britain 36th out of 190 countries in terms of the percentage of female MPs following the 2015 general election. That put the UK below most of the rest of Western Europe, broadly defined, although still above countries such as the US, Canada, Australia or Ireland, and in the top 20 per cent overall. In the European Parliament, the UK's figure of 41 per cent makes the UK (joint) ninth, out of the 28 EU countries.

The absolute number of out LGB MPs at Westminster has been the highest anywhere in the world since at least 2010 (Reynolds 2013). It is slightly less impressive if measured in relative terms as a percentage of the chamber, with the record for the highest percentage figure in the world set by the Scottish Parliament elected in 2016. (The London Assembly

LGB percentage figure is even higher, but it is not normally classed as a parliament.) Lastly, one study of eight countries in Europe showed that Britain had a higher proportion of MPs of 'immigrant origin' (a definition wider than the classification used in Table 7.1) than all but one (Sobolewska 2016): Westminster's record was better than Belgium, France, Germany, Greece, Italy and Spain, being knocked off top spot only by the Netherlands.

In other words, British political institutions *are* unrepresentative, but they are not noticeably worse than comparable professions and, while lagging behind many European countries on female representation, are ahead of the same countries when it comes to the representation of other previously excluded groups.

Box 7.1   Intra-group differences

The data discussed in the main text are overall figures, but these can often mask important differences *within* groups. For example, in the UK and elsewhere, gay men have been better represented than lesbians; all the current British LGB MPs are white; and the normal LGBT acronym would be misleading, given that there have been no transsexual MPs – although Nikki Sinclaire became the first transsexual elected politician in Britain when she was elected to the European Parliament in 2009.

Similarly, while there has been an increase in the number of female MPs, there is even greater under-representation of mothers, at least those caring for children: women MPs are less likely to have children than male MPs; more likely to have fewer children than male MPs; and enter Parliament when their children are older than the children of male MPs (Campbell and Childs 2014).

And while the proportion of non-white MPs has also been growing, they were, until very recently, overwhelmingly male. Before 2010, there had been just two black female and no Asian women MPs. Plus, nonwhite MPs have been disproportionately of Black African origin rather than of, say, Indian or Caribbean origin (Sobolewska 2014). It took until 2015, for example, for a single MP of Chinese heritage to be elected.

To the opponents of descriptive representation, this all shows the difficulties of attempting to create political institutions that are more representative than in the past. But even for supporters, it is a reminder of what is known in this field as intersectionality – the idea that there are multiple, often overlapping (or *intersecting*), social identities, which can often have the effect of multiplying forms of discrimination or exclusion. The phrase may be a piece of clunky jargon, but the concept is an important one.

Change, and its causes

One of the ways in which political bodies are most unrepresentative of the wider public is that they are packed full of members of political parties – something that is true of all MPs compared to just 1 per cent of the population. One consequence of this is that political parties are central to most questions of representation. There is next to no evidence that women candidates, for example, suffer at the ballot box, although there is still evidence of a small electoral penalty paid by ethnic minority candidates standing in predominantly white areas (Curtice, Fisher and Ford 2015). For the most part, however, the reason various groups are under- or over-represented in Parliament is because parties select them as candidates at differing rates – and the story of the changing composition of Parliament is therefore in large part a story of the differing ways parties have approached the issue. For those who want to see political institutions which broadly resemble the population, change in Britain has been generally in the right direction, if slower than they might like; yet this has not occurred by chance, but following considerable pressure within and without political parties.

Until the late 1980s, the percentage of women in the Commons had never been as high as 5 per cent; it rose to 18 per cent following the 1997 election; and after the 2015 election, there were 191 women MPs, 29 per cent of the total – and a tenfold increase on the 19 women MPs after the 1979 election. There has been a similar increase in the European Parliament, with the proportion of British MEPs who are women rising election-on-election since 1999. The figures for the devolved bodies in Scotland and Wales – which were set up with high hopes of being more representative – have always been higher than at Westminster, but have not shown any noticeable increase since their establishment in 1999. The proportion of women has varied between 33–40 per cent in the Scottish Parliament and 40–50 per cent in Wales; the latter's boast in 2003 that it was an assembly in which a full 50 per cent of its members were female was not sustained in 2007, 2011 or 2016.

The number of non-white MPs has also increased tenfold and in an even shorter period of time. In 1987, just four ethnic minority MPs were elected; that figure rose, election-on-election, reaching 41 in 2015. The change in the numbers educated at private schools is less dramatic, but on the Conservative side of the Commons the percentage of Conservative MPs who went to a private school has been falling fairly constantly since 1979, down to 50 per cent in 2015, with only a minority of Conservative MPs elected for the first time in 2015 having been educated at private schools. And although David Cameron may have been educated at Eton, there has also been a noticeable decline in the number of Old Etonians. This applied to just 6 per cent of Conservative MPs elected in 2015; in 1959, the equivalent figure had been 23 per cent (Criddle 2015).

Change over time is less clear-cut with gay and lesbian MPs. Ever-present in politics (Bloch 2015), the combination of legal prohibition (until 1967 in England and Wales, and later still in Scotland or Northern Ireland) and social stigma meant that relatively few were open about their sexuality – and so it is not clear whether the increase in recent decades is an increase in the actual number of LGB MPs or in the numbers who are open about their sexuality. But there has, at least, been a clear increase in the number of out MPs, and the current figure of 32 is higher than the 24 in the 2010 Parliament, which in turn was higher than the 2005 Parliament.

Some of this change has resulted from broader societal changes. Yet it also occurred as a result of considerable pressure exerted within political parties, by activists and campaigners. The dramatic increase in female representation, in particular, occurred as a result of the Labour Party adopting a system of all-women shortlists (AWS) to be used in certain constituencies, as well as adopting other measures to deliver increased female representation in the devolved elections. AWS has now been used by Labour in every Westminster election since 1997, with one exception. That exception was 2001, and it is not a coincidence that 2001 saw the number of women MPs fall, for the only time since 1979. The introduction of AWS was controversial: it involved considerable political battles; saw the policy fall under a legal challenge; and required the Labour government to reform the law to enable it to continue. Individual selections have also often been controversial, most obviously in the constituency of Blaneau Gwent in the 2005 general election (where, after Labour imposed an AWS, a local male candidate resigned from the party and fought and won the seat as an independent), but that was only the most high-profile example of a more widespread tension. Quotas or similar policies are not popular – with either men or women – but they do work. Fears that they bring in unqualified or otherwise poor quality candidates seem largely to be untrue (Nugent and Krook 2016); by most objective measures the quality of the candidates who succeed through AWS seem to be identical to those who prosper through open competition (Allen, Cutts and Campbell 2014).

Labour had long had a slightly better record on female representation than the Conservatives, but the introduction of AWS caused the gap to become much larger, and much more obvious. When David Cameron became Conservative Party leader in 2005, there were still just 17 Conservative women MPs, compared to 98 for Labour. Cameron's response fell short of quotas – a policy that would have been even more controversial in the Conservatives than in Labour – but a series of reforms in candidate selection, including the so-called A List of candidates, who were disproportionately female and from ethnic minorities, helped to drive up the number of both groups sitting on the Conservative benches (Childs and Webb 2011). For the 2015 election, there was no formal A List, but Conservative Campaign Headquarters exerted considerable informal pressure behind the scenes, and there was a further increase in both Conservative women and ethnic minority MPs. The effect of the last two elections has been to reduce the party disparities, but not to eliminate them. There are still more Labour women MPs at Westminster than in all the other political parties put together. The same is true of ethnic minority MPs.

The arrival of the large Scottish National Party (SNP) cohort, following the tsunami in Scottish electoral politics in 2015, had less impact than some *parti pris* commentators liked to pretend. There was lots of talk about the arrival at Westminster of lots of Scots, as if the MPs they replaced had all come from Australia. But there were some differences: the SNP MPs were less likely to have been educated at private school than other MPs – this applied to only four of the SNP's 56 MPs – though this still exceeded the proportion of Scots who do so – and at 13 per cent, the SNP's Westminster group could then boast the highest proportion of LGB MPs anywhere in the world (Reynolds 2015), although Westminster already held the record for LGB representation, even before their arrival.

These various interparty differences often help explain what can appear to be counter-intuitive overall trends. To take one example, a few years ago it was noted that the number of privately schooled MPs in the Commons had risen. This was generally felt to be a Bad Thing. But it had occurred because Conservative MPs are more likely to have been educated at private schools and as the Conservatives had started to do better in elections, so the number of Conservative MPs had risen. Within Conservative ranks, the number of privately educated MPs had fallen. Similarly, in 2013 it was pointed out that the proportion of women in the Cabinet had fallen under the coalition compared to the government of Gordon Brown. But this was because David Cameron – and Nick Clegg – had far fewer women MPs to recruit from to form their government than had either Tony Blair or Gordon Brown. Even after the relatively large expansion in Conservative female MPs in 2010, the new arrivals were too inexperienced to serve straight away in the Cabinet, and it took time for them to progress up the ranks.

This last example is a good illustration of the pipeline that exists in political recruitment. Comparative evidence shows there is a clear relationship between the number of women in a country's parliament and in its government. The relationship is not perfect, but the two correlate extremely closely at 0.7 (Deegan-Krause et al. 2016). Some institutions outperform their overall percentage, including many of the more recent

British examples. The Cabinet is (at the time of writing) 32 per cent female, a higher figure than the 20 per cent of women in the Conservative parliamentary party. The SNP Cabinet formed in Scotland in 2014 was gender-balanced despite the Parliament as a whole then only being 35 per cent female and the SNP parliamentary grouping only being 25 per cent female. Jeremy Corbyn's first Shadow Cabinet in 2015 was slightly more than 50 per cent female (although he got flak for appointing men to all of the senior positions), but with a Parliamentary Labour Party that is now more than 40 per cent female, this is much easier than it used to be. Similarly, as well as its relatively high number of LGB MPs, Westminster can also claim more out gay ministers than any other country in the world; again, these two facts are not unrelated.

More generally, although there are frequent claims about there being a glass ceiling at Westminster – another phenomenon, which, even if it existed, would not be specific to Westminster – there is currently no evidence of such an effect. Even before Theresa May became Prime Minister, analysis of the career paths of women MPs shows they progress through the parliamentary ranks just as quickly as men, once they are at Westminster (Allen forthcoming). The problem is not at Westminster; it is getting into Westminster. There may be a glass door, but there does not appear to be a glass ceiling.

A broadening debate

Early concern about the politics of presence (albeit not using that terminology) focused almost entirely on social class (see, for example, Guttsman 1965). This was the original piece of identity politics: the creation of the Labour Party was designed to secure the representation of the working class. But class then fell largely off the agenda, both in 'real world' and academic debates, to be replaced, first, by gender, and then, second, by ethnicity. The consultative paper on constitutional reform issued by Gordon Brown's government, *The Governance of Britain* (2007) mentioned both women and ethnic minorities but listed no other group as requiring descriptive representation.

Discussion of representation has begun recently to include a more varied range of characteristics. The Speaker's Conference on Parliamentary Representation set up in 2008 to focus on the representation of sex and ethnicity soon adopted a wider focus on diversity, which included the representation of both disability and sexuality (and, albeit to a lesser extent, social class and age) (House of Commons 2010). Ed Miliband's interventions on this subject were also framed much more broadly than has been usual in British political discourse, stressing the importance of class representation. In 2012, Labour launched an explicit search for more working-class candidates, and its National Executive Committee changed party rules so that selection panels had to take social class into account, as they already do race and gender. The idea of all-working-class shortlists, similar to all-women shortlists has also been mooted; one former MP argued that only people on the minimum wage should be allowed to stand for Parliament in 10 per cent of seats.

In some ways, what is most striking about the return of social class to the agenda was that it took quite so long. It is moot whether the most important development in political representation over the last 30 or so years has been the rise of female representation in the House of Commons – or the decline of working-class representation, a decline which is much sharper than the decline of the size of the working-class population in the population as a whole, to the point where just 3 per cent of MPs elected in 2015 had a background in manual work. One reason why there has been not quite the same focus on class as on sex or ethnicity is that it is harder to get agreement on what exactly is meant by class – or how we should measure it. (The justification for the focus on the percentage of public school educated politicians is often because it is a crude proxy for class.) This is not helped by the tendency among some observers to talk about the working class like something out of an episode of *Steptoe and Son*, rather than the more complicated reality of modern-day life. But however it is measured, there is little doubt that working-class representation has been sharply in decline and its return to the agenda was overdue.

This has all resulted in a discussion around the politics of presence that is broader than at any time for 100 years. The broadening of the terms of the debate in this way brings with it certain difficulties. Most obviously, these various identities can come into conflict, as they compete for representation – and axiomatically the more identities that are considered important, the more they are likely to clash. Moran (2006), for example, argued that the process of feminising Westminster had simultaneously been one of increasing exclusion for the manual workers and the very poor. The desire to increase the representation of ethnic minorities has similarly been thought to retard the number of women candidates, although the evidence for this is, in practice, limited (Sobolewska 2016).

Even focusing, as the debate usually does, on marginalised or excluded groups does not help reduce the scope of debate all that much. As Kymlicka (1996) pointed out, the list provided by the theorist Iris Marion Young of those to whom arguments for descriptive representation could validly apply in the US – women, blacks, American Indians, old people, poor people, disabled people, gay men and lesbians, Spanish speakers, young people and non-professional workers – included almost everyone in the population except white middle-class able-bodied professional men. (Add in some of the other criteria mentioned by writers on this topic – such as geographic location, drug use, criminal records and religion – and the net becomes wider still.) This provides plenty of criteria by which groups can insist that their presence is important.

At times, this can all become self-serving, as members of Group X sees Group Y's representation being treated as important and wonder why Group X is being ignored, or as ambitious candidates prioritise the characteristics that they possess and downplay the importance of others. I was once at a seminar in which someone observed that there were relatively few MPs who knew what it was like to be worried about having money to put in the electricity meter. A woman MP on the panel objected, and said that it was not necessary to have personally experienced such hardship, as long as you tried to demonstrate empathy and worked in the best interests of such people. She would never have accepted such an argument being applied to women's interests. But if politics becomes about presence, then we should not really be surprised to discover that the ambitious will find a way to justify *their* presence.

One useful way of looking at this is to consider the groups that the public think are important. Table 7.3 draws on the British Election Study

Table 7.3   *To what extent do you believe that Parliament should have more or fewer MPs with the following background?*

	Fewer	Same	More	More minus Fewer	Don't know
People who come from the area they represent	4	19	63	+59	14
Working-class people	4	22	61	+57	12
Women	3	32	54	+51	11
People with disabilities	3	31	49	+46	16
Young people	11	34	41	+30	14
Ethnic minorities	13	37	36	+23	14
Gay, lesbian, bisexual or transgender people	13	39	26	+13	23
Christians	10	47	15	+5	28
People with university degrees	15	52	12	–3	21
Muslims	24	37	16	–8	24

Source: British Election Study, wave 6, core weighting. Fieldwork: 8–26 May 2015. N=5088.

in 2015, and shows the responses to a question about the representation of variety of different groups. Not everyone cares about who is in Parliament – or wants massive change. A decent chunk of people – often the plurality – say that they would like things to stay the same, and another group (between 11 per cent and 28 per cent depending on the characteristic) say they don't know. But majorities wanted more local MPs, more working-class MPs and more women MPs, and pluralities wanted increases in the representation of people with disabilities and young people.

Note that the groups that the public want to see represented in Parliament in greater numbers are not necessarily the same ones that much of the debate has focused on thus far. The top priority in Table 7.3 is for MPs from the local area, and in second place comes working-class MPs. More women MPs comes third on the list, closely followed by more disabled and younger MPs. Some of these are areas where progress has been made in recent years, but some of these issues have been basically ignored by both parties and academics, perhaps for the reasons discussed in Box 7.2, or, as with class, where things have been going backwards. This is all evidence of how much the politics of presence matters to voters, but just maybe not the same types of presence that most of the debate has been concerned with.

Why it matters, or doesn't

Of the three arguments for political presence, the first – that on grounds of justice there would need to be grounds for exclusion – is perhaps the easiest to understand. As Phillips famously wrote, we should ask 'by what "natural" superiority of talent or experience men could claim a right to dominate assemblies?' (Phillips 1995). This is a hard position to argue against in principle – although, in practice, given that British political parties are themselves disproportionately male, it is easier to see how assemblies drawn from within their membership can be male dominated. The most recent figures from Tim Bale and Paul Webb's Party Members Project estimate just 29 per cent of Conservative Party members are female and just 38 per cent of Labour members. Similarly, given that political parties are overwhelmingly middle class – the same survey estimated 75 per cent of Conservative members were in the middle-class ABC1 category used by market researchers, along with 70 per cent of Labour members – it is easy enough to see how MPs chosen from the same people can themselves end up as a skewed sample of the wider population. We may regret this state of affairs, and wish that political parties better represented the wider population – and their own

Box 7.2 Not being, or getting, local

The number one priority for a changed House of Commons in Table 7.3 was a desire for local MPs. It also came top in another study which found that being local was the main demographic people wanted from their own MP, almost as significant as sharing voters' political views (Cowley 2013) – yet it almost never features in discussions of representation.

The journalist David Goodhart has argued that British political elites simply did not understand this sense of place among many voters. The political elite, he argued (2014), like other members of the upper professional class, mostly leave home in their late teens to go to university and then onto a world of 'physical and social mobility with an identity based on career and achievement'. He contrasted that with most non-graduates, who are less mobile 'and draw their sense of themselves much more from place and group'.

Goodhart claimed that about 60 per cent of Britons live within 20 miles of where they lived when they were 14. We lack a similar statistic for MPs – but we know enough about their background to know that they are a) more likely to be local than they were a few decades ago but b) still a lot less local than their voters. Just under half of British MPs in 2010 even represented a constituency in the region of their birth, and regions are pretty sizeable places (Gandy 2014).

It might be just as revealing to find out the equivalent figure for those who write on politics – both academics and journalists. Richard Fenno noted this problem in *Home Style*, the classic investigation of US House Members and their relationship with their voters, published as long ago as 1978:

> Compared to academics, nearly all House members are locals. Compared to a university, most congressional districts are less cosmopolitan. Members tend to be rooted in the values and the institutional life of local communities. They belong; they know where they belong; and it is the very strength of our representative institution that they do. The academic, on the other hand, is likely to be less locally rooted, more mobile, more attached to free-floating academic communities, an outsider in any context beyond the scholarly one.

Perhaps it is because academics, who frequently lack deep roots in the communities in which they live, sometimes struggle to understand the importance that locality can have for individuals with deeper roots. The same is almost certainly true for many political journalists, who equally rarely write about this topic, despite its importance to voters.

voters – but in terms of explaining the injustice of selections, it might make sense for these to be the figures we judge parties against, rather than the data for the wider population.

When we get onto the question of whether it makes a difference, things become less straightforward. Most of this research in this area, at least in the UK, has focused on women's representation. In terms of any substantive effect, those researching this subject undertook to discover whether the presence of women actually affected the decisions taken by parliaments. After decades of research, the answer is a pretty unequivocal yes. Multiple studies – in the UK and elsewhere – have comprehensively demonstrated that the presence of women MPs in legislatures makes a difference. Women MPs prioritise different issues and push different causes compared to men; they use different language and behave in different ways in Parliament; and they vote differently to men. Similar findings come through in the research on ethnic minorities and LGBT politicians. This is all now so well-established that it should no longer need to be debated. Presence matters.

Less often discussed is a second, related, question: how *much* does it matter? Because the very same studies often showed that the differences between men and women MPs were rather small. Yes, women politicians vote differently from men on some issues, but only in a minority of cases (and, as Box 7.3 shows, not always in the ways that women in the electorate might want). Yes, they prioritise different issues, but again the differences are relatively small. Yes, they (sometimes) use a different tone in debate, but they mostly behave pretty much as male MPs do. As Anne Phillips noted, summarising much of this research, 'the empirical material on representation has not established enormously strong correlations between descriptive and substantive representation' (2012). She went on: 'When there are more women in a legislature, there tend to be more initiatives on employment equality or against domestic violence. Styles of doing politics change to some extent, and new issues appear on the political agenda. But on the less overtly gendered political issues, there is rarely a striking difference between the sexes, and on the most obviously gendered issues, there are pretty sharp areas of disagreement.'

A similar observation could apply to many of the supposed symbolic benefits of increased group representation, a concept encompassing the idea that greater descriptive representation of a group can lead to a variety of different positive effects, ranging from an increase in political engagement to a greater sense of efficacy to a heightened interest in politics, and from a greater faith in the political system to an increased belief that politics is for that group. It is clear that such benefits do exist. Studies have variously shown that women feel more positive about parliaments containing more women; young women are encouraged to enter

Box 7.3   The curious case of abortion voting

One of the few areas where there is a clear sex difference in MPs' voting is the issue of abortion.

This might not seem surprising. Abortion is the archetypical women's issue – and exactly the sort of issue that makes people say that it is important to have women in Parliament in order to ensure that women's perspective is accurately reflected.

Women MPs are – and have been for a long time – more liberal on the issue than male MPs (Pattie, Johnston and Stuart 1998). In a vote in 2011, not only were women MPs more likely to participate, but compared to male MPs of all three main parties they were more likely to vote in a liberalising direction. Conservative women MPs in particular were roughly 50 per cent more likely to vote in a liberal direction than Conservative men, with similar, if weaker, differences existing in other parties. All other things being equal, the effect of having more women MPs in the Commons therefore is to make the Commons more liberal on abortion.

What is curious about this is that we find no similar difference with the electorate at large. Women voters are not more liberal than male voters on abortion. Indeed, often, the opposite. In 2012, for example, YouGov found that 49 per cent of women wanted a reduction in abortion time limits, compared to just 24 per cent of men. Other polls do not always produce such stark differences, but the direction is usually the same (Wells 2012).

Abortion is often held up as a prime example of 'substantive representation', both because it is so obviously an issue that affects women disproportionately (some would say solely) and because it is one of those issues (of which there are relatively few) where there is indeed a noticeable difference in behaviour. But the one thing women MPs are certainly *not* doing is reflecting the issue preferences of women in the electorate. They would, of course, argue that they are reflecting women's *interests* as they see them, but it is a curious irony that to better represent the views of British women on abortion, we probably need more male MPs.

politics if they see women involved in politics (the so-called role model effect); and women feel more engaged in politics if there are more women in a parliament. But, again, even where studies find such effects – and not all do – the differences are never very large. It is worth noting that in the UK the rise in the number of women in political bodies has not exactly coincided with a rebirth of trust in politics or politicians, among men or women. Trust in politicians and politics remains persistently low, shows no sign of increasing and on some measures is even decreasing.

Moreover, these conclusions are from the studies that get published. There is a well-known effect in academic research of publishing bias – for studies that demonstrate effects to be published, while those that show no effects (so-called null findings) not to make it into print (Franco, Malhotra and Simonovits 2014). This is either because researchers simply do not write up null findings – what the psychologist Robert Rosenthal (1979) called the 'file drawer problem' – or because academic publications reject null findings as uninteresting. In this case, researchers have gone looking for differences of women MPs making a difference; have often looked in the very places where they might expect to find such differences; routinely do not publish (or are not able to get published) null findings; and even then the research literature reveals relatively minor effects.

One line of defence for such small differences is to say that looking at behaviour in an individual parliament is not helpful. Instead of looking at the difference between (say) men and women or white and black politicians at any one point in time (a cross-sectional analysis), we should look at the difference between parliaments over time (a longitudinal analysis). The claim is that increasing the presence of one group can make politicians from the other groups behave differently, and so only a longitudinal analysis can pick up the way that institutions begin to discuss different topics or pass different laws as their composition changes – although separating out the effect of increased group presence from the mere passage of time is a significant practical problem with such claims.

Of course, for some even these various small cross-sectional effects may be significant enough. But the question of scale matters, because achieving increased descriptive representation for women or minority groups is not cost free in political terms. Most of the mechanisms to achieve it involve some push back from either voters or (especially) party activists, and all of the more effective mechanisms for increased representation are suboptimal and involve restrictions on choice that few people would otherwise support. Few people actively *like* quotas; even their advocates tend to argue that they are an unpleasant necessity, like traffic wardens or seat belts. Given that there are costs, we might want to be sure that the benefits outweigh them. As Phillips concluded: 'There are gender differences, but it is not clear from the evidence so far that these are large enough to justify making descriptive representation a priority.' If we end up arguing that the substantive and symbolic benefits are marginal, but that the case for quotas or other similar measures depends largely on the justice argument, then we essentially end up with two injustices squaring off against each other – the collective injustice of a group's under-representation versus the injustice of individuals being prevented from standing for office – with the potential that they just cancel each other out, and fail to be seen as important.

Career politicians

Running alongside the debate over the demographic composition of political bodies is another debate – intellectually distinct, but in practice often conflated – about the emergence in Britain of a 'political class'. The phrase is widely used, but usually in an ill-defined way. As Allen and Cairney note (2015), it has multiple meanings – although all of them are negative. It encapsulates the idea that politicians are somehow a class apart, have never had 'real jobs', do not understand 'normal' people's concerns and are distant and cut off from their voters.

Although the sense of a distinct political class no doubt intensified after the expenses scandal of 2009, such complaints are not new (King 1981). Career politicians have long been part of politics – and there have always been criticisms of politicians for being detached or distant. Ironically, in terms of their actual contact with voters, today's MPs are much more closely connected, as a result of the extensive constituency work they undertake, and which no MP in the 1940s or 1950s would have even considered – and the rise of the career politician has coincided with a much more assertive House of Commons, as Meg Russell's chapter in this volume discusses – but that is not the perception.

Where there has been a change is in terms of the routes into politics. Research used to note that career politicians came disproportionately from a small group of occupations – known as 'brokerage' or politics-facilitating occupations, such as law, lecturing or journalism – which provided both skills useful in politics and other advantages such as flexible work patterns or access to Westminster. More recently there has been a rise of more directly 'instrumental' occupations, those which have an even closer links to Westminster – such as working for an MP or for a minister as a Special Adviser, the so-called SpAd (Cairney 2007). In 1979 just 3 per cent of MPs from the main parties had previously worked as politicians or political organisers; by 2015 this figure had risen to 17 per cent (Audickas 2016). In part, this is because there are now more such positions – in the 1970s, parliamentary allowances were minimal, so few MPs employed researchers and SpAds were much less numerous; but the growth of the political staffer has brought with it fears of MPs who have not done anything much outside of politics. As Box 7.4 shows, this is one of the main concerns the public have about the political class.

However defined, career politicians remain a minority of MPs, but they are an increasingly large minority – and one that enjoys fast-track career progression. Like in cycling, two types of politicians now exist at Westminster: the elite and the *domestiques*. Those with pre-parliamentary political experience are more likely to reach the Cabinet, and at a faster rate (Allen 2013). The three main UK party leaders who fought the 2015 election all had such instrumental career paths: Nick Clegg had been an MEP and before that worked as a lobbyist and for the European Commission; Ed Miliband had worked as a SpAd to Gordon Brown (on and off) since Labour entered government in 1997 (and had worked before for Brown in opposition); David Cameron had worked in the Conservative Research Department and later as a SpAd. All three had spent only a very limited amount of their pre-parliamentary careers working outside of politics; and all then had extremely brief careers in the House of Commons itself before becoming leaders of their parties (Cowley 2012).

Political parties claim to take concerns about the political class seriously, and to want a wider pool of candidates for Westminster, but remedial action here – unlike with gender or ethnicity – remains largely exhortatory. The coalition's plan to introduce 200 all-postal primaries, part of a plan designed to open up politics to non-standard candidates, was one of its very first reform proposals to be discarded after 2010, both on grounds of cost and because it had begun to dawn on those involved that candidates selected through this route might be worryingly independent-minded (Cowley 2015). There is anyway an irony in very senior politicians, who themselves are almost always career politicians down to their fingertips, calling for there to be fewer people like them involved in politics. It is a political version of St Augustine: Lord, elect fewer people like me, but not just yet.

In candidate selections for the general election in 2015, there was a slight backlash against career politicians; it was noticeable how few Downing Street staffers managed to get selected as MPs and candidates tended instead to pepper their CVs with references to how local they were (Criddle 2015). Several political leaders have managed to ride this backlash, although in each case their credentials as a non-career politician are, at best, dubious. Nigel Farage, for example, would routinely rail against the political establishment – UKIP, he said, were a threat to the 'entire political class' – but he was a privately educated city trader who had been a Member of the European Parliament since 1999. Nicola Sturgeon – another politician often praised for her authenticity – was able to campaign during the 2015 election condemning politicians and the political elite, despite having been a member of the Scottish Parliament since 1999 – and *in government* in Scotland consistently since 2007. And last there is Jeremy Corbyn: an MP since 1983, and whose pre-parliamentary career consisted almost entirely of work for trade unions and as a councillor. In many ways, Corbyn is the very epitome of the career politician – living both for and off politics for decades – just one who until very recently had not enjoyed much of an upward career trajectory.

Box 7.4 What voters want

In 2014, the pollsters YouGov asked people which professions they wanted represented in Parliament. There were clear preferences for more doctors (61 per cent wanted more, just 11 per cent fewer), scientists (57 per cent more, 8 per cent fewer) and factory workers (57 per cent more, just 14 per cent fewer). At the other end of the scale, they wanted fewer lawyers (46 per cent wanted fewer, just 24 per cent more), and reporters (48 per cent wanted fewer, 18 per cent more). Both of the last two groups are already disproportionately represented in the Commons.

Another YouGov survey, also in 2014, asked people what they thought were 'unsuitable' characteristics in a politician. Out of a list of 14 characteristics, respondents could choose three or four that they thought were 'most unsuitable in a leading politician'. The characteristics that most people thought unsuitable were all perfectly legal activities; indeed, some of them — such as earning or having large amounts of money – might be otherwise considered by some to be signs of success. They were:

That they had never had a 'real' job outside the worlds of national politics/think tanks/journalism/local government before becoming an MP (chosen by 55 per cent)

That they have a few million pounds and use legal methods to minimise their tax bill such as setting up trust funds for their children (41 per cent)

That they went to Eton and don't understand how normal people live (38 per cent)

These easily trumped the things on the list that were actually illegal, but which were not considered by voters to be important – such as taking cocaine or heroin when younger (14 per cent) or being caught shoplifting when a teenager (5 per cent). The irony, of course, is that the first three clearly do not limit political attainment, whereas the illegal ones do.

Conclusion

It is common to discuss political representation in Britain in terms of the *under*-representation of certain groups – women, ethnic minorities, the working class. But the corollary of this is the *over*-representation of other groups – especially middle-class ethnic majority men. Rainbow Murray (2014) has argued that we should stop talking about the groups that are under-represented and instead focus on the problems caused by the groups who are over-represented. As she writes: 'The focus on women's underrepresentation has the unintended consequence of framing men as the norm and women as the "other." With men's presence already accepted as the status quo, the burden of proof for justifying presence lies with the outsiders wishing to enter politics (women), rather than with those already present in excessive numbers (men).' Instead of advocating quotas for women, Murray therefore advances quotas for men – an explicit maximal limitation on the number of men who could stand for elected office.

The idea seems far-fetched, yet so too did the idea of AWS a few decades ago, and yet they are now widely used and broadly accepted. Indeed, even as this chapter was being written, the Liberal Democrats – previously resistant to quotas – adopted a set of reforms including AWS in some seats, and quotas for other under-represented groups. Moreover, as this chapter has demonstrated, the debate has broadened significantly in recent years, and now encompasses a much wider range of characteristics.

Yet one of the paradoxes of this topic is that the idea of the politics of presence has become increasingly accepted in Britain at pretty much the same time as its practical limits have become clear. The more diverse parliaments have become, the more obvious it is that diversity does not matter quite as much as some of its advocates used to claim.

None of this is to argue that composition does not matter – or that there are not good reasons to try to change the composition of political bodies. But when it comes to what political institutions do or the way people see them – trust, satisfaction, a sense of connection – changes in composition will at best make a very small difference. Anyone who thinks otherwise is setting themselves up for a fall.

Chapter 8

Political Participation

MARIA GRASSO

Political participation involves all those actions carried out by citizens to influence political decision-making (Pattie, Seyd and Whiteley 2004). It is the central means whereby citizens can articulate and act to promote their interests, whether individual or collective. Political participation includes more mainstream, or conventional, types of activities such as voting or being a member of a political party, as well as more confrontational, or unconventional, modes of participation such as occupying a square or taking part in a protest or demonstration. Political participation is typically seen as fundamental for a healthy democracy, since without it there is no effective representation of the people.

Given the importance of political participation for democratic practice, it is particularly concerning that in recent years Britain, like many other polities, has witnessed a steady decline in political engagement. There is clear evidence that conventional forms of political participation such as turnout and involvement with political parties have declined. While protesting and other forms of unconventional participation such as occupying have been more visible in the news, only a small minority of individuals are actively engaged in such forms of activism. This chapter will examine recent developments in political participation in Britain. While on the one hand it might seem that recent events such as 'Corbynmania', and protest against public spending cuts and student fees, signal a resurgence of activism, we need to be careful not to extrapolate too readily from short-term trends and anecdotal examples. In examining prominent explanations for political disengagement in Britain as well as other concerns about inequalities in political action, this chapter argues that political disengagement continues to characterise the British political landscape. The chapter will show that the roots of political disengagement and the decline of political participation in Britain are to be found not in the character of citizens – young or old – but rather in the characteristics of the current political conjuncture.

The chapter is structured as follows: the first section examines the ways in which participation has evolved in Britain in recent decades. It examines how previous conceptions and categorisations of political participation are being questioned in light of recent developments such as 'the normalisation of protest' and the proliferation of 'new social movements' including more recent incarnations such as Occupy London. In the second part, we turn to the most recent trends in participation – both the well-documented decline in youth participation through conventional means and the theorised rise of unconventional participation. In the third, we look at the determinants of political participation according to most recent research. This focuses on young people's politics specifically, as well as the question of generational differences in participation, reflecting on the implications of both for the future. It also examines whether inequalities in participation both within the general population and among young people are deepening. The impact of the crisis and the politics of austerity on forms of participation will also be considered. Finally, the chapter examines the future of political participation. Will participation continue to decline? What can we expect from young people's politics and our democratic future?

The evolution of political participation

The literature on political participation is vast and growing rapidly. Yet despite this diversity and the conceptual profusion (if not confusion) to which this has led, almost all accounts draw a core distinction between 'conventional' forms of participation, such as voting and joining and participating in political parties, on the one hand, and 'unconventional' forms of participation, such as protesting and joining and participating in social movements on the other. Table 8.1 summarises this distinction and presents some examples. While the conventional–unconventional distinction has itself proved conventional since the 1960s, it has nonetheless attracted criticism on the basis that it is rather reductive and groups together a great diversity of forms of political and civic engagement (Fox 2014). Thus, even when we use it, we need to keep an eye out for other relevant distinctions and variables which the twofold categorisation might lead us to overlook. With these cautionary thoughts in mind, we can now turn to examining trends in participation over time. Is the British public becoming increasingly disengaged from politics? And to what extent does such disengagement vary according to age, generation, gender, class and other socio-economic variables?

Table 8.1   *Examples of conventional and unconventional political participation*

Conventional	Unconventional
• Voting	• Demonstrating
• Contacting a politician	• Joining an occupation
• Member of a party	• Joining a strike
• Volunteer work for a party	• Signing a petition
• Member of a union	• Joining a boycott/buying for ethical reasons
• Volunteer work for a union	• Member of an environmental organisation

Understanding the roots of political disengagement

In the late 1960s, Butler and Stokes (1974: 26) wrote of Britain that 'blurred ideas of popular sovereignty and universal suffrage are so interwoven in prevailing conceptions of British government that the obligation to vote becomes almost an aspect of the citizen's national identity'. This could not be said today. Between 1992 and 2001, turnout fell from 78 per cent to 59 per cent, the lowest level ever recorded in a British general election since 1918. Since then, turnout has recovered, a little, to 61 per cent in 2005, 65 per cent in 2010 and 66 per cent in 2015, despite a very close race. Voting is, of course, still the most common form of political participation, but it is seemingly less important to citizens today than at any time since the franchise was extended to women in 1918 (Franklin 2004; Mair 2006; Hay 2007).

Studies now consistently show that the majority of citizens have little or no contact with political bodies or organisations and that most forms of political participation are on the decline if we take into account generational differences (Grasso 2016). Plunging party membership is also taken to show the extent to which citizens have grown increasingly disenchanted with formal politics (Dalton and Wattenberg 2000, Van Biezen, Mair and Poguntke 2012).

In stark contrast to the picture painted by Butler and Stokes of Britain in the 1960s, there is mounting evidence that the British public is increasingly disengaged from mainstream politics. Table 8.2 presents summary data on forms of political participation in Britain in 2015. It shows that only two activities other than voting are practised by over half of the

Table 8.2   *Levels of political activism (last 12 months) in Britain, 2015*

Conventional	
Party member	9.1%
Volunteer work for party	7.4%
Contacted or visited a politician or government official (online or offline)	27.3%
Donated money to a political organisation/party or action group (online or offline)	17.3%
Displayed/worn a political or campaign logo/badge/sticker (online or offline)	12.8%
Attended a meeting of a political organisation/party or action group	10.9%
Unconventional	
Member of an environmental organisation	7.9%
Volunteer work for an environmental organisation	2.3%
Signed a petition/public letter/campaign appeal (online or offline)	52.7%
Boycotted products for political/ethical/environment reasons (online or offline)	30.4%
Deliberately bought products for political/ethical/environmental reasons (online or offline)	26.3%
Attended a demonstration, march or rally	3.8%
Joined a strike	2.0%
Joined an occupation, sit-in or blockade	0.6%
Damaged things like breaking windows, removing roads signs etc.	0.2%
Used personal violence like fighting with the police	0.1%
Online activism	
Searched for information about politics online	52.5%
Visited the website of a political party or a politician	38.1%
Discussed or shared opinion on politics on a social network site, e.g. Facebook	30.1%
Joined or started a political group on Facebook/followed a politician or party	14.2%

Source: UK data 2015, LIVEWHAT project (Giugni et al. 2013)

British public: searching for information about politics online and signing a petition (whether online or offline) – an unconventional activity. Both are simply and costlessly achieved. Despite the growing popularity of online petitioning platforms such as 38 Degrees and Change.org, it is telling that petitioning this activity is not more widespread. Other online activities are also reasonably easy and therefore popular, but even the next most popular only involve around a third of citizens. Contacting an MP, hardly a strenuous activity in an email age, is practised by scarcely a quarter of British citizens. Moreover, despite the ubiquity of free trade products and the popularity of 'green living' campaigns, fewer than a third of citizens said that they practised some form of ethical consumerism. From Table 8.2, it is clear that the more demanding an activity in terms of effort, time and other resources, the lower the proportion that practise it. The more challenging activities, such as attending a demonstration, damaging property or fighting with the police, are reported by only a tiny fraction of the population (though for the last two, one might anticipate under-reporting of participation in comparison due to social desirability bias).

Turnout decline, low participation levels in both conventional and unconventional types of political activism, as well as the sense that social cohesion and community in Britain are increasingly at risk have put the problem of political disengagement at centre stage. Already in the 1990s some had begun to speak of an 'anti-political' zeitgeist with growing apathy and widespread cynicism about politics. More recently, Stoker (2011) has identified the features of an 'anti-political' culture in Britain: alienation from the mainstream political parties, a growing disdain for formal politics and an increasing disengagement from all modes of conventional political participation. Evidence now consistently shows that trust in parties and government in Britain is extremely low (Norris 2011). These observations, along with falling levels of participation, have prompted a number of authors to speak of a crisis of citizenship (Macedo, Alex-Assensoh and Berry 2005, Stoker 2006) and of our hate for politics (Hay 2007). This crisis has been linked to many factors including declining civic life and associational participation (Putnam 2000), low trust in institutions (Pharr and Putnam 2000), an increasingly individualist culture and the rise of post-material values (Inglehart and Welzel 2005), the depoliticisation of the public sphere and the rise of technocratic managerialism (Mair 2006; Hay 2007), as well as growing cynicism (Stoker 2006, Grasso 2011).

So how did we get here? In order to understand the roots of political disengagement in Britain, it is particularly important to look at the transformation of political parties (Mair 2006). What is especially relevant in this respect is their withdrawal from civil society and their willingness to favour a form of centralised managerialism instead of mediating and representing group-based interests (Whiteley and Seyd 2002). What this means is that whereas in the past MPs were much more closely linked to the interests of their constituents and sought to represent these in Parliament, today they are more separate from their grass roots and more likely to be driven by other factors. This process is also linked to declining membership and activism in parties: the pressure on people's time has made party activism undesirable and, at the same time, since major parties have become more managerial in style, they are less in need for volunteers and have thus reduced joining incentives (Mair 2006; Whiteley and Seyd 2002). Together, these processes have contributed to the distancing between increasingly professionalised parties and party voters and activists 'on the ground', in constituencies.

Hay (2007) has answered the question implicit in the title of his book, *Why We Hate Politics*, with reference to the depoliticisation of public policy. Politicians, he argues, tend increasingly to portray their decisions as above contestation in an effort to evoke consensus. In the process, they avoid *political* arguments in favour of technocratic reason, often appealing to external economic constraints that they are powerless to shape in the process. This avoids the disagreement that has traditionally been at the heart of politics and presents elite decision-making as void of ideology. In turn, this undermines the possibility of challenging decisions on political or ideological grounds since the case is hardly ever made on those terms. In this way, depoliticisation has further contributed to alienate the public from politics in presenting the impression that there is no normative underpinning to elite decision-making.

The diminishing sovereignty of governments in a globalised world characterised by supranational bodies also contributes to the decline of political engagement since elections appear less relevant to citizens. Franklin (2004: 179) argues that globalisation and the growing powers of supranational bodies such as the European Union can be seen to have a depressing effect on turnout since 'a globalised world in which governments surrender powers to bodies such as the WTO is also a world in which elections are less meaningful as vehicles for achieving or blocking policy change'. In other words, in a world where governments surrender more and more powers to other bodies, political participation pertaining to government appears increasingly ineffective.

The diminishing relevance of class for the structuring of voting patterns in Britain is also likely to be linked to declining levels of conventional participation. Traditionally, the middle class has tended to vote for the Conservative Party, whereas the working class has tended to vote for the Labour Party. The politicisation of class identities over issues such as the redistributive role of taxation or the extent and form of the welfare state has meant that the class cleavage has largely shaped British politics at least since the industrial revolution. Changes in the class composition of society or the declining relevance of class in political debates (Evans and Tilley 2012b) are likely to have contributed not just to the decline of class voting but also to the growth of abstention among those sections of the working class that did not feel particularly strong levels of attachment to the centrist politics of new Labour.

Growing political disengagement in Britain is thus understood in terms of the 'twin processes of popular and elite withdrawal from mass electoral politics' (Mair 2006: 25). This has changed the way individuals see politics: as politicians retreat from civil society, citizens feel that party politics has less and less bearing on their lives (Pattie and Johnston 2001). This is in sharp contrast to classic democratic theory. In Schattschneider's (1942: 1) famous argument, democracy was not merely linked to, but *unthinkable* without parties: 'The most important distinction in modern political philosophy, the distinction between democracy and dictatorship, can be made best in terms of party politics. The parties are not therefore merely appendages of modern government; they are in the centre of it and play a determinative and creative role in it.' In contrast to this, with the growing withdrawal of political elites from civil society, and the severing of the links between citizens and parties, we witness a 'hollowing out' of democracy (Mair 2006).

The breakdown of the link between politicians and the communities they are meant to represent in Parliament can be seen as part of a broader decline in social cohesion. As organisations that reflected specific and well-delineated interests within society, traditional mass parties were embedded in a complex network of other organisations: trade unions, churches, business associations, mutual societies and social clubs, for instance. Mass parties were rooted in society, while their electorates were relatively stable and easy to distinguish. Over the past few decades, however, and in parallel to an increasing individualisation of society, traditional collective identities and organisations have weakened. While parties were usually understood to integrate and mobilise the citizenry (to articulate collective interests, translate them into public policy and organise the institutions of government), they can now be said to focus much more on the procedural aspects of democracy (Rogers 2005). As Pitkin (2004: 339) has argued: 'The representatives act not as agents of the people but simply instead of them ... They are professionals, entrenched in office and in party structures. Immersed in a distinct culture of their own, surrounded by other specialists and insulated from the ordinary realities of constituents' lives, they live not just physically but also mentally "*inside the beltway*" [the phrase used to describe the politicians who inhabit Washington DC].' The gulf between the represented and the representatives would appear to be growing.

Such developments not only provide the backdrop for understanding declining political engagement, they also suggest that the very nature and meaning of democratic politics is changing. The rising professionalisation and managerialism of the major political parties is associated with declining ideological differences between parties competing for power in advanced Western democracy. In Britain this has led to citizens' growing indifference to both the major political parties. The declining influence of political parties, partisan dealignment and increasing voter volatility now define the landscape of contemporary electoral politics.

This changing landscape is not simply marked by political disengagement with respect to the old politics; it is also associated with the rise of new political cleavages (Heath et al. 1990, Inglehart and Welzel 2005). With respect to this, a prominent argument in the literature is that the 'old' politics of class has given way to a 'new' politics conducted largely by social movements rather than parties and around questions such as environmental degradation, the use of nuclear technologies, gender equality, sexual and civil rights and so forth. These developments are seen to define the post-war period, particularly the period since the 1960s. As Della Porta and Diani (2006: 6) observe, 'even the most super-ficial observer of the 1960s could have not helped noticing that many of the actors engaged in those conflicts (youth, women, and professional groups) were only partially related to the class conflicts, which had con-stituted the principal component of political cleavages in industrial socie-ties'. Marxist and other left-wing scholars had tended to argue that the pressure for social change would come from the working class's struggle for socio-economic equality. However, by the 1960s and 1970s, the paradox was that the pressure for social change did not come from the working class, but rather tended to emerge from a struggle for 'recognition' of culture and identity groups disproportionately drawn from the highly educated middle classes. New social movements were understood to be the main actors channelling these types of new demands in society.

Is participation declining or are young people simply participating in different ways?

The above discussion of the changing nature and content of democratic politics prompts an important question: are we truly witnessing the decline of political engagement or has political involvement simply changed? Here it is instructive to examine the new body of scholarship examining the participation patterns of the youngest generations com-ing of age in the current political context. This offers a glimpse into the future. Analysing the way in which generations differ from each other in the way they participate allows us to gauge the likely effects of generational substitution (the replacement of elderly age cohorts by younger ones). For, as Mannheim (1928) famously explained in terms of the impressionability of youth, the events of an epoch leave the greatest imprint on those undergoing socialisation. Thus, while political disengagement is understood to affect all citizens, it should be most evident among the young who are coming of age in the current political context.

In Britain, young people's disengagement from politics has been an increasing worry. While some have argued that the young are still active in politics, just not in mainstream politics (Marsh, O'Toole and Jones 2007), more widespread is the view that the young are simply apathetic. Youth disengagement in Britain, as reflected in low voter turnout, is particularly acute. Evidence shows that the vast majority of young people in Britain have little or no contact with political organisations of any kind, and only about 40 per cent turn out to vote. These findings have led to the development of groups such as Bite the Ballot and campaigns to raise awareness of National Voter Registration Day (#NVRD) for over 16s. Bodies like the British Youth Council are also active in trying to raise youth political participation particularly through youth parliaments.

One of the key social processes influencing the changing nature of political participation particularly among the young is individualisation. For younger citizens, participation is more likely to be conducted on the basis of personal interests and to be single-issue focused than it is to be an expression of group solidarity, such as a shared class interest or identity (Furlong 2009, Marsh, O'Toole and Jones 2007). Young people's experiences of their social world, including the institutions of the state and what they seem to perceive to be its diminishing powers in the face of external pressures, all influence their understanding of and relationship with the world of politics. Thus, while they may be interested in politics, they are less likely to transform these feelings into political action. In this respect, some have suggested that young people prefer single-issue campaigns that deal with practical issues in concrete and personal ways (Bang 2005).

One strand of argument in the literature on recent developments in political participation suggests that, while voting is still the most common form of participation today, individuals and particularly young people are increasingly turning to alternative modes of engagement such as occupations, sit-ins, protests and boycotts. These unconventional modes of engagement are, in turn, associated with social movements and other forms of identity or lifestyle politics. Additionally, the rising prominence of social media, particularly for young people, is said to have contributed to 'clicktivism'. More generally, the development of digital technology, particularly social media, is understood to have wide-ranging repercussions for the way young people not only choose to participate in politics but also how they express themselves politically.

Yet, despite the growing availability of technologies that should make participation easier and cheaper – coupled with other secular trends such as the rise in education, particularly tertiary education, among British youth – this has not served to hold up levels of participation at an aggregate level. Put slightly differently, despite multiple factors supporting an *expansion* in the political involvement of youth, the trend is for decline. This suggests that something deeper must be occurring in terms of the wider political landscape and the choice that young people perceive they are faced with. In the past, it was impossible to escape politics. Communities were divided along political lines and 'left' and 'right' had real resonance in the daily lives of people. Today, by contrast, things are very different. Whatever professional politicians might say, it is hard for people to become passionate about different types of managerial strategies, whereas arguments over how best to organise society, who should and should not count as a citizen, what rights citizens should have, to what extent we should redistribute from rich to poor, and what scope is there for universal welfare systems, are just some of the perennial questions of politics which might reignite the passions of young citizens for politics, both formal and informal.

While protesting has never been particularly popular among British youth relative to other European countries, a number of large-scale protests have made the news since the largest ever Stop the War in February 2003 in Central London, attracting over 1 million protesters. These other prominent demonstrations in Britain were Make Poverty History in 2005, linked to the Global Justice Movement in Edinburgh (estimated at 200,000), Fund Our Future in 2010 against tuition fees and spending cuts in education in London (estimated at 50,000) and, recently, Occupy London 2011 (estimated at 2,000–3,000). On 20 June 2015, over 250,000 were thought to have joined the capital's anti-austerity protests, with more attending similar events across the United Kingdom. In 2015, on 12 September, and joined by a the newly elected Labour leader, Jeremy Corbyn, the Refugees Welcome rally is said to have attracted over 100,000 protesters in Central London. This rise of protest in the news should not, however, obscure the fact that these developments do not on the whole signal a newfound rise in youth political involvement, since the number involved in these activities are still very small.

Table 8.3 shows levels of participation by generation. In order to examine generational patterns in participation, we need data spanning a longer period of time so that we can examine different generations in different moments of their lives, so here we use data from the British Social Attitudes from 1983 to 2012. We pool the data from all the different surveys so we can actually compare generations in their patterns

Table 8.3   *Levels of political activism by political generation, 1983–2012*

Years of birth	Pre-Consensus Generation 1910–1924	Early Consensus Generation 1925–1944	Wilson/Callaghan's Children 1945–1958	Thatcher's Children 1959–1976	Blair's Babies 1977–1990
Contacting					
contacted your MP	14%	20%	21%	14%	6%
contacted a government department	3%	5%	6%	4%	2%
contacted radio, TV or newspaper	3%	6%	8%	5%	2%
contacted an influential person	3%	6%	7%	4%	3%
Group activism					
raised an issue with group you belong to	4%	6%	7%	4%	2%
formed a group of like-minded people	1%	2%	3%	1%	1%
Protest activism					
gone on a demonstration	3%	7%	15%	12%	9%
signed a petition	27%	39%	48%	46%	39%

Source: British Social Attitudes 1983–2012

of participation using data from when they were in different life stages. In this way we avoid the pitfall of comparing 'generations' examined only in one cross-section of time – normally a survey year – and extrapolating from this generational differences when really what is being compared is one generation when they are young and another when they are old. By pooling data from the 1983–2012 surveys across several years instead, we can examine members of different generations as having experienced different life stages. As Table 8.3 shows, the youngest generation, Blair's Babies, are less likely than older generations to be involved in political activities across the board. This is particularly true for conventional political activities such as contacting MPs but, importantly, is also true of unconventional activities.

The evidence presented in Table 8.3 and in other studies of political participation across generations (Grasso 2014; Grasso 2016) challenges the idea, popular in some of the literature, that while being detached from mainstream party politics, younger generations engage in protest activism and other avenues (Dalton 2009; Marsh, O'Toole and Jones 2007; Sloam 2007). Evidence such as this goes against the argument that young generations are more likely than older ones to engage in unconventional activism such as sign petitions, join boycotts or participate in demonstrations (Inglehart and Welzel 2005).

While there does not seem to be robust empirical support for the argument that young generations are more likely to be involved in unconventional politics, there may be some traction to the argument that young people's political involvement is increasingly mediated through new technologies and online social networking opened up by Web 2.0 and linked to what some have called 'clicktivism'. According to some authors, the rise of lifestyle politics twinned with the popularity of social networking sites such as Facebook and Twitter has meant that young people can construct their own sense of community through the internet often based around identity politics and campaigning around issues surrounding the politics of recognition.

Related to these trends, and in particular the emergence of the New Politics discussed earlier, is the rise of post-materialism. Post-materialism is understood as a set of values emphasising self-actualisation and higher-order needs instead of survival and material necessities. This transition is linked to the move from industrial to post-industrial societies and to the increasing affluence of the post-war period. The development of this type of new values is charted in Inglehart and Welzel (2005) who show that between 1970 and 1999 each new birth cohort is more post-materialist than the previous one and remains so. This helped produce a shift towards post-materialist values as younger cohorts replace older ones in society. These patterns are linked to the rise of organisations championing what are seen as post-material concerns including nature protection. So, for example, the rise in support for the Greens, the environmental and anti-war movements as well as many others can be traced back to the growth of post-materialist values supporting these types of concerns over material redistribution issues.

However, while post-materialism emphasises the importance of 'new' values for drawing people, and young people in particular, to unconventional political action, the 'global financial crisis' hitting Britain since 2007/08 would rather suggest a resurgence of material concerns (Grasso and Giugni 2016). The crisis can be seen to have acted as a catalyst, spurring the young to political action against political elites. Young people in Britain are increasingly alienated from mainstream politics. Yet they have many grievances: their diminishing prospects of home ownership; rising university tuition fees; soaring rents, particularly in the big urban cities; the abolition of the Educational Maintenance Allowance; their diminished prospects in even more competitive labour market and so forth. The generation coming of age in the current period is understood by many to face a dire future: young people may come to be worse off than their parents for the first time since the Second World War (Sloam 2007). Precarious employment is also most widespread among this age group.

However, movements such as those against tuition fees, spending cuts in education or Occupy are unlikely to change the overall patterns of participation of young people since they only attract very small numbers of participants. Moreover, these types of participation are less likely to have an impact than voting and are all too easily be ignored by mainstream political parties. Since young people are perceived as a lost constituency and the least likely to turn out to vote, it becomes easier to sacrifice services and provisions for young people in an age of retrenchment and austerity. Britain's plurality electoral system arguably compounds the problem. Small parties, and particularly small progressive parties, that may appeal disproportionately to younger voters are under-represented. Entry points such as local politics are also problematic for young people since they tend to be dominated by older and more resource-rich individuals. As such, they do not provide much space for grass-roots campaigns. While young people active in social movements have contested the austerity message, there remains no widely identified alternative. While that remains the case, the young and other marginalised and less economically powerful groups seem set to continue to suffer disproportionately from the retrenchment of public services.

Deepening inequalities in political participation?

The importance of generational effects, however, should not lead us to overlook other inequalities in political participation. Arguably these, too, are on the rise. In this context, a crucial variable is occupational class.

As Table 8.4 shows, there is a clear and consistent difference (or gradient) in participation levels between individuals with manual and non-manual occupations. There are gaps of about 10 per cent or more for contacting a politician, donating money, signing a petition, ethical buying, searching for information about politics online, visiting a politician's website or discussing politics online. This evidence supports claims that while unconventional participation does not particularly seem to attenuate age-based inequalities in participation (as we have seen demonstrations only attract very small numbers in society overall, and even fewer as a proportion of the youngest generations), these modes of participation are still characterised by considerable socio-economic inequalities. This is almost certainly since they tend to be more demanding of resources and, accordingly, more likely to be practised by highly educated, well-off citizens. This suggests a potentially alarming feedback effect, in which only the already well-off and highly educated have the time and resources to defend their interests. Whereas almost everyone has the opportunity

Table 8.4   *Levels of political activism by occupational class (last 12 months), 2015*

Conventional	Non-manual	Manual
Party member	9.8%	6.0%
Volunteer work for party	7.9%	5.0%
Contacted or visited a politician or government official*	29.4%	17.3%
Donated money to a political organisation/ party or action group*	18.9%	9.9%
Displayed/worn a political or campaign logo/badge/sticker*	13.1%	11.5%
Attended a meeting of a political organisation/party/action group	11.5%	8.2%
Unconventional		
Member of an environmental organisation	8.2%	6.4%
Volunteer work for an environmental organisation	2.7%	0.3%
Signed a petition/public letter/campaign appeal*	54.2%	46.0%

Boycotted products for political/ethical/ environment reasons*	30.6%	29.3%
Deliberately bought products for political/ ethical/env't reasons*	28.3%	17.3%
Attended a demonstration, march or rally	4.1%	2.4%
Joined a strike	1.9%	2.5%
Joined an occupation, sit-in or blockade	0.7%	0.2%
Damaged things like breaking windows, removing roads signs etc.	0.3%	0.0%
Used personal violence like fighting with the police	0.1%	0.21%
Online activism		
Searched for information about politics online	55.4%	38.8%
Visited the website of a political party or a politician	39.6%	30.8%
Discussed or shared opinion on politics on a social network site	31.8%	22.4%
Joined or started a political group on Facebook/followed politician	14.4%	12.8%

Source: UK data 2015, LIVEWHAT project (Giugni et al. 2013); *online or offline

to vote, fewer citizens engage in more radical political actions. As such, recent developments and the emergence of social movements do not look likely to improve existent problems of voice and equality in political action (Verba, Schlozman and Brady 1995).

Gender and education have also historically been identified as important socio-economic predictors of political participation (Almond and Verba 1963). As politics has historically been the domain of men, women have traditionally been more excluded from politics (Verba, Nie and Kim 1978). However, others have argued that more recently, with the growing liberalisation of gender roles, the gender gap should diminish, and more so among the young (Inglehart and Welzel 2005). Following Almond and Verba (1963), research evidence has generally confirmed that educational attainment is linked to a citizen's level of political knowledge, interest and sophistication, and the better-educated have been found to be more likely to have the time, money, access to political information, knowledge and the ability to become politically involved

(Dalton 2008, Grasso 2013). These types of influences are unlikely to diminish in importance for political participation.

Additionally, party attachment has normally been found to influence participation in conventional politics (Dalton 2008). As such, there is likely to be growing inequalities in participation between those that support political parties and those instead that feel like they have been left behind. Similarly, membership in voluntary organisations offers the opportunity to develop skills which play a key role in prompting more overtly political participation (Verba, Schlozman and Brady 1995). Individuals with greater resources will thus have more time and money to be involved in these types of organisations and, in turn, this will lead to growing inequalities in participation between party members and non-members. Moreover, ideological identification, satisfaction with the way democracy works in one's country and other political values may help explain variations in levels of political involvement. While dissatisfaction with the way democracy works in one's country has been said to influence participation, some argue that satisfaction increases support for the political process and thereby participation, whereas others suggest that dissatisfaction might stimulate efforts for change (Dalton 2008). The literature has also discussed the role of ideology and political values; if participation influences the law-making processes, then the question of whether activists are drawn equally from different political camps also has implications for democracy.

Conclusion: The future of political participation in Britain

As we have seen, younger generations are particularly detached from conventional politics. In Britain, in particular, young people's disengagement from politics is well documented. Against this picture of youth political disengagement, some have argued that while young people vote and participate in conventional politics less than older people, they may be more active in unconventional forms of participation. As we have seen, evidence does not appear to support this idea. Moreover, social movements only attract small numbers and studies examining generational differences in political values have shown that the generation coming of age under New Labour are even more right-wing than Thatcher's Children and older generations (Grasso et al. 2016).

In order to know what to make of this, it is important that we introduce one final, and crucial, distinction: that between 'age' and 'cohort' (or 'generation') effects. Should age or generation effects be thought to be responsible for explaining the differences in participation between younger and older people, this has major implications for future participation. To attribute current trends to age effects would suggest that young people participate less than older people simply because of factors related to their comparative youth – and that they will, in effect, grow out of their current disaffection. For example, some have argued that lower levels of political involvement can be expected among young people because they are more concerned with challenges such as establishing themselves in their careers, finding a job, committing to a partner or defining their identity. But there are other credible explanations for why young people are less engaged in conventional politics than other age groups. One is that, following the professionalisation of politics and the introduction of increasingly marketing-led campaigning methods, the campaigning strategies adopted by political parties tend to be geared more towards middle-aged voters, therefore marginalising young people and leading them to consider formal politics as remote and irrelevant. However, it may also (or instead) be the case that parties tend to cater less for young people's interests, since they perceive them as a lost constituency. If age effects are responsible for young people's lower levels of participation, we have less to worry about, since the implication of this type of reasoning would be that once young people become older, they will participate at the same levels.

On the other hand, attributing current trends to generation or cohort effects suggests that these differences are the product of socialisation. On this reading, there is something about the current political context that breeds new, more politically disengaged generations. Generational theories share the idea that some attitudes are formed early in one's life and remain relatively stable over time (Grasso 2014; 2016). Mannheim (1928) argued that adolescence and young adulthood are critical periods for the development of values, attitudes and beliefs, and that once established, these beliefs and values crystallise and stabilise, persisting throughout people's lives. On this reading, 'formative experiences' leave a lasting imprint on the political behaviour of generations coming of age in specific periods. Alwin and Krosnick (1991: 171) show how the unique political characteristics of certain eras 'provide a basis for the assumption that birth cohorts achieving political awareness during the ascendancy of one particular political party will be affected by the different popularity of parties'. Similarly, Russell, Johnston and Pattie (1992) show that socialisation during Thatcher's ascendancy meant that first time electors in 1979 and 1987 were more Conservative relative to other cohorts in their youth. Grasso (2014) has shown how the youngest generation coming of age since the fall of the Berlin Wall is less likely than the highly politicised generations coming of age in the 1960s and 1970s even to demonstrate and engage with social movements.

The fall of the Berlin Wall, in particular, is seen as a historical turning point in terms of shaping the wider political context we live in. This event has, for many, come to be seen as the symbol of the end of the struggle between competing visions of left and right that had traditionally structured class voting and democratic debate between progressive and conservative forces. As argued by Mouffe (2005), the left–right dimension is normatively important because it represents recognition of the antagonism inherent in the sphere of politics, and provides the partisan dimension that in turn politics requires to politicise and mobilise the citizenry. She contends that 'to be able to mobilise passions towards democratic designs, democratic politics must have a partisan character. This is indeed the function of the left/right distinction.' Most importantly, she contends that 'what is at stake in the left/right opposition is not a particular content ... but the recognition of social division and the legitimisation of [political] conflict' (Mouffe 2005: 6, 11). On this reading then, the socialisation of the 1990s generation was marked by and took place in a context of the distinct pervasive shrinking of political alternatives or depoliticisation (see also Hay 2007). This in turn contributes to explaining this generation's lower propensity for political action, both conventional and unconventional, relative to, say, the more politicised generation of 1968 (Grasso 2016). For Britain, there is some evidence that while the rightward shift marked by the Thatcher government's commenced a process of political withdrawal of younger generations, this shift was completed in the post-ideological times of new Labour (Clarke et al. 2004).

Only the future will show whether movements such as Occupy London or the left-wing turn in Labour signalled not only by Corbyn's election but also the support of the SNP in Scotland can begin to foster the basis for new political movement to challenge the current mainstream parties and provide an institutional locus to focus the participation of young people. Social change comes from youth; they hold the key to the future. The only question is in what new direction, if any, this change will take.

Chapter 9

Developments in the Civil Service

CATHERINE HADDON

The UK civil service is 'both a component and a product of the UK's constitutional system' (Burnham and Pyper 2008: 5). The constitutional basis for UK government is reflected in the role of officials, who are employed by and serve the Crown but are directed by ministers. In line with the traditions of the UK constitution, the principles underpinning the role of the civil service depend to a great extent on precedent and convention. Unlike other countries, aspects of its role have only recently been put on a statutory basis.

Many of the principles that are seen to lie behind today's UK civil service hail from a seminal 1854 report, referred to as the Northcote-Trevelyan report (after its authors). This formalised a system in which there would be a clear demarcation between democratically elected ministers and the permanent body of officials who reported to them, advised on policy and were responsible for its implementation. At the heart of this reform was the principle of appointment on merit, based on skills and experience, in place of political patronage. It solidified the idea of officials' roles separate from those of politicians and impartial in serving whatever government they served.

The core principles of today's civil service are expressed in different ways to the actual Northcote–Trevelyan report, but are seen to represent the spirit of that reform. The 2010 Act, which put the management of the civil service onto a statutory basis, and the code that accompanies it, describe these as integrity, honesty, objectivity and impartiality. More broadly, the 'Whitehall model' has been characterised as a permanent, career service providing the main form of support and advice to ministers on policy matters, recruited largely as generalists and trained on the job.

This chapter will look at developments in four key areas to examine what changes have occurred since 2010, and how they fit into the wider academic debates about the civil service's development over a longer perspective:

- **Changes to size and shape**
  In 2010, government departments faced a massive cuts programme. This section will look at how it was managed and how it has changed the civil service.

Box 9.1   Understanding the civil service

Academics exploring how the civil service of today differs from its predecessor 40 years ago contrast it with a traditional model of the civil service, enjoying a monopoly of advice to ministers and in the implementation of those policies (Chapman 1997; Bevir and Rhodes 2003; Richards 2008; Burnham and Pyper 2008). By the middle of the last century, civil servants' role also included overseeing and managing public services and nationalised industries. Over time, this has changed, both because of the privatisation of those industries and because of changes in how some public services are managed at arm's length. There is now a complicated landscape of public servants and civil servants working across a range of bodies.

In May 2010, the civil service comprised about 485,000 people. The majority were 'front-line' civil servants working all over the country doing things like running employment and benefits offices, collecting taxes and administering tax-credits, running prisons and probation, in departments with big direct-delivery roles – for example the Department of Work and Pensions, Ministry of Justice and Ministry of Defence.

At the higher end of the civil service are around 50,000 people mostly in London who work in their department's main buildings in and around Whitehall. They do more of the policy and support roles close to ministers, in helping to make sure that policy is delivered and in overseeing the various organisations that might directly deliver public services.

At the head of government departments are the dual roles of the Secretary of State – a politician – and the Permanent Secretary – the chief civil servant. Historically, ministers, as the democratically elected representatives of government, have been accountable to Parliament for government action; officials act in the minister's name and are only themselves accountable through the role of the Permanent Secretary, who accounts to Parliament for the department's expenditure, value for money and propriety. Ministers are most immediately supported by their private office, which performs a secretarial and diary function, but also can provide some additional policy advice in helping the minister sift through the work the department sends his or her way.

In the UK system, departments are somewhat autonomous, with individual statutory powers residing with the Secretary of State. Hence, Permanent Secretaries also have quite a bit of control over the management of their own department. The Prime Minister is minister for the civil service and so has overall statutory authority over aspects of it. Likewise, a Head of the Civil Service (HCS) post has existed since 1919, but this has at times been honorary. A separate post, since 1983 combined with the HCS role, is that of the Cabinet Secretary, who is often seen as the most senior civil servant. The structure mirrors the Prime Ministerial and Cabinet relationship of *first among equals*.

- **Changes to skills and role**
  Both policy and technology have driven change in the tasks and, therefore, skills of civil servants. What does this say about the longer-term evolution of the civil service?

- **Management, leadership and reform**
  At various times in its history, the civil service has veered between autonomy for departments to manage their staff and resources, and greater centralisation and uniformity. Since 2010, pressure has increased, and there have been a number of different efforts to bring more corporate-style leadership into managing the civil service. Do the developments since 2010 suggest a more significant change than past attempts?

- **Impartiality, politicisation and the relationship with ministers**
  Fears about 'politicisation' go to the core of the principle of an impartial civil service. Since 2010, there have been both specific changes to appointment processes for senior officials and public spats played out in the media. But how far have these actually undermined the core principle of impartiality and appointment by merit?

These themes provide a useful way to examine how trends have continued since 2010, what new developments have occurred, and how the core principles of a Whitehall model can be used to benchmark these changes and consider whether the UK civil service has or is likely to fundamentally move to a new model.

Changes to size and shape

When the coalition government was formed, its central policy theme was deficit reduction, which became the hallmark of its relationship with the civil service. The government stated its intention to balance the budget within four years, with £81 billion of cuts to be achieved by 2014/15. It was the largest planned public-expenditure reduction since the end of the Second World War. The scale and pace of deficit reduction implied a massive challenge for the government and especially for the civil service. The civil service was under great pressure to deliver on the cuts, and sensitive to concerns that it would be seen as resistant to change or overly influenced by the experience of 13 years under a Labour government (Riddell and Haddon 2011). The incoming Prime Minister, David Cameron, had already spoken of his aim to reduce the size of government and therefore to 'get rid of the centralised bureaucracy that wastes money and undermines morale' (Cameron 2010).

Over the summer of 2010, departments had to start thinking about what and how to cut. The government set out cuts of about 33 per cent for departments' administrative budgets, which included their workforce (Thornton et al. 2015: 20). Departments were told to expect future cuts as well. This required changes to the size and shape of the civil service.

Cutting the civil service

As Figure 9.1 shows, there has been a steady reduction in the overall size of the civil service since the late 1970s, though with some growth in the mid-2000s. Reductions included a decline in the number of industrial civil servants, as industries were privatised, and moving functions out from the civil service to different kinds of external bodies. In 2010, the government set a target of 380,000 staff by 2015 – a reduction of about 20 per cent. In comparison, the Conservative government of Margaret Thatcher (remembered for its radical cuts) had aimed to reduce civil service numbers by around 10 per cent between 1980 and 1984. So the challenge for Whitehall in 2010 was huge.

Departments moved fast on the issue (see Figure 9.1). Between the end of 2010 and the end of 2012, some 54,000 posts were scrapped: a

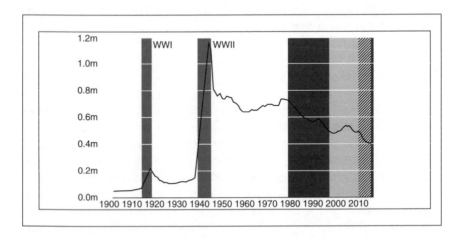

Figure 9.1   *Civil service staff numbers, 1902 to March 2015 (full-time equivalent) – governments 1979–2015 highlighted*

Source: Institute for Government analysis of Cabinet Office compilation (Civil Service Statistics, 1902–1990; Public Sector Employment, annual, 1991–1998 and quarterly, from 1999).

reduction of 11 per cent. Cuts slowed down over the following two years, but by 2015 the civil service had been reduced to 406,150: an overall decline of 15 per cent. Most of this had been achieved by reduced recruitment and natural turnover, though some departments ran redundancy programmes. The Department for Communities and Local Government (DCLG) and the Department for Culture, Media and Sport (DCMS) both achieved cuts of over 35 per cent, but these were two of the smallest departments (totalling about 1,600 and 400 staff, respectively, by mid-2014). Bigger delivery departments saw greater overall reductions. By mid-2014 the Department of Work and Pensions (DWP) had reduced staff by over 30,000 (27 per cent), the Ministry of Defence (MoD) by more than 15,000 (25 per cent), the Ministry of Justice (MoJ) by 18,000 (25 per cent) and HM Revenue and Customs (HMRC) by nearly 8,000 (12 per cent).

These reductions had important effects on the remaining civil service. Notably, they slightly changed its make-up, with the recruitment pause seeming to have reduced the number of civil servants under 30 (Freeguard et al. 2015).

Changes within departments

The cuts to numbers have clearly in one sense reduced capacity, in that there are fewer people. But changes within departments were also focused on trying to do more with less. Such 'transformation' programmes were not entirely new; some of them stemmed from a greater focus on 'capability' from the mid-2000s onwards. However, the focus on deficit reduction and massive cuts to expenditure for various departments put much greater pressure on departments to reform (Page et al. 2013).

Many of these reform efforts had broad features in common: some were about new structures, new ways of working, changes to culture and the elimination of practices that were felt to contribute to inefficiency. Some focused on IT reforms, others to changes to the management of finances; and all tended to address issues around the leadership and management of the department.

In the MoD, reform aimed not just to deal with cuts but also to address what was seen as systemic failings in the department. In August 2010, a review was launched to look at how to achieve the savings called for in the spending review and Strategic Defence and Security Review, but also to address fundamental problems in budget estimates. The review made 53 recommendations for change. These would be implemented alongside other reforms, and ongoing operations, altogether amounting to a vast programme.

A separate, but related, question that civil servants had to explore with ministers was where the cuts might mean stopping doing things they had done previously. For the most part, this was a question about spend on policies. However, in at least one department, reforms to the workforce were driven by criticisms from politicians about the quality of the department and a desire to look more fundamentally at what it should and shouldn't be doing. In June 2012, the Department for Education (DfE) launched a review that aimed for a 50 per cent reduction in its administrative budget by 2015, with an emphasis on cutting out 'bureaucracy' and eliminating tasks that were not ministerial priorities. Reports at the time were that the review was a guinea pig for what the Secretary of State Michael Gove felt was needed in the civil service as a whole (Hurst and Sherman 2012).

The phrase often used was that these reforms were about achieving 'better for less'. But objective measurement of whether by 2015 departments were better or worse as a result is difficult. Departments are not rated against each other in terms of their capability, and the data on what has changed is complex and piecemeal.

In some cases, it is possible to view how well the department delivered on policy during this period. DCMS began implementing a 50 per cent cut in its budget while delivering the 2012 London Olympics. For the DfE, there was qualified policy success. The department went from a standing start to the first free schools opening in the autumn of 2011. The number of academy schools also rocketed, so the department shrank while nonetheless delivering government policy. However, the question of whether this could be sustained, whether the governance for those schools is in place and what that will mean for the department's capability and the policy's longer-term success is more difficult to say. House of Commons select committees have been very critical on the oversight and intervention ability of the department (Adams 2015).

Changes in skills and role

As well as simply cutting, the incoming government brought an ambitious policy agenda, and the civil service was under pressure to implement it effectively and efficiently. This meant not only massive policy reforms in major areas – particularly in welfare, NHS and education – but also pressure for new skills and new ways of working. The preceding decade had seen many a clarion call for a fitter, more effective and more modern civil service. However, the combination of deficit reduction, the scale of

Box 9.2 The history of civil service reform in the UK

In the early twentieth century, the role of the state expanded in the delivery of pensions and benefits and, by the mid-twentieth century, into the direct administration of nationalised industries and social and health services. The First and Second World Wars saw increases in the number of civil servants brought in to tackle the administrative challenges of each (Figure 9.1).

In the 1960s, attention became more focused on the adoption of management skills. The 1968 Fulton report, named after the chair of its Commission, criticised the UK civil service for relying on a 'generalist' model where career officials were expected to tackle all policy issues. It called for more use of specialists in economics, scientific and statistical skills. It also instituted the development of a Civil Service College to train civil servants and a Civil Service Department to manage the service. It was critically received and not wholly implemented.

From 1979, the Conservative government brought further pressure for managerial approaches through an Efficiency Unit and changes to financial management. Other policy changes such as the privatisation of previously nationalised industries also had a major impact. The late 1980s saw a particular drive to separate the traditional functions of policy advice and some of the operational roles of the civil service. A greater number of Executive Agencies were formed to focus on delivery, at arm's length from government and headed by Chief Executives. This challenged the constitutional model of ministers accountable for all that occurred in their department.

Throughout this period, and through the 1990s, changes to grading and management and a greater opening-up of appointments for external recruitment further challenged the idea of a career civil service. The 1990s also saw changes to government services that affected the role and function of the civil service, emphasising public users as consumers and introducing market mechanisms for the delivery of services.

The early 2000s saw greater pressure for modernisation. A Prime Minister's Delivery Unit and Public Service Agreements provided a focus for departments to deliver the government's priorities. The government was particularly keen to focus more on the 'outcomes' policies were meant to achieve.

the government's programme and the vocal critique on current capability accelerated and in some cases exacerbated these existing trends – under both the coalition and the subsequent Conservative government.

Delivering policies

In the early 2000s the Labour government placed particular emphasis on the role of the civil service in the 'delivery' of policy, trying to ensure that more of the policies devised in Whitehall achieved the outcomes government wanted. The Labour government tried to achieve this through a central unit which would monitor particular policy priorities and look in more depth at the 'delivery chain' between policy idea and the results for public services and the public. While the original machinery under Labour was discontinued, aspects of it, now called implementation, did continue under the coalition government.

From 2001, the newly-established Prime Minister's Delivery Unit (PMDU) sought to chase delivery in priority areas and help departments think about how to improve it generally. Public Service Agreements (PSAs) set out priorities and targets devised to measure success in achieving the changes or outcomes that policies were devised to tackle. As the PMDU and PSAs were both closely associated with the previous government, they were quickly abolished by the coalition in 2010. Subsequently, with the loss of personnel and bodies associated with the previous delivery machinery, Whitehall had to relearn some lessons. After a hiatus, and some criticisms of how well David Cameron's No 10 was keeping the Prime Minister informed of policy progress, an Implementation Unit was established. This bore similarities to the PMDU in its basic aim and approach; collecting and analysing performance data, undertaking 'deep dives' into particular implementation problems and working with departments. The big difference compared to the previous version (apart from a massive change in staff) was the coalition government's preference for avoiding targets.

Commercial, project management and digital skills

As well as a broad focus on delivery, Whitehall after 2010 also had to focus on particular skills. One was in the creation of markets where public services are outsourced to third parties – the private sector and charities. Increasing the range of service providers has been policy under successive governments; the coalition sought to hasten and deepen efforts in this area. For example, they increased the number of free schools, building on the academies model of the previous government. This resulted in more schools directly granted money by central government, but also allowed businesses or groups of individuals to establish and run them. The coalition also increased the use of other providers to support unemployed people getting back to work, through a scheme that paid by results. In

December 2014, the Ministry of Justice signed contracts to manage parts of the probation service, a controversial new expansion of the market approach.

These programmes required more commercial skills in procurement, contracting and managing markets. The Department for Work and Pensions initially had great success in implementing back to work policy rapidly in its first year. However, in late 2012 it became apparent that providers had failed to meet the minimum performance objectives. There were problems in contract design, developing the payment mechanism and inaccurate forecasts, as well as later regulation issues (Gash et al. 2013; 40).

In January 2012, the government announced a Commissioning Academy to train and support civil servants responsible for commissioning public services, and thereby to address some of these skills deficits. The Academy is notable because it fits in with a traditional Whitehall approach of learning in-house. In other areas, such as defence procurement where huge sums are spent on decades-long major defence equipment programmes, there has been greater emphasis on bringing in specialists.

A second area where skills have been challenged is policy management and delivery. Since 2010 there has been an increased emphasis on the idea of project management of policies, and therefore a focus on private-sector style approaches.

The Major Projects Authority (MPA) was introduced in March 2011 as a response to concerns over how government managed its highest-risk, large-scale projects. Annual reports have since provided Red Amber Green (RAG) ratings for all major projects, showing what was on track and what at high risk. It also aimed to help support departments to develop more project and programme management capability. By 2015 the MPA was overseeing 188 projects with costs of around £489 billion. Nearly a quarter of them were rated as being at risk (i.e. red or amber).

As with commercial skills, there has been a tension within Whitehall between improving project management in-house and appointing new people with those particular skills. The government brought in private-sector expertise to manage the MPA, through John Manzoni, previously a senior executive at BP. The Major Projects Leadership Academy was introduced to lead in-house training for civil servants and provided a handbook for how to manage such projects.

Whitehall was also under pressure to become more technically minded. In early 2011, the Government Digital Service was created to reform how government uses and presents itself via digital service. This new body recruited developers and designers to take a different approach to developing digital services. It worked to create a single web platform for government, where all departments and services were transferred to gov.uk by late 2013. It also aimed to work with government departments to help them use digital skills in better ways.

Policy advice – opening up Whitehall

The pressure on delivery and implementation, and the pressure for new commercial and project management skills, strengthened existing trends in the evolution of the civil service since the 1990s. But their development needs to be seen alongside the continuing role for the Whitehall-based top echelons of the civil service in providing policy advice. While a government's main policy proposals will often be developed inside the political party, and ministers may have their own ideas and priorities, the job of costing these, working them up into legislation, and considering how they are implemented is largely the role of officials. This policy advice, which depends on ministers for decision, can be a complex process. In essence, ministers seek advice on how best to make policy work and achieve the desired outcomes.

The importance of policymaking to the identity as well as the role of Whitehall-based civil servants is most apparent in the attempts to professionalise that role, which emerged in the early 2000s. Other skills had long been seen specialisms. For example, scientists, economists, statisticians and those with accountancy skills were differentiated from the 'generalist' civil servant that the 1968 Fulton report had famously criticised. The idea in the 2000s was to distinguish the role of civil servants providing policy advice and to recognise it as an expertise in itself. The policy 'profession', like those other skills, was hence given a Head in each department to champion the role and lead on improvements, and an overall 'Head of Profession' who would do this job civil service–wide. However, both had limited formal powers. In October 2013, further ways to improve the culture, skills and accountability of those undertaking policy were proposed, which gave these postholders a bit more power, and provided clearer standards to which departments should be held on how they devised policy.

The renewed emphasis on policy expertise was accompanied by increased pressure for Whitehall to open itself up through initiatives like the Open Data Initiative, launched in 2012. This sought to make government data more open and accessible, so that the organisation and its sources of information would be more transparent. Likewise, an Open Policymaking initiative of the same year was designed to widen the range of people from outside government who might be involved – through bringing sources of evidence, or providing new techniques for analysis or design of policy. A network of 'What Works' centres were set up to examine and challenge the effectiveness of policy in various areas of crime, education, social care, local economic growth and health. This focus on 'evidence-based policy' was not new; it was a mantra of the previous Labour government.

How well these various initiatives were taken up and whether they improved policy is difficult to judge. More standards were set out for what was considered good policymaking, and the civil service became much more prolific in blogging and tweeting about its work. In theory, various changes provided more insights into policymaking processes and means to measure and judge policy outcomes, but not as many as critics had wanted. It is not clear as of 2016 how far practice has caught up with the rhetoric of change set out in 2012. Many aspects of how Whitehall does policy remained the same, and other indications suggest that openness and transparency have their limits. A review launched in 2015 of the UK's Freedom of Information Act suggested that there were parts of the policymaking process, including advice to ministers, that those in government wanted to keep closed off from public scrutiny.

The continued importance of policy development to Whitehall can be seen in how civil servants categorise themselves. They were asked to do so between 2010 and 2015, in terms of things like 'operational delivery' (so departments where staff are collecting taxes or paying benefits), 'other' (which included things like people who specialise in human resources or as media and communications civil servants) and those who saw themselves as policy specialists. Some departments struggled, meaning that many of their staff were still categorised as unknown. The results (see Figure 9.2) show changes to that categorisation over time (both because of changes in staff make-up and also just changes in how they do that categorisation). It also shows the importance of delivery in big departments and how, in the smaller ones, many civil servants continue to identify policy as their main role. The policy profession reforms seem designed to strengthen rather than change that.

Management, leadership and reform

Since 2010, there has been a long-running discussion about whether and how the civil service can be managed as a corporate entity, and indeed whether it should be, given its historic federal structure. In the past, departments had greater autonomy over their own recruitment, grading and pay, management and estates. At various times in its history, management functions for the service as a whole – pay, terms and conditions – have lain with either the Treasury or the Cabinet Office.

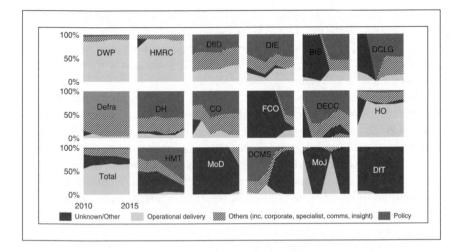

Figure 9.2   *Professions to which civil servants belong, 2010 to 2015 – percentage headcount by department*

Source: Institute for Government analysis of Office for National Statistics (ONS) Annual Civil Service Statistics 2010 to 2015.

Three aspects of corporate oversight have been important in the civil service since 2010: first, the role of the Cabinet Office in overseeing aspects of administration by departments; second, the role of the Cabinet Secretary or Head of the Civil Service in providing leadership; third, the role of the centre in civil service–wide reform.

Corporate leadership – the role of the Efficiency and Reform Group

Since 2010, the use of the Cabinet Office to provide some kind of corporate management has had a chequered history: a strong minister provided impetus, but the continuing model of decentralised departmental authority provided any uneasy balance.

In 2010, the minister for the Cabinet Office, Francis Maude, entered government with an agenda for reform. He immediately created an Efficiency and Reform Group (ERG), jointly headed by himself and the Chief Secretary to the Treasury. ERG brought together various functions in Whitehall with the aim to try and help departments reduce costs and drive improvements in public service provision.

Having this area headed by a relatively powerful minister was a distinct break with past efforts at greater control. Previous ministers for the Cabinet Office have varied in their seniority or, importantly, in their interest and enthusiasm for the role and what to achieve with it. Even more significantly, few lasted as long as Maude remained in post. He left the position only when he left the government, after the 2015 election.

The role of the ERG says much about the relationship between the centre and departments. Some ERG measures were about the centre trying to get a grip on the different approaches, duplication and inconsistencies across Whitehall in administrative expenditure. There was a centrally mandated freeze on consultancy and marketing and IT spend above £1 million. Procurement for goods and services were centralised, and reviews were to be undertaken on changes to civil service pay and conditions and the simplification of human resources functions across Whitehall. ERG came to epitomise the harsh reality of austerity across the civil service, but also repeated an older tale of centre versus departments in how best to achieve change.

Corporate leadership – the roles of the Cabinet Secretary and Head of the Civil Service

The other experiment with management of the civil service was through changes to the posts of Cabinet Secretary and Head of the Civil Service. Since 1983, the roles had been combined. Prior to that, the Head of the Civil Service was for a period a role in its own right, as the senior official in the Civil Service Department – abolished in 1981. The Cabinet Secretary is officially the Head of the Cabinet Office, Secretary to the Cabinet and often the Prime Minister's chief adviser. In the UK, the Head of the Civil Service role has not carried the same kind of corporate powers as the equivalents in other systems, such as New Zealand.

In October 2011, it was announced that when the current postholder Sir Gus O'Donnell retired, the roles of Head of the Civil Service and Cabinet Secretary would be split. In January 2012, Sir Jeremy Heywood, previously the most senior official in No 10, took over as Cabinet Secretary. Sir Bob Kerslake was appointed as Head of the Civil Service on a part time basis alongside his continuing role as Permanent Secretary of the DCLG.

There were criticisms of the split, based on arguments that leadership of the civil service should not be a part time role and that Kerslake would lack the access and clout that came with Cabinet secretaryship. For others it was a plausible reaction to the fact that Heywood's strengths were in performing the role of senior policy adviser and that the combination of both HCS and Cabinet Secretary roles was more than one person could achieve. Previous holders of both posts had found ways to delegate aspects of the two roles.

Recent years have seen attempts to find a private-sector solution to these long-standing leadership concerns. In 2010 a Chief Operating Officer post was created. The role was effectively Head of the ERG with a remit that mirrored it. But alongside the role of Minister for the Cabinet Office, Cabinet Secretary and Permanent Secretary of the Cabinet Office, the remit lacked the kind of clarity that might exist in a private corporation.

By mid-2014, briefings against Kerslake preceded the announcement that he would resign as Head of the Civil Service. In October that year, after more pressure for a business solution, a Chief Executive of the Civil Service was appointed following a much publicised search for someone with private-sector skills. John Manzoni, the previous Head of the MPA, was appointed to the position, but would report to the Cabinet Secretary.

These various efforts to find the right role and person to fulfil it went to the heart of the government's desire to inject more external, private-sector skills. They also reflected the long-running debate about whether it is possible to manage the civil service from the centre.

Reforming from the centre

The difficulties of managing the civil service as a coherent entity are perhaps most visible in the question of service-wide reform.

In its first couple of years, despite calls for improvements and changes to departments resulting from spending and headcount reductions, the government did not look to instigate comprehensive reform. In early 2011, Francis Maude told the House of Commons Public Administration Select Committee that this was because he didn't see change coming through 'plans and blueprints and reports and White Papers ... I am more interested in us doing stuff' (Public Administration Select Committee 2011:EV 38). By early 2012 the government had changed its mind and produced a civil service reform plan.

The civil service reform plan chimed with the changes already set in train. Policymaking was criticised as drawing 'from too narrow a range of views and evidence'. There was to be more focus on commissioning and contracting skills. Culture was to be 'pacier, more flexible, focused on outcomes and results rather than process'. Finally, on leadership, the reform plan stressed the accountability of Permanent Secretaries and the Head of Civil Service and Cabinet Secretary in seeing through these reforms. Private-sector style boards overseeing departments, which already existed, were to have a greater emphasis on non-executive members and provide scrutiny and oversight over how the reforms were being implemented (Cabinet Office 2012).

The plan had 16 specific action points, some of which were about prompting departments into action, for example in publishing plans to make parts of their services 'Digital by Default'. Others were about increasing the powers of the centre to oversee progress, such as the role of the MPA. Some set out very specific reforms: making the accounting officers, usually the Permanent Secretary, sign off implementation plans for policies and reviews of progress. Others were more aspirational, including some of the plans to improve policymaking. A year later, the government acknowledged that the pace of change was lacking. The reforms were suffering what many saw as age-old problems of managing centrally-driven change in a federal organisation. Other reasons for slow progress were the very culture that the reform plan wanted to change. The *One Year On* review called for clearer signals and commitment from leaders in achieving change.

Maude argued that the changes did not undermine the core model of the civil service, addressing the question directly in a public speech:

> Do we want to uproot the Northcote-Trevelyan model that has lasted 150 years: a permanent, politically impartial civil service where appointments are made on merit? I'm not persuaded. (Maude 2013)

With the arrival of a Chief Executive for the civil service in 2014, the reform agenda became part of his remit. By 2015, there had been much activity. This was highlighted in 'report cards' showing specific changes; but whether the reforms were achieving their broader outcomes was difficult to judge objectively.

Impartiality, politicisation and the relationship with ministers

The principle of an impartial, apolitical civil service is what differentiates the UK and similar models from systems like the United States in which the majority of senior officials are appointed by the incoming government. These traditions often feature in debates about 'politicisation': the concern that if officials are beholden to ministers, they will cease to speak truth to power, be coerced into political activities beyond their constitutional role or prove unable to serve future governments effectively.

Post-2010, various developments raised issues at the heart of the impartiality concept within the Whitehall model. These included questions about the appointment by merit of senior officials, the role of direct political appointments and, more widely, pressures on the relationship between officials and ministers.

Appointment of senior civil servants

During 2010–2015, debates about the role of ministers in the appointment of senior civil servants touched on an iconic issue for civil service status – appointment on merit only and the avoidance of political patronage. For some this was a threat. For others, it represented an attempt to achieve a more reasonable balance between the role of ministers and Permanent Secretaries in managing departments, and a logical extension of current practice.

The June 2012 *Civil Service Reform Plan* set out the government's aim to strengthen the role of ministers in the appointment of the Permanent Secretary and others in their departments. The plan stated that greater influence would improve the relationship at the top of departments – hinting that one concern was over ministers getting on with their Permanent Secretary and having confidence in them. The plan was ambiguous on what changes were needed, acknowledging that 'Ministers already have involvement in the recruitment process but we believe there is a case to go further' (Cabinet Office 2012: 21). It indicated that the Civil Service Commission, the body that oversees and runs the appointment process for the civil service and acts directly in recruitment for senior officials, would be consulted on what the changes should be.

Despite the formal concept of appointment on merit, in reality ministers already played a role in influencing appointments (Paun, Harris and Magee 2013: 11). The existing process for recruiting Permanent Secretaries involved an advertisement period, recruitment rounds and interview panel consisting of other senior officials, civil service commissioners and the Cabinet Secretary. During this process, the views of ministers would be canvassed and taken into account. In some cases, they might already know or know of an individual; in others, they might be consulted over what type of person, skill set and background they thought would be best for the role. Choosing someone who would work well with the current minister might be desirable, but it had to be borne in mind that that minister might move on. The appointment panel would decide on a single candidate to put to the Prime Minister for approval, but it was then for the Prime Minister to make the appointment or reject it. Other appointments to senior roles occurred outside this process, known as 'managed moves'.

The proposed changes were largely driven by Maude, the Minister for the Cabinet Office. He argued that without greater ministerial influence, officials might not be held accountable for their failures in terms of their career advancement:

[Y]ou can preserve in all its purity the model of ministers being accountable to parliament for their department. But it seems to me you cannot do that and at the same time deny ministers, to the extent the system currently endeavours to maintain, the ability to have any serious choice over the people who are responsible for delivering the performance of their department. (quoted in Wintour 2012)

The government could not make such changes without the Civil Service Commission. That body published revised guidance on the issue in late 2012, which didn't go as far as Maude had proposed but set out consultation with ministers in the appointment process in a more explicit fashion. Rather than one name going to the Prime Minister, the names of all suitable candidates were to be offered. Again, more informal processes might play a role: though the Prime Minister was the only person who could formally make the decision, he or she would have knowledge of what the relevant minister felt on the subject. Describing this change, Sir David Normington, the First Civil Service Commissioner, suggested that it 'stops short of allowing ministers to choose from a list of recommended candidates ... [and] maintains the essential balance between involving ministers fully in the process, while safeguarding a non-political civil service, selected on merit' (Civil Service Commission 2012).

Views vary about how significant a change this is: it clarifies the existing but opaque influence of ministerial views in choosing their Permanent Secretary. However, for critics, it represents a totemic issue that may lead to further erosion of the principle of an apolitical civil service.

Direct political appointees

Further questions about the line between political patronage and impartial civil service were raised in other methods of providing support to ministers. In the UK some political appointments do occur in the form of special advisers (SpAds), technically temporary civil servants but directly appointed by ministers and operating under a code of conduct that differentiates them from other civil servants. In practice, this requires them to abide by the Civil Service Code, but provides exceptions in terms of the ability to engage in party political activity.

Since the first use of special advisers in the early 1960s, their role has added to debates about politicisation. They are, by and large, considered a useful way of helping the minister handle the burden of work, helping the department understand the motives of the minister, and bringing either useful additional experience or political understanding into the department. However, under the 1997–2010 Labour government, political scandals surrounding a few special advisers, and their increased overall number, became a leitmotif and a cause of criticism.

In 2010, David Cameron entered office claiming that he would cut the number of special advisers in his government as a deliberate break with the previous government's approach. However, with office, their value became more apparent and the pressures of coalition and creation of a Deputy Prime Minister's office for Liberal Democrat Leader Nick Clegg eventually led to an increase in the use of SpAds. Meanwhile, media controversies involving the actions of advisers to the DfE and Home Office briefing against each other, and the boundaries between advisers' government and party political work, renewed complaints about special advisers' effect on the politicisation in government. By early 2016 the question also came up of the role of special advisers in terms of the planned referendum on British membership of the European Union. Guidance set out by the Prime Minister on how ministers who wished to campaign against the government could do so stated that they could be supported by their special advisers in this, but also placed restrictions on access to government resources and the civil service in doing so. SpAds and the dividing line between political activity and government activity were again in the spotlight.

Extended ministerial offices

Potentially blurred lines between civil servants and political appointments were confused by another development: the idea of an Extended Ministerial Office (EMO) instead of the traditional private office. Private offices are staffed by civil servants picked out by the Permanent Secretary. Some ministers preferred the idea of a European-style *Cabinet*: an extended version of the private office in which there are a larger number of directly appointed advisers. The EMO model enabled this: it allowed for more policy advisers within the office, alongside the more traditional Private Secretary role. However, this was to be enabled through ministerial involvement in the appointments, which would in effect blur the line between the special adviser role and the civil service Private Secretary. This would mark an extension of the overt role of ministers in appointments similar to the changes on Permanent Secretary appointments. Unlike SpAds, these appointments could not be party political, but rather would be about the minister getting the type of person he or she felt would do the best job; critics felt the line was too easily blurred between the two.

In the DfE, a number of appointments to key civil service roles and into the Secretary of State's private office were seen as another precedent in allowing politicians to influence civil service appointments. Subsequently, in November 2013, the Cabinet Office issued guidance allowing ministers a role in making appointments to private offices that would effectively be EMOs. Appointments were still to abide by codes of conduct, civil service or special adviser codes and contracts, but ministers could appoint directly and appoint a special adviser as Chief of Staff.

Again, critics were quick to point out the politicisation dangers. For the Head of one of the civil service's trade unions, Dave Penman, the risks of a politicised civil service were that 'loyalty to a minister' would outweigh 'evidence-based objective advice' (Penman 2013). The change was seen to put civil service objectivity at risk because the careers of those recruited to an EMO might be more dependent on political approval, with personnel changing when a minster was reshuffled or sacked.

By December 2015, few departments had taken up the full plan. But the DWP developed a Ministerial Policy and Delivery Unit, while the Department for Environment, Food and Rural Affairs (Defra) and the DfE each remodelled their Secretary of State's office. The latter also directly appointed a Director of Strategy, Performance and Analysis, from outside of the civil service in a move that was seen to be the clear choice of the Secretary of State.

Relations between government and civil service

Debates about politicisation were also exacerbated by reports in the media during this period in which relations between ministers and officials became the story. Combined with the pressure from job losses and pay freezes, many interpreted such stories as indicating a breakdown in relations between the two. Whether or not the reality was as bad as represented, the stories contributed to suggestions that the civil service was changing in fundamental ways.

Some ministers were vocal in criticising the civil service. In November 2011, Francis Maude referred in a speech to cases where 'permanent secretaries have blocked agreed government policy from going ahead or advised other officials not to implement ministerial decisions' (quoted in Mason 2012). By early 2013, briefings to *The Times* led to a story about Whitehall being in its 'worst crisis', with reports of difficulties at the Home Office, in the DCLG and DfE, as well as at the centre (Watson, Sylvester and Thomson 2013). Though rejected by other ministers and the Cabinet Secretary, the impression of bad relations in some parts of government increased calls for more fundamental reform.

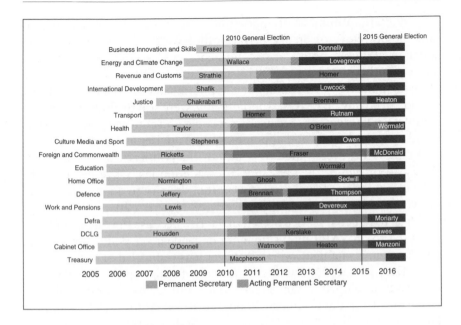

Figure 9.3   *Tenure of Permanent Secretaries, 2010 to 2016*
(from first appointment, projected)

Source: Institute for Government analysis of Permanent Secretary appointments, 2005 to 2016.

The appearance of many of these stories needs to be viewed in context. In 2010, as in 1997 and 1979, the civil service had to adjust to new language and ways of working. There was certainly a high turnover of Permanent Secretaries after the 2010 election (see Figure 9.3). But many of these changes were a result of anticipated retirements.

New governments bring a desire to challenge the status quo and can become frustrated with the official machine, not necessarily with individual civil servants (Riddell and Haddon 2011). The media attention since 2010 was perhaps about breakdowns in personal relationships and broader internal power clashes, rather than something more fundamental.

A more politicised service?

Arguing that these changes have led to tangible politicisation is difficult at this distance. The appointment process will be more significant if it leads to controversial appointments or departures of Permanent Secretaries. The use of EMOs and influence of direct appointees could be the slippery slope to a more substantial use of direct appointments, but this has not happened yet. In some respects, it mirrors the initial inclusion of special advisers into government in 1964, when similar concerns were voiced. The fact that few ministers have taken up the limited opportunities for more involvement in the appointment of the civil servants close to them suggests that they may prefer the existing mechanisms. Likewise, while the media's representation of a clash of culture and personalities was serious, it concerned limited grievances and briefing against individuals.

Conclusion: Future trends for the civil service

Civil service reform is a theme that has ebbed and flowed throughout the history of the service, particularly when external pressures accumulate. Changes to the civil service since 2010 need to be put within that historical context.

Since 2010 there have been big efforts to increase and diversify the types of skills needed in order to provide changing public services, as well as pressures for more private provision and more digital approaches. Another issue is the degree to which civil servants retain, or should have, a monopoly of advice to ministers. The open policymaking agenda suggests that ministers think that they should not. Wider societal, technological, devolution or decentralisation change continue to affect Whitehall, just as the development of the fax, computers and email, or entry into the European Union, have altered its role in the past.

Developments since 2010 also show different views of the Whitehall model and its traditions of permanence, impartiality and merit-based appointment. Changes to appointment and the role of direct appointees, in isolation, may not alter the basic foundations of the civil service any more than Prime Ministerial influence over senior appointments did in the past. For some these changes clarify what already occurred: senior officials see getting along with ministers as part of their job. However, concerns do exist about a fundamental breakdown in the impartiality of the civil service, and controversy over the role of the civil service in supporting the government's remain position during the EU referendum campaign again put this issue in sharp relief. Fears of politicisation may prove to be no different than under previous generations and previous governments; but much will depend on how future governments use the processes that have been developed.

When looking at developments since 2010, there are clearly many continuing themes and concerns from earlier eras. However, the austerity implications were substantially different in scale. If the pressure for deficit reduction continues, then the civil service will continue to be under great pressure to innovate and seek efficiencies, more so given the pressure on resources and capability that will come with the UK's decision to leave the EU. It may even need to look to more fundamental change in how it operates. Changes to the civil service in Scotland have seen a move away from a departmental structure towards directorates which cut across the strategic themes of the government. Developments in Whitehall since 2010 focused more on practices and culture than structural solutions. But the continued pressure to cut, and be more innovative and efficient, might in the end result in fundamental change from the hierarchical, departmental structure of the UK government. Moves towards more corporate leadership of the civil service may also change this traditional structure. At the moment, the course of civil service reform and the difficulties in achieving its outcomes show that there remains a fundamental tension between departmental autonomy and a more corporate civil service.

All of this suggests that there are many ways in which the civil service, particularly the Whitehall 'core', is moving away from the traditional Whitehall model. However, the tensions in doing so and the way in which developments since 2010 have run their course, show that many of the existing characteristics of that model remain intact. Perhaps most fundamentally, the tone and comments of ministers are revealing – neither in statement nor in action have they called for a more fundamental move away from the civil service that they inherited.

Chapter 10

Politics and the News Media: Messages and Messengers

RICHARD HEFFERNAN

Online platforms change the way the media makes and communicates news and how citizens access it. The 'mainstream' media, however, still reports and explains politics. Having migrated online, television and newspapers, if supplemented by newer forms of communications, continue to be the principle way politicians speak with the public and the means by which electioneering takes place. Traditional reportage and commentary (now reported in non-traditional fashion) thus continues to have a key role in creating *a* space for politics. Often, however, the news media is *the* space within which politics takes place. Especially when, being a watchdog, charged with holding politicians accountable, the news media is a political actor in its own right. Because it participates in the politics it reports, not merely spectating them, the news media remains for politicians both obstacle and resource. It continues to influence the ways in which 'they' (and 'we' citizens) 'do' politics.

Age old questions of bias and partisanship, patterns of ownership, especially for newspapers, continue to attract attention, but the online format of the modern news media, the means by which it enacts its traditional functions, prompts further consideration of its role in contemporary politics. Particularly so, when the 'print' and broadcast news increasingly form part of the same 24/7 news culture reflecting the speeding up of the reporting of news at a time when the notion of 'newsworthy-ness' continues to be challenged and reconstructed.

Plus ça change, plus c'est la même chose...

Citizens, increasingly finding their news online by browser or app, no longer need buy the hard copy of a particular newspaper (or have it delivered in the morning). Nor need they wait for the TV or radio bulletin broadcast at a specific time on a particular channel. *Guardian* editor Alan Rusbridger, retiring in 2015, claimed 'the essentials of newspaper life were the same in 1995, when I took over from Peter Preston, as they had been in 1821'. Some 20 years later, however, online realities mean his newspaper 'still tell[s] stories in text and pictures, but the words are as likely to be in the form of live blogs as stories. We have learned to use moving pictures as well as stills. We work in audio, interactives, data, graphics and any combination of the above. We distribute our journalism across multiple channels, platforms and devices, including live discussion and debate ... Two thirds of our readership is now outside of the UK: We publish continuously' (2015). Reporting deadlines, especially those of newspapers, can now fall every minute, no longer once a day. The physical printing of Rusbridger's newspaper, the mainstay of news production for 500 years, is petering out. 'Hard copy' news is soon to go the way of music on vinyl, with online provision blurring the distinction between print and broadcast news as newspapers use video and broadcasters the published word.

Citizens now access information instantaneously in ways previously unimaginable. By 2015 some 90 per cent of British citizens were online, with some 65 per cent of internet traffic being generated by smartphones and tablets (Reuters Institute 2015). This has transformed the way we live, work and play. One survey reports that while 'the majority of UK adults (85 per cent) still get their news from television, in 2015, four in ten adults (39 per cent) said they got news from a website or app' (theMediabriefing 2015), so there has clearly been a 'quickening of the pace towards social and mobile news ... and significant growth in video news consumption online' (Reuters Institute 2015). This can only increase: the reporting of news is always improved by technological change, but the internet enables news to be produced and accessed faster, more easily.

There is now a 24-hour, seven-days-a-week news cycle. Certainly, in terms of British news, a cycle operating continuously between 6AM and 11PM. News can now be broken beyond the mainstream media, by social media, but the mainstream catches up fast. Like a poacher turned gamekeeper, however, the mainstream media uses social media, especially Twitter, to break news before it posts or publishes it. *The Guardian* has proven particularly adept at this, but so too the BBC, *The Telegraph* and the *Mail*. Reporters report in real time via Twitter, often trailing the report they post. Thus the news is finally reported in the hard copy of a newspaper some considerable time after it has happened (usually when new news has broken to replace it). The hard copy of a morning newspaper reports yesterday's news, but its website covers today's news (often news broken that minute). So news, being both local and global, now rolls online in real time, being ceaselessly updated by providers, and instantaneously accessed via an app or browser anywhere (coverage permitting).

Failing business and established regulatory media models?

If news organisations can now report more effectively, more quickly, being online has had significant consequences for the business model which hitherto sustained newspapers (Cage 2016). Newspaper readership, in terms of the purchase of hard copy, is in serious decline. Some say it is presently 'falling off a cliff ... By October 2015 analysts found the British daily market is declining by more than 8% a year and the Sunday market by a little over 9%' (Greenslade 2015). Online readership grows a newspaper's readership, but shrinks its revenue; only 6 per cent of online readers pay for such news and only the *Daily Mail* seemingly exists profitably outside of a paywall. British newspapers, barring exceptions such as the *Financial Times*, *The Times* and *Sunday Times*, *The Telegraph* (and previously *The Sun*), provide their content free via browsers and charge only for accessing their product through an app (charging much less than for purchase of the hard copy). In February 2016, selling only 40,718 daily copies saw the demise of *The Independent*. In April 2015, *The Guardian* sold only 174,941 copies a day, but was read that month 'by more than 7 million unique browsers a day' (Rusbridger 2015). But money cannot easily be made from unique browsers, so for most newspapers, digital revenue fails to replace revenues lost through declining sales. In 2014–2015 *The Guardian*, reporting an upturn in income, recorded a loss of £19.1 million and lost £69 million in 2015–2016 (prompting plans to cut costs by 20 per cent). Newspapers not only fail to make money, but lose money, something which is problematic when such newspapers, whatever their vices, continue to provide a social good and quality reportage remains a valuable resource requiring continual investment.

The news media environment, especially in regard to the blurring of print and broadcast, is one of established regulatory regimes. The behemoth that is the BBC, its TV, radio and online services used by 97 per cent of UK adults each week in 2013–2014 (boasting a global audience of 308 million) (BBC News 2015), faces financial pressures from ministers eager to reduce its size by cutting its budget. Newspapers, now online, reporting in real time, even after the phone hacking scandal, still have no statutory obligation to be fair, impartial or non-partisan. Factual reporting for 'print' remains a matter for professional pride and reader requirement, more likely to be found in the 'quality' end of the market (*The Times*, *The Telegraph*, *The Guardian*) than the 'popular' end (*The Sun*, *The Star*, *The Mirror*). If newspapers continue to 'campaign', broadcasters still face enforceable regulations that require them to strive for political balance; they, unlike newspapers, cannot prefer to be 'free to comment' rather than 'obliged to inform'. More significantly, especially in the short term, the news media being a social good, it remains unclear what will happen when producers can no longer rely upon their traditional forms of funding, such as cover price, subscription fee, advertising revenue or, in the case of the BBC, the present level of licence fee. Responsible journalism, being a craft, requires financial resource. News gathering remains an expensive profession that has to be paid for.

The internet and the mainstream media

One of the truly staggering effects of the internet is the radical proliferation of non-traditional online information sources. Commentary produced by social media aside (which is discussed below), such sources provide citizens who have both time and inclination with unmediated access to a wealth of political information and comment. The internet provides more open platforms for the likes of bloggers, such as Guido Fawkes (now too a *Sun* columnist); institutions, such as Parliament; organisations, such as political parties, campaigns, charities and think tanks; activists, such as Labourlist, Conservativehome; and numerous experts and academics. Such online information sources feed off traditional media sources (and it them), but they provide those possessing some celebrity or expertise, however small, with more opportunities to participate in *a* public conversation. Those with opinions can 'speak' to those who wish to 'hear' them. Such people are often others with similar celebrity or expertise. But the opinions of those with some pre-existing cache usually have to be taken up by others, principally the mainstream media, to take some small part in *the* public conversation.

In terms of the online consumption of mainstream media, commentators make much of the role of social media such as Twitter and Facebook. Facebook reaches 97 per cent of those with a social profile, followed by Twitter at 26 per cent (Ofcom 2015: 34). Social media plays some part in 'finding, discussing and sharing news' (Ofcom 2015: 34), but the impact of this on the consumption of news can be easily exaggerated. The internet is put to innumerable uses other than the consumption of news; news presently ranks only seventh out of the ten internet uses listed by Ofcom. And news, however it is found, online or off, is still more likely to be consumed by the better educated and more professional (Ofcom 2015: 34). It may be consumed faster, but many people are not consuming it.

Even wired citizens remain either information-rich or information-poor. This reflects social status, occupation or education, but also being time-rich rather than poor. Citizens have online things to do other than read news, something easily facilitated by social media. So the information-rich are richer and faster, but the information-poor remain poor; easier, faster accessibility of news is of little interest to them. Consideration of online news consumption too often fails to account for the quality of news found online. Much of it involves reportage of non-political events and the provision of infotainment. Maybe more people access the *Daily Mail*'s 'Sidebar of Shame' than its actual news and comment. Much 'news' that is shared over social media is often for fun. Often it is not political.

Surveys too often over-report social media use while under-reporting traditional media use. Those who research in the field of internet studies tend to inflate the importance of their subject. The relevant literature ludicrously defines digital participation as 'sharing a news story by email, text or social media at least once in a week' (Reuters Institute 2015). It is undeniable, however, that the online migration of news reportage – something increasingly facilitated by the mainstream media – has significantly impacted the production, distribution and consumption of news. But the purchase of traditional platforms – particularly television – persist even amid 'generational divides over the way news is found, consumed, and distributed' (Reuters Institute 2015). Non-traditional online information empowers folk beyond the mainstream media; social media lends itself brilliantly to the early reporting of a news event (it can make every citizen an 'on the spot reporter'), but further information and explanation remains the domain of that mainstream media (even if that media is online and uses social media to link to their reports and stories): 'TV becomes more popular for younger people when they are seeking accuracy and reliability; social media use is mainly for breaking news' (Reuters Institute 2015). If the internet has changed the ways in which citizens consume news, it has significantly altered how news is produced – but less so, by whom news is produced. Collectively, the traditional media, especially television, if increasingly accessed online, remains the trusted arbiter of what is news, and is still the principal reporter of it.

Politicians and the mainstream media: news being both obstacle and resource

From what little is known about media effects, scholars suggest mainstream media reinforces political opinions and preferences, rather than changes them. A committed leftist isn't going to change his or her mind by reading the *Daily Mail*. Nor a conservative shift leftwards reading *The Guardian*. Often the very opposite happens. Partisans, those holding committed, stable politics, seek out news chiming with their world views. Non-partisans, free floating voters, can be more open to being influenced, but more often than not their opinions reflect their own experience and interests. The apathetic, being uninterested in politics, largely avoid political news, so are unlikely to be influenced by a medium they fail to engage with. The principal effect of the news media seems to be its collective ability to frame stories. In constructing the news people and politicians read or watch, the media, rather than tell 'us' what 'to think', can exert an influence on what 'we' collectively 'think about' – the issues we are considering and which other people and politicians are discussing.

The news media enables politicians to communicate with the public, so is the primary means by which they electioneer. Playing the key role of helping set the political agenda, the media is a resource politicians can use, but because it factually reports politicians, and also challenges them, it is simultaneously an obstacle they must circumvent. Political news reflects the interaction of politicians and the news media in light of such events and opinions. This interaction owes everything to the relationship between politicians and journalists. This relationship, born of each needing the other to make and report political news, is symbiotic. But it is adversarial, and has, over many years, become increasingly antagonistic. It is even, at times, hostile – so much so that Tony Blair felt the media sometimes behaves like 'a feral beast, just tearing people and reputations to bits'. It 'increasingly and to a dangerous degree is driven by "impact". Impact is what matters ... [S]candal or controversy beats ordinary reporting hands down. News is rarely news unless it generates heat as much as or more than light ... [A]ttacking motive is far more potent than attacking judgement. It is not enough for someone to make an error. It has to be venal. Conspiratorial' (Blair 2007).

So politicians, eager to be favourably reported, not critically reviewed, engage with the news media in the often forlorn effort to ensure it prioritises the former, not the latter. Blair contests that a major aspect of the politician's job, 'outside of the really major decisions, as big as anything else – is coping with the media, its sheer scale, weight and constant hyperactivity. At points, it literally overwhelms' (Blair 2007). He suggests 'not to have a proper press operation nowadays is like asking a batsman to face bodyline bowling without pads or headgear' (Blair 2007). Thus politicians employ communications strategies to try to secure media reportage they hope can win them public approval. Chief amongst these is news management. Party leaders believe they have to 'sell' themselves and their parties. Blair and David Cameron have been the two most successful Westminster politicians of the past 20 or so years. Both are proven communicators, something considered the essential skill for any successful political leader. Less successful party leaders invariably fall short on their ability to craft and sell themselves. They, whatever their other virtues, lacked the marketable, voter-friendly personality considered to be the focus of the electable party brand.

By providing information – but then spinning it – politicians seek to create a buzz through information. Spin is the most common form of news management, being supplied by politicians and their advisers, and often required by journalists. To this end, rather as landowners once made poachers their gamekeepers, parties employ strategists with experience of the news media. Cameron, seeking his own Alistair Campbell, the *Mirror* journalist who spun for Blair (and much more), had Andy Coulson, the former *News of the World* editor as the Tories Director of Communications. Coulson entered No 10 with Cameron, but was forced out following renewed allegations about his former paper's involvement in phone hacking. Eventually sentenced to 18 months in prison, Coulson was one of the very few newspaper reporters and/or executives convicted of wrongdoing. For his replacement, Cameron employed Craig Oliver of the BBC and Graeme Wilson of *The Sun* as press secretary. Tom Baldwin of *The Times* was Labour leader Ed Miliband's chief media strategist, Bob Roberts of the *Mirror*, Labour's director of communications and Patrick Hennessy of *The Telegraph*, Roberts's deputy. On succeeding Miliband, Jeremy Corbyn made *The Guardian*'s Seamus Milne his media strategist. Each is a partisan as well as an experienced media operator. The relationship is not entirely one-way; other former political staffers, such as the Tories' Danny Finkelstein and Labour's Philip Collins, have ended up as newspapers columnists.

Such is the purchase the media has over politics (and vice versa); personal relationships can be forged by the interactions of politicians and media folk. Tony Blair became godparent to Rupert Murdoch's children. Cameron, whom it was revealed had met with News International executives 26 times in 15 months, regularly socialised with Rebekah Brooks, the chief executive, considering her a personal friend and frequently exchanged familiar texts with her. For similar reasons of schmoozing, Blair had to endure the company of Piers Morgan, meeting him privately some 56 times, over 10 years, when Morgan was editing the *Mirror*. Such interactions between the elected and the unelected wielders of power is something radical critics of the system point to when suggesting that media ownership is 'one of the most devastatingly effective forms of political power and influence in modern Britain' (Jones 2015b: 90)

Politicians try to challenge the media's efforts to critically interpret their messages and actions. They and their communications strategists know that 'media judgments are no objective science; they are a collective view formed by the most influential people at different [news] outlets – the editor, political editor and key columnists – based on their conversations with each other and with key [political] players' (McBride 2013: 246). Thus, senior politicians try to 'maintain strong and friendly relationship with those key people' (McBride 2013: 246) but also strive to manage and manipulate, befriend or threaten them. By such means, politicians try to influence the news agenda by creating a good news narrative or stopping a bad one. Sometimes these succeed, but often they do not.

Being knowledgeable about politics, Ed Miliband strove valiantly to turn media pathologies to his advantage. For the BBC's Nick Robinson, his speeches invariably contained 'carefully honed and market-researched lines' (2015: 182), such as when he claimed, 'I'll fight (I'm strong) for you, (I'm on your side), and to change Britain (things can be better than this)' (Robinson 2015: 182). But to his dismay (and disadvantage), Miliband clearly struggled to project himself through the news media, something crystallised by the now famous photograph of him struggling to eat a bacon sandwich. Lynton Crosby, the Tory strategist, observed (once the election was safely won) that Britain had 'the most aggressive press in the world' and that the coverage of Miliband and the sandwich was 'unfair, unwarranted [and] irrelevant' (Sparrow 2015). Trying to recast the popular notion that, if pleasant, he was 'geeky', 'other worldly', the Labour leader tried to turn the negative into a positive, conceding that 'You could probably even find people who look better eating a bacon sandwich. If you want the politician from central casting, it's just not me, it's the other guy. If you want a politician who thinks that a good photo is the most important thing, then don't vote for me' (Wintour 2014).

Miliband's media depiction played some part in his failure to connect with the electorate. But, if he was placed at a disadvantage, the point has to be emphasised that things were largely reported as they were. Polling showed that 'by more than four-to-one, voters regard Miliband as weak rather than strong and by three-to-one they say he is not up to the job of Prime Minister' (Wintour 2014). Newspapers, mixing comment and reportage, sometimes report crudely (especially the more partisan tabloids), but polls bore out the fact that many electors had a poor opinion of Ed Miliband. Critical, 'campaigning' reportage of him in the *Daily Mail* or *The Sun* probably reinforced any *Mail* or *Sun* reader's negative opinion of him, but such reportage by itself was not responsible for their holding such opinions. However, critical, unsympathetic reportage, frequently repeated, clearly hamstrung Miliband. Amplification, perhaps unfairly, helps reinforces reality – especially so when the mediatisation of politics plays its part in encouraging a celebrity culture. This was apparent in Andrea Leadsom withdrawing from the Tory leadership race (so enabling Theresa May to succeed Cameron as Prime Minister) when she appeared to claim in a *Times* interview that her being a mother gave her an advantage over the childless May. This triggered an anti-Leadsom backlash, and played some part in her decision to pull out. Supporters of the little known Leadsom cried foul, claiming it was not the job of media commentators to either 'big up' or 'trip up' politicians in politics, but for many the *Times* interview merely brought home the fact that a naive Leadsom, an MP for only six years, a minister outside the Cabinet for only two, lacked the experience a Prime Minister requires to avoid falling into media elephant traps.

The centrality of the news media to modern politics means Enoch Powell's familiar trope, that 'for a politician to complain about the media is like a fisherman complaining about the sea', has much to commend it.

Box 10.1 The news media as an intraparty political bulletin board

Politicians make use of the media to communicate with the electorate, but they make as much use of it to communicate with each other; intraparty communication is common. The political class utilise the media as a 'bulletin board' or 'message centre' through which ministers and shadow ministers communicate to each other or about each other, often trying to frame the political agenda in their individual or factional favour. Prime Ministers brief against their colleagues in order to assert their authority (McBride 2013), but other politicians brief to promote themselves, so encroaching on the Prime Minister's – or party leader's – privileges. Political infighting by media is rife in modern politics. In Australia, ousted as Prime Minister by his own parliamentary caucus, Tony Abbott observed that media coverage of politics was increasingly driven by reportage and commentary that was 'mostly sour, bitter, character assassination'. Complaining that 'a febrile media culture has developed that rewards treachery', he suggested reporters should 'refuse to print self serving claims that the person making them won't put his or her name too. Refuse to connive at dishonour by acting as the assassin's knife' (Chan 2015). Such things reflect the fact that the media is as interested in how politicians act as in what they do, that it reports 'process' as much as 'policy'. The efforts of a shell-shocked Parliamentary Labour Party to come to terms with Corbyn's election as leader (in which perhaps no more than 20 of 232 MPs cast their vote for him) has been endlessly played out in the news media. Critics, both anonymous and named, from both frontbench and back, consistently make plain to reporters and pundits their displeasure with him and his team.

The media's relentless pursuit of news means parties and government have to grapple with a news agenda which is often not of their choosing. Ministers and their media managers endlessly seek to stay ahead of the curve. One former No 10 media staffer, Theo Bertram, said of Labour's planning efforts to react to the news, 'It was as if new Labour operated in a different time zone – we were ahead of GMT, responding to tomorrow before it had even begun' (2015a). Politicians make enormous efforts to prepare their common line and to rebut unfavourable stories. For said staffer, however, such planning 'doesn't achieve much. But it's all about preserving the myth that No10 is in control' (Bertram 2015b). Politicians seek to manage the news in order to make the news more of a supportive resource and less of a troublesome obstacle. But the right of news organisations to report and comment cannot be controlled in a liberal democracy. Their autonomy to report can be at best only restrained by politicians. It can rarely be restricted and can never long be curtailed. Sisyphus, it could be said, had the easier task, than have politicians obliged to try to manufacture a supportive story line or challenge an unfavourable one.

Elections, political personalisation and 'authenticity'

Political celebrity is clearly reinforced by news reportage. Party leaders receive much more coverage than their parties, and parties use their leaders (plural as well as singular) as the prism through which to make their electoral pitch by way of news reporting. This helps create a 'leadership stretch', magnifying modern political leaders while 'marginalizing other political actors to the periphery of public attention' (Foley 2000: 293). Of course, because the media can only amplify or reinforce reality, not invent or change it, reportage cannot make the strong party leader weak, or the weak leader stronger. But by amplifying and reinforcing reality, reportage can, however, make the strong leader stronger and the weak leader weaker. So political leaders can find themselves either empowered or else weakened by the news media. Even the most one-time powerful party leader or Prime Minister, Blair, say, can eventually find themselves the butt of negative news reportage.

The media reportage of politics plays some part in encouraging political disaffection, something registered in low, declining levels of trust in politicians, or poor electoral turnout. Only 15 per cent of voters today feel close to the main six parties (the Conservatives, Labour, the Scottish National Party (SNP), the Liberal Democrats, the Greens and United Kingdom Independence Party (UKIP)) (Bale, Webb and Politti 2015). The media, being the space in which politics is done, can help bring politics into disrepute. Fairly reporting wrongdoing such as the parliamentary expenses scandal undermines trust in politicians, but too often, the news media encourages the negative enactment of politics. Political correspondents too easily employ a hyper-aggressive interrogative style, more often than not challenging the interviewee as if he or she is on trial for their life (Lloyd 2004). One such example is Channel 4's Michael Crick, who has made haranguing politicians, invading their personal space, his stock in trade. Adversarial encounters produce heat, but too often insufficient light, especially when skilled politicians possess counter-techniques enabling them to avoid searching questions (even at the price of being seen to be inveigling). It is then no accident that politicians, eager to make the media more resource than obstacle, manoeuvre, play safe and stick to their script. But stonewalling interrogative questions, however unfair the questions, can make politicians seem shifty and untrustworthy.

For one senior Blair staffer, the necessity to engage with the media meant:

> centralized parties constructed around national advertising cam-
> paigns displaced the direct, movement-building politics that had
> kept Labour – and the Conservatives – alive at the grass roots. In
> government … Labour's success in attracting bright new politicians
> became a vice when too many jumped straight into advisory roles
> and ministerial posts, in which the highest ambition was to get a well-
> honed soundbite on to the evening news. It is not surprising that so
> many appeared ill-prepared and inauthentic when they offered them-
> selves up for leadership. (Mulgan 2015)

For too long conformity and loyalty, reinforced by eager partisanship, has been the means by which politicians climbed off the backbench and up the frontbench ladder. This political career path churns out bland, identikit male and now female politicians who can parrot the party's message, but not inspire the public, nor enthuse the remnants of the party faithful. This may help explain how the backbencher Jeremy Corbyn unexpectedly trumped the frontbenchers Yvette Cooper, Andy Burnham and Liz Kendall when succeeding Ed Miliband as Labour leader. Corbyn, presenting himself as honest and authentic, lacking personal ambition, easily eclipsed the other three poor candidates. His election was as much a repudiation of them as it was an endorsement of him. Perhaps the same mediatised phenomenon lies behind much of the success enjoyed by UKIP's Nigel Farage in the last Parliament (or Nick Clegg's 'newness', in terms of personal ratings, at the 2010 election).

Box 10.2 Bad news and scandal

'Politician sleeps with spouse' is not a news story. Much political news reflects the reportage of 'scandal'. Even the political cognoscenti struggle to
recall the reasons behind, say, pensions secretary David Blunkett's second
resignation from the Blair Cabinet. The five resignations from Cameron's
Cabinet following personal failings were those of Chief Secretary David
Laws, Defence Secretary Liam Fox, Chief Whip Andrew Mitchell, Energy
Secretary Chris Huhne and Culture Secretary Maria Miller. Each owed
much to the tone of their news media reportage. Cabinet resignations can be
invariably precipitated by news media exposés, and numerous examples can
be cited. Both Laws's and Miller's were the results of the reporting of their
various expense claims, so their falls began and ended with the news media;
Huhne's was from the marital fall-out that followed an affair and the reportage of his (and his wife's) perjury following a newspaper investigation.

Thus, authenticity, the supposed preparedness to speak straight, is valued by some of the public. This is a repudiation of the established political class, as they are presented by (and present themselves in) the media.

The news media and the 2015 general election

General elections often seem to be celebrity contests. Now, as ever, the news media personalise the campaign agenda by enabling party leaders to command their party's public profile. Opinion polls, commissioned and reported by the news media, help shape the narrative of the campaign. The scripted election campaign has become predictable – some say tedious. Once more in 2015 it was built around staged-for-camera events showing each party leader variously visiting factories (Hi-Viz and hard hats); hospitals (patients and nurses) and schools (teachers and children); being interviewed by the media; and him (with two hers) speaking to handpicked, ticketed, supportive groups of party people. Campaign events, often being in themselves god-awful small affairs, are brought to a significantly larger public by the media. Thus they are enacted by communications strategists eager to shape the news agenda. One worker, part of the audience for a cerebral Miliband speech on her shop floor, told the BBC's Nick Robinson she couldn't follow what he was saying: 'They don't speak to the public do they? It's all for t'media, i'n't it?' (2015: 58). She was not wrong. One election stunt which backfired was Miliband's unveiling of the infamous 'Ed Stone'; the 8ft 6in, two-tonne limestone block on which were chiselled Labour pledges (or commandments...), which was to be mounted in the No. 10 garden in the event of Labour winning (Baker 2015).

The 2010 election had seen the novel introduction of the party leader's debates, but the media's eagerness to reprise these in 2015 were stymied by Cameron. In the end, the compromise reached saw Jeremy Paxman on Channel 4 place the Prime Ministerial candidates, Cameron and Miliband, on trial for their political lives; a BBC *Question Time* special featuring them, plus the Liberal Democrat's Nick Clegg; a one-off debate between the seven party leaders, excluding the Northern Ireland parties; and a six-way 'challengers' debate in which Cameron declined to take part. If the debates reinforced the fact that Britain's two-party system was long over and its three-party one breaking up, they lacked the traction that they had enjoyed in 2010.

Anecdotal evidence suggests print journalism was more influential than broadcast in 2015. It is suggested that it was the other way round in 2010 largely because the debates cast far more of a shadow on the campaign last time round. Press coverage in the 2015 election was clearly skewed towards the Conservatives and more likely to be hostile to other parties; broadcast news focused on the two main parties and the three main party leaders. The 'big winners of the media coverage were the Conservatives. They gained the most quotation time, the most strident press coverage, and coverage focussed on their favoured issues (the economy and tax, rather than say the NHS)' (Deacon et al. 2015: 12).

Social media now plays a key and growing role in the organization of intraparty factionalism, but in spite of its many cheerleaders, it continues to fizzle as an electioneering tool. If in US politics the internet plays a huge part in outreach and fundraising, British parties and candidates, needing less money to campaign, mostly use it to broadcast their messages. They rarely, if ever, use it to receive the public's opinions (Jensen 2016). The Conservatives reportedly spent some £100,000 per month on Facebook advertising. This investment put the party in front of millions of people, but the return is largely unknowable; Labour apparently spent only £10,000 per month. Such efforts came a poor second to the traditional means of communicating by direct mail and the mainstream media. Campaign materials posted online seemingly had little effect. For instance, of the election broadcasts posted on Labour's YouTube channel in 2015, one featuring Ed Miliband recorded only 125,808 views by December 2015, with a mere 565 comments posted. Another, featuring the celebrity Jo Brand, registered a scant 26,561 views. By contrast, Bohemian Carsody, a YouTube sketch by the Australian comedians Sketchshe, was viewed some 27.5 million times in the same period.

Social media enables parties to communicate with the public, but they still largely use the mainstream media – plus direct mail – to do so. At the last election, press and broadcasters (plus social media) briefly made much of another Brand, Russell, interviewing Ed Miliband online (or rather, his inanely speaking at him). *The Guardian*'s Owen Jones claimed Brand's endorsement of Labour was big news: Brand 'has nearly 10 million Twitter followers; his YouTube interview with Ed Miliband received well over a million hits and counting; he is listened to by hundreds of thousands of disillusioned Britons, particularly young people' (2015a). Others, more realistically, considered Brand's inchoate, infantile leftism so unappealing to 'middle' England that 'Agent' Brand should be thanked by the Tories for helping them win the election. But, of course, the reportage of Brand's 'intervention' had no measurable effect other than to feed the ego of another leftist 'celeb' while enthralling those with a fetishism for internet politics.

Truth be told, the effect of the election campaign 'proper' (the period from the prorogation of Parliament to polling day) can be overrated. So too the impact of the media coverage. Tim Bell, Thatcher's election strategist, says of the Tory winning campaign of 1987, 'The reality was that the result was in the bag months before polling day. We could have stuck a huge poster up in Piccadilly Circus saying "Fuck off" and people would have still voted for us' (Delaney 2015: 141). The same could be said for

Labour's victories in 1997 and 2001, and probably that of 2005. Elections, if neck and neck, are won and lost over years, not weeks. And not only by or in the media. The 'quiet Tories' of the 2015 election had been Tories for some time before the starting gun was fired on the actual campaign.

Human fallibility: Getting it wrong

Helping 'make' news makes the media a political actor in its own right, but newspapers, being beyond state regulation, must in some way balance their freedom to comment with their obligation to inform their readers (or 'infortain' in the case of tabloids). For publications still called broadsheets, the opinions they express reflect their partisanship in terms of left or right, but their reportage must be cool-headed and factual; this is what their readers expect. Being made by humans means some form of bias is inevitable in the manufacture of news. For instance, the BBC's social liberalism, reinforced by its executives and creatives being socially liberal, middle class, metropolitan professionals, fosters the politically correct bias it eagerly displays. However, in the field of party politics, it and other broadcasters remain resolutely non-partisan, even if an inbuilt predilection for the 'centre' makes the party extremes on both sides somewhat unpalatable. The BBC's earnestly worn social liberalism is reflexively displayed, but like every broadcaster, it strives to fairly report electoral politics. Newspapers, too, have to be factual. Commentary involves punditry: presenting a variety of voices and opinions, the best both partisan and non-partisan. Punditry, often more critical of politicians than supportive of them, is now part and parcel of the political conversation. So much, much political coverage involves pundits interviewing each other. Commentary tends to the negative rather than the positive and focuses on 'process' (who's in/out or up/down) rather than 'policy'. Too often, however, it involves forecasting what is to happen tomorrow, as much as analysing what is happening today.

Predictions, inevitably, can be more often wrong than right. For instance, coverage of any election concerns the 'horse race' of the campaign: who is winning or is likely to win. Almost half of all television and newspaper coverage of the 2015 campaign focused on this (Deacon et al. 2015: 13). But, unusually for Britain, the common expectation of a hung parliament meant close attention was paid to possible post-election scenarios. Almost no pundit, pollster or politician foresaw that any party would achieve a Commons majority, so speculation was rife as to the coalition or minority government that would result. So much so, calling the outcome of the 2015 horse race wrong might well have impacted the running of the race. For instance, inaccurate polls forecasting a hung parliament fed the notion that the SNP could prop up a Labour minority, even participate in some form of Labour-led coalition. This may well have prompted some middle-England electors to vote Conservative in larger numbers than expected. The Tories, taking their cue from the polls, clearly played to this 'narrative, especially in the closing stages of the election: the fear of Labour taking office with SNP support. This was supported by an advertising campaign that depicted a diminutive Ed Miliband as being either in the pocket of or having his strings pulled by the SNP leader' (Wring and Ward 2015: 225)

So punditry is too often proved spectacularly wrong – perhaps never more so than in the last Parliament. For instance, in the past six years, the Conservative–Liberal Democrat coalition was not predicted; the persistence of that coalition was often doubted; few foresaw that the Alternative Vote would be so resoundingly rejected in the referendum, that the SNP would win a majority in the Scottish Parliament, that a referendum on Scottish independence would be held, nor that the yes vote in that referendum would be so large; no one expected a Conservative victory in 2015; no one, not even the candidate himself, expected Jeremy Corbyn to become Labour leader following that election; few, if any, pundits foresaw Brexit winning the referendum; and, in spite of endless speculation that Cameron's successor as Prime Minister would be either George Osborne or Boris Johnson, neither man proved politically viable enough to even seek the crown when it fell from Cameron's head.

Each erroneous opinion, every one honestly held, was reported by the news media – and thereby the purchase of each error considerably

Box 10.3   News beyond Westminster

The 15 per cent of the British population living in Scotland, Wales and Northern Ireland turn to Edinburgh, Cardiff and Stormont, not merely Whitehall and Westminster, to find out how they are governed. The devolution of political power has brought about a separate, distinctive Scottish, Welsh and Northern Irish form of politics, something seen in the very distinctive party systems that have been established (for some time in the case of Northern Ireland). It is also seen in terms of the emergence of specific news agendas – and news providers – that cater to the particular needs of those nations and that province. For instance, the British news media reporting in England largely spectated and reported on the Scottish independence referendum campaign, but the Scottish media participated in it. Technology easily allows the news media to provide Scottish, Welsh and Northern Ireland news tailored to Scottish, Welsh and Northern Ireland politicians and people, something which may in some way further encourage, perhaps reinforce, centrifugal forces challenging the unity of the UK.

magnified. Two such errors may well have been considerably significant. First, the fallout from one single, perhaps rogue YouGov *Sunday Times* poll, giving the 'yes' campaign the lead in the referendum campaign, saw the unionist camp panic and party leaders scramble to offer all sorts of hasty, ill-thought-out promises. By this means, following Cameron, Clegg and Miliband's 'vow' in the *Scottish Herald*, was devolution max launched. Second, the opinion polls were horribly inaccurate at the election, which was the most polled in history. Learning of the exit poll, which correctly contradicted every opinion poll, the head of pollster ICM tweeted two words; 'Oh, shit' (Rawnsley 2016). The polls could well have been wrong for much of the 2015 Parliament. Every single one of the over 1,000 polls reported in 2012–2015 put the Conservative vote well below the 38 per cent won at the election. Had the Conservatives true standing been more accurately reported, politics may well have played out differently in the last Parliament. For instance, the Tories may have been far more robust in their handling of their Liberal Democrat coalition partners. Or Labour far more fearful of being led at an election by Ed Miliband. The reported possibility of a hung Parliament could well have played some part in rallying reluctant conservatives to the Conservatives at the election. Such can be the power of the mediated story. Especially when the news media's real potential for influence (invariably an unintended influence) results from its ability to shape and frame the issue agenda both politicians and the public follow. Thus, because the 'horse race' has to be studied, the news media has to take greater care in calling it accurately.

Noises off? Social media and its political impacts

The need to make sense of an exhausting pace of change prompts grandiose claims suggesting social media is part of a 'revolution in technology that has ... destroyed the traditional means of disseminating ideology that persisted through two hundred years of industrial capitalism, and has made social media the irreversible norm' (Mason 2013). Such claims ought to be taken with the proverbial pitch of salt. Voices can be cast further, faster, but the claim is too lazily made that social media of itself enables citizens to more effectively participate in politics. In non-democratic authoritarian regimes like Egypt and Iran, where a mainstream news media colludes with elites to prop them up, the likes of Facebook and Twitter can help mobilise opposition to the regime by organising opinion and protest. In Britain, however, the political class, long held to account both by the election cycle and free-flowing information and opinion, is criticised by social media use, not seriously challenged. Here, humour, as much as anger, is often behind the comments going viral. Being online certainly enables some degree of horizontal communication, but it complements, not replaces, vertical communication. If reporters are no longer needed to make media, reporters still make media. Change in communication forms, however startling, tends to the incremental, not the revolutionary.

Social media certainly makes some people more present than previously. But bear in mind that of June 2016 David Cameron had 1.4 million Twitter followers, but Justin Bieber 82.8 million. And Kim Kardashian 45.9 million. Commentary may be less restricted to professional journalists working for a newspaper or broadcaster, but there is still a gap between the making of news and its consumption. Comments below newspaper stories usually object to or support the writer's argument; such comments rarely prompt fruitful exchanges. Writers never engage with commentators (many seemingly never read them); readers of such comments invariably have their opinion reinforced, rarely changed. Some assert that something referred to as 'dual screening', someone using an online device to comment while watching a live broadcast, can 'reconfigure' a media event (Chadwick and Vaccari 2015), but exactly how remains largely unexplained. If social media can provide a 'second screen' to comment while viewing the mainstream media, so what? Who reads such comments? There is very little evidence of any meaningful feedback loop in operation. The huge gap between broadcasting and receiving remains, especially when much social media comment forms part of a private, not a public, conversation. Only those with some wider knowledge capital, if you will, can likely find an audience wider than friends and family – usually by way of the mainstream media. Not everyone with a typewriter wrote *War and Peace*. People still 'spectate' events others 'create'; pundits and journalists still report news, but others, even should they comment on that news, or reproduce it, still consume it.

One curious feature of Twitter and Facebook is that people use them to publicly advertise their private virtue. Such 'virtue signalling' 'consists of saying you hate things. It is camouflage. The emphasis on hate distracts from the fact you are really saying how good you are' (Bartholomew 2015a). For instance, should a left-liberal post that they 'hate the *Daily Mail* or UKIP, they are really telling you that they are admirably non-racist, left-wing or open-minded. One of the crucial aspects of virtue signalling is that it does not require actually doing anything virtuous ... It takes no effort or sacrifice at all' (Bartholomew 2015b). Social media campaigns reflect this phenomenon. For Rod Liddle, they invariably tend to be organised by the 'maniacally obsessive, relentlessly involved liberal left ... There is never a right-wing petition to be signed ... There are no normal people at all in this online activism: normal people are all at work or down the pub. It is a tiny fraction of the population ... much less than 0.5 per cent – and they are all psychotically furious about everything' (2015). Critics of social media rightly lament this 'era of emoji politics, where identity and emotion suffocate debate and rationality' (Hunt

2015). Twitter, used politically by the convinced and committed – too often the obsessional, egotistical – sits well with the modern notion that the self is all-important. Thus, social media facilitates the scourge that is identity politics: helping promote the 'intellectual and generational shift away from objective principles of action and expression towards subjective notions of interpretation and feelings' (Anthony 2016). Via Twitter 'I' must make plain my opinion to 'my' followers. Narcissus, one notes, chose to privately admire his reflection. Identity politics lends itself to ever louder cyberactivism and vice versa. Far less digital space is devoted to, say, economic growth and other such valence issues which far broader number of citizens take into account before casting their vote.

We now live in a 'world of constant chatter, everyone has a view, all of us are bombarded with messages and messengers fighting for our attention' (Campbell 2016). Part of such chatter is too often a culture of political complaint, fermented by social media, which is part of the online 'outrage' industry (Hume 2015). Such complaint, invariably led by the politically correct, is something seen in what is called a 'Twitter storm', a form of mob rule. Such mobs, usually small, wholly unrepresentative, can make social media feeds ever more 'loud, shrill, reflexive and ugly' (Manjoo 2015). Such shrieking of nothing can encourage 'a cycle of action and reaction. In just about every news event, the internet's reaction to the situation becomes a follow-on part of the story, so that much of the media establishment becomes trapped in escalating, infinite loops of 140-character, knee-jerk insta-reaction' (Manjoo 2015). Strident, uncivil expressions of outrage by a small minority become the norm in an 'era of internet preening, out of control partisanship, and press a button punditry, when anything and everything becomes prompt for a "plaint, a rant, a riff"' (Bruni 2015). By such means can the left parade their offence at what someone has said (far less often what they have done). Outrage is often confected; offence gleefully taken. Named individuals find themselves called out for offending words often without regard to context. No allowance is made for foolishness or error, but retribution sought for transgression, often in the form of calls for professional ostracism and loss of livelihood. All lacking due process. And without judge and jury. In such circumstances, freedom of speech is significantly threatened by the freedom of communication (Hume 2015; O'Neill 2015). Such censorious, politically motivated complaint could, in time, even threaten the 'sometimes ugly, but ultimately amazing world of internet freedom' (O'Neill 2016; Pickles 2016).

How can social media influence thinking about politics?

The traditional news media reinforces political opinions and preferences and frames what we collectively 'think about', but the outrage industry reflects a form of 'groupthink'. It owes much to people seeking out only certain types of news and opinion. For decades, left liberals read *The Guardian* and conservatives the *Mail* or *Telegraph*, but the exclusivity by which news and information can now be selected means pre-existing, firmly held opinions can more easily be reinforced. Politically minded social media users, often being in Britain of a leftist persuasion, can find themselves inside 'online filter bubbles'. Such bubbles, by filtering out unfavourable opinions or bad news, reinforce existing beliefs by carelessly substituting the ideas of a vociferous few for those of the silent many. Labour's Corbynistas typify this, endlessly substituting the beliefs of a few for the opinions of the many, preferring the certainties of their own social media over the realities reported by other media.

Social media can thus tell users what they should 'think'. On the day Corbyn became Labour leader, some 270,000 tweets mentioned him, of which 90 per cent were positive (Sparrow 2015b), but in his first poll rating, Corbyn scored minus three, worse than every other party leader since 1980. Filter bubbles encourage false hope or expectation when such 'associative news gathering' obscures the true state of public opinion. Labour MP Tristram Hunt warns against 'algorithm politics' where activists gravitate only to views that confirm their own: 'If social media were politicising the many as well as radicalising the few; were it significantly growing the number of people engaged in politics in the first place, rather than confirming pre-held bias, then Ed Miliband might now be sitting in 10 Downing Street' (Wintour 2015). Prime Minister Cameron rather gleefully made the same point, when expressing the view that 'Twitter is not Britain' (BBC News 2015a).

Rather worryingly, for reasons explored above, social media offers the chance for activists to not only challenge, but seek to criminalise other opinions; the zealous eagerly seek to police the discourse. Such activists, however, tend to inhabit small communities organised around narrow subjects of interest to very few. But social media can facilitate public brawling between people who would previously have had to be in the same room as one another to fight (or on the same newspaper story or television or radio programme). Others can now join in said brawl, usually to less effect. Politicians can tweet themselves into hot water – and can find themselves sacked from the frontbench for a 'snobby' tweet, such as Labour's Emily Thornberry. On certain topics, social media can clearly be an accelerant, if less a catalyst. This is especially so when issues aired through social media are taken up by the mainstream media. The political conversation that results, however, is still dominated by politicians and pundits. If added to and amplified by social media, that conversation remains largely driven by a mainstream media which has now migrated online. The use of social media, for all the exaggerated emancipatory claims made for it, still involves citizens 'pulling' information and opinion out, rather than 'pushing' information and opinion in. One is still more likely to 'follow' a political event, rather than 'lead' it: to 'comment' on events rather than 'shape' them. But the vast majority of people still neither follow nor comment.

Conclusion

Produced faster, consumed quicker, news is in danger of becoming increasingly hyperactive. Stories come, stories go, but news and comment are increasingly interwoven. When Prime Minister Cameron observed:

> I don't want to be consuming media all day. I want to run a country, not a television channel. With all the modern tweeting and blogging, and 24-hour news, politics is in danger of being too short term anyway. I sometimes take people into the Cabinet Room and say, 'This is the room where Churchill decided in 1940 to fight on, and they [the cabinet] sat there for five days and discussed it.' And imagine now – after about half an hour the modern equivalent of Alastair Campbell will come in and say, 'Sky News are outside and they want to know if you're going to surrender or not'. And after an hour someone will probably have tweeted from the meeting. (Mount 2015)

If, as Cameron suggests, politicians 'can't follow the media all the time, because you'll never take a decision' (Mount 2015), no politician can ignore the mainstream media either. Jeremy Corbyn's eagerness to do so could help bring about his downfall.

In hindsight, Tony Blair thought new Labour devoted inordinate time to 'courting, assuaging, and persuading the media. In our own defence, after 18 years of opposition and the, at times, ferocious hostility of parts of the media, it was hard to see any alternative' (2007). This was because, for good or ill, the news media, in its many forms, online as much as off, remains the principal means by which politics is reported and explained. For politicians, it is an important resource, but also a formidable obstacle – and something for which most politicians retain a strange fascination. But in all its variety, the news media is still as indispensable as ever, largely because it provides a window through which people can see the world, but also because it actively helps frame how both politicians and the public perceive that world. Politicians still prefer less effective 'command and control' methods of media management to 'engage and explain' strategies. But both necessitate politicians engaging with the media, both 'old' and 'new', 'mainstream' and 'social', in order to make their electoral pitch and undermine that of their opponents.

Chapter 11

Governing in Times of Austerity

DEBORAH MABBETT

In 2015, as the general election was being fought, a drama unfolded in the euro area. Greek voters rejected austerity imposed by the country's creditors, and debt default and euro exit looked likely. Critics argued that austerity had crippled the Greek economy and, indeed, slowed the recovery of the euro area as a whole. Policymakers in Northern Europe, particularly in Germany, were said to be in the grip of the 'dangerous idea' (Blyth 2013) that the norms of good housekeeping should be the basis of economic management, and that governments should therefore not spend more than they raised in revenue, regardless of the condition of the wider economy.

The tenor of the debate about austerity in the UK presents a striking contrast. Policymakers might have believed for a time that austerity was necessary to satisfy creditors, but any threat of a government bond crisis quickly faded after 2010. Austerity was a policy choice, made by the Conservatives, supported by the Liberal Democrats, and not categorically opposed by Labour. The 2015 election result suggests that it was not devastatingly unpopular. This chapter considers several possible explanations of why this was. One is that austerity has not actually taken place: for all the talk, the really damaging cuts to public expenditure have yet to come. This claim is largely rejected on the basis of the evidence presented below, but the government did soften the blow of cuts in public expenditure by also cutting taxes. This suggests a second explanation: that 'austerity' in the UK has been more about shrinking the state than balancing the budget, and has therefore been popular with some political constituencies. In so far as austerity did mean hardship, this was not distributed over the whole population: on the contrary, austerity was accompanied by increased inequality. Complementing this is a third distinctive aspect of the UK's austerity: that while it might initially have slowed the country's recovery from the financial crisis and induced a 'double-dip' depression, the economy did begin to recover in time for the election, while much of the euro area economy still languished.

In the following discussion, I consider first whether austerity would have been forced on any government by the parlous condition of the government finances in 2010, and explain the differences between Labour's fiscal plans and those of the coalition. I then review the government's choice of targets for cutting spending. After documenting the effect of austerity on public services and living standards, I come to the question of why austerity was apparently so difficult for the opposition to oppose effectively. Before the election, Nicola Sturgeon of the Scottish National Party (SNP) gave the country a brief masterclass in how the dominant narrative of austerity might be challenged. But the Conservatives responded vigorously by portraying a possible Labour–SNP coalition as incompetent to govern. This was 'statecraft' (Gamble 2015): instead of reacting to public opinion, Conservative politicians were proactive and strategic in defining their programme. Austerity worked as a policy that portrayed the Conservative Party as uniquely competent to govern, thereby attracting sufficient voter support for victory in the 2015 election.

Finally, I turn to the relationship between austerity and growth. While persuading the public that austerity is a necessity is made easier by the apparent common sense of balancing the books, it is made harder by the negative effect of austerity on the economy. If public expenditure cuts dampen growth in the economy, one effect is that tax revenue falls, the deficit does not fall and the debt burden continues to rise. These 'Keynesian' effects of austerity on the economy (see Box 11.1) are one of the main reasons why, for all the government's expenditure-cutting efforts, the target of eliminating the deficit by 2015 was not met. The new target for a surplus by 2020 will not be met either, unless there is a sustained upturn in economic growth.

The budget presented by the Chancellor contains projections for revenue and the deficit that depend on forecasts of growth. A positive growth forecast will make the government's financial plans look better than a gloomy prognosis for the economy. Since 2010, a specialised independent body, the Office for Budget Responsibility (OBR), checks the growth forecasts used in the budget. In the final section on growth, fiscal rules and fiscal monitoring, I discuss the possible effects of the OBR's oversight of the government's claims and promises about the budget.

One reason for the public to accept the pain of austerity is that it might help to put the UK on a more sustainable growth path than that taken in the 2000s, which ended with the disaster of the financial crisis. But, in the final section, I argue that the effect could be exactly the opposite: restrictive fiscal policy means a heavy reliance on monetary policy to stimulate the economy, and that may result in new asset price bubbles and set the economy up for a reprise of the instability of the late 2000s.

Austerity and the bond markets

The 2010 election took place in exceptionally bad fiscal conditions. The financial crisis had contributed to a large fall in tax revenue, and the previous government had also increased its own spending to counteract the crisis-induced fall in private consumption and investment. The result was that the government's deficit had increased to some 11 per cent of GDP in 2009–2010. In turn this meant that debt was mounting every year, reaching nearly 53 per cent of GDP by 2009 even with financial rescue measures excluded (HM Treasury Budget 2011, Table 1.3: 24). The Conservatives fought the election promising to tackle 'Labour's debt crisis'. The Liberal Democrats joined the coalition embracing essentially the same analysis of the urgency of 'acting now on debt'. In the last budget of the Labour government in March 2010, Alastair Darling announced a long-term plan for restoring the public accounts to balance. The new Chancellor, George Osborne, brought in an 'emergency' budget in June 2010 which preserved Labour's plans but added substantial immediate cuts, particularly in funding for local government, along with longer-term plans to bring down social security spending. The more popular spending areas of health and schools were protected, but the axe fell heavily on some areas traditionally favoured by the Conservatives, such as defence and policing.

Why did the main parties disagree about the timing of retrenchment? The Conservatives cultivated the idea that there was an urgent need to take steps to reassure financial markets: a claim which apparently helped to convince the Liberal Democrats that they should join the coalition for the sake of the country (Gamble 2015: 46). In mid-2010, the euro area was in the midst of a government bond crisis (see Box 11.1). In May 2010, as the country went to the polls, the interest rate on UK government debt was less than 1 per cent higher than the rate on German government debt, the lowest in Europe. This did not prevent mounting anxiety about the prospect of the bond market crisis spreading to the UK. With the benefit of hindsight, these fears seem overblown, because the Bank of England could step in and buy gilts. Since 2010 it has done this on a large scale, not to rescue the government but as part of the expansionary monetary policy technique known as 'quantitative easing'. But in 2010 quantitative easing was in its infancy, and few would have forecast that interest rates would remain low for years.

The Labour opposition argued that premature austerity damaged the recovery from the financial crisis. A slight recovery was underway by the time of the election, but this ended and the economy entered a 'double-dip' recession. By January 2011, there was already much talk in the business press of the need for a 'Plan B' that would promote growth. By

---

Box 11.1   The language of austerity

Austerity is implemented through *fiscal policy*, which refers to the government's decisions about the spending it undertakes and the taxes it sets. The difference between spending and revenue is the *fiscal (or budget) deficit*. To pay for spending that is not covered by tax revenue, the government borrows an amount equal to the deficit, which increases its stock of *debt*. Borrowing is done by selling government bonds, known as *gilts* in the UK, to savers and institutions that manage savings, such as pension funds. Normally, the interest rate or *yield* that the government has to pay on gilts is lower than the rate that other borrowers (firms or households) have to pay, because gilts are regarded as 'safe': the government will always repay its debts (mainly by issuing new debt). However, if buyers lose confidence that the government will repay, the interest rate they demand will go up. When the interest rate is greatly in excess of the economic growth rate, the government's finances rapidly get into a worse and worse state. Bond buyers know this, and demand an even higher interest rate, provoking a *government (or sovereign) debt crisis*.

The government can raise taxes and cut expenditure to reduce the deficit. However, higher taxes and lower spending will reduce demand in the economy, causing lower growth or even an economic contraction (negative growth). This *Keynesian effect* of fiscal policy on the economy can be offset by an expansionary *monetary policy*. Monetary policy is controlled by the Bank of England, and refers to the decisions it makes about interest rates and other measures to promote or suppress borrowing and spending by firms and households.

---

the end of 2012, the Chancellor had to admit that, because growth was lower than expected (and tax receipts therefore remained depressed), the plan to eliminate the deficit by 2015 would not be met. One consequence was that the UK lost its triple-A credit rating early in 2013. In normal times, this would have damaged the government's finances further by pushing up the yields demanded by bond buyers. This did not happen largely because there was nowhere else for buyers to turn. Many major economies were experiencing similar downgrades.

In the face of these pressures, the coalition insisted that it would stay the course in restraining public spending. But it did create some stimulus via tax cuts. In the 2011 budget, the chancellor began a staged reduction in corporation tax, from 28 per cent to 26 per cent in 2011, with further steps down to reach a rate of 20 per cent in 2015. From the first budget in June 2010, the government also began the implementation of the central Liberal Democratic policy of raising the personal tax allowance, taking more low-paid workers out of the tax system. The headline figure of a £10,000 allowance was reached in 2014.

Thus austerity took on a distinctive shape, with the focus on cutting expenditure rather than raising revenue. Projections to the end of the decade show that more than 90 per cent of the reduction in the deficit will come from expenditure reductions, and less than 10 per cent from tax increases (OBR 2014a: 17). This strong expenditure-reduction bias in the government's approach is indirect evidence that austerity has been more about seizing the opportunity to reduce the size of the public sector than addressing a pressing financial threat.

How much austerity has there been?

The last Labour budget in March 2010 set out plans to restore budget balance in ten years. Labour proposed some £21 billion in tax increases and £51 billion in expenditure reductions (Crawford 2010). Soon after the election, the coalition produced an emergency budget which shortened the time horizon for eliminating the deficit to five years (the term of the Parliament). This target was not achieved, despite the announcement of dramatic additional expenditure cuts. There are two main reasons why a deficit might not come down as planned. First, plans may not be implemented, so that actual expenditure is higher than anticipated. Second, if expenditure cuts depress the economy, they will also reduce tax revenue, so the gap between expenditure and revenue does not close.

Planned and actual expenditure cuts

Cuts were not applied uniformly across all areas of government spending. Real-terms spending on health and schools was 'ring-fenced'. Some spending is not at the government's discretion, such as interest payments on debt. Social security spending cannot simply be cut in cash terms by announcement. The amount the government spends is determined by legally binding rules. Those who meet the legal conditions are entitled to benefits, and cannot just be told that the money has run out. Cuts have been implemented in social security by changing the rules, in the expectation that the new rules will disqualify people or reduce their entitlements, but sometimes these expectations are confounded. If the economy does not perform as hoped, or people do not get the jobs that are forecast, or rents go up more than expected, then savings are not realised.

One effect of these constraints was that, in the 2010–2015 Parliament, cuts were concentrated in departments where spending is subject to

Table 11.1   *The changing composition of government expenditure*

% current or projected expenditure	2010–2011	2015–2016	2020–2021
Health	15.0	16.6	*
Education	7.9	8.0	*
Total spending subject to departmental expenditure limits	51.7	46.7	45.1
Social security benefits and tax credits	30.7	32.1	29.7
of which – not subject to welfare cap (mainly old age pensions)		14.3	14.7
Interest on government debt	6.8	5.1	7.1

* The allocation of departmental spending to 2020 had not yet been announced at time of writing.

Sources: OBR 2011: table 4.15; OBR 2015: Table 4.13 and Chart 4.9.

'departmental expenditure limits', meaning that it is set in cash terms. Heavily affected were policing, defence, environmental protection, central government administration and grants to local government. In the 2015–2020 Parliament, the rate of cutbacks in these areas is set to slow down, and there is heightened attention to social security spending. The government has created a cash limit called the 'welfare cap' to indicate its target of reducing spending on benefits other than old age pensions. Table 11.1 shows how the composition of government spending is projected to change further in the coming five years. The projections are subject to considerable uncertainty. Strikingly, the share of government spending on debt interest went down between 2010 and 2015, despite rising government debt, because interest rates were low. The amount is projected to rise, but there will be savings on interest payments if rates stay low for an extended period.

There was some, but limited, scope to cut social security spending in politically popular ways. The government tapped into resentment by working people of others who received their living from the state. This was cultivated by the policy of imposing a 'benefit cap' which limited the total amount that a household could receive in benefits relative to the average wage, drawing attention to the position of some benefit recipients relative to working people. This was largely a symbolic policy: it saved a mere £330 million a year (see Table 11.2). Less symbolic, but

Table 11.2 *Planned cuts in social security in the 2010–2015 Parliament*

	Projected annual saving in 2014–2015
	in £s million
Indexation changes (2010)	5,840
Freeze in child benefit	975
1 per cent uprating (2012)	2,175
Benefit cap	330
Reforms to incapacity benefits and Disability Living Allowance	2,885
Child benefit cut for higher-rate taxpayers	2,445
Tax credit reforms	3,220

Sources: Table 2.1 of successive budgets and autumn statements.

also apparently politically acceptable, was the 'affluence testing' of child benefits, which are now not paid to households containing a higher-rate taxpayer.

The bulk of savings in social security spending were achieved through methods that did not attract public attention. Cuts in the level of benefits would be very noticeable if done in money terms, but benefits can be eroded with low visibility by failing to index them fully to inflation. In the June 2010 budget, the Chancellor announced that the index used to adjust benefits would be changed to one that tends to produce lower increases. Furthermore, some benefits were frozen for three years, including child benefit. In the 2012 autumn statement, the Chancellor turned to indexation again to achieve further savings, announcing that benefit increases (other than old age pensions) would be capped at 1 per cent per annum for three years. All in all, freezes and caps on indexation had a much bigger effect on the social security budget than all other measures combined.

The government hoped to achieve reductions in expenditure on disability benefits by conducting a programme of reassessments, identifying those who could be working rather than relying on benefits. But many of those who were ruled capable of work in reassessments appealed successfully against these judgments, the process attracted public criticism, and little money was saved. Here the government trod in the footsteps of previous governments, both Labour and Conservative, who had thought they could identify 'shirkers' by reforming assessment procedures. These policies have never succeeded in producing significant and sustained reductions in the growth of benefit expenditure. Thanks to the creation of the OBR, there is now much clearer evidence than there used to be of how projected savings may fail to materialise. In 2011, the government planned to save about £2.9 billion a year in disability-related expenditure by 2014 (as shown in Table 11.2). By 2013, the expected saving had fallen to less than £2 billion. In 2014, the figures were revised again: in place of savings, the projections show a slight but steady growth in expenditure (OBR 2014b: chart 4.5).

Looking for savings after the 2015 election, the government's eye alighted on tax credits. These are benefits (or 'negative taxes') paid to people who are working, whose earned income is inadequate for their family's needs. As Table 11.2 shows, there were substantial cuts to tax credits in the 2010–2015 Parliament, achieved through numerous small adjustments to the various thresholds that calibrate the system. These cuts were opposed by Labour, but it was unable to rally a wider movement against them. However, when the government proposed further cuts to tax credits after the 2015 election, the House of Lords rejected the enabling regulation. If the welfare cap is to be complied with, cuts will have to be found elsewhere.

Planned and actual revenue

Government revenue depends on the state of the economy: thus the double-dip recession in 2011–2012 reduced tax receipts. Furthermore, as economic growth has resumed, tax receipts have not kept pace, and the tax-to-GDP ratio has fallen. Only part of this is due to policy changes, such as the increase in income tax personal allowances. Striking examples of other changes include declining revenue from tobacco duties, as the tax base (spending on cigarettes) has fallen due to the decline in smoking. Another tax 'underperformer' has been Stamp Duty paid on house sales: although house prices have recovered, transaction volumes have stayed low. But perhaps the most important and profound source of revenue shortfall has been income tax, because wages and salaries have declined as a share of GDP.

There is not much the government can do to stimulate growth in those parts of the economy that produce the most tax revenue. Obviously, it does not want people to start smoking more, or even drinking more – spending on alcohol has also declined relative to the size of the economy (OBR 2014a: 109). It has tried to increase transactions in the housing market with a scheme to help first-time buyers. Perhaps its most audacious move to improve revenue has been the increase in the minimum wage announced in the new Conservative government's summer 2015 budget. The fiscal effects of higher wages are expected to be positive if small: the OBR (2015: 98) predicts an increase of £0.1 billion in income tax and national insurance by 2020.

In summary, has austerity really happened? The basic answer is surely yes: there have been substantial direct cuts in expenditure. However, it may not be quite that simple. For there are at least three reasons to modify the answer: there have been tax giveaways, too; not all planned expenditure cuts have happened; and the deficit has not come down as forecast because of slow growth, particularly in some economic activities which have a strong effect on tax revenue.

The impact of austerity on public services and living standards

Given that the government's deficit has not fallen as planned, it is tempting to conclude that austerity has not been as bad as all that. But the size of cuts in expenditure can understate the real impact of austerity on public services. Cuts in services can take place even when spending is constant, if demand for services is rising. Thus the real-terms protection of the NHS budget will not ensure the maintenance of services, given the increasing needs of a rising and ageing population. Hidden cuts in services are also occurring in schools, where the government committed itself to maintaining spending. The number of schoolchildren is going up, so stable expenditure means a decline in per-pupil spending. The impact on many schools was heightened by the introduction of a flagship Liberal Democratic policy, the pupil premium. This policy means that schools with the most disadvantaged pupils get more money, but this leaves less for other schools (Crawford 2010).

As well as being partly hidden in this way, the impact of austerity has also been highly unequal. A number of studies have sought to establish how austerity has affected the distribution of income and welfare in the UK. The most straightforward results are from studies of the effect of tax and social security changes on households across the income distribution. Using the technique of 'microsimulation', researchers take models which include a representative sample of UK households, and apply the tax and benefit changes to their income and circumstances.

An authoritative study of the impact of austerity using microsimulation highlighted two striking conclusions (De Agostini, Hills and Sutherland 2014). First, direct tax and benefit changes since May 2010 did not contribute to deficit reduction. The measures were fiscally neutral because reductions in benefits and tax credits have been 'spent' on raising the personal income tax allowance. Second, people in the bottom half of the income distribution lost out overall, while those in the top half of the distribution gained. This seems surprising as it might be assumed that poorer households would gain from the tax allowance as much as they lost from the benefit changes. Certainly the Liberal Democrats aimed to present themselves as the tax-cutting party for the low-paid, with their focus on raising the personal allowance. However, higher tax allowances do not benefit those who earn too little to take advantage of them, and they bring the biggest benefits to two-earner households in the middle of the income distribution, as each earner can claim an allowance. Lone parents, with only one tax allowance, are among the major losers.

Analyses such as this focus on austerity in the government budget, which has an effect on households when services and benefits are cut and public sector employees lose their jobs. Households are also affected by austerity in other ways. As the economic downturn has continued, many households have been affected by unemployment, underemployment (having to take part-time instead of full-time work, or obtaining only intermittent work) and declines in real wages. While it is possible to get a general sense of the magnitude of these changes from statistics on wages and prices, studies of their impact have to piece together an account based on indicators such as the expanding use of food banks and reports from schools about the welfare of children, or they rely on interviews (Clark 2014). Some accounts are policy-oriented, focusing on the spread of practices which disadvantage poor households such as delays in paying social security benefits (All-Party Parliamentary Inquiry into Hunger in the UK 2014).

While these studies give a picture of how austerity affects the poorest, it is less often noticed that some households have benefited from the characteristic policy mix of this period of austerity: specifically from very lax monetary policies. For example, those with 'tracker' mortgages gained from lower mortgage interest rates, while holders of financial assets benefited from central bank measures to support the economy. Efforts have been made to calculate the effects of monetary policy on inequality. There has been a particular focus on the effects of quantitative easing (QE) which works (if it works at all) by boosting the value of financial assets, which in turn is hoped to make the holders of those assets more inclined to spend or invest. Estimates by the Bank of England in 2012 suggested that QE had boosted UK households' net financial wealth by £600 billion. Financial wealth is very unequally distributed: the top 5 per cent of households have 40 per cent of the financial assets of the household sector (Bank of England 2012: 11). This means that the direct benefits of QE were also very unequally distributed. Ben Chu of *The Independent* updated the Bank's figures and calculated that the top 10 per cent of households benefited from QE to the tune of nearly £350,000 each (Chu 2012). While this is a very approximate calculation, it is consistent with the Bank's own methodology.

These estimates suggest that austerity has had very differentiated effects on the population, with a pronounced pattern of public poverty and private wealth. Since private wealth is very concentrated, while poorer households rely more heavily on public services, the overall impact of austerity has undoubtedly been to magnify inequality. One might expect that this would have political implications. Gains for a small minority and losses for a large group would normally be a recipe for political disaster in a democracy, but this was not the case.

The political consequences of austerity

Mark Blyth (2013) offers a powerful and influential critique of austerity, arguing that it is not necessary and does not work. Why, then, do governments embrace austere policies? Blyth never really answers this question. He focuses on the prescriptions of economists, tacitly assuming that politicians are heavily influenced by economic arguments and prone to conclude that 'there is no alternative'. This analysis might be persuasive in heavily indebted countries that rely on international lenders for support, although even then it fails to explain why the lenders are so enamoured of evidently counterproductive policies. Yet his account explains very little about the UK, where it has been clear that the government has had choices about the timing of fiscal retrenchment and the balance between expenditure reductions and tax increases.

Andrew Gamble (2015) takes a different approach to explaining the attractions of austerity, specifically in the context of the UK. He sees austerity as a strategy to win and hold office. Its key feature in the context of the 2010 election was that it enabled the Conservatives to blame Labour for the economic crisis, claiming that they had persistently overspent during the 2000s and were now in denial about the extent of the reversal that was required. Any attempt by Labour to rebut this argument and point to the role of the financial crisis in causing the deterioration of public finances could be portrayed as self-serving and delusional. Labour had proven itself incompetent to manage the economy; only the Conservatives had the courage to take the necessary steps to restore health and balance.

Gamble frames his analysis with the concept of 'statecraft'. This concept draws attention to the strategic choices governments make in defining their political agenda. Their central problem is to maintain their distinctive partisan identity, and thereby satisfy their core supporters, while pursuing sufficiently centrist policies to win future elections. A party that wins power and then concentrates on providing payoffs to its core voters can expect to be punished at the next election: in this sense, the UK does not have 'winner-take-all' politics, despite the lack of formal limits to the powers of the winning party in government. The statecraft of austerity worked by satisfying centrist or swing voters that the policy was competent, while also offering to the Conservative heartland the prospect of a smaller state and tax cuts.

Competence and partisanship

Gamble's account helps to explain why Labour had great difficulty in putting forward opposing arguments. They accepted much of the austerity agenda, ending up arguing over details about scale and timing. But austerity is also risky for the Conservatives, particularly because of its predictable effect in dampening growth. The claim that austerity was a responsible policy would lose its attraction if the economy went into a sustained decline. Here the opinion poll data is potentially illuminating. Ipsos MORI has regularly asked which party is best at managing the economy. Their data show that the Conservatives overtook Labour in 2008 and held their lead (sometimes fractionally) right through into 2014. There was a pronounced upturn in approval between March and October 2010, suggesting that the emergency budget was well-received (Ipsos MORI n.d.a), and there was also a very strong positive verdict for George Osborne in June 2010 (61 per cent; net outcome +32). However, this faded as economic optimism declined. The coalition's rating for economic management in October 2011 was poor: just 36 per cent said it had done a good job compared with 55 per cent assessing it as bad, a net score of −19 (Ipsos MORI n.d.b).

Similarly, using data for the period 2004–2013, Whiteley et al. (2015) assessed how each government's rating for economic management correlated with political support, measured by voting intentions. They found that there had been a strong relationship during Labour's term of office but, at the time they did their analysis, the coalition did not appear to be benefiting from the nascent improvement in the economy. Assessments of economic management were, in other words, slow to shift: while economic growth was restored in 2013, the government's net score did not scrape into positive territory (+1) until March 2014. Whiteley et al. (2015: 22) suggest that the government was not reaping political rewards because the recovery had 'not reached the wallets and purses of the average voter'. However, by 2015, the government's ratings had picked up strongly: in March 2015, the net score stood at a healthy +19 per cent (Ipsos MORI n.d.b).

Was economic growth the key to winning the 2015 election? The perspective of 'valence' politics suggests that it was. The (reasonable) assumption here is that all voters want a thriving economy, and their decision about which party to support is based on their assessment of which they deem the most competent to deliver that outcome. But, as shown above, austerity also had pronounced distributional effects, suggesting that there might be some role for a spatial analysis of voter preferences. A simple spatial model supposes that voters have different redistributive preferences related to their income. On the low-income end of the spectrum, voters favour redistribution; on the high-income end, they seek tax and expenditure cuts.

There is a reason to think that there is a right-wing, small-state bias in the UK's first-past-the-post electoral system that the Conservatives have managed (yet again) to exploit. The reasoning runs as follows. The electoral system means that two main parties dominate the political contest, one centre-left and the other centre-right. Each tries to appeal to the median voter, but faces a problem of commitment: can it be trusted to maintain a centrist policy once in office? The centre-left party in office may pander to its core constituency by adopting strongly redistributive policies that are costly to the median voter. The right-wing party may also have a bias, towards cutting back benefits and services that are not favoured by its core constituency but are valuable to the median voter. The key argument is that the costs of the right-wing bias are likely to be seen by the median voter as smaller than the costs of the left-wing bias. A right-wing bias means a smaller state and lower benefits and services, but it also means lower taxes. It means a system where you 'keep what you earn' whereas the left-wing party holds out the galling prospect of paying taxes with the proceeds going to other people (Iversen and Soskice 2006).

The logic of this analysis is not watertight. It assumes that the right-wing party does not engage in regressive redistribution, taking from the middle and giving to its wealthier core constituents. It also neglects other policies than taxing and spending, where the right-wing government may be drawn into measures that those in the middle see as costly, such as leaving the European Union. Nonetheless, it suggests that there are political gains to be had from a fiscally conservative policy that go beyond establishing a reputation for economic competence.

Locking-in austerity?

'Small state' politics and distrust of government spending may have self-reinforcing elements. As the government becomes less well-funded, the services it provides fall in quality, and more people turn to private alternatives. Haffert and Mehrtens (2015) present a study of countries that experienced severe fiscal crises in the 1980s or 1990s, imposed austerity, and gradually worked their way to positions of budget surplus and debt reduction. They show that the fiscal space thereby created was not used to revitalise public services; instead, an austere approach to expenditure was maintained, and the fruits of fiscal improvement were disbursed in tax reductions. They suggest that austerity has a number of 'lock-in' effects which mean that the size and capacity of the government is permanently reduced. Expenditure reduction becomes an obsession, pursued to the exclusion of other goals. Politicians who have invested political capital in making the case for austerity do not want to risk their reputations for responsible fiscal guardianship by changing course. Radical reforms to some public services lead to the development of alternative private provision, and political constituencies shift to support these changes.

The experience of Conservative governments between 1979 and 1997 suggests that these 'path-dependent' processes have some power, but also some limitations. Not all public spending is unpopular with voters on the right, and there is little evidence that demand for public services has fallen with private purchasing filling the space. While privatisation of funding is well underway in higher education, middle-class resistance is high in other potential areas such as care services provision. The policies advocated by the Conservatives' right-wing competitor, the United Kingdom Independence Party (UKIP), do not indicate that the ground of public service provision has shifted radically. In the 2015 election, UKIP focused on the government's failure to meet its deficit and debt reduction targets, but it also drew attention to pressure on public services, although it attributed this to immigration rather than underspending.

Towards the end of the coalition's term in office, senior Liberal Democrats sought to put some clear water between their party and the Conservatives. One of their criticisms was that the latter's embrace of austerity was 'ideological', implying that it went beyond what was necessary for sustainable public finance and that it was politically extreme (see, for instance, Alexander 2014). The discussion in this section has suggested, on the contrary, that Conservative policy was calculated for electoral advantage.

Growth, fiscal rules and fiscal monitoring

The Chancellor began his term of office in 2010 by announcing an intention to eliminate the deficit by the next election. Since then, he has had to abandon this target, setting out instead a 'fiscal mandate' that requires that the government plan for balance in the future, without necessarily ever achieving it. This section addresses two questions. First, why do governments persist in announcing fiscal targets? Do they mean that future governments will be locked in to austere policies? Second, what does austerity mean for growth? Spending cuts may have played a part in the 'double-dip' recession, soon after the coalition came into office in 2010, but does austerity ultimately create the basis for more sustainable growth?

Fiscal rules and the Office for Budget Responsibility

Soon after the election in 1997, Labour announced a 'golden rule' for fiscal policy, whereby the government committed itself to maintaining a balanced budget over the course of the business cycle. Economists and political scientists have long debated the desirability and significance of such rules, bearing in mind that they are unenforceable. Lohmann (2003) argued that such commitments are the political equivalent of getting married. It is not that anything really changes in the relationship, but making a commitment in the presence of others binds the partners by raising the costs of breaking up. Fiscal rules can impose political costs if they are not complied with. This was the experience of Labour: Alastair Darling had a torrid time explaining the 2009 budget, which projected a long slow return to balance. The golden rule was junked, and the opposition made great capital out of this, even though many economists believed that a substantial fiscal stimulus was needed to avert a depression on the scale of the 1930s.

One inference that George Osborne might have drawn is that fiscal rules are best avoided. Arguably, Labour had more reason to tie its hands with economic rules than the Conservatives. Labour was always vulnerable to the suspicion that its left wing would pull it towards an expansionary economic policy. Thus it made sense for Labour to set an inflation target and delegate the task of hitting it to the Monetary Policy Committee of the Bank of England, whereas Margaret Thatcher had resisted proposals for central bank independence as unnecessary constraints on the government's freedom to choose the most politically expedient monetary policy. The same argument would seem to apply to fiscal hand-tying.

On the other hand, it was tempting to press home criticism of Labour's economic policy by trumping the golden rule with something that looked even better. Labour had been accused of manipulating the rules by using over-optimistic growth projections. By creating the OBR in 2010, an independent body to verify and sign off growth forecasts, the new government protected itself against such criticisms. There would, the message went, be no cheating on the rules under the coalition.

Some observers see the OBR as tightening the constraints on the government. Berry (2013) has claimed that the OBR is an agent of austerity, which 'institutionalises the misleading analogy favoured by Conservative politicians between the public finances and a household budget'. But this argument can be turned on its head. Labour was accused of cheating, but its forecasts, while wrong, were not unreasonable in the light of the information available at the time. It would arguably have been better for Labour if its forecasts had been signed off by an independent body. It is beneficial to have independent verification of the government's projections and forecasts, to safeguard it against claims of bad faith. In other words, the OBR could protect the government's credibility if targets could not be reached.

This argument has been taken further by Wren-Lewis and Portes (2014). They suggest that governments have difficulty in providing sufficient stimulus in an economic downturn because of pressure to rein in the deficit. This pressure can come from public opinion – which might be excessively swayed by the 'common sense' of austerity – or it can come from the bond markets. Either way, governments need a way of avoiding immediate cuts in a downturn while setting out credible long-term plans, and fiscal institutions might provide this.

The working methods of the OBR have an inbuilt Keynesian element, in the form of cyclical adjustment. The aim is to give a 'structural' or medium-term view of the public finances that is not affected by booms and busts in the economy. In 2013–2014, an adjustment factor of 1.6 per cent of GDP was applied, which meant that the OBR took the view that, if the economy had not been in recession, the government would have received that amount in extra revenue or savings in benefit expenditure. The worse the OBR estimates the cyclical state of the economy to be, the larger the adjustment factor that is applied, so the adjusted fiscal figures look better than the raw data. At various points since its foundation, the OBR has been accused of applying adjustment factors that are too large, making the government's performance look better than it really is (O'Connor 2012). These criticisms suggest that the OBR is not a hawkish agent of austerity.

Austerity and sustainable growth

One does not have to be a raging fiscal conservative to worry about whether continuing deficits and rising levels of government debt are sustainable. However, it is clear that, if austerity reduces growth, it does not improve the sustainability of the public finances. To bring about growth while the government is imposing a fiscal contraction, the Bank of England has pursued an exceptionally expansionary monetary policy. But will this lead to sustainable growth?

In the first phase of recovery from the financial crisis, there was a tantalising possibility that the UK economy would not only recover, but also 'rebalance'. The buoyant economic conditions of the 2000s had been built on a debt-fuelled boom in household consumption. The country as a whole was a net borrower from the rest of the world, with a small but persistent current account deficit. The crisis in the financial services sector and the depreciation of the pound in 2009–2010 seemed to present an opportunity for more industrial investment and a revival of exports.

At time of writing (late 2015), this has not happened. In early 2015 the country achieved the highest current account deficit recorded since 1948, at 5.5 per cent of GDP. Adverse external conditions – particularly the prolonged recession in the euro area – are largely to blame. But there are also concerns that austerity is delaying investment in public infrastructure that is needed for industry to thrive (LSE Growth Commission 2013). In 2015, the new Conservative government reversed tax and subsidy measures to combat climate change: a reversal that appeared to be financially driven. These policy changes will not improve the sustainability of UK growth in the long term, and may also discourage investment in the short term (Harrabin 2015).

If the investment climate is adverse, then monetary policy can work in undesirable ways. In the UK, monetary stimulus is felt primarily through rising house prices, increased mortgage lending, and higher consumer expenditure sparked by optimism brought about by rising housing wealth. Despite the Conservatives' criticism in their 2010 manifesto of the old growth model built on debt, inflated housing equity and private consumption (Hay 2011: 24; 2013), it seems that the government is just as reliant on this channel for recovery as its predecessors.

Conclusion

Gamble (2015) argued convincingly that austerity was a politically astute policy, particularly in the way it assigned blame for the after-effects of the financial crisis to the previous Labour government. However, he also saw risks for the Conservatives, as they have staked a lot of political capital on reducing the deficit. This will not occur until the end of the decade: possibly not in time for the next election. This is not something that the government can do much about. If it cuts spending more sharply, it risks strangling growth. Austerity 'effort' does not necessarily produce a good fiscal outcome.

The Conservatives' 'statecraft' of austerity blamed Labour for high debt and deficits, and suggested that it was not competent to govern. Under Ed Miliband, Labour struggled to establish its credibility, insisting that its plans would also bring the deficit under control. One consequence was that the opposition did not categorically oppose austerity. This changed with the election of Jeremy Corbyn to the Labour leadership in September 2015. Labour's rejection of austerity is now unequivocal. In some ways, this was a timely change. The passage of time has made the Conservatives' insistence that Labour is to blame for the deficit less convincing. Furthermore, the second round of expenditure cuts is likely to be more politically damaging than the first, as more households are affected and valued services lost. The rising tide of opposition to cuts in tax credits illustrates this.

This chapter began with the question of why austerity in the UK has not brought more open dissent and political failure for the leading party associated with it. The primary answer is that austerity has been a tailored and targeted process. It may also be self-reinforcing. Expenditure cuts can provoke a downward spiral: voters become increasingly disillusioned with the provision of public services, and vote for a smaller and smaller state. However, there are countervailing tendencies. The UK's central-ised system of government makes it easy to attribute blame. Ministers in overstretched departments fight hard for more resources, even while they may continue to assert their support for the overall policy of austerity. In the background, low growth intensifies the pressure; economic revival could ease it. The prognosis for the next five years is uncertain, but one thing is sure: political calculation, rather than ideological commitment, will determine the Conservative government's choice of policies.

Chapter 12

The Politics of Immigration: Old and New

MARIA SOBOLEWSKA AND ROBERT FORD

Immigration has been one of the dominant issues on the British political agenda over the past decade – the numbers of newcomers coming to Britain has never been higher, nor have the numbers of voters naming the issue as one of the nation's political priorities. Anxiety about immigration was also a key driver behind the dramatic rise in support for the United Kingdom Independence Party (UKIP), the most successful new political party in a generation, and was a central issue in the referendum on British membership of the European Union (EU). Much of this reflects recent structural shifts such as the expansion of EU free movement rights to new countries in 2004, the demand for labour generated by the economic boom of the mid-2000s and the decline in the costs of cross-border travel.

Yet immigration is not a new issue in British politics. The first wave of sustained mass migration began over 60 years ago, and the changes it sparked continue to reverberate in debates over multiculturalism, discrimination and identity. The new political conflicts generated by the recent surge in immigration have interacted with, and sometimes reinforced, older divisions, the political salience of which has also been rising. The public is fundamentally divided over the impact of immigration; consecutive governments have struggled to meet public demand for immigration limits; and political parties struggle to respond to a polarised electorate whose views are changing rapidly.

The rise of immigration as a political issue

Immigration was a fairly dormant issue for most of the 1990s, but shot up the political agenda in the early 2000s, as both migrant inflows and public concern rose rapidly. The importance of immigration reached its peak in 2006, 2007 and then again in 2015 when it was cited as the most important problem facing Britain by more than 40 per cent of the public, according to the pollster Ipsos MORI. While the economy became more important after the onset of the global financial crisis in 2007, displacing immigration as the most important issue named by respondents, once the economy recovered it once again topped the agenda for voters. By June

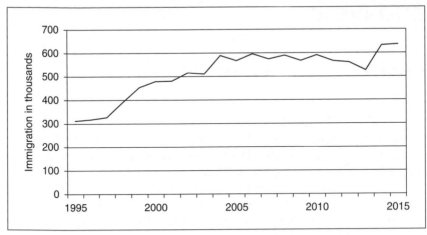

Figure 12.1   *Increases in immigration levels to Britain*

Source: ONS 2015.

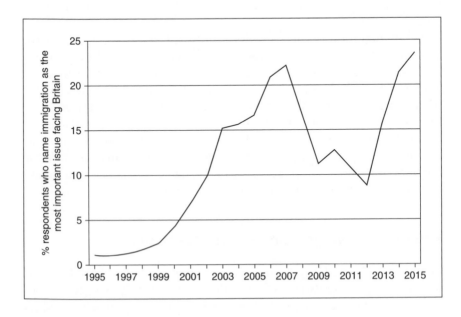

Figure 12.2   *The rising salience of immigration as a political issue*

Source: adapted from Ford, Jennings and Somerville 2015: 1396.

2015 immigration had come back as the most frequently named most important problem that Britain faced. Immigration has been in the top three most important issues as volunteered by the public for nearly 15 uninterrupted years.

One of the key factors that drove immigration up the national agenda in the first decades of the twenty-first century is numbers: immigration inflows have dramatically increased over the past two decades, and the British public have noticed and reacted to this. While Britain has, over the centuries, experienced many waves of immigration, from the Ancient Romans, Angles and Saxons, through the influx of Huguenot Protestant refugees in the 1800s to the settlement of migrants from Britain's former colonies in the Commonwealth since the 1940s, the wave of immigration experienced in the last 15 years has been very substantial. Indeed, it is arguably a larger and more rapid influx than any previously experienced. From about 200,000 immigrants arriving in England and Wales every year throughout the 1980s, numbers tripled to almost 600,000 a year between 2004 and 2015. Comparing Figures 12.1 and 12.2 shows how immigration flows and public opinion track each other closely in this period.

The new wave of immigrants who have arrived over the past 15 years is quite distinct from the earlier post-war migration inflows. These came primarily from the Commonwealth countries, whose residents were given extensive rights to settle and work in Britain by the 1948 British Nationality Act. The largest new element in the most recent influx is the result of a similar extension of work and settlement rights – this time to the central and Eastern European countries which joined the EU in 2004. Britain was by far the largest of the three existing EU members to grant immediate unrestricted settlement rights to the new members in 2004. It did so at a time of rapid economic growth. Citizens of Poland, the Czech Republic, Hungary, Slovakia and the Baltic countries responded by moving to Britain in large numbers in search of better pay and job opportunities. The Labour government of the day failed to foresee the magnitude of this inflow, and paid a significant political price: according to the pollster Ipsos MORI, public confidence in Labour's handling of immigration collapsed after 2004 and has not recovered since.

Not all immigrants are equal

However, while European immigration is now a focal point of political debate, less than half of all immigrants come from the EU, and inflows from the 2004 accession countries were not the only factor driving the sharp increase in migration rates in the past two decades. Large numbers

Box 12.1   Old and new immigration to Britain – the two waves of immigration

Modern immigration to Britain is traditionally thought to have begun after the Second World War.

First wave

Although many immigrants arriving after the Second World War were from Europe, the truly distinguishing feature of the first wave of post-war migration is that it was the first very significant influx of non-white people from the former colonies in the Caribbean (West Indies) and South Asia. While before the War there had been a steady, but slow, trickle of colonial subjects arriving at British shores, the arrival of the ship *Empire Windrush* in 1948 with 492 West Indian British subjects holding British passports was quickly identified as the symbolic start of first wave of a mass migration from the colonies. Many of these first arrivals had served in the British Army during the Second World War, and some were responding to the call for labour from the Old Country, as Britain has suffered severe post-war labour shortages. The late 1960s and 1970s saw a particular upturn in immigration from so-called African Asians: middle-class South Asian people who immigrated to Africa during colonisation and who were forced out by Uganda's and Kenya's newly independent governments. Many of the former colonies are still significant sources of immigration, with the exception of the Caribbean countries, immigration from which is now very insignificant. Due to work visa restrictions (see Box 12.2) the majority of these immigrants now come as fiancées, spouses and dependent children.

Second wave

The symbolic date for the beginning of the second wave of immigration to Britain is the 1997 general election after which the new Labour government introduced selective liberalisation of the immigration policy regime. The politically salient immigration source in this period has been the EU. In April 2003 an Accession Treaty was signed, enlarging the EU on 1 May 2004 by adding ten countries, the largest of which was Poland. This treaty offered the 'old' EU members a right to introduce transition periods before the citizens of these countries could benefit from freedom of movement within the EU. While the majority of EU members introduced transitional periods, Britain did not. As a result, an unprecedented influx of new immigrants came to Britain. The Labour government of the day has since been blamed for what many now see as a miscalculation. However, immigration from outside the EU remains the main source of immigration even after EU enlargement.

of migrants continue to arrive from Commonwealth countries such as India, Pakistan and Bangladesh that were among the main sources of the first wave of immigration (see Box 12.1), while other Commonwealth countries such as Nigeria are now among the largest new sources of migration. While much public debate has focused on 'Polish plumbers' coming to work in Britain, foreign students on British campuses have also been an important and rapidly growing source of migration in official statistics. These are important distinctions to remember, as the make-up of the immigration inflows is crucial to how immigration is perceived by the British public.

The origins of immigrants matter, because native voters have a clear hierarchy of preference between immigrants based on their ethnic and cultural distance from the majority group (Ford 2011). Most people in Britain prefer immigrants from other Anglo-Saxon countries such as the US, Canada, Australia and New Zealand origin, followed by Western Europeans such as the French or Germans. Eastern Europeans, like those from the 2004 accession countries, are on the whole perceived to be the least desirable of the white immigrants, but are nonetheless generally regarded as more desirable than most black and Asian immigrants. In fact, Asian immigrants, particularly of Muslim origin, are the most negatively perceived of all groups (Ford, Morrell and Heath 2012). The persistent ethnic hierarchy in views of immigrants has led some to argue that hostile reactions to some non-white migrant groups seem out of proportion to their size or social impact, suggesting prejudice may play a large role in driving them. Similar arguments have been extended to immigration policy, as migration restrictions have tended to impact more heavily on non-white migrants. However, the public and political controversy over 2004 EU accession immigrants has changed the nature of this debate, as race and immigration are clearly not as closely intertwined as they were in the first wave migration period of the 1950s–1970s.

The second element shaping public perceptions is the reason for migration. Immigrants come to Britain for a wide range of reasons, and these motives influence both the social and economic impact of migration and how migrants are viewed. Generally, the public are more positive about highly skilled and educated immigrants, including students, than they are about unskilled workers, family reunion migrants and asylum seekers. The public, however, misjudges the relative numbers of immigrants from each of these categories coming to Britain – overestimating the numbers of refugees and unskilled jobseekers whom they dislike most, while underestimating the relative numbers of the groups of more welcome immigrants. Figure 12.3 shows the estimates of the relative size

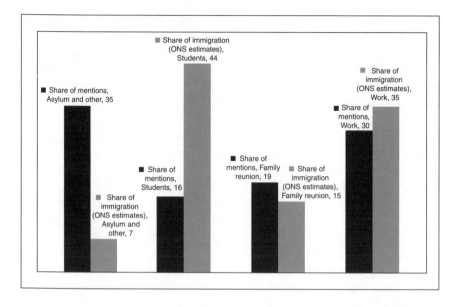

Figure 12.3　*The perception gap: perceived (black) and actual (grey) shares of migrants coming to work, study, join family and seek asylum in the UK (2011)*

Source: Office for National Statistics and Ipsos MORI/Migration Observatory survey data (2011).

of the four main migration streams to Britain – students, workers, family reunion and asylum – in official statistics and in a 2011 Migration Observatory survey asking people which groups of people they had in mind when thinking about immigrants.

As we see in Figure 12.3, the biggest motive for migration in the year the survey was conducted was education: 44 per cent of arrivals in that year were students coming to study in British colleges and universities. Asylum was the least common motive for migration – only 7 per cent of the arrivals in Britain that year were refugees. However, these two groups are reversed in the public imagination – asylum seekers loom largest, with 35 per cent of the total mentions made in the survey, while students were the least important migrants in voters' minds, with only 16 per cent of the total mentions. (Note that respondents could mention more than one group, and usually did so. Accordingly, we rebase the figures to reflect shares of all the mentions made by all respondents in the survey.) Voters' perceptions about the nature of migration to Britain are very different to the reality shown in official statistics.

Impacts of immigration: Evidence and perceptions

Public misperceptions about the mix of migrants settling in Britain have consequences for their assessments of the economic impact of migration, which tend to be negative. Of those polled by Ipsos MORI in August 2015, 38 per cent thought immigrants were good for the economy over-all, while 68 per cent in the same poll thought that immigration put too much pressure on public services. The actual impact of migration is complex and often hard to measure accurately. It depends on a wide variety of factors, including why migrants come, what they do while here, the taxes they pay, the public resources they use and how long they remain in the country.

Students are the category for which the economic contribution case is clearest: students pay high fees to universities and schools, and spend money in the economy. Most leave on completing their studies, while those who want to stay must work in well-paid jobs in order to get a visa to do so, thereby contributing skilled labour to the British economy, and taxes to the British state.

Those who migrate to Britain in order to work have very different economic impacts depending on their skill level and origin. The Migration Advisory Committee, in their report from 2012, show that highly skilled immigrants of all origins contribute positively to the living standards of the existing residents of Britain in the long term. However, low-skilled immigrants from outside of Europe have a net negative impact, equivalent to a modest loss of jobs for the existing British residents. Newer evidence on EU migration suggests a positive impact overall (Dustmann and Frattini 2013). While it is now easier for low-skilled immigrants to come from the EU accession countries, it has also become much harder for low-skilled jobseekers to migrate to Britain from outside the EU.

An even harder category to assess in terms of net economic contribution is that of migrants coming to Britain for family reunion. These immigrants could be foreign spouses coming to join British citizens, or dependants such as elderly parents or children who come and join the immigrant already settled in Britain. Migrants coming into Britain via this route are less likely to work, are generally less highly skilled and qualified, and often have relatively poor English language skills. The economic contribution of this group is therefore likely to be smaller, and their costs through use of public service and consumption of benefits will be higher. However, keeping families separated also risks imposing costs on the state, for example reducing household incomes and increasing the need for state support and childcare. In addition, families who remain separated are more likely to send money out of the country to support the relatives they are unable to bring to Britain.

Asylum seekers are the category of migrant where the economic case is often weakest: they are less likely to be fluent in English, and their potential economic contribution is curbed by the fact that they cannot work in Britain for the first year while their claims are processed. While the financial support for this group offered by the state is very limited, they are clearly net beneficiaries before they are granted legal status and allowed to be economically active. The evidence is more mixed after this point. But some do struggle to integrate into the labour market and find work commensurate with their skills (Bloch 2008). However, the case for accepting asylum claimants is not usually based on their economic contribution.

Despite these variations, most economic analysis finds little conclusive evidence that immigration depresses wage levels overall (Dustmann and Frattini 2013), although some low-wage occupations with large concentrations of migrants may experience significant downwards pressure. There is also little conclusive evidence that migration has damaged employment prospects for the British-born, with Migration Observatory research suggesting that the most recent immigrants largely compete with more established migrants, who tend to work in similar sectors. There is also fairly conclusive evidence that immigrants are, on the whole, net contributors to the state, paying more money in taxes than they take out in benefits and public services (Rowthorn 2014). Yet opinion polls repeatedly show the public think that the opposite is true. This reflects the demographic profile of migrants, who tend to be young, healthy and usually have higher rates of employment, than the native population. Most economists believe that, taken as a whole, the economic impact of migration is either neutral or modestly positive. The positive national view, however, does not mean that there aren't real negative impacts on the daily lives of native Britons in local areas with high migration rates, for example from shortages in school places (Migration Advisory Committee 2012), or rising local rents.

This disjuncture between economists' fairly sanguine assessments of the economic impacts of immigration and the public's clearly negative assessments is linked significantly to misperceptions about the motives, qualifications and origins of migrants. The public tend to overestimate the size of groups such as refugees and unskilled workers whose net economic contribution is less clear-cut, while underestimating the size of groups such as students and skilled workers where the economic case is more obviously positive (Ford, Morell and Heath 2012). The disconnect between the actual mix of migrants Britain accepts and the perceived pattern of inflows creates a problem for policymakers – one of the reasons voters want migration numbers restricted is the mistaken belief that most migrants are a burden on the economy and the public purse. Yet actually pushing down the number of arrivals recorded in migrant statistics requires restricting the arrival of groups such as students and skilled workers who make a positive economic impact, one which is recognised by voters, who are much more positive about such groups. The growing political polarisation over migration, which we consider next, only sharpens this dilemma.

The growing polarisation of the British electorate

While negative views of immigration are widespread, they are far from universal. British public opinion is divided over immigration and its effects, and such divisions have deepened as immigration has risen up the political agenda. These divisions are multiple and have very different effects on the political life of the nation. Age, education, social class and ethnicity all influence views of immigration. The old worry about it more than the young, those with few qualifications worry more than those with university degrees, the working class worry more than the middle class, and white Britons worry more than ethnic minorities. All of these divisions have deepened since the early 2000s and all show the same dynamic: concern has intensified in the groups who started out most worried, while attitudes in the less worried groups have remained stable. This has generated a large and growing divide between older, white, working-class voters with low education levels, for whom immigration has become an all-encompassing political concern, and young, ethnically diverse university graduates, who seldom worry about it at all.

Generational divisions

One of the most prominent divides in public opinion is the generational gap: younger generations are a lot more comfortable with immigration, even though they are much more likely to face direct competition from migrants, who also tend to be young. Changing attitudes about identity and diversity are one major driver of this generational divide. The British Attitudes Survey has been asking white British people how comfortable they would be having a black or Asian neighbour, boss or in-law since the 1980s. The data reveal large and consistent generational differences in attitudes. Those who have grown up since the 1970s, after the first great wave of migration began to transform Britain into a multicultural society, express much less discomfort about social contact with minorities. This generational gap is also found in national identity attachments, with younger cohorts much less likely to see birthplace or ethnicity as important markers of Britishness. This more inclusive, multicultural outlook is also reflected in views of new immigrants. Younger generations are not only generally more comfortable with contact with immigrants, but they also do not seem to discriminate on race: while older generations show a strong preference for white European and Australasian migrants over non-white migrants from Asia and the Caribbean, younger cohorts discriminate much less, though some racial bias does persist (Ford 2008).

The rapid expansion in higher education is another driver of the generation gap. On the whole, university graduates find immigration less threatening, in addition to having more liberal and tolerant attitudes towards ethnic minority groups, so the dramatic expansions in university education in the 1960s and again from the 1990s onwards have had important long-term consequences for British social values. Another explanation for the generational gap is the much higher level of contact that younger generations have with minority groups and immigrants. Generally speaking, people born in the 1950s and 1960s had much less contact with other ethnic and religious groups when they were growing up, as Britain was a more homogenous country, both ethnically and culturally. From the 1980s onwards, a larger portion of each cohort attended ethnically diverse schools and grew up in ethnically diverse neighbourhoods. It is usually argued that such contact promotes trust between the different groups and allays any fears of difference, a relationship which has been confirmed in Britain by a range of studies (Laurence 2011; 2014). The positive effects of social contact on attitudes also helps to explain the otherwise paradoxical finding that the local areas where opposition to migration is highest tend to be those which have received the fewest migrants – regular social contact with migrants in high immigration areas tends to produce more accepting attitudes. Geographical proximity can, however, cut both ways. While those who live in diverse and rapidly changing neighbourhoods tend to adopt more liberal attitudes, those who live close to, but not actually among, immigrants often emerge as one of the most anti-immigrant groups, a phenomenon known as the 'halo effect'. People who live in homogenous areas neighbouring areas of high immigrant inflow can feel threatened by the change they see in the neighbouring areas (Biggs and Knauss 2012), but do not experience the direct everyday social contact with migrants which offsets these negative reactions in the more diverse neighbourhoods themselves.

Ethnicity

A related, but often overlooked, divide in public opinion on immigration is the ethnic divide. Established immigrants are often the most likely to have to compete for jobs and housing with new immigrants, who tend to settle in diverse areas with large existing migrant populations. Established immigrant-origin minority groups may also worry that a backlash against migrants will harm their interests too. Greater opposition to new immigration from earlier migrant communities therefore seems rational. On the other hand, many immigrants may still maintain loyalties with other immigrants more generally, or from their country of origin, or may worry that restrictions will prevent their own families from joining them in Britain. Thus, one would expect a rather complex attitude towards immigration from immigrants. And complex it is. Immigrant-origin Britons are not immune from worrying about the levels of immigration and generally support restricting the numbers of new immigrants to some extent. The 2011 British Social Attitudes (Ford, Morrell and Heath 2012) survey shows that 60 per cent of ethnic minorities polled agreed that immigration should be reduced and an Ipsos MORI sample of immigrants of all ethnicities, who arrived before 1970, shows an even starker picture, with 70 per cent of them calling for immigration restrictions. Ethnic minorities, however, tend to hold less intense preferences – they tend to say migration should be reduced 'a little' rather than 'a lot', and are much less likely than white respondents to name migration as one of the most important issues facing the nation.

Established immigrants and ethnic minorities are also much less likely to see the economic and social impact of immigration as negative: while only 26 per cent of white people said immigration has been good for British economy and 31 for British culture, 55 and 56 per cent of ethnic minority Britons thought this, respectively. This big difference in views of the impact of migration has important political implications which we will consider later (see also Heath et al. 2013).

Cross-pressured elites and the 'policy gap'

Given the widespread consensus around limiting the inflow of immigrants, it is perhaps surprising that the political class has not responded to intense public anxiety with stronger restrictions on inflows, despite having promised to do so many times. This is not unusual: in most countries, immigration policy tends to be less restrictive than the public opinion would like it to be. This well documented 'policy gap' has been observed in the US and many European countries (Hampshire 2013). The explanations offered for this phenomenon usually centre around two issues: the country's economic interests and elite preferences. While immigration may be unpopular, it is usually beneficial for the economy, businesses and employers, who have a lot of influence on governments' policies and use this influence to press for higher immigration than the general public would otherwise like to see. The elites who run political parties and governments also tend to be more liberal on this issue than the general public. However, there is a third possibility: that the policy gap is not so much between restrictive public opinion and liberal policy, but between policy reforms which attempt to be restrictive and the outcomes of such reforms, which fail to deliver the desired reduction in numbers. The reason for this failure stems particularly from Britain's international obligations, which place growing constraints on how restrictive immigration policy can be.

The first two explanations for a 'policy gap' provide a plausible account of liberal immigration policy during the first immigration wave, from 1948 to 1983 (Hansen 2002). The 1948 British Nationality Act set up a remarkably expansive definition of British citizenship, which granted rights to migrate and settle to citizens of territories that were currently or formerly part of the British Empire, including the Indian subcontinent, much of Africa and a large number of Caribbean islands. Public opposition to migration from these regions became clear almost as soon as significant inflows began, yet Britain's political elites resisted demands to restrict this migration or reform the citizenship laws. This reflected both liberal values and pragmatic politics. Britain's political elites, many of whom had served in the Second World War, regarded public opposition to black and Asian migration as reflecting racial prejudices which they did not want to legitimise through political action. Each step towards restricting migration was heavily criticised as a victory for racism, and when Conservative MP Enoch Powell began to campaign for drastic immigration restriction, Labour politician Tony Benn drew an explicit comparison with the German Nazi regime: 'The flag of radicalism which has been hoisted in [Powell's seat of] Wolverhampton is beginning to look like the one that fluttered 25 years ago over Dachau and Belsen' (Schofield 2013: 284).

Elite resistance to restriction was not just, however, a matter of values. It also reflected practical political judgement: Britain was suffering from labour shortages in the 1950s and 1960s and so had great need for migrant workers – Enoch Powell himself had lobbied for the recruitment of Caribbean migrant nurses to the NHS when he was Health Minister in the Macmillan government. Many leading politicians in both parties also regarded the Commonwealth as Britain's main future source of post-imperial political and economic influence (Britain was at the time outside the then EEC, which it finally joined in 1973 after two previous applications were vetoed by French President Charles De Gaulle). Restricting Commonwealth citizenship rights would alienate Britain's former colonies, and jeopardise this project. As a result of this elite resistance, reform proceeded slowly despite rising public pressure, with a series of incremental steps towards restriction starting in 1962, and finally culminating in comprehensive reform to abrogate Commonwealth citizens' rights by the Thatcher government in 1981, 33 years after the original British Nationality Act, and 8 years after Britain joined the EEC (see Box 12.2).

Policy responses to the second wave of immigration however, suggest a different explanation for a 'policy gap', with international obligations playing a larger role. Once again, however, the responses are a product of both value commitments and political pragmatism. The values include a normative commitment to EU membership (and the obligations which come with it) and a commitment to oppose racism and xenophobia (and hence to any policy predicated upon such assumptions). Yet economics continues to play a role, too: there is a widespread recognition among policymakers (and indeed many voters) that many forms of migration, particularly of university students and highly skilled professionals, bring significant economic benefits and restricting them would do more harm than good.

Ultimately, however, the biggest factor behind the persistence of open immigration policy in the current era was the widely shared, although not unanimous, belief that the political costs and risks of renegotiating or unilaterally reneging on Britain's international commitments are too great. As a result, despite large and persistent increases in EU immigration since 2004, governments have focused restrictive policy responses on non-EU immigration. As in the earlier wave of migration, persistent and intensifying public concern has produced a steady stream of restrictive reforms, despite the countervailing forces acting on elites (Ford, Jennings and Somerville 2015).

The Labour government of 1997–2010 passed three major pieces of legislation reforming the asylum system in an effort to respond to public anxiety about rising inflows and perceived abuses. They acted to restrict family reunion migration, twice raising the minimum age for marriage and introducing additional language requirements and citizenship tests for family migrants. After introducing liberal reforms on labour migration in the late 1990s, Labour reversed course after 2004 following the sharp rise in EU migration, consolidating a complex economic migration system (22 categories and 80 entry routes) into a five-tier points-based system, phased in between 2008 and 2010. The new system provided clearer skill-based rules for entry from outside the EU and facilitated restriction of numbers, which could now be done through cutting quotas in individual tiers or eliminating tiers entirely.

The subsequent Conservative–Liberal Democrat coalition government of 2010–2015 continued these restrictive reforms. It began by toughening existing rules governing all the main non-EU migration streams – study,

---

Box 12.2   A brief history of British immigration policy

Until 1905 there were no legal instruments to limit immigration into Britain. In 1905 the first act limiting right to entry was passed in response to the influx of Jews escaping pogroms in Eastern Europe and Russia. Key British and European legislation since World War 2 include:

1948 British Nationality Act: introduced the concept of 'Citizenship of the UK and Colonies' for all people born or naturalised in either the UK or its colonies. This unusually broad conception of citizenship extended full right to enter (called Right of Abode in law), reside and work in the UK to all those who were citizens of current or former colonies who were members of the Commonwealth of Nations (similar rights were extended to Republic of Ireland citizens in the Ireland Act 1949). Nonetheless, immigration from these countries was often subsequently discouraged using diplomatic and bureaucratic strategies (Hansen 2002; Hatton and Price 2005).

1962 Commonwealth Immigration Act: limited the right to entry of Commonwealth citizens to three categories of labour immigrants, who needed to obtain work vouchers, and their dependants.

1968 Commonwealth Immigration Act and 1971 Immigration Act: further restricted rights to enter and settle in Britain to those Commonwealth citizens who could prove 'patrial' links to Britain – a parent or grandparent born in Britain was decisive in retaining unrestricted right of entry to Britain. Commonwealth citizens who could not prove such ancestral links to Britain – the vast majority of whom were non-white Commonwealth citizens in former colonies – lost their rights to settle in Britain.

1972 European Communities Act: British accession to the European Economic Community in 1993 meant that EEC workers' rights to freely

→

---

family reunion and work. Rules for student visas, which Labour had left alone, were severely tightened in March 2011, which particularly hit applications to further education colleges or English language schools, where applicant numbers fell by over 80 per cent from 2011 to 2015. The coalition also introduced strict new rules on family reunion migration in 2012, introducing an income requirement of £18,600 a year for the British sponsor of the reunion. To restrict labour migration, the government introduced numerical limits on some tiers, increasing the qualifications required in others, and closing some off altogether. However,

→

work in other member states, defined in the 1957 Treaty of Rome, were thereby extended to Britain.

1981 British Nationality Act: abolished the concept of 'Commonwealth and UK citizenship' (though two residual categories relating to Commonwealth citizens were retained). It also replaced the *jus soli* principle – which gave anyone born in the UK citizenship – with a *jus sanguinis* principle, which limited citizenship to British-born children of citizens and permanent residents.

1992 Treaty of Maastricht (EU): further expanded the rights of freedom of movement within the EU from an economic right reserved to workers to a right for all citizens.

1999 Immigration and Asylum Act: was the first restrictive immigration legislation passed by a Labour government.

2002 Nationality, Immigration and Asylum Act: introduced English language and citizenship tests as requirements for naturalisation as a British citizen.

2003 Treaty of Accession (EU): Britain chose not to impose transitional restrictions on freedom of movement for the citizens of the ten new EU members to join in 2004 (see Box 12.1). Britain, however, exercised the right provided for by this treaty by introducing restrictions in 2007 for Bulgaria and Romania (expired in 2014) and in 2013 for Croatia (due to expire in 2018).

2006 Immigration, Asylum and Nationality Act: introduced the five-tier points system for visas issued to migrants outside the EU that is in operation to this day with minor amendments. For more discussion of restrictive immigration policies since then see pages 231–235 in the main text.

while these changes produced some reduction in migration from outside the EU in the early years of the coalition, the reduction was not lasting and, in any event, was more than offset by sharp rises in EU immigration from 2012 onwards (Office for National Statistics 2015). Immigration was high during the Labour and coalition governments not due to liberal attitudes on the issue, but because both governments' repeated efforts to restrict it failed due to an inability to control some of the largest migration inflows without triggering major disputes with international partners – fights neither government were prepared to start.

Immigration policy: Made in Brussels?

Freedom of movement is one of the principal building blocks of the European project, enshrined in the core treaties of Rome (1957) and Maastricht (1992). It provides EU citizens with full rights to settle and work in other EU member nations; although, since 2004, existing members have been able to impose 'transitional restrictions' on migration from new members, which can be active for up to seven years. Moreover, to discriminate between EU citizens on the basis of nationality is expressly forbidden. Thus, preferential treatment for British jobseekers over Italian or German applicants, or charging different fees to British students over Dutch or Polish students, is illegal. This also applies to welfare provision: any EU citizen who can show that they are normally resident in Britain is eligible for the same assistance as a British citizen. This is, of course, entirely reciprocal – a British immigrant to Spain or France will receive the same treatment as citizens of those countries (although not all EU countries have free healthcare for everyone, for example). These fundamental treaty rules made it very difficult for Britain meaningfully to restrict migration from the EU without prompting a major legal and political conflict with Brussels. Even in the face of Britain's exit, it is unclear how quickly EU regulations and obligations in this area can be changed, given we are facing a lengthy negotiation about the timing and details of withdrawal.

Britain also has other international obligations. The European Convention of Human Rights (ECHR) has in the past acted against some efforts to limit immigration, particularly after the passage of the Human Rights Act 1998, which incorporated all the ECHR rights into British law. Even before this, however, the Convention was used to apply pressure on Britain: in 1985 a primary purpose rule, which had been designed to ascertain that fiancés and spouses entering the UK do not plan to or did not get married primarily for the purpose of immigration into Britain, was challenged in the European Court of Human Rights for gender discrimination as it focused on male applicants more than female applicants, and it was ruled discriminatory. Attempts to limit asylum or family reunification rights regularly bring about legal challenges in this court, which has repeatedly ruled against them.

The main practical consequence of both the EU and the ECHR on immigration policy has been external constraint: both greatly limited the government's ability to control migration. Changes to freedom of movement or the protection of human rights were nearly impossible while Britain remained a member of the EU, as a retreat from free movement rights would require EU treaty change agreed by all member states – including many which regard the current system as very beneficial. Given the persistence of public concern about immigration, and the inability of politicians to respond fully to this under EU rules, it is no surprise that pressure grew for a referendum on Britain's continued EU membership from the mid-2000s onwards, resulting in the vote on 23 June 2016 in which a majority voted to leave the EU. Yet it is far from clear that even the vote to leave the EU will deliver the immigration changes anxious voters demand, as the EU insists on free movement rules applying to major non-members states such as Norway and Switzerland as a condition for full access to the EU's 'single market'. Withdrawing from this would be economically costly and very disruptive for Britain.

Political party best on immigration

The modern constraints on policy pose a dilemma for the political parties who must balance the public desire for reduced levels of immigration against the limits of their abilities to respond. All the main political parties advocated more or less restrictive policies including, unusually, the Liberal Democrats in their 2015 general election manifestos. The commitments varied significantly between the parties, however: the Liberal Democrats and Labour emphasised a 'firm but fair' approach, while in 2010 the Conservatives made a commitment to bring down immigration numbers 'from the hundreds of thousands to the tens of thousands' – one they later came to regret. Yet there is little evidence that these commitments did much to improve the public's assessment of any of the mainstream parties on the issue.

Since 2005 the pollster Ipsos MORI has asked its respondents which party they think has the best policies on asylum and immigration. This data shows us that the Labour government's efforts to reassure voters with steadily tougher policies on immigration did not have the desired effect. The percentage of people naming Labour as best on immigration was virtually unchanged at around 18 per cent from 2005 to 2010; it did not improve after Labour went into opposition. While the majority of voters had stable opinions about Labour's ability to tackle immigration, they began with higher hopes for the incoming Conservative-led government. In 2005 the Conservatives were widely thought to be the best party on this issue, and as such they 'owned' it. However, despite a consistently hard-line approach in rhetoric and, as we have seen, a large set of restrictive policy reforms, the public were unimpressed by the failure to reduce immigrant numbers and turned against the party in office. In 2005, 36 per cent of Britons believed the Conservatives had the best policies on immigration, but by 2015 this has fallen by more than half to just 17 per cent (Ipsos MORI 2015b). Persistent high migration levels have exacted a big political price: both main parties of government have now lost the faith of the electorate on the issue. The main beneficiary from this loss of faith in the Conservatives is the new challenger on the right: UKIP. Even though we have no data from 2005 to 2012, the share naming them as the best party on immigration has risen sharply from 11 per cent in 2013 to 20 per cent in 2015, overtaking the Conservatives to become the most widely named best party on the issue, and coinciding with a period where the party's overall poll ratings also rose sharply. So, what gives UKIP a unique advantage on this issue?

An anti-immigrant and anti-politics party

Before UKIP's rise, the voters who felt ill at ease with the new, cosmopolitan and immigrant-friendly Britain had limited political options. Some of them allied with the Conservative Party, which was the most openly anti-immigration out of the three established parties, and had a long established reputation as being 'tough' on immigration, a legacy of Enoch Powell and Margaret Thatcher. The Conservatives have long been happy to court voters anxious about immigration, as evidenced in the 2005 general election campaign, when they fielded billboards with the (somewhat defensive) slogan, 'It is not racist to impose limits on immigration'. However, as we will discuss in more detail below, by the 2010 election the Conservatives became worried that their anti-immigrant reputation could hurt them with more liberal voters and ethnic minorities who deemed them a 'nasty' party. Thus, they started to tone down their rhetoric on the topic, although they did pledge to dramatically reduce net migration into Britain. As we have seen, this pledge came back to haunt them as their inability to deliver on the promise in government deeply damaged their credibility as the party best able to restrict immigration after 2010. The other option for anti-immigration voters in the mid-2000s was the far-right British National Party (BNP), whose support surged between 2005 and 2010 (Ford and Goodwin 2010), but whose appeal was limited by a legacy of fascism and open racism, the often violently intolerant behaviour of its activists, and a weak and unstable party organisation. The party collapsed after the 2010 election and has not recovered since. Between 2010 and the most recent election, UKIP have emerged as a new option for voters worried about immigration – one willing to voice an uncompromising opposition to immigration, but not hindered by a fascist or racist legacy. UKIP provide a political outlet for voters opposed to immigration and disappointed by the Conservatives' failure to control it.

How did UKIP come to be seen as a politically acceptable option for anti-immigration voters, mobilising them in record numbers yet largely (although not completely) escaping the accusations of racism and bigotry that hampered the BNP? The answer lies with the party's history, and the reputational legacy of that history. UKIP began life in 1993 as a single-issue party focused on campaigning for Britain's withdrawal from the EU. UKIP's defining issue for over a decade from its inception was therefore not immigration, but leaving the EU. However, as the two issues became fused in the public mind following the post 2004 surge in EU migration, UKIP was presented with a new opportunity. Since this time, the party has been able to run stridently anti-immigration campaigns, while also focusing these on its core issue of Britain's EU membership, providing it with a credible defence from the charge that it is mobilising intolerance. This does not mean that such accusations were lacking. Intolerant outbursts by UKIP members or activists have been regularly reported in the press, and senior political figures both outside and within UKIP have criticised the prevalence of prejudice and intolerance within the party. Yet, when UKIP gained momentum after the 2012 local elections it was more easily accepted as a mainstream political voice than the BNP had ever been. While the BNP's one high-profile mainstream media appearance, when party leader Nick Griffin appeared on the BBC's *Question Time* in 2009, triggered high-profile public protests, UKIP leader Nigel Farage has been a regular (and largely uncontroversial) guest on this and many other politics programmes and also took part in the televised party leaders' debates during to the 2015 general election campaign.

The issue of reputation aside, UKIP has had a mixed electoral record. Research by Ford and Goodwin (2014) has shown that the typical UKIP voter is an older, white, working-class man with few educational qualifications. UKIP's support is strongest among voters who have lost faith in traditional politics, intensely dislike the EU and regard immigration as having a very negative effect on Britain. In their book, Ford and Goodwin call such voters the 'left behind': those who did not benefit from UK's growing globalised economy with its cosmopolitan workforce, and who resent the fast-changing world around them. They are more sensitive to growing immigration, but are also less likely to trust the existing political elites to do anything about it. A populist party like UKIP has a unique appeal for these disaffected voters as it is by definition an anti-establishment party. Given UKIP's elite and Eurosceptic origins, however, this new portrait of its voters went against the previously adopted assumption that UKIP supporters were mainly disaffected Conservative Eurosceptics. It suggested the party could equally pose problems to Labour by poaching working-class Labour voters anxious about immigration. That UKIP secured nearly 13 per cent in the 2015 general election, the largest vote by a new party for a generation, is testament to the political power of unresolved immigration concerns. However, its haul of nearly 4 million votes delivered only one Westminster seat, suggesting an inability to broaden its appeal enough to win elections under Britain's first-past-the-post system.

The legacy of the first wave of immigration and the BME vote

While UKIP poses a new source of competition for older, white, working-class voters, Labour and the Conservatives also must worry about how to win or hold support from the rapidly growing and diversifying immigrant origin and ethnic minority electorate. As we have seen, they have much more positive views of immigration. Britain is in a unique situation in that a large share of its immigrant population – those from Commonwealth countries and Ireland – are eligible to vote in Parliamentary elections from the moment they settle in Britain, without having to take up British citizenship to do so. This is one of the legacies of the 1948 British Nationality Act which has survived all subsequent reforms.

At the 2010 election, black and Asian ethnic minority voters from Britain's largest Commonwealth migrant communities constituted 8 per cent of the electorate (Heath et al. 2013). These voters have historically been treated as a distinct group in the electorate, the 'black and minority ethnic' (BME) vote. The rapid rise of this BME electorate is set to continue, due to both continued migration and natural population growth. Significant numbers of family-reunion migrants continue to arrive from South Asia, while large numbers of new primary migrants from the Commonwealth also arrive to work and study in Britain each year – with African countries such as Nigeria and Ghana a particularly fast-growing source. The settled BME population also tends to be younger on average than the white British, and to have somewhat larger families. The cumulative effect of all these factors is very rapid population growth: between the 2001 and 2011 censuses, the size of the BME population nearly doubled. Although many BME groups are less likely than the white British to register to vote, they do turn out to vote at high rates once registered. The ethnic minority electorate also tends to cluster geographically, giving them even higher political influence in the constituencies where their populations are concentrated.

Traditionally, the vast majority of the ethnic minority electorate has been loyal to Labour, a loyalty which repeated Conservative efforts have failed to erode. This has been a source of mounting concern for the Conservatives, with many in the party recognising that continued hostility from such a rapidly growing segment of the electorate represents a serious and growing electoral problem. Senior Conservative and major party donor Lord Michael Ashcroft commissioned several studies investigating the drivers of minority opposition to the Conservatives and concluded that the historical reputation of the Conservatives as intolerant towards migrant minorities continues to hurt the party with BME. In recent years, right-wing think tanks such as Bright Blue and Policy Exchange have added further research, commissioning reports on how the party can boost its appeal with rapidly growing BME communities. The US Republicans constitute a cautionary tale of what happens to right-wing parties who fail to build an appeal to minorities in a diversifying society: Mitt Romney won the support of 59 per cent of white voters in 2012, more than any Republican since George H. W. Bush's 1988 victory (Roper Center 2012), yet still lost to Barack Obama. Since the 1980s, Republican support among African Americans is around 10 per cent, and although they had high hopes for the supposedly more conservative and fast-growing Latino electorate with Ronald Reagan in 1980 winning 37 per cent of their voters and George W. Bush winning a record 44 per cent in 2004, they on average win around 30 per cent of that vote (Roper Center 2012).

Both the Republicans and the Conservatives face a paradox – they need to build their appeal to minorities, yet at the same time their firmest support comes from numerically declining sections of the white electorate who find the rapid cultural change associated with immigration and ethnic diversity threatening. As we saw earlier, generational change in attitudes means that the newer generations are more liberal, cosmopolitan and open to immigration. In the US this problem is described as 'death by demographics': the core support for the Republican party is diminishing purely on the basis of wider demographic changes in society. In the long term, to avoid this 'death' the Conservative Party – just like the Republicans in the US – needs to attract more support both from ethnic minorities and the growing sections of the white electorate with more liberal views on race and immigration issues.

The Conservative Party has made a number of efforts to attract the ethnic minority vote, organising campaign events at mosques and temples and making appeals on policy areas where they perceived a disconnect between ethnic minorities and Labour. Their initial attempts were based around the idea that while the Labour Party focused on a person's race, the Conservatives looked at an individual in their own right, and not through the lens of their origin. The best examples of this were the 1983 Conservative election leaflets bearing the title 'Labour say he's black. Tories say he's British.' This colour-blind approach proved unpopular, however, as ethnic minorities experienced multiple disadvantages and everyday racism, which the Tory campaigns did not address. BME voters were more impressed by Labour's approach, which recognised such discrimination as a problem, and passed legislation to combat it. The second attempt to win the ethnic minority vote, in the 1990s, therefore centred less on colour-blind meritocracy and more on the ideological similarities between the Conservatives and some immigrant-origin communities, particularly South Asians, whom the party saw as natural small 'c' conservatives – entrepreneurial, often self-employed and less supportive of rises in taxation that the usual Labour voter. While this perception has (or, at least, had at the time) a grain of truth to it, the social conservatism found among South Asian voters seldom determined (even then) their vote choices, and the Conservatives' more recent embrace of liberal policies on issues such as gay marriage has in any event weakened this source of appeal.

The Conservatives under the leadership of David Cameron were more ambitious in their efforts to win minority voters, focusing on changing the image of their party with minority voters rather than looking for new audiences for their traditional messages. They sought in particular to increase the number of minority MPs, with a good deal of success: numbers rose from just two in the 2005–2010 Parliament to 11 after the 2010 elections and 18 after 2015. The party took a further step forward in 2015, when David Cameron embraced the issue of racial discrimination, one the party has in the past avoided, by pledging to tackle it in the coming Parliament. However, despite regular Conservative appeals to British Indians over two decades, in 2010 a majority of 54 per cent of them backed Labour in 2010 (compared to under 30 per cent of whites), with less than half of this number, 25 per cent, supporting the Conservatives. Figures for Conservative support among other South Asians and non-Asian minorities were even lower (Heath et al. 2013). Although definitive numbers from 2015 do not exist, available estimates suggest that Conservative gains among South Asians were again very modest (Ford et al. 2015).

A diversity divide in British politics and a 'Brexit'

Given high migration inflows, and limited options for reducing them, immigration is likely to remain high on the political agenda, with important consequences for politics. Growing ethnic polarisation, internal party disputes and declining public trust in a political system which has failed to deliver the reductions in migration they demand make this a toxic issue for most mainstream parties. A swift resolution to these problems is hard to see, as all mainstream political parties are caged in by the political and legal legacies of past choices.

The core immigration dilemma for the mainstream political parties is this: appearing tough on immigration has short-term appeal, particularly given rising competition from UKIP, but does long-term harm, alienating liberal and minority voters and eroding the trust of 'left behind' voters when electoral promises are not kept. UKIP's success in taking votes from all mainstream parties in the 2015 general election highlights the costs of inaction. However, any action on immigration which would be credible to such voters would be either difficult to deliver or harm prospects with liberal graduates and minorities. Winning back the anti-immigrant working-class vote from UKIP and appealing to the more liberal BME vote and the educated, cosmopolitan middle class are both politically essential for a stable majority, but are more or less mutually exclusive strategies. This is a danger particularly for the Labour Party, which has traditionally relied on a coalition of voters from the working class and the liberal elites. As Labour's appeal to these very different groups of voters may become an impossible balancing act, the issue of immigration may take a larger toll on this party's future.

Finally, given that solving the immigration question to the satisfaction of the large proportion of voters has now resulted in withdrawal from the EU, the question of Britain's place in Europe post-Brexit will most likely dominate the political agenda in the short-to-medium term. Given the difficult negotiations to come over the ways in which withdrawal can be finalised, and Britain's need to remain part of the single European market, it remains to be seen how much control Britain will really gain over their immigration rules, and how quickly. Will the momentum behind UKIP solidify to make them one of the main political players for years to come, or will they be victims of their own success? How will the parties on the losing side of the referendum, such as Labour, respond to the result? Given the mood of the last few weeks of the campaign further polarisation of the electorate is the most likely outcome as we face prolonged uncertainty about the practicalities and consequences of Brexit.

Chapter 13

The United Kingdom after the Scottish Referendum

CHARLIE JEFFERY

The territorial constitution of the UK has been radically reshaped since the late 1990s and has yet to find a settled equilibrium. The biggest challenge to that equilibrium so far was the referendum on Scottish independence held in September 2014. Although in the end the result was clear, with 55 per cent of Scots opting to remain in the UK versus 45 per cent voting for independence, the debate prompted by the referendum was long, intense and divisive, and the outcome was for a time quite uncertain. The question – 'Should Scotland be an independent country' – drew a stark dividing line through complex and nuanced issues. It pitted the UK and Scottish governments, pro- and anti-independence campaigns and, often, friends and families against one another. In doing so it prompted perhaps the most comprehensive popular engagement with a political question the UK has ever seen. Ordinary Scots took political participation to a new level amid formal campaign events on either side of the debate, in countless community-level meetings and ultimately in a record electoral turnout in Scotland of over 85 per cent. For many the intensity of the debate energised a political commitment which has extended beyond the referendum and shifted the terrain of Scottish politics, invigorating the Scottish National Party (SNP), the party that pressed for but lost the referendum. It also severely undermined the Labour Party which had dominated Scottish politics for most of the period since the Second World War and had been the biggest player in the victorious anti-independence campaign. The SNP followed up by winning 56 out of 59 Scottish seats in the 2015 UK election (with Labour falling from 41 seats to just one), and then consolidating its grip on the Scottish Parliament with a third victory in a row in the 2016 Scottish election. The reinforcement of the SNP's position as the dominant party in Scottish politics since 2014 means that the constitutional question remains an open one. The powers of the Scottish Parliament are now again under review and set to be boosted significantly. And the debate about a second independence referendum has never been far from the surface – and erupted into plain view following a UK-wide Brexit decision opposed by a majority of Scots in the 2016 EU membership referendum.

This chapter provides an analysis of the 2014 Scottish referendum and the aftermath which has redefined Scottish politics. It uses the analogy of a chain reaction in which one event of constitutional significance catalyses the next and in due course a sequence of successor events. Yet it is not just Scotland that lacks constitutional equilibrium. Wales is now debating the features of what is likely to become the fifth variant of Welsh devolution since the National Assembly for Wales was founded in 1999. And 2015 saw England gain a form of institutional recognition as a distinct political unit for the first time in centuries with the introduction of English Votes for English Laws (EVEL) in the House of Commons. Northern Ireland has nudged on more slowly, constrained by a history of conflict now institutionalised in an unwieldy form of power-sharing, but it too saw an extension of its powers in 2015. So the UK is now host to a set of distinct, evolving and increasingly divergent internal political arenas.

The chapter explores how and why this wider process of divergence has unfolded. Some of the explanation lies in the Scottish debate. The effects of the constitutional chain reaction there spilt over into England, giving life to what had been a moribund debate about EVEL. But more generally, and standing back from the drama of the Scottish referendum, it is clear that the UK's territorial constitution has been evolving in an ad hoc and uncontrolled way for at least the last two decades. In other words, there has been a longer-term, slower-burning chain reaction, both preceding and then running alongside the events prompted by the Scottish referendum. The chapter argues that this seemingly open-ended process of change has much to do with the approach – and the weaknesses – of the central government in Whitehall and Westminster in managing the UK's different territorial challenges. It finishes by exploring where this mix of territorial divergence and a weak centre might lead the UK, considering the additional impetus for change given by the EU referendum outcome in June 2016.

The Scottish referendum debate

The Scottish independence referendum was a direct consequence of the SNP winning an absolute majority in the May 2011 Scottish Parliament election. The Scottish government under first minister Alex Salmond quickly claimed a mandate to hold a referendum. But it just as quickly became bogged down in a debate about whether it could legally do so under its own authority given that constitutional matters remain a prerogative of the UK Parliament. In the end, in October 2012, and following protracted negotiations, the UK and the Scottish governments agreed a framework under which a referendum could be held beyond legal challenge, through authorisation under UK legislation. The UK government insisted on only one major condition: that there was a straightforward yes/no question. This was to head off the idea mooted by Salmond of having a middle option between status quo and independence, often known as 'devo-max', on the ballot sheet. All the other key issues – the precise wording of the question, the timing of the referendum, the franchise (which extended the vote for the first time in UK politics to 16- and 17-year-olds) and rules on campaign funding – were left to the Scottish government. Both governments committed to work together constructively in light of the outcome, whichever way it went. Some were surprised that the UK government was so obliging given that the outcome could have been a loss of its own territory. But the calculation was clear enough: if the UK government had frustrated what was a clear mandate for a referendum, it could well have stoked further passion and support in favour of independence and the SNP. It was also confident it would win, buoyed by Scottish opinion polls showing 60 per cent-plus support for Scotland remaining within the UK.

The two governments then became major players on each side of the debate. The Scottish government published a mammoth 649-page White Paper in November 2013, ten months ahead of the referendum which was scheduled for 18 September 2014. The White Paper combined the government's case for independence with a policy prospectus on what it would do with the enhanced powers of independence (Scottish Government, 2013). The UK government responded with, in total, 14 substantial papers in its Scotland Analysis series between February 2013 and May 2014, each focused on a key theme in the debate and each at least the size of a short book. The most prominent was the paper of February 2014 which ruled out a sterling currency union between an independent Scotland and the rest of the UK, as discussed further below (HM Government, 2014) Separate from, but coordinated with, the two governments were two lead campaigns: Yes Scotland in favour of independence, and Better Together in favour of Scotland remaining in the UK. Yes Scotland was centred on the organisational and financial strength of the SNP, but acted as an umbrella for other pro-independence parties (the Scottish Greens and Scottish Socialist Party) and a range of non-party campaign groupings. A number of these – the Radical Independence Campaign, the National Collective (a grouping of artists and creatives) and Women for Independence – played a prominent role, giving the wider Yes side a clear left-leaning tone. Better Together likewise drew together the unionist parties – Labour, the Conservatives and the Liberal Democrats – and other groups.

The governments and the campaigns set out their stalls on an electoral terrain that was a little more nuanced than the headline polls suggested. These put No ahead at around 60:40 per cent in late 2013, a pattern that appeared to have moved little since the SNP's 2011 victory. But subtler survey research showed a different picture. The Scottish Social Attitudes survey has for some years used a question which sets out a spectrum of constitutional possibilities for Scotland. These range from the Scottish Parliament making 'all decisions for Scotland' – implying independence – to the UK government making all decisions for Scotland, implying a return to the pre-devolution situation, with two options in-between: the Parliament making all decisions except on defence and foreign affairs, an approximation to what has become known as 'devo-max' and the Scottish Parliament making all decisions except on taxes, benefits, defence and foreign affairs, an approximation to the status quo at the time of the referendum.

Table 13.1 reports survey findings on these options for 2013 and 2014. It shows minimal support for turning the clock back to before devolution, but also, at best, 25 per cent support for the status quo. Support for 'all decisions' being made in Scotland rose significantly from 2013 to 2014, but around 30 per cent of Scots continued to favour a 'devo-max'

Table 13.1   *Constitutional preferences in Scotland 2013 and 2014*

	2013 %	2014 %
The Scottish Parliament should make all decisions for Scotland	31	41
The UK government should make decisions about defence and foreign affairs; the Scottish Parliament should decide everything else	32	29
The UK government should make decisions about taxes, benefits, defence and foreign affairs; the Scottish Parliament should decide everything else	25	22
The UK government should make all decisions for Scotland	8	6
Don't know/refused	4	3

Source: Eichhorn and Paterson 2014: 4.

option that extended beyond the status quo but left Scotland within the UK. The median voter in the referendum – the individual whose vote is needed to achieve a majority – was in the devo-max category. This suggested an incentive for the two sides in the referendum debate to appeal to a median voter situated beyond the status quo but not in favour of full independence. Using the 2014 figures as a guide, the Yes side needed to convince a third of devo-max supporters to achieve a majority for independence, and the No side needed to ensure its offer appealed to the great majority of devo-max supporters – who wanted more, but were not convinced by independence.

Table 13.2 summarises the messages the two sides in the debate sought to project to voters. It shows how the Yes side – the Scottish government and Yes Scotland – portrayed both its vision of independence ('what yes meant') and its criticism of the status quo ('what no meant'). It shows the same for the No side: its interpretation of independence and the problems

Table 13.2   *Positions of the two sides in the referendum debate*

	What Yes Meant	*What No Meant*
Scottish government/Yes Scotland	We get the governments we vote for Different values: social justice, public services, foreign affairs Tailored economic policy, so Scotland better off Continuing partnership with the rest of the UK, including currency	Governed by Conservatives from Westminster Flawed values: bedroom tax, food banks, NHS privatisation, nuclear weapons London's economic interests above all else No new powers, cuts in Scottish funding
UK government/ Better Together	Independence risky – and Yes side understating the risk Scotland would be worse off No shared currency and sceptical about other continuing partnership Loss of international influence	It ain't broke … Celebrating shared heritage Best of both worlds – strong devolution in a strong UK Better to share risks in a bigger pool More powers coming Scotland's way, funding guaranteed

it saw with it; and the reasons it advocated a No vote. The Scottish government's independence White Paper set out an optimistic vision of independence. Independence would bring greater democratic accountability (which is Scottish code for not being governed from Westminster by a Conservative Party lacking support in Scotland). It would also bring the opportunity to pursue different values in domestic and foreign affairs and to put Scotland's economic interests first, rather than them being subordinated to those of London.

Also striking was the White Paper's vision of an independent Scotland's relationship with the rest of the UK. Across a wide range of fields, from the economic fundamentals of the pound sterling to the administrative detail of vehicle tax administration through the Driver and Vehicle Licensing Agency, the White Paper envisaged the negotiation of continuing partnership with the rest of the UK. In that vein, Salmond identified six forms of union that Scotland shares with the rest of the UK:

- the parliamentary union;
- the social union of family and cultural ties;
- the sterling currency union;
- the shared monarchy;
- the defence union realised in NATO; and
- shared membership of the European Union (EU).

Of these, independence (in his view) would end only the parliamentary union; the rest would remain in place. With that, the Yes side could portray independence simultaneously as a fundamental change in Scotland's national status, yet still leave much *un*changed.

This combination of change amid continuity was a formula designed to appeal to the median voter in favour of devo-max to move into the Yes camp. It sought to offer reassurance by presenting independence as involving extensive continuity and little risk, close in a continuum of options to devo-max. The No side just as obviously had an interest in presenting independence as a rupture, identifying risks, especially economic risks, and querying Salmond's vision of partnership and continuity. Evoking this sense of risk and uncertainty was the linking theme of all the Scotland Analysis papers. In February 2014 the No side amplified that message in a landmark intervention on currency union. In a coordinated series of statements by George Osborne, Conservative Chancellor of the Exchequer, Danny Alexander, his Liberal Democrat deputy, and Ed Balls the Labour Shadow Chancellor, each explicitly rejected currency union, chanting the mantra 'it is not going to happen'. In addition, and confounding standard practice around confidential civil service advice, a letter from the then Treasury Permanent Secretary, Sir Nick

Macpherson, to Osborne which argued that a currency union would not be in the UK's interest was also published.

The aim of this concerted attack was to prevent defection from the devo-max group to the independence camp. The No side clearly felt that the economic argument for independence was their opponents' Achilles heel. A related theme was to raise concerns about how much an independent Scotland's economy would depend on the tax receipts from resources – oil and gas – whose price was volatile (a concern underlined since the referendum by the collapse in oil prices and of UK tax receipts from the oil and gas sector). Likewise, doubts were raised about whether an independent Scotland would maintain its membership of the EU or would be forced to leave and reapply for membership with all the economic disruption that could involve.

An important backdrop to this messaging about economic risk was the insight from the so-called £500 question used initially by the Scottish Social Attitudes survey. This asked survey respondents whether they would support Scottish independence if it made them £500 better off, £500 worse off, or made no difference. The answers were striking (Table 13.3). Imagining being £500 better off as a result of independence produced a majority in favour of independence. Imagining being £500 worse off produced a big majority against. It would, of course, be wrong to read too much into these numbers, but this polling did suggest that people were at some level considering personal risk and benefit as part of their calculation about how to vote in the referendum. So trying to frame

Table 13.3   *The £500 question, 2013*

View on Inde-pendence	Better Off %	No Difference %	Worse Off %
In Favour	52	34	15
Neither	12	9	16
Against	30	40	72
Sample Size	*1497*	*1497*	*1497*

Question wording: 'Say it was clear that if Scotland became an independent country (separate from the rest of the UK), the standard of living would be lower [higher] and people would on average be £500 worse [better] off. In those circumstances would you be in favour or against Scotland becoming an independent country?'. The third option supposed that independence would make no difference on either of these points.

Source: Curtice 2013: 10.

independence as an economic risk likely to make people worse off was an obvious tactic for the No side.

The negative framing of independence as economically risky earned the No side and in particular the Better Together campaign the nickname 'project fear' (Pike 2015), contrasting sharply with the more positive and optimistic messages relayed by the Yes side. What was striking about the latter phases of the referendum campaign was how the balance of positive and negative campaigning flipped. In that period, the Yes side found it was winning real traction by focusing on what it presented as the problematic consequences of staying in the UK, in particular around questions of social justice. Scotland staying in the UK was presented as meaning more inequality – with spending cuts, the bedroom tax, food banks and child poverty highlighted – and more privatisation of public services, in particular the NHS. So voting Yes was increasingly framed as a negative – voting against inequality and privatisation – rather than the optimistic vision the White Paper had set out.

At the same time, the No side, stung by a closing of the gap in the polls, complemented 'project fear' with a more positive agenda. One feature of this was the entry of former Prime Minister Gordon Brown into the fray, with his strong message (reiterating arguments he had been making for many years) on the benefits of pooling risks on a UK-wide scale (Brown 2014). Another was the profiling of the proposals the Liberal Democrats, Labour and the Conservatives had each separately made on more devolution for Scotland in the event of a No vote. These had considerable common ground in the areas of tax and welfare devolution but were set to remain three distinct initiatives until one YouGov poll on 6 September 2014 showed a lead for the Yes side. This – and a series of other polls the same weekend showing a neck-and-neck race – prompted the three Better Together parties to firm up their intentions in a jointly expressed commitment to rapid cross-party talks (to conclude by the end of November 2014) and draft legislation (drawn up by late January 2015) on additional Scottish devolution.

Here too was an appeal – a rather last-minute one – to the median voter which moved from the negative message of deterring a Yes vote by evoking economic risk to a positive of incentivising a No vote by offering at least some of the additional powers that devo-max supporters might be expected to favour. That appeal was then underlined yet further in 'the Vow', a set of pledges made by the three pro-union party leaders David Cameron, Ed Miliband and Nick Clegg on the front page of the Scottish tabloid newspaper, the *Daily Record*. The Vow – issued two days before the referendum – underlined the commitment to deliver additional powers for the Scottish Parliament on the promised timetable, and also to continue the mechanism by which the Scottish Parliament was funded.

The latter pledge was designed to blunt Yes-side arguments about possible spending cuts should Scotland vote No. But it also protected a system for funding devolution which allocated Scotland more public spending per capita than England, a point noted by Conservatives in England who already felt that Scotland's treatment was overgenerous. We return to this point below. But in the Scottish context, the Vow seemed to do its job. The opinion polls widened out from the neck-and-neck race of 6–7 September back to a lead for No, with the referendum itself delivering the relatively comfortable No majority of 55: 45 per cent.

However, the impact of the Vow is easily overstated. The Scottish Referendum Study, which tracked Scottish voters' views over the four weeks running up to the referendum, recorded only a modest increase in those thinking more powers likely in the event of a No vote, from 36 per cent to 40 per cent, with those thinking more powers unlikely falling slightly from 41 per cent to 39 per cent (Henderson and Mitchell 2015: 19). The other factors which strongly drove No voting were age – older voters were disproportionately opposed to independence – and a belief that Scotland would be worse off economically under independence. In that sense, 'project fear' looked to have succeeded in tying devo-max supporters into the No camp. To put it a different way, the Yes side had failed to convince enough voters that it had a compelling enough economic case for independence. The Scottish Referendum Study shows that Yes voting was associated with the belief that an independent Scotland would actually be better off. But not enough held that view for Yes to win. The strongest association with Yes voting was the belief that inequality in Scotland would increase if there was a No vote, and the next strongest the belief that inequality would reduce if Scotland voted Yes (Henderson and Mitchell 2015: 21). This confirms the traction that the Yes side was finding in the latter stages of the campaign around issues of social justice and, as discussed below, set a clear trajectory for post-referendum politics in Scotland.

The constitutional chain reaction unfolds

Returning to the analogy of a chain reaction of constitutional events, the 6 September YouGov poll takes on special significance. Put bluntly, it sparked outright panic on the No side. Better Together was plunged into disarray (Pike 2015: 121–147). Convention was torn up when Prime Minister's Questions in the House of Commons was cancelled on 10 September to enable the three No side party leaders, Cameron, Clegg and Miliband, to zoom up to Scotland to campaign for the union. The Vow of 16 September was the next stage in this panicked reaction. Even if it did not do much to change voters' opinions, its prominence in the final days of the campaign established it as a marker stone for what was to follow immediately after the referendum. On 19 September, two further, and divergent, paths in that reaction followed, both announced by Prime Minister David Cameron on the doorstep of No 10 Downing Street: one pursuing the direction set out in the Vow, the other opening up a path of change in England.

Towards the next Scotland Act

Outside No 10, Cameron announced that Lord Smith of Kelvin, fresh from his successful delivery of the 2014 Commonwealth Games in Glasgow, would convene a cross-party group to deliver on the Vow. The Smith Commission included nominees of the three pro-union parties in Scotland – the Conservatives, Labour and the Liberal Democrats. It also included nominees from the SNP and the pro-independence Scottish Greens. Working across the pre-referendum Yes–No divide, Smith managed to deliver a set of agreed proposals on schedule by the end of November 2014 (Smith Commission, 2014). The UK government then produced a draft bill, on schedule and based on the Smith proposals, by the end of January 2015. And a formal bill was introduced to Parliament, again as anticipated in the timetable to which the Vow had committed, after the UK general election of May 2015.

This was rapid progress and enabled the former No side to claim plausibly enough that the Vow had been delivered. But these developments occurred against a shifting backdrop in Scotland which put the Vow, and Smith's recommendations, into a very different context. This was signalled already at the launch of the Smith proposals in November 2014, when the lead SNP representative, Scottish Finance Secretary John Swinney, argued that the proposals in the report he had co-authored did not go far enough. This was not a surprise; a pro-independence party can always seek more powers up to the point independence is achieved. What was a surprise was the political momentum that accumulated behind the SNP after the referendum. The party that lost the referendum it had called emerged rapidly as the big winner in post-referendum politics. Some of that was due to Alex Salmond's resignation as SNP leader on 19 September and the anointment of Nicola Sturgeon, his deputy, as his successor. With that, Salmond took the whiff of the defeated with him (though he has since reinvented himself as a feisty contributor in the House of Commons, to which he returned at the 2015 UK general election). His departure also enabled the SNP to renew itself around the figure of Sturgeon – a generation younger than Salmond, the first female leader of the SNP, and someone (unlike Salmond who had a pro-business reputation and enjoyed engaging with prominent businesspeople) who had nurtured credentials on the left of the political spectrum. Sturgeon had also developed a reputation as a straight-talking, highly competent leader, whether as Cabinet Secretary for Health in Scotland or a key figure in the Yes campaign.

Nicola Sturgeon contributed significantly to the SNP's phoenix-like quality. It rose from the ashes of referendum defeat to capture and organise much of the enthusiasm for political participation that Yes supporters had discovered in the referendum campaign. Her left-leaning credentials both appealed to some of the campaigners around the Yes banner, bringing them in to conventional party politics, and also harnessed the appeals to social justice which had been so prominent towards the end of the campaign. This fed a quadrupling of SNP membership from less than 25,000 before the referendum to over 100,000 by November 2014. And the SNP began to buck a trend in the opinion polls that had been evident since the start of the devolution era. Over that time, the SNP had generally fared worse in voting intentions (and election outcomes) for UK elections in Scotland than it did in Scottish Parliament elections, with the Labour Party in Scotland doing better in UK elections and worse in Scottish ones. This was widely interpreted as an example of 'second order' politics; Scottish voters used Scottish elections to experiment or express protest by voting SNP because the Scottish Parliament was a secondary arena where less was 'at stake', returning to Labour for the more important, 'first order' Westminster arena (Reif and Schmitt 1980; Jeffery and Hough 2009). Indeed, the SNP had only been ahead of Labour in Westminster voting intentions in Scotland on two occasions between 2007 and 2014. In 2014 that pattern was broken intermittently in the run-up to the referendum, and then consistently and decisively from October 2014. From then to 2016, the SNP was (way) ahead of Labour in Westminster voting intention, regularly reaching and exceeding 50 per cent in the polls. Significantly, this left little difference between Scottish and Westminster voting intentions in Scotland; UK-level voting behaviour in Scotland appears to have aligned itself to Scottish Parliament voting behaviour, leaving the SNP ahead – and Labour far behind – on all counts.

This pattern was reflected in the 2015 UK general election, when the SNP achieved 50 per cent of the vote (and Labour just 24 per cent, its worst performance since 1918). With that, the SNP won an astonishing 56 out of 59 Scottish seats, 50 up on the 2010 election, with Labour losing 40 and the Liberal Democrats ten. These results say something about the Labour Party, which for many lost credibility when it allied with the Conservative Party, which had been generally disdained in Scotland since the Thatcher years, in the Better Together campaign. It also says something about Scottish views of the UK-level political system. Many of those who voted SNP in 2015 had previously voted Labour in UK elections in order to have an influence in the formation of the UK's government. The SNP is not a party capable of forming a UK government. Voting SNP was a statement that influencing the formation of such a government is not the way in which Scottish interests are best secured. While the SNP group at Westminster has in many respects appeared a more coherent and effective opposition than a Labour Party convulsed by its 2015 defeat, the primary – or 'first order' – arena for the SNP remains the Scottish Parliament. Many Scottish voters appeared to have come to the same conclusion by the 2015 election. And if the Scottish Parliament is now the primary arena for the pursuit of Scottish interests, the type and extent of powers it can wield will inevitably remain high on the Scottish political agenda. That gives the SNP a powerful platform to continue to press for additional devolution and, should it calculate it can win it, a second independence referendum.

So the period since the 2015 general election was marked by skirmishes, carefully coordinated by the SNP at Edinburgh and Westminster, to (in Salmond's words) 'hold feet to the fire' and deliver as powerful a version of the Smith proposals via the post-election Scotland Bill as possible. There were also calls from some quarters in the party to seek a mandate for a second independence referendum. Nicola Sturgeon responded carefully to these calls, arguing that 'material change' would be needed before a move to a new referendum. Such change appeared to have two components: a sustained pro-independence lead in opinion polls; and a significant change in circumstances, with the most obvious trigger an EU referendum outcome where a UK-wide vote to leave, driven by the weight of voters in England and their now markedly more Eurosceptic views, pulled a more pro-EU Scotland out of the EU against its will. Such, indeed, was the outcome of the referendum, and we return to this point below.

Thinking of England

So the Scottish path of the constitutional chain reaction continues to unfold. As Prime Minister Cameron gave it a further nudge on 19 September 2014, so he also opened up the English path of the chain reaction as he announced his commitment to EVEL. EVEL is a response to the so-called West Lothian Question, which is what many saw as the undue role Scottish MPs had on English matters once many of the same matters had been devolved in Scotland and were beyond the influence of

MPs from England. EVEL offers an answer to that question by excluding Scottish MPs (and in principle Welsh and Northern Irish MPs, but the emphasis in practice is always on Scotland) from at least some parts of the legislative process on English matters in the House of Commons.

Given that the Conservatives were and are so weak in terms of Scottish representation in the House of Commons – they have had one Scottish MP since 2001, improving on the count of zero they achieved in 1997 – it is not difficult to see why EVEL might appear attractive to them. They lose the voice of one MP, while other parties potentially lose far more. This in effect gives stronger voice to MPs from the part of the UK where the Conservatives have most strength: England. So while the timing of Cameron's announcement on EVEL surprised many, the logic should not have. Indeed, the Conservative Party had advocated (half-heartedly, it has to be said) a version of EVEL in all its general election manifestos since 2001, and then in 2012 the Conservative–Liberal Democrat coalition government set up what became known as the McKay Commission to explore how EVEL might be implemented (McKay Commission 2013). While an early response to McKay foundered on disagreements within the coalition, the Scottish referendum debate – and in particular the offer of more powers to Scotland in return for a No vote – brought the issue back up the agenda. Influential Conservatives like Boris Johnson expressed concern that the situation of Scotland – already receiving more public spending per head than England, and now offered both more powers over tax and a guarantee of current funding levels – was increasingly unfair to England. Others like John Redwood saw this perception of special treatment for Scotland as a lever to push for compensation for England in the form of EVEL.

Those rumblings of discontent were given a particular potency by the threat the United Kingdom Independence Party (UKIP) posed on the Conservatives' right flank. The 2014 Future of England Survey (conducted in April 2014, a few months ahead of the Scottish referendum) reported considerable dissatisfaction in England about Scotland. Some 38 per cent felt Scotland got more than its fair share of public spending, 56 per cent that public spending in Scotland should (counter to the commitment made in the Vow) be reduced to the UK average, and 62 per cent that MPs from Scotland should not be able to vote on laws affecting England. What was striking was how strongly UKIP supporters held these views, and how close the views of Conservative supporters were to UKIP supporters on these issues (Table 13.4). What was striking also in the Future of England Survey findings was how these resentments about Scotland aligned to other resentments in England – not least about European integration – and were linked by an association with strength of English, as opposed to British, national identity, as also set out in

Table 13.4 *English attitudes on Scotland and national identity*
in England by party (2014)

	England Total %	Labour %	LibDem %	Cons %	UKIP %
Agree Scotland gets more than fair share of spending	38	30	43	52	53
Agree Scottish spending to be reduced to UK average	56	50	54	69	70
Agree Scots MPs not to vote on English laws	62	52	67	73	81
English identity	43	37	29	50	60
British identity	43	48	47	44	33
Sample size	*3705*	*934*	*385*	*969*	*415*

Source: Jeffery et al. 2014: 28.

Table 13.4. UKIP supporters were by some way the most resentful and the strongest English (and weakest British) identifiers. With that, UKIP – a little inadvertently perhaps, given the 'UK' in its title – had become a gathering point for a set of specifically English concerns. And over two-fifths of UKIP respondents in the April 2014 survey reported voting Conservative in the 2010 general election (and just 19 per cent Liberal Democrat and 14 per cent Labour) (Jeffery et al. 2014: 26–30). UKIP had become a material threat to the Conservative Party in England.

This was a threat Cameron sought to head off in England through his announcement on EVEL on 19 September. His subsequent attempt to establish a cross-party framework for developing proposals for EVEL – like Lord Smith's process in Scotland – quickly foundered. Nor could agreement be reached on a specific proposal in the coalition. So in the end the Conservative Party struck out on its own and set out its preferred version of EVEL in January 2015, which was then included in the Conservatives' manifesto for the May 2015 general election. This proposed a double-majority system for legislation certified as applying to England: to be passed, such legislation would require a majority of

MPs in England to endorse it, as well as a majority of the whole House of Commons. An initial proposal to implement this system by changing the standing orders (the rules of procedure) of the House of Commons was introduced in July 2015, withdrawn for further consideration, then reintroduced and approved in October 2015.

The effect of all this on parliamentary business may well be minimal. There are in fact few laws whose reach is limited to England. But that may not be the point. The debate about EVEL may be a signal of a deeper change underway in the UK's territorial politics. Strikingly, EVEL was presented by the Conservatives as one of a set of issues in an 'English manifesto' in the 2015 general election. The manifesto also included the idea of an English rate of income tax (analogous to tax devolution in Scotland) and the 'Carlisle Principle' which would institute a periodic review of the cross-border impacts in England of policies enacted by the Scottish Parliament, so that action might be taken to redress any negative impacts (quite how was not made clear). At the same time, speculation that a Labour minority government relying on SNP support might be an outcome of the 2015 election was used deliberately as a scare tactic in England, most vividly in election posters depicting Alex Salmond pickpocketing (what we presume was) an English taxpayer to pay for (we presume) Scottish largesse, and Ed Miliband as Nicola Sturgeon's puppet. So the Conservatives did not just mobilise distinctively in England, but did so also *against* a Scotland symbolised by the SNP leadership. The Conservatives – conscious of the UKIP threat on their right flank and UKIP's particular resonance in England – were identifying England as a distinct electoral arena and using Scotland to define that distinctiveness.

This combination of distinctive electoral competition and an institutional form – EVEL – through which to respond to the specific concerns of the English electorate might be seen as the basis of an incipient English analogue to the distinctive political systems that have emerged since devolution in the other parts of the UK. The Conservative Party's role in this emergent political institutionalisation of England is remarkable. It is worth recalling the comment of Robert Hazell on EVEL in 2006, when he suggested that the difficulties of its implementation 'seem insuperable at both a technical and a political level'. Most would agree on the technical point; it is difficult to disentangle English from non-English business in the House of Commons. What Hazell saw as the political insuperability is more interesting. This was something 'unlikely ever to be implemented by a Conservative government ... If they seriously wanted to end the equal voting rights of all MPs, the Conservatives could no longer claim to be unionist, but would have become an English party' (Hazell 2006: 43).

The chain reaction continues?

It remains to be seen how far the Conservatives will develop a more general profile and purpose as an 'English party'. EVEL and the wider language of an English manifesto may well have been more a superficial, short-term tactical response to head off internal party dissent and the electoral challenge of UKIP than a deeper and enduring change. But in a sense, each step in the chain reaction described above was superficial and tactical, a short-term response to an immediate problem. Once a step has been taken, future options may be limited. So, once the precedent of responding to a distinctive pattern of opinion in England has been set, it may make it more likely that political issues subsequently are framed as English and requiring responses in and for England, rather than capturing their UK-wide dimensions. Such a pattern is already well-established in Scotland, driven on further by the referendum and its aftermath. The effect – unplanned and largely uncontrolled – is one of divergence of institutional structures, party competition and the terms of political debate in different parts of the UK. The final section below offers an account of why these divergences are uncontrolled and their likely trajectory in future.

There was one issue around which these English–Scottish divergences might be exposed in the short term: the referendum on UK membership of the EU on 23 June 2016. It had become increasingly clear that English and Scottish opinion on the EU had veered sharply apart (Henderson et al. 2016). This was confirmed in pre-referendum polling which showed that England and, increasingly, Wales were leaning towards a leave vote. Polling in Scotland, however, showed 60 per cent-plus support for remaining in the EU. There was scant survey data for Northern Ireland, but the few polls that were conducted there also suggested clear majority support to remain (but also a stark division within Northern Ireland between overwhelmingly pro-remain nationalists and strongly pro-leave unionists).

Given England's preponderant share of the UK's population, the likelihood grew that different UK nations would find themselves divided by the referendum outcome. Indeed this turned out to be the case. Wales voted 52.5 per cent to leave and England 53.4 per cent (with every region of England, except London, in favour of leaving). Northern Ireland voted 55.8 per cent and Scotland by 62.0 per cent to remain. The UK-wide vote, given England's preponderant share of the UK population, was 51.9 per cent to leave, outweighing the popular will in Scotland and Northern Ireland to remain. As Nicola Sturgeon put it the day after the referendum, this was 'significant and material change'. It was, she said, 'therefore a statement of the obvious that the option of a second referendum must be on the table. And it is on the table.' Nonetheless Sturgeon also committed to looking at other options, including scenarios in which Scotland as part of a UK outside the EU might have some form of privileged relationship with the EU. Such options look politically and constitutionally implausible. Exploring them – including in a high profile visit by Sturgeon to Brussels in June 2016 – looked to have two rationales. The first was to give the SNP and the Scottish Government breathing space to develop a renewed vision of independence within the EU in the circumstances of Brexit. Surprisingly neither party nor government appeared to have given much thought to developing that vision, perhaps expecting a UK-wide vote to remain. The second was to build the other aspect of 'material change' that Sturgeon had identified after the 2014 Scottish referendum: increased public support for independence. A reasoned exploration of other options for maintaining a close Scottish relationship with the EU while remaining part of the UK – and the likely conclusion in due course that there are no plausible such options – may be a precondition for persuading those who voted No in 2014 but prize EU membership to switch sides in a second independence referendum. Some of the early post-Brexit polling suggested that such a shift in opinion may indeed by underway. Against that background it is difficult to escape the conclusion that the EU referendum has widened yet further the territorial divide between Scotland and England.

Reforms without end

With that, the trajectory of the UK's territorial politics remains disintegrative. There is no sign of a stable equilibrium. Scotland is set for its third stage of devolution, now involving substantial tax powers, as the Smith Commission reforms are enacted, with the independence debate now also reignited by Brexit. An intermittent debate on regional devolution in England is now accompanied by a first (but likely not the last?) version of EVEL which treats England as a whole as a political unit. Wales, remarkably, is now debating the fifth variant of devolution since 1999. The first, in force from 1999, was quickly deemed unwieldy and was subject to a formal review through a commission which published proposals for change in 2004. The second variant, subsequently enacted in the Government of Wales Act of 2006, was, if anything, even more complicated. The 2006 Act also provided for variant number three under which Wales would move closer to the cleaner-cut distinction of devolved and UK-level powers that existed in Scotland. This third stage came into force following a referendum in March 2011. In November 2011 another reform commission was set up with its agenda in part following the trajectory of tax devolution underway by then in Scotland. Variant four followed in 2014 with initial provisions for tax devolution. Debate on variant five – now focused more directly on a Scottish model of devolution which 'reserves' specific powers to the UK Parliament and leaves anything not so 'reserved' to the Scottish Parliament – produced a new Draft Wales Bill by October 2015. And even Northern Ireland has moved from the initial form of devolution of 1999 through a second stage agreed in 2006, now supplemented by a limited amount of tax devolution in 2015. It remains to be seen how Brexit will be digested there given the divisions on the EU question between Northern Ireland's communities and the prospect – anathema to the nationalist community – of the hardening of border arrangements between the north and the Republic of Ireland that Brexit implies. Pressures for further constitutional change may follow. Looking across the four parts of the UK, this is an extraordinary amount of change in less than 20 years. Why?

One part of the answer lies in pressures for change in the different parts of the UK. There was a rapid acceptance in Wales that the initial forms of devolution were not fit for purpose and needed to be changed. Changes in Northern Ireland in 2006 and 2015 were in part the outcome of deals by the Northern Ireland parties to hold a fragile settlement together. EVEL began to be taken seriously when politicians recognised that people in England were dissatisfied with how they were governed. And changes in Scotland were directly prompted by the SNP's successive Scottish Parliament election victories in 2011 and 2015.

The mystery of the missing centre

But another part of the answer lies with the UK central government and extends back in some respects to long before devolution. The UK is a state that emerged, over centuries, as a multinational union. And over centuries, its central governments have had to manage territorial challenges of different kinds in different places. They have not typically responded in a uniform way, but have tailored different responses to local circumstances. Stein Rokkan and Derek Urwin (1983) coined the term 'union state' to challenge the easy imagery of the UK as a 'unitary' state by recognising the territorial differentiation that had always existed. Jim Bulpitt (1983) pointed in a similar direction by exploring the 'codes' which helped assimilate and pacify local elites in order to maintain the autonomy of the centre in the 'high' politics of economic management and external affairs. James Mitchell (2009: 6) nuanced this understanding further in his phrase 'state of unions', a state in which distinct unions had been struck, revisited and remade between centre and component nations, each with their own dynamic. In all these under-standings, the management of territorial pressures by the UK government has been piecemeal, reactive and bilateral, lacking any overarching strategic purpose.

Devolution brought an important change. While there may have been no grand strategic purpose before devolution, there was a basic level of coordination that came from the consideration of territorial interests in a single central government, latterly in the form of Cabinet ranking departments for Scotland, Wales and Northern Ireland. While those departments remain, they no longer bring the growing list of matters that are now devolved into collective discussion through the UK Cabinet and its sub-structures. Post-devolution, a different approach was required. As Robert Hazell put it at the outset of devolution: 'If devolution is to lead to a stronger union, not a fragmenting one, new consultative inter-governmental regimes and mechanisms need to be developed' (Hazell 1999: 19). This would 'require some imaginative re-engineering at the centre ... It is a matter on which the government needs to give a lead, in its actions and in its words, to bind the union together in order to counterbalance the centrifugal political forces of devolution' (Hazell and O'Leary 1999: 45).

That lead has never been given. Joint Ministerial Committees linking governments across the UK were established but have been underused and have mostly fallen into disuse. Governments across the UK do inter-act intensively, but at an operational level through civil servants, not a strategic level through political leaders. Hazell and his colleagues, who reported annually in the early years of devolution, looked in vain for a response to their call for *political* leadership: 'there is an absence of any strong sense of vision in the government of how the centre needs to change' (Hazell 2000: 281); 'Westminster and Whitehall carry on much as before' (Hazell 2001: 269); 'there is no coherent approach at the cen-tre, with no one who thinks about devolution in the round and no one to give it strategic vision' (Hazell 2003: 296); 'the adjustments made have been the smallest possible, both in degree and extent' (Trench 2004: 189). All of the major enquiries or commissions which have looked at the implementation and operation of devolution have identified the absence of meaningful institutional structures for political coordination across the UK as a failing. There is, in Hazell's words, no counterbalance to what have emerged as the – perhaps unexpectedly strong – 'centrifugal political forces of devolution'. Commenting on the 2015 draft Wales Bill, Cogbill et al. (2016: 10) write of 'the confusion, incoherence and frustration associated with a constitutional journey that in turn reflects and reinforces the pervasive sense of no overall direction in UK devolu-tionary development'. Enid Blyton might have called it the mystery of the missing centre.

Outlook: The UK as a disintegrating state

The result has been a succession of piecemeal changes which have been pursued and implemented in each part of the UK with no regard to the other parts, and as short-term tactical reactions with little regard to possible longer-term consequences (Jeffery 2008). This pattern of short-term reaction to centrifugal pressure finds clear illustration in the Scottish referendum debate and its consequences. The ways in which far-reaching change not just in Scotland but also England can be traced back to a single YouGov poll in Scotland on 6 September 2014 is an extraordinarily focused and accelerated variant of a more general pattern. Wales offers its own, seemingly madcap, variant of piling reform on reform to address the inadequacies of whatever the most recent reform were. The UK government, under whichever political party, does not *lead* in UK territorial politics. It has not been capable of sustained focus and instead jolts into action from time to time without thinking much through. Tellingly none of the candidates to succeed David Cameron as leader of the Conservative Party and Prime Minister appeared to have given any thought to the territorial divisions revealed by the Brexit vote in June 2016. And without an effective capacity at the centre to hold the ring, the inevitable effect is one of disintegration. Each part of the UK – now England as well – is developing as a distinct political arena with, as time passes, fewer points in common with the others. The trajectory is towards a significantly looser relationship of the UK's component parts to one another than now, and with that a progressive diminution of the grip of central government over the different parts of the UK. What is unclear is whether this trajectory will unfold as a loose union combined in a single state, or two or more different states. What is clear, though, is that the UK is now embarked on a seemingly inexorable process of disintegration.

Chapter 14

Britain beyond the European Union?

ANDREW GEDDES

On June 23 2016 Britain voted to 'take back control' and to leave the European Union (EU). For good or ill, this epoch-making decision, taken by 52 percent of the people to 48 on a 72 percent turnout, will reshape British politics and the country's place in the world. The scale of the decision was made evident by the resignation of Prime Minister Cameron being only the third item on the BBC evening news bulletin on June 24. Referenda, however, do not necessarily provide verdicts that are conclusive and definitive. The 'yes' vote made by the British people at the 1975 referendum on membership of what was then known as the European Community (EC) or 'Common Market' was neither whole-hearted or unequivocal. The outcome of the 2014 Scottish independence referendum hardly put that matter to rest. While highly unlikely that the decision to leave can be reversed, the leave vote raises as many questions as answers and requires fundamental renegotiation with the EU to redefine the relationship. A criticism of the leave campaign was that there did not seem to be a plan for Brexit. The future of the UK itself has been be plunged into doubt as a Scottish government led by the Scottish National Party (SNP) is almost certain to push for another independence referendum.

The dust had barely settled on the 2015 general election campaign before battle lines were drawn for the referendum on Britain's EU membership. The Conservatives' 2015 general election manifesto proposed 'real change' in Britain's relationship with an EU characterised as too big, bossy, bureaucratic and undemocratic (Conservative Party 2015). In government, 'change' for the Conservatives meant renegotiation of some of the terms of membership followed by an in–out referendum. In September 2015, the Electoral Commission approved the wording of the referendum question:

Should the UK remain a member of the European Union?

With two options – either:

Remain a member of the European Union

or

Leave the European Union

In November 2015, Prime Minister Cameron wrote to the president of the European Council, Donald Tusk, outlining the issues on which the British government would seek renegotiation, including the very thorny issue of access to welfare benefits for citizens of other EU member states that move to the UK. Cameron and his team participated in a series of renegotiation discussions with the other 27 EU member states and with EU institutions, which resulted in a settlement arrived at by the European Council in February 2016. Cameron, claiming Britain should remain within the EU, had then to fight the referendum while trying to manage divisions within the Conservative Party, consider media reaction and think about the broader implications of the deal for public opinion and for the nations of Britain. Add to this the views on Europe of influential interests such as business and the trade unions, then it becomes clear that the politics of Britain's role inside or outside the EU are complex and multidimensional.

Attitudes towards the EU have changed since the 2000s. Euroscepticism has become mainstream in British politics, particularly within the Conservative Party. On the eve of the referendum, the BBC calculated that, of those that declared, 185 Conservative MPs favoured remain while 138 advocated a vote to leave. The Parliamentary Labour Party was overwhelmingly in the remain camp (218 of those who declared favoured remaining while just 10 argued for a leave vote), but the United Kingdom Independence Party (UKIP) has mounted an anti-EU challenge to the political mainstream. Scepticism has been further emboldened by the eurozone and refugee crises. Beneath the surface of the EU debate is a debate about the future of Britain itself – the UK – as a political union within which the EU also plays a part. Euroscepticism in the Conservative Party and UKIP can, at times, appear a distinctly English phenomenon, while debate in other nations of the UK can be different.

Visions of Europe

The history of British relations with the EU is complex and does not present a reliable guide to the future. While history clearly matters, there has been no single, shared vision or narrative that can both explain and justify

Britain's relationship with the EU and that all British people agree with. There are ardent Eurosceptics, equally ardent – albeit probably fewer – Europhiles, plus many – perhaps the majority – of people for whom the EU is neither a top priority nor something about which they have very strong feelings or know very much. There are also many different and competing versions of the nature and implications of the historical relationship between Britain and Europe that are filtered and mediated by key variables such as age, education, social class and national identity, as well as the ways that the EU can become entangled with other issues such as trust in political leaders or attitudes to immigration.

British relations with the EU could be understood as elite-driven and reflecting liberal and internationalist values. These elites and their values were challenged during the referendum campaign as too was the role and value of expert opinion that largely lined-up behind the remain campaign but was systematically attacked by the leave camp. From the pro-EU side, the EU was seen primarily as a vehicle for economic growth and competiveness. But even on the pro-EU side there was little enthusiasm for the more overtly political or federalising dimensions of EU integration. On the anti-EU side, the EU was seen as irredeemable precisely because it erodes national sovereignty, leads to 'uncontrolled immigration' while also threatening the operation of markets through over-regulation and burdensome bureaucracy.

Over time, British governments have demonstrated three long-standing British positions on the EU: a preference for intergovernmentalism; a belief that the EU should be about markets not politics; and concerns about sovereignty and national identity. These three factors shaped both pro- and anti- versions of British relations with the EU. They also meant that decades of equivocation by British governments about the EU's value, direction and purposes were difficult to turn into a positive case for continued membership during a 4 month referendum campaign.

A preference for intergovernmentalism

British governments have exhibited a long-standing preference for intergovernmental cooperation rather than supranational integration. This means preferring a more state-centred vision of the EU within which national governments have the upper hand compared to a more supranational vision that sees a much greater role for EU institutions such as the Commission, European Parliament and Court of Justice. The problem with this preference for intergovernmentalism is that the history of the EU since at least the 1980s has seen a growing role for supranational institutions. The EU's 'Ordinary Legislative Procedure' means that legislative power is shared between the Council of Ministers representing the member states and the directly elected European Parliament representing

Europe. The EU's Court of Justice has also seen its role and remit grow as the ambit of the EU Treaties has expanded. Confirming the ambitions of the founding member states in the 1950s, the EU has become a political system in its own right (Hix and Høyland 2011). When declaring his support for the Vote Leave campaign, Justice Secretary Michael Gove focused on this question of who makes laws and argued that EU supranationalism was an unacceptable erosion of the sovereignty of Parliament. In response, David Cameron suggested that such a stance was based on an 'illusion of sovereignty' in a global and interdependent world. An achievement of the Vote Leave campaign was to turn abstract debates about sovereignty into the powerful and ostensibly more understandable slogan of 'take back control'. This meant taking back control of decision-making from a Brussels elite, of the UK contribution to the EU budget and control of borders to stem 'uncontrolled immigration'. This message cut through to potential leave voters.

Markets not politics

The Conservatives' 2015 general election manifesto opposed what were seen as the EU's bureaucratic and undemocratic tendencies while expressing support for the European single market in capital, goods and services: 'We are clear about what we want from Europe. We say: yes to the single market. Yes, to turbo charging free trade' (Conservative Party 2015: 74). Euroscepticism erupted as a political force in British politics precisely because of the plans in the late 1980s to move beyond market integration to create a 'social dimension' to the then European Community (EC). This social dimension reinforced a longer-standing suspicion of and opposition to deeper political union and the EU's aspiration to attain 'ever closer union of the peoples of Europe'. Eurosceptics will often claim that the 1975 referendum was based on a false prospectus because British people thought they were endorsing being members of a free trade area. This is misleading because, to join the EC in 1973, Britain actually left the free trade area that it had formed in 1959, the European Free Trade Area (EFTA), in response to the creation of the EC in 1957. The political ambitions of the EC were clearly stated in the founding treaties agreed in the 1950s and that Britain didn't sign precisely because of these ambitions.

National identity

Geographically, Britain is clearly a European country, but if this question is thought about in social and political terms then the answer is less clear. The historian Timothy Garton Ash (2001), posing the question of whether Britain is a European country, came up with the answer:

'yes, but not only'. Britain's relationship with the EU rests alongside relationships with Commonwealth countries, with the US and a lingering attachment to a great power status as marked, for example, by Britain's permanent membership of the United Nations Security Council. Conservative MEP Daniel Hannan (2013) has argued that Britain should leave the EU and align with Anglophone countries such as Australia, Canada, New Zealand and the US that 'invented freedom' and share, as he sees it, a fundamentally different conception of liberty to more state-centric continental European countries. This thesis neglects the influence of post-enlightenment continental European political thinkers such as Montesquieu and Voltaire on US advocates of independence from the despotic British monarchy and colonial rule. The idea that there is an alternative for Britain outside the EU requires the right to 'dream up a new world order'. Liberated from the EU and allied with the rest of the Anglosphere, the argument runs, 'Britain could reinvent its open trading heritage, harnessing its colonial history to integrate itself into the new global economy of the Asian century' (Kenny and Pearce 2015).

Whether the 'Anglosphere' would be receptive to Britain's advances is another matter. In July 2014, US President Obama stated that Britain should stay in the EU if it wanted to maintain global influence and that the US saw Britain's presence in the EU as important for European stability and prosperity. Obama said the same when intervening firmly on the remain side during the EU referendum campaign. The leave campaign attacked Obama's intervention as an unwelcome foreign intervention in a UK debate and also pointed out that the US was very unlikely to cede sovereignty in the ways required by EU membership. US strategic priorities have also developed a strong Asia–Pacific focus. Similarly, both Australia and New Zealand have an important regional dimension to their trade and economic relationships and are actively seeking to build even stronger relations with their regional neighbours, such as Australia's 2015 free trade agreement with China. For many people in these countries, particularly those whose roots do not lie in Britain such as the Hispanic population in the US or people of Asian origin in Australia and New Zealand, ideas about an Anglosphere hark back to cultural connections that mean little or a colonial order that no longer exists.

Bringing together these three themes within debate on the EU - intergovernmentalism, markets not politics and national identity – shows how they continue to exert powerful influences on both the pro- and anti-sides of the EU debate. While they differ in their view on the necessity of British EU membership, a deeper commitment to European integration has not formed a significant component of the debate for even the pro-EU forces.

Growth in popular opposition to the EU

Fundamental shifts and realignments both domestically and internationally during the 2000s have led to intensified Euroscepticism in Britain. Support for the EU in Britain rested on what has been called a 'permissive consensus' that essentially allowed British political elites (such as ministers and civil servants) to get on with the business of negotiating within the EU and participating in decision-making. The permissive consensus was never too deeply grounded in the UK. It was challenged at elite and popular level, and became a more-open conflict during the tortuous ratification of the Maastricht Treaty after 1992. Since the 1990s, there has been an 'uncorking of the bottle' of popular opposition to the EU giving rise to an era of 'constraining dissensus' with increased popular opposition to European integration evident not just in Britain but in other member states too (Franklin, Marsh and McLaren 1994; Hooghe and Marks 2009).

Attitudes to European integration vary in relation to, for example, age. Data breaking down the Brexit vote from polling by Lord Ashcroft showed that 76 per cent of people aged under 24 voted to remain while 60 per cent of people aged 65 or over voted to leave. The relationships between age, turnout and voting to leave are striking. The higher the

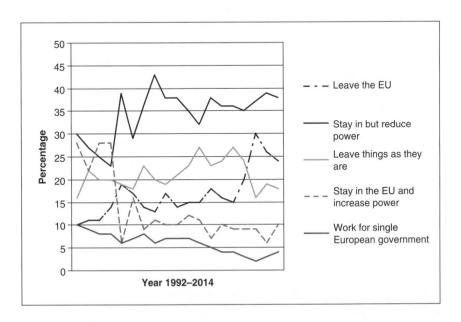

Figure 14.1 *Attitudes to EU Membership 1992–2014*

Source: British Election Study adapted from Curtice and Evans (2015).

median age in each of the 328 counting areas the more likely it was both that turnout was higher with a leave vote the likely outcome. Young people could claim that it was their future that was the subject of the vote, but very few turned out to stake a claim in this future.

The referendum presented a binary 'leave or remain' choice, but drilling down a little deeper into attitudes shows some of the challenges facing the leave and remain campaigns. British Election Study data allow exploration of attitudes to a range of options varying from leaving the EU to moving to single European government. Figure 14.1 shows a doubling between 1992 and 2014 of those supporting outright exit from the EU (10 per cent to 24 per cent) but, also, growth in those who wanted to see the EU's powers reduced (30 per cent to 38 per cent in the same period). Figure 14.1 also shows a precipitous decline dating to the mid-1990s in those who wanted to see increased powers for the EU. This was initially linked to public anger about the EU-wide ban of 1996 on British beef exports as a result of bovine spongiform encephalopathy (BSE) or 'mad cow disease'. Cameron's renegotiation and referendum strategy in 2016 depended on convincing enough people in the 'stay but reduce power' camp that his renegotiation amounted to a substantive change in Britain's terms of membership and a reduction in EU power or, failing that, to make the point that the future outside of the EU would be too risky and uncertain.

Figure 14.1 for the remain campaign suggests that it would not be credible to make a case for staying in the EU based on leaving things as they were or, more improbably, increasing EU powers. Key referendum voters were those who were not necessarily averse to staying in the EU but would also want to see some reduction in its powers. These are the voters who needed to be persuaded by Cameron's renegotiation, but it was also possible that some softer Eurosceptics, seeing the need to support the status quo, largely for economic reasons, 'holding onto nurse for fear of something worse', could reluctantly defect to the remain camp. It was received – albeit mistaken – wisdom that there would be a preference for the status quo that would favour Remain.

There have been a number of developments since the 2000s that represent a significant change in British relations with the EU and that pushed Britain to the EU's exit door.

The effects of crises

'Crises' can possess different meanings, enabling new ideas to take root in political debate while also reinvigorating or empowering political actors that may have been marginal. The eurozone and refugee crises enabled Eurosceptics to point to what they see as the EU's failings, inadequacies and inefficiencies. It was quite hard for the pro-EU camp to counter these claims. The financial and economic crisis that began in the US with the sub-prime mortgage scandal of 2007 and spread to Europe had profound implications for British relations with the EU. Britain did not join the euro but has not been able to escape the implications of the transformation of the banking and financial crisis into a sovereign debt crisis with hugely damaging effects on EU members of the eurozone states, particularly Greece. Having to be bailed out by the EU had considerable consequences for countries like Greece, not least in terms of the erosion of their political and economic sovereignty following their obligation to set a budget largely dictated by their EU partners. Eurosceptics in Britain represented the sovereign debt crisis as a failure of the EU model.

The refugee crisis possessed different potential meanings as, for example, a human rights crisis or, alternatively, as a threat to borders and security in Europe. The refugee crisis caused principally by conflict in the Middle East, particularly Syria after 2012, led millions of people to flee and for over a million people in 2015 alone to make perilous journeys to Europe and seek asylum in EU member states. More than 3,700 people lost their lives. The refugee crisis led to a political crisis for the EU as its members found it difficult to work together and to respond effectively. The sight of hundreds of thousands of people moving through Europe and then making chaotic journeys by whatever means necessary towards, in particular, Germany, fed into Eurosceptic argument that the EU was losing control. Terror attacks in Paris and Brussels in 2015 and 2016 intensified fears about security and also led to support for tougher border controls by EU member states.

Separately from refugee flows, Britain found itself bound by EU free-movement laws that enable citizens of each of the 27 member states to move freely between them. This has allowed upwards of 2 million people from other EU member states to move to the UK and around 1.4 million Brits to go to other EU countries. Eurosceptics, especially UKIP, claim that this creates an 'open door' policy for upwards of 450 million people from other EU member states. While it is unlikely that the entire EU population would move to the UK, it is clear that immigration, including EU free movement, has become a key public concern and that Britain, like other member states, cannot control or restrict intra-EU migration. For many, a vote to leave was a vote to 'take back control' of borders.

While Britain is bound by EU free-movement laws, it has an 'opt-out' from the relevant EU treaty provisions on asylum and refugees that meant that it was not covered by EU plans agreed in September 2015 for the mandatory relocation of up to 160,000 asylum applicants from Hungary, Greece and Italy to other EU member states. The UK government announced its own scheme in 2015 to take 20,000 Syrian refugees over a 5-year period. Foreign Secretary Philip Hammond claimed that an effect of the refugee crisis in Britain had been to compound concern about immigration, including EU free movement. Concern about immigration and EU free movement has fuelled public opposition to the EU (Curtice and Evans 2015: 14). Ipsos MORI polling in September 2015 showed 58 per cent of respondents wanting to see greater controls on free movement compared to 11 per cent who wanted to see free movement provisions stay as they were (Ipsos MORI 2015b). Hammond said that the refugee crisis could further hit support for the EU in Britain and that refugee flows could get mixed-up with debates about free movement. This was evident in misleading claims by the Leave campaign that Turkey was poised for EU membership, perhaps as soon as by 2020, and that this would lead to more than 80 million Turks having free movement rights and potentially being able to move to the UK. Cameron's renegotiation secured agreement to introduce new EU laws on access to welfare benefits for EU citizens living in the UK via the potential imposition of an 'emergency brake' when EU migration was of an 'exceptional magnitude'. The brake itself could last for up to seven years, while the exclusion of individual EU migrants from welfare benefits could last for up to four years. Strikingly, Cameron's deal was almost irrelevant during the campaign. It lacked credibility as a way of dealing with the issue of numbers of EU citizens moving to the UK while the leave campaign played on the fear of Turkish membership.

These crises intensified debate about the legitimacy of the EU project. Political institutions can be viewed as legitimate because they reflect or represent the views of the people, i.e. possess popular legitimacy. This issue of popular legitimacy has long been an issue for the EU because, aside from the directly elected European Parliament, EU institutions are either indirectly elected (the Council) or not elected (the Commission). This means that the EU has, to some extent, relied on what could be called its moral legitimacy bringing peace and security to Europe after the Second World War and as a vehicle for the progressive idea of European unification. The EU has also sought to generate legitimacy via the efficient and effective performance of tasks. The moral basis used for EU legitimacy and progressive ideas about 'ever closer union' have never held too much sway in the UK. The eurozone and refugee crises raised questions about the EU's credibility and thus hit its legitimacy because it was seen by many as failing to respond effectively.

The mainstreaming of Euroscepticism

A second trend has seen Euroscepticism move from the margins to the mainstream of British politics. This is certainly the case for the governing Conservative Party, which has become increasingly a Eurosceptic party (if during the referendum campaign led by a leader, Cameron, supportive of continuing EU membership), but Euroscepticism has also become a more complex organism with maximalist and minimalist variants that have implications for the meaning of Brexit. Being a Eurosceptic does not necessarily mean advocating leaving the EU. To say that there has been a mainstreaming of Euroscepticism is not to claim that there was not previously opposition to the EU, but, rather, that Euroscepticism was a marginal concern for groups of people on the margins of mainstream politics who would sometimes be dismissed as cranks, obsessives or both (Geddes 2011). In his victory speech to the European Parliament five days after the referendum, UKIP leader, Nigel Farage, said that pro-Europeans used to laugh at his campaign for Britain to leave the EU. 'Who's laughing now', he asked. Euroscepticism as a force on the right of British politics can be traced back to a speech given by Margaret Thatcher at the College of Europe in Bruges in 1988 when she opposed the wider political ambitions for European integration of the then Commission President, Jacques Delors, and instead asserted a trade-based and intergovernmental vision of the then EC. She particularly feared that European integration would be a vehicle for what she saw as a Socialist-inspired re-regulation of the British economy via the back door of European regulations.

As the Conservatives became more Eurosceptic – and tore themselves apart between 1993 and 1995 ratifying the Maastricht Treaty – Labour renounced their opposition to an EC and EU that they had once seen as a 'capitalist club' and, instead, under Neil Kinnock, John Smith and Tony Blair embraced a pro-EU position. This means that the statement at the top of this section ought to be qualified because Euroscepticism did become mainstream, but within the Conservative Party. This highlights a more general point: European integration has tended to be a divisive issue within political parties – particularly the Conservatives – rather than between them. The substantive debate within the Conservative Party has been about the form of Euroscepticism and not a debate between pro- and anti-EU elements. This is not simply an 'in' our 'out' debate because there are distinct Eurosceptic positions that had important implications for Prime Minister Cameron's renegotiation and the 2016 referendum. Four main strands of Eurosceptic thought have been identified with implications for the shape of Brexit.

- *outright rejectionists* want Britain to leave even if that also means leaving the EU single market;
- *maximal rejectionists* want a new settlement with the EU, perhaps with the UK in a position similar to Switzerland or Norway that form part of the single market while not being full EU members and accepting free movement of goods, capital, services and, importantly, people;

- *minimal rejectionists* would like to see some repatriation of powers and an end to commitments such as that to 'ever closer union';
- *minimalists* look to existing opportunities such as opt-outs from aspects of the treaty or enhanced procedures for scrutiny at national Parliamentary level to resist further EU integration (Lynch and Whitaker 2013).

Outright and maximal rejectionist could be labelled as 'hard' Eurosceptics. Michael Gove and Boris Johnson fell into this camp. More minimal visions would be 'softer' Eurosceptics. Minimalists such as David Cameron, George Osborne and Theresa May saw the EU as reformable, while maximal and outright rejectionists tend see the EU as incapable of serious reform.

Cameron's flirtation with harder-line Euroscepticism was brief. As soon as he was elected party leader in 2005, Cameron had warned his party to stop 'banging on about Europe'. Cameron's modernising project meant talking a little more about the issues that mattered most to people's daily lives such as the economy, health and education, and a little less about immigration and European integration. Conservative modernisation emerged prior to David Cameron's leadership, but after his election in 2005 became a vehicle for Cameron to project an alternative image of the party as a way of 'decontaminating' the brand. The party's arch modernisers (Cameron, Chancellor George Osborne, plus other key figures at various times in the party's history such as Michael Gove, Francis Maude and Oliver Letwin) all claimed to be Eurosceptic. The main debate within the party was between softer, minimalist and reformist Eurosceptics such as Cameron and Osborne and maximalist Eurosceptics in Cabinet such as Iain Duncan Smith, Gove, Chris Grayling, Andrea Leadsom, Priti Patel and Theresa Villiers and on the party's backbenches such as Bill Cash, Bernard Jenkin and Jacob Rees Mogg. Cameron might have stopped banging on about Europe, but this didn't mean that his MPs and party members had stopped being concerned; rather, it was not to the fore in party campaigning (Bale 2011).

Tensions simmered during the Conservative–Liberal Democrat coalition government between 2010 and 2015. The coalition agreement's section on the EU was more a reflection of Conservative than Liberal Democrat thinking, stating that no further powers should be transferred to the EU without a referendum. To that end, the 2011 European Union Act provided for a 'referendum lock', meaning that any future changes to the EU treaties or changes in the power of the EU that affected the UK would require Parliamentary approval and a referendum for them to become law in the UK. Previously ratification by Parliament had been sufficient. Cameron had issued a 'cast iron guarantee' that he would hold a referendum on the 2009 Lisbon Treaty, but said, before he came to office in 2010, that it was too late to do so because the treaty had already been ratified by the UK by Gordon Brown's government.

The referendum lock was unlikely to appease the more maximalist Eurosceptic MEPs favouring exit from the EU, or at least an in or out referendum on Britain's EU membership. Significant numbers of Conservative MPs were prepared to rebel against their own party on EU issues. In the 2010–2015 Parliament, a total of 103 Conservative MPs (60 from the 2010 intake) rebelled on EU issues with rebellions on 49 EU-related votes (Lynch 2015: 193). The largest rebellion occurred in October 2011 when 81 Conservative MPs defied a three-line whip to support a private member's bill proposed by David Nuttall calling for an in–out referendum. In October 2012, the coalition also lost a vote on the EU budget when 53 Conservative rebels voted with Labour to demand a real terms cut in the EU budget. In response, as noted earlier, Cameron stiffened his position, and the Conservatives' 2015 manifesto criticised the undemocratic, bureaucratic and bossy EU, pledged a renegotiation and in–out referendum while making it clear that a reformed EU with a strengthened single market would be the party's main objective in government.

Referenda may seem relatively simple mechanisms for testing the public view and securing consent, but referenda have more complex causes and consequences. Wellings and Vines (2015) argue the referendum lock introduced by the 2011 EU Act actually eroded the Parliamentary sovereignty that ostensibly it sought to defend and that it also had the effect of embedding a populist and nationalist opposition to European integration within British political culture. The same argument could be made about the outcome of the 2016 referendum. They see provisions for the use of referenda in Britain as part of a wider EU trend that has increased the impact of Euroscepticism on domestic and EU politics (see also Leconte 2010). A potential problem is that votes in referenda may have little to do with the question at hand but rather reflect domestic politics and be a mid-term popularity or unpopularity contest for the governing party (Hobolt 2009). Referenda have also been portrayed as a more modern form of direct democracy enabled by technological developments. Conservative MP David Nuttall suggested that people would be 'baffled' that they can pick up their phone or press their red button on their TV remote control to vote for a TV talent show contest but could not have their say on big issues such as EU membership (cited in Wellings and Vines 2015: 13).

New groups emerged within the Parliamentary Conservative Party after 2010 to provide a forum for Eurosceptic thinking. For example, the Fresh Start Group advocated a more rejectionist critique of the EU to include opting out of the EU's Charter of Fundamental Rights, reforming free movement, overhauling the Common Agricultural Policy and 'repatriating' regional policy from the EU to national level (Fresh Start Group 2013). Fresh Start provided a form of 'licensed Euroscepticism' with their Manifesto for a Fresh Start published in January 2013 containing a fulsome endorsement in a preface written by then Foreign Secretary William Hague who noted that many – but not all – of the proposals were already government policy and lauding the group for its ideas about how to reform the EU in line with Conservative instincts.

Eurozone governance was a source of tension in 2011 when tighter fiscal rules were proposed as part of the so-called Fiscal Compact, or *Treaty on Stability, Coordination and Governance in the European Union* as it was more formally known. Cameron threatened a veto of the treaty, which led the European Commission to propose a complex legal manoeuvre that allowed the compact to be agreed by the member states while Britain and the Czech Republic stayed outside. The British government was also on the back foot with proposals such as the so-called Tobin Tax on financial transactions charging 0.1 per cent against the exchange of shares and bonds and 0.01 against derivatives contracts with 11 member states, including France and Germany, agreeing to go ahead using EU treaty provision for 'enhanced cooperation'. Chancellor George Osborne said that such a tax could work only if it were global and challenged the Commission's proposals in the EU's Court of Justice.

For much of 2012, Cameron was expected to make a major speech outlining his position on the EU. The much delayed speech, known as the Bloomberg speech, was finally delivered in January 2013 when Cameron said: 'The next Conservative manifesto will ask for a mandate from the British people for a Conservative government to negotiate a new settlement with our European partners in the next Parliament' (Cameron 2013). An in–out referendum would then be held on the renegotiated terms. This Bloomberg speech made it clear that Cameron thought that Britain was stronger in the EU but that the EU needed to be reformed. Five broad themes for reform, rather than specific areas for renegotiation, were identified: competitiveness; flexibility; powers back to the member states; democratic accountability; and protections for non-eurozone countries within EU decision-making.

The rise of UKIP

UKIP's rise is both a cause and effect of the important shifts that have occurred in British relations with the EU. It is a cause in that UKIP, with its call for Britain to leave the EU, became the third party in terms of vote share, if not in seats (the SNP is the third largest party in the House of Commons) at the 2015 general election and was Britain's leading party at the 2014 European Parliament elections (Dennison and Goodwin 2015).

UKIP's rise is an effect in that UKIP capitalises on the mainstreaming of Eurosceptic sentiment that occurred within, mainly, the Conservative Party and that can be traced to the 1990s, which has helped to legitimise UKIP's cause. For its supporters at least, UKIP's success challenged David Cameron's assertion in a 2006 LBC radio interview that UKIP supporters were 'a bunch of fruitcakes, loonies and closet racists, mostly' (BBC News 2006).

UKIP does more than capitalise on hostility to the EU because it draws too from opposition to immigration and a deeper sense held by some people that they have been 'left behind' in contemporary Britain (Ford and Goodwin 2014). UKIP voters are typically male, elderly and working-class people that were, at one time, seen as Labour's core constituency. UKIP has also capitalised on high levels of immigration to the UK to make connections with the case for exit from the EU as a way to reassert control over the UK's borders. The UKIP component of the Leave campaign – which was effectively a separate operation from the Conservative campaign fronted by Johnson and Gove – was strongly and powerfully focused on 'uncontrolled immigration' and taking back control of borders.

Clearly UKIP capitalises on disillusion with and alienation from mainstream politics and also exemplifies wider populist tendencies across Europe, particularly since the onset of the economic crisis. The focus for right-wing populist parties such as UKIP has typically been on both immigration and European integration that exemplify in their eyes the ways in which 'ordinary people' have been sold out by the political elite. As such, this is clearly populism understood as a reaction on behalf of 'the people' against the perceived failings of representative politics (Taggart 2004). The history of populist movements across Europe shows that they can be episodic, experience rapid rises but also similarly rapid falls in appeal while being heavily dependent on a leader. A vote to leave the EU would be a justification of the party's arguments, but could ultimately also be its death knell. Stating that he had 'got his country back' and now 'wanted his life back', on July 3 2016 Farage resigned as UKIP leader, albeit for a third time, with some seeing potential for a future comeback.

Leave and remain: Alignments in the pro- and anti-EU debate

Two main leave groups emerged when preparations for the EU referendum campaign began in 2015. One, Vote Leave, a cross-party group with backing from business and UKIP's one MP, Douglas Carswell was eventually designated the 'official' campaign by the Electoral Commission.

The Vote Leave battle bus toured the country emblazoned with the claim that leaving the EU would save £350 million a week that could instead be invested in the NHS. Even though it was untrue, the continual repetition of the claim cut through to public perceptions of the potential benefits of Brexit. The second, Leave.EU, was funded by a prominent UKIP donor and fronted by UKIP leader Nigel Farage. In-fighting between the Vote Leave and Leave. EU campaigns led to the foundation in January 2016 of the Grassroots Out organisation aligned with the Leave. EU organisation and drawing cross-party support, including from the Conservatives, UKIP, including Farage, as well as maverick figures such as ex-Labour MP George Galloway. Farage claimed that Vote Leave was a vehicle for the political establishment and that the Grassroots Out campaign – ideally with him to the fore – reflected the anti-mainstream, insurgent characteristics of UKIP. For the Vote Leave campaign, Farage was seen as a potentially divisive figure whose views on issues such as immigration and religion could polarise opinion and alienate the undecided rather than build a winning anti-EU coalition. Major Conservative figures in favour of leaving the EU, such as Michael Gove and Boris Johnson, were always unlikely to align themselves with a Farage-led leave campaign that had an anti-immigration focus.

There were no such distinctions and divisions on the remain wing of British politics. The Britain Stronger in Europe campaign, led initially by the former Marks and Spencer chief executive Stuart Rose, projected a non-party political image bringing business people to the fore. In the campaign itself, David Cameron became the focus of the remain campaign. The result was that the campaign resembled a battle within the Conservative Party. Cameron was keen to limit blue-on-blue conflict, which meant that he didn't participate in TV debates alongside Conservatives in the leave camp, such as Gove and Johnson. The Britain Stronger in Europe campaign had three key components. The first component was the politics of fear: identifying the risks of leaving as a 'leap in the dark', the costs of changing or damaging trading relationships with other EU member states, the absence of a credible alternative to EU membership and the consequent cloud of uncertainty over Britain's role in the world outside the EU. The second component was the politics of hope: a reformed EU with a 'turbo-charged' single market could be an engine of growth for the UK economy while the EU could provide the UK with a wider global influence than it could have acting alone. And the third component was the politics of trust. Polls suggested that David Cameron enjoyed relatively high levels of public trust, so a campaign in which Cameron was to the fore and sought to assure the people of the value of the renegotiation and to trust him could pay off. Boris Johnson's decision to support the leave campaign was very damaging because he, too, was a relatively trusted figure. There was much speculation about Johnson's real motives, namely what some saw as a desire to succeed Cameron as party leader and Prime Minister that was stronger than his desire to leave the EU. Johnson's post-referendum bid for the party leadership was brutally undermined by his erstwhile ally Michael Gove who announced his own candidacy based on what he saw as Johnson's lack of leadership qualities. Johnson did not stand.

A brief flirtation with the Eurosceptic wing of his party did help Cameron become party leader when he pledged that the Conservative MEPs in the European Parliament would leave the federalist European Peoples' Party grouping, but Cameron, being a minimalist and a reformist, strongly supported Britain remaining in Europe, largely for pragmatic reasons. Harder-line Eurosceptics doubted the extent to which he embraced even the softest forms of rejectionism when his main purpose in his EU renegotiation was to secure a 'yes' vote in a referendum. From this point of view, in order to maintain a credible position in the run-up to the referendum, Cameron did have to say that he could countenance the UK leaving the EU. The problem for Cameron was that, after years in which he had nothing positive to say about the EU, he then had to become in a four month campaign an ardent advocate of the necessity of continued membership. There was, though, little doubt on both the leave and remain sides of the debate that his key objective in the renegotiation of Britain's relationship with the EU was to claim he had had substantive effects and that he could then make the case for Britain to stay in the EU at the subsequent referendum.

In January 2016, Cameron found himself obliged to concede a free vote on the referendum to Conservative ministers: the suspension of collective Cabinet responsibility, which similarly allowed Labour pro- and anti-Europeans to take different sides in the 1975 referendum. This time, of the 29 people eligible to attend meetings of the Cabinet, 6 declared for Brexit while the others elected to remain. Labour's Jeremy Corbyn had voted 'no' in the 1975 referendum because of his concerns that the EC was a capitalist club, but Corbyn undertook to back remaining in. Labour, unlike the Conservatives, was firmly and fully found within the remain camp, even if being acutely aware that issues of sovereignty and identity were precisely those upon which UKIP has been able to capitalise on when challenging Labour in its heartlands. Five days after the referendum on June 28 Labour MPs, by a margin of 172 to 40, supported a vote of no confidence in Corbyn's leadership and a challenge from Owen Smith MP then ensued. The head of Labour's Remain campaign, Alan Johnson MP, had condemned Corbyn's 'risible' campaigning and claimed that his team actively undermined its own campaign.

Euroscepticism has not remotely been mainstreamed in either Scotland to the same extent as in England. In Scotland both before and after the 2014 referendum, politics has been subsumed by the constitutional question. The SNP, the dominant party in Scotland, is a pro-EU party and campaigned for a remain vote. The Scots voted 62 per cent to 38 per cent vote in favour of remaining in the EU. A decision to leave taken on the basis of a vote in England and against the wishes of the Scottish people hastened calls for Scottish independence. SNP leader Nicola Sturgeon repeatedly made it clear that a leave vote in an EU referendum that went against the wishes of the Scottish people would mean another independence referendum would be 'probably unstoppable'. The SNP's objective of Scottish independence could thus be hastened by the UK leave vote even though the SNP was strongly committed to a remain vote. In Wales, 52.5 per cent voted to leave the EU while 47.5 voted to remain. While not in as strong a position as the SNP, Plaid Cymru supported EU membership. Both the SNP and Plaid had unsuccessfully argued that all four nations of the UK should vote in support of leaving the EU for it to occur. Northern Ireland also voted to remain in the EU by a margin of 56 per cent to 44 per cent. Leaving the EU raises questions about the status of the border between Northern Ireland and the Republic of Ireland and whether it would become a 'hard' border. Some also feared for the future of the peace process. Clearly, the referendum result asks basic questions about the UK's future with a third referendum on Scottish independence a likely accompaniment to Brexit.

Renegotiating the terms of EU membership

Between 2004 and 2013, EU enlargements brought in 13 new member states that tended to accord with a long-standing British preference for a wider, more economically liberal and more Anglophone EU to dissipate federal impulses. Britain, it was argued, had 'the most privileged terms of membership of any member state in the EU', which means that 'the British are seemingly able to have their cake *and* eat it' (Copsey and Haughton 2014: 75). Britain's privileged position saw it outside the single currency, eurozone and Schengen area of passport-free travel with a rebate on its budget contributions.

When contemplating Cameron's renegotiation, other EU member state governments could wonder why Britain needed more special treatment, which bounces us back to the point made earlier. Cameron's renegotiation required playing a complex multilevel game at EU level, getting other member states and EU institutions on board. At home, the bulk of the Cabinet, the Parliamentary and wider Conservative Party also needed to be signed-up while it was necessary to get key interest groups, particularly business, on board too. The trade unions sent a warning shot in September 2015 when they mooted opposition to the EU if social and employment rights were watered down as part of a renegotiation. The remain camp was based on a cross-party coalition of support for the EU via the Britain Stronger in Europe organisation and couldn't afford for the main trade unions to be outside this organisation. Media reaction is also important. While 'old' media have lost some of their influence, a key difference between the 1975 and the next EU referendum is that 40 years ago the main newspapers all advocated British membership while now the *Sun*, *Daily Mail*, *Daily Telegraph* and *Daily Express* were at the maximalist end of rejectionism. Cameron needed to muster enough support along each of these dimensions at EU and national level to secure a believable renegotiation and then a remain vote.

Box 14.1 The economic pros and cons of leaving or remaining

The economic case for or against EU membership was central to the referendum campaign. There is no single magic number that encapsulates either the costs or benefits of membership, with key issues less tangible or subjective. There is a baseline cost of membership, which is the UK's £9.8 billion pound 'net' – meaning after rebates and EU income flowing to the UK – contribution in 2014 to the EU budget (House of Commons 2015). To put this in context, the UK spends £150 billion, £130 billion and £90 billion on pensions, health care and education, respectively.

For the remain camp, the costs of leaving could be high. Other EU member states are the UK's largest trading partners: 43 per cent of exports and 55 per cent of imports of goods and services either go to or come from other EU member states (House of Commons 2015). The UK government has estimated that up to 3.5 million jobs are linked either directly or indirectly with the EU (House of Commons 2015). Foreign Direct Investment to the UK could also be threatened if UK access to the single market was jeopardised.

For the leave camp, the UK is the world's fifth-largest economy, and could still trade with EU member states while EU exit would allow it to forge trading relationships with rising economies such as China and India. This would be more attractive than being saddled with declining EU economies and red tape arising from EU regulations. The think tank Open Europe (2015) put the cost of the 100 most-burdensome EU regulations at £33.3 billion a year.

In late 2015, Cameron was reluctant to reveal his renegotiating position because he could be subject to sniping from other EU leaders and would almost certainly find UKIP and Conservative Eurosceptic maximalists arguing that he was not going far enough. At some point, however, he had to say what he was after. In November 2015 he could put it off no longer and provided a list of the areas in which he would seek renegotiation. Predictably, Eurosceptic backbench Conservative MPs immediately denounced the suggested changes for being, as Jacob Rees Mogg MP put it, 'pretty thin gruel'. Cameron's letter, entitled 'A new settlement for the UK in a reformed EU' identified four priorities:

- protection of the rights and interests of non-eurozone members, including recognising that the EU has more than one currency, that EU businesses from outside the eurozone should not be at a disadvantage and not making taxpayers in non-eurozone countries liable for the costs of bailouts;
- a strengthened commitment to single-market integration including in services, reflecting the long-standing UK preference for markets not politics;
- on national identity and sovereignty, an opt-out for Britain from the EU's commitment to an 'ever closer union of the peoples of Europe', a greater role for national Parliaments and a renewed commitment to subsidiarity, meaning, as Cameron's letter put it, 'Europe where necessary, national where possible'; and
- controls on EU migration with citizens of new member states not able to move freely until their economies had converged with those of other EU member states, and most importantly, not allowing citizens of other EU member states to move to the UK and access in-work benefits or social housing for four years (Cameron 2015; 2015a).

Given the high level of public concern about immigration, a key component of the renegotiation deal was the 'emergency brake' on EU migrants accessing welfare benefits and enough people being convinced that this was a substantive change in Britain's relations with the EU. Evidence suggests that EU citizens predominantly move to the UK for work and, when in the country, make a net fiscal and welfare contribution (Dustmann and Frattini 2014). The wider point is that free movement (for goods, capital, services and people) is not only central to the EU's legal framework, but is jealously guarded by key member states and EU institutions such as the Commission. UK governments have also long been advocates of much greater liberalisation within the single market for goods, services and capital. Whether the 'emergency brake' would make much difference to migration to the UK from other EU member states was a key referendum campaign issue. While member states can determine their social security rules, they must do so in a way that does not contravene EU rules by discriminating against citizens of other EU member states. Cameron claimed victory in the renegotiation deal secured at the February 2016 European Council, but that victory changed the minds of very few of those backing Brexit, including Brexit supporting members of his Cabinet. Cameron's deal only partially met his renegotiation agenda. The package of changes to the UK's membership of the EU would have included changes to:

- **the Eurozone:** sterling would be protected, as the EU agreed that the EU had more than one currency while the UK government could not be forced to participate in bailouts for eurozone countries – it was also agreed that eurozone members could not act as a bloc to undermine the single market;
- **free movement:** the 'emergency brake' mechanism referred to above was bolstered by agreement that child benefit payments for the children living in other EU countries of EU citizens working in the UK would be paid at the rate of their home countries – this would apply to newly arrived EU workers and to existing workers from 2020; and
- **sovereignty:** EU treaties would be amended to state explicitly that references to ever closer union would not apply to the UK, marking recognition that the UK is not committed to further political integration in the EU.

Ultimately the leave vote means that this deal became null and void, but Cameron made it clear his would be the strongest voice campaigning for a Remain vote. Of course, as Remain supporter Timothy Garton Ash (2016) conceded, Cameron's renegotiation could never have achieved 'a fundamental redefinition of Britain's relationship with the EU. Nor would we [the UK] suddenly find ourselves in "a reformed Europe". On this, Eurosceptics are right: Cameron's demands were less than he pumped them up to be, and inevitably, given that 27 other European countries had to be satisfied, what he achieved is even more modest. But it was foolish to let a decision about the economic and political future of Britain for decades ahead hinge on the detail of an "emergency brake" on in-work benefits for migrants. Cameron's deal seemingly persuaded no one in the political class to change their opinion on Britain's place in Europe. Some career-minded Conservative MPs may have chosen to damn their principles to stick with their leader, but it was the public, harangued by both the leave and remain camps, that decided the matter of Britain's EU membership at the referendum.

To where does the exit door lead?

Britain has decided to leave the EU, but it's not clear where the exit door leads. A leave vote is only be the beginning of a highly complex debate not only about the future of the UK but also about Britain's future relations with the EU. From its previous obscurity, EU treaty Article 50 governing the procedure for leaving the EU, became a subject of fierce public debate. Eurosceptics are not arguing that Britain should simply leave and thereafter have nothing more to do with the EU. 'In', 'out' or something in between, Britain will still be closely tied to other EU member states, not least as the UK's major trading partners. Most argue that it will be essential to maintain these trading relationships and maintain access to the EU's single market. The think tank Open Europe (2015) developed various scenarios for Britain outside the EU and found that the economically most positive 'out' vision required that the UK enter into liberal trade arrangements with the EU combined with large-scale domestic deregulation to maintain a competitive edge. This 'positive' vision mirrors a Thatcherite view of European integration that is present within Conservative 'rejectionist' thinking that sees the EU as an obstacle to rolling back the frontiers of the state. Such an approach could encounter opposition at EU level if the UK was seen as undermining social and welfare standards while, within the UK, further deregulation and market-oriented reforms would mean, as Open Europe put it: 'exposing firms and workers to whole new levels of competition from low cost countries and would therefore be politically sensitive' (Open Europe 2015). Deregulation could also require liberal rules on labour migration, which might also be politically controversial if EU exit were to lead to continued high levels of immigration. The alternative, narrow protectionism outside the EU, would, according to Open Europe's scenarios, be highly damaging to the UK economy.

The mechanics of leaving the EU are far from straightforward. Box 14.2 shows the key text from Article 50 on provisions for a member state to withdraw from the EU. To leave after a vote in a referendum requires the British government to notify the European Council (comprising heads of state and government) of its intention. The Commission would then negotiate and conclude an agreement with Britain that would set out the arrangements for British withdrawal, but this agreement would require a qualified majority in the Council of Ministers and approval from the European Parliament. The EU, not the British government, would be in charge of negotiations that could take up to two years, but could actually take much longer, and of the final vote in the Council with the risk that

Britain gets a take-it-or-leave-it deal two years or more after a leave vote. There is no guarantee that the leave deal would be favourable to the UK. Arguments advanced by Boris Johnson prior to the campaign that a leave vote in the referendum would give greater leverage to the UK government to extract concessions in the exit negotiations, perhaps even leading to a further referendum on the re-re-negotiated terms, were dismissed as fanciful by David Cameron.

Box 14.2 EU Treaty provisions for a member state leaving the EU

Article 50(1) of the Treaty on the Functioning of the European Union

A Member State which decides to withdraw shall notify the European Council of its intention. In the light of the guidelines provided by the European Council, the union shall negotiate and conclude an agreement with that State, setting out the arrangements for its withdrawal, taking account of the framework for its future relationship with the union. That agreement shall be negotiated in accordance with Article 218(3) of the Treaty on the Functioning of the European Union. It shall be concluded on behalf of the union by the Council, acting by a qualified majority, after obtaining the consent of the European Parliament.

'Maximal rejectionist' Eurosceptics think it is possible to be outside the EU, but still participate in the European single market, as do Norway and Switzerland, which, unlike the UK, are both also members of the Schengen zone of passport-free travel. Conditions for Norwegian and Swiss access to the single market is that they pay into the EU budget and abide by EU single-market rules, including on free movement. In February 2014, Switzerland had a referendum on 'mass immigration' and voted for quotas on immigrants, including on EU citizens. Subsequently, the Swiss government sought to negotiate on this issue with the EU, but the Commission has made it plain that there will not be a negotiation because the issue of free movement is non-negotiable. A lesson from this could be that, outside the EU, Britain would need to maintain trading relationships and, to get single market access, could be required to adhere to free movement rules guaranteeing the rights of both EU and UK citizens. Britain could then be outside the EU but still bound by rules on free movement of people that were a key reason for it to leave.

Conclusion

The decision to leave the EU leaves British politics clouded by huge uncertainty and asks fundamental questions about the established precepts both of the British political system and of political analysis. Long-standing concerns configured British relations with the EU: a preference for intergovernmentalism; a preferred vision of a market-oriented EU; and questions about sovereignty and national identity. These were compounded by the confluence of three factors in the 2000s that, taken together, have energised Eurosceptics and meant that the debate about the EU was placed on a different footing leading to Brexit. A series of crises, especially in regard to the movement of people and the management of the eurozone, eroded confidence in the EU and weakened its legitimacy. Euroscepticism intensified and became mainstream in British politics. And UKIP's rise signified not only the emergence of right-wing, anti-EU populism in the UK but also the appeal of such parties to those feeling alienated from mainstream politics.

Cameron's renegotiation of Britain's membership before the referendum on continuing membership was ultimately futile and exposed complex multidimensional politics. These entailed dealing with EU institutions and other EU member states, as well as an array of interests within the UK stretching from the Parliamentary Conservative Party to devolved governments and taking in key interests such as business and the trade unions. A crucial concern was EU free-movement provisions on which there was no settled consensus within Britain or agreement amongst EU member states.

Difficult as it might be to accept for those that are not captivated by debate about British relations with the EU, the referendum on Britain's EU membership may well not be conclusive. A vote to remain would not have led to a period of harmony and stability in British–EU relations, particularly if the result had been on a knife-edge. A leave vote will undoubtedly lead to high levels of turbulence and opens the door to an even more complex renegotiation with the EU once Article 50(1) is invoked. And the break-up of the UK is much more likely with a further vote on Scottish independence almost inevitable. There is an exit door for Britain from the EU, but it's far from clear where it leads. In the immediate aftermath of the leave vote it swiftly became clear that even its most ardent advocates were unsure about the meaning of Brexit.

Chapter 15

Developments in (33 years of) British Politics

COLIN HAY

If, according to Harold Wilson's political calculus, 'a week is a long time in politics', then 33 years is an eternity. Yet it is now almost exactly a third of a century since the very first edition of *Developments in British Politics* (henceforth *Developments 1*) was published. It appeared just before the 1983 general election, though with a hastily revised re-edition published early in 1984 to take account of the re-election of Margaret Thatcher. Much, of course, has changed since then. The task of this concluding chapter is to gauge quite how much – how, if you like, developments in British politics have ... *developed*. In so doing, I return to and draw on the concluding chapter of the original volume, Patrick Dunleavy's characteristically crisp, lucid and still extremely useful 'Analysing British Politics' (1983). My central question is whether and, if so, to what extent, we can still make sense of and analyse British politics today in and through the categories, terms and theoretical perspectives that he set out so clearly a little over three decades ago.

To start with, however, it is useful just to remind ourselves a little of the world in 1983. Ronald Reagan was President of the US, and Peter Davidson was Doctor Who. The Cold War was at its height, the Berlin Wall had yet to fall, Gorbachev was not yet general secretary of the Soviet Communist Party and the terms *glasnost* and *perestroika* were, as yet, entirely unfamiliar even to Western diplomats. The European Union (EU) was still the European Economic Community (EEC), the debate on European Monetary Union would take a further five years to begin in earnest, and although trade volumes as a share of global GDP were rising steeply, the concept of globalisation was only just beginning to enter academic parlance and had yet to become part of the lexicon of political debate (it does not appear in the index, nor even the text, of *Developments 1* – and it would have been very strange if it had). Domestically, Margaret Thatcher was on the verge of being re-elected British Prime Minister for the first time – something that had seemed very unlikely until the turning in the tide of the Falklands conflict of 1982 (even if this was far from being the sole determinant of that outcome). Moreover, the term 'Thatcherism' would have been unfamiliar to all but a handful of her most ardent critics on the left (though it was, in fact, first used by Thatcher herself in 1975). Indeed, strange though it might seem today, it, too, appears neither in the index nor the body of the text of the original *Developments 1*, not even in the section on the Conservatives' embrace of neo-liberalism in Raymond Plant's authoritative chapter on the 'resurgence of ideology'. The Liberal Democrats and United Kingdom Independence Party (UKIP) had yet to be founded, the Scottish National Party (SNP) and Plaid Cymru are referred to three times, respectively, but only in passing and in one chapter; and the predecessor to the Green Party (the Ecology Party) is referred to just twice, again in passing, in a chapter on new protest groups.

A team of time-travelling political scientists stepping out of their time machine in 2016 having just read, on its date of publication, *Developments 1* would no doubt be shocked and surprised by the contents of *Developments in British Politics 10*. It is difficult to gauge what they would deem most remarkable. That an anti-establishment party of the right that did not exist in 1983 (UKIP) would win nearly 13 per cent of the vote in the 2015 general election (having won scarcely 3 per cent in 2010)? That the SNP would win 56 out of the 59 available seats in Scotland in the very same election? That Britain's third party (now, the Liberal Democrats) would suffer the largest single drop in vote share (15 per cent) ever recorded in a post-war British general election, having been in a coalition administration with the Conservatives until the election? That a Conservative Prime Minister could resign having held and lost an in/out referendum on Britain's membership of the EU? That the break-up of Britain itself could be a very distinct possibility?

Yet there is a deep and profound irony here too. For one does not have to travel forwards in time three decades to the present to find any of these current realities shocking. The brutal truth is that none of them would have seemed very likely and virtually none of them were predicted before the 2010 general election – indeed, very few were predicted even after 2010, *by anyone*. The time-travelling editors of *Developments in British Politics 9* (my time-travelling alter ego included) would be scarcely less amazed. As Richard Heffernan suggests in this volume, 'in the past five years, the Conservative–Liberal Democrat coalition was not predicted; the persistence of that coalition was often doubted; few foresaw that the [referendum on the] Alternative Vote (AV) would be so resoundingly rejected ...; that the SNP would win a majority in the Scottish Parliament; that a referendum on Scottish Independence would be held, nor that the yes vote in that referendum would be so large; almost no one expected a Conservative victory in 2015; and no one, not even the candidate himself, expected Jeremy Corbyn to become the Labour leader following the election' (197).

This raises a fascinating question – much easier to pose than it is to answer. Is British politics today (perhaps, even, politics more generally today) different in kind than it was until very recently – more contingent, more unpredictable, more prone to radical change? Or was it ever thus – was British politics (and/or politics more generally) always more contingent and less stable than we tended to give it credit for?

Much of the rest of this chapter is concerned with trying to answer that question. But, to give a hint of the argument, I think there is much in the view most clearly endorsed by Alan Renwick in his chapter on electoral behaviour (but more broadly representative of *Developments 10*) that much of what appears exceptional is in fact explicable in terms of broader long-term trends. Exceptional outcomes may, in other words, be the product of familiar processes. What makes outcomes so difficult to predict today, in this understanding, is not so much a sea change in the degree of political contingency in the British polity as a product of the complexity which comes from the interplay and interaction of a number of factors (including partisan and broader political disaffection and the disintegration of any single British political culture) which are themselves long-term tendencies. This is illustrated in Table 15.1 in which I seek to show how a series of seemingly exceptional political outcomes in the period 2010–2015 might be seen as the manifestation of broader political trends identified in the proceeding chapters. If this is right, and the 'exceptional' is in fact explicable in more general terms, the impression of a new condition of radical contingency afflicting our polity and our politics may well be misleading and something of an illusion. It could also prove rather transitory.

In a sense, we have been here before. And herein lies a second irony. For, despite the indisputable and massive transformation that has occurred in British politics since the 1980s (to say nothing, for now at least, of the international/global context in which British politics is embedded), there are also considerable echoes of that past in the present. The introductory chapter of *Developments 1* in 1983 begins as follows:

> British politics in the 1980s differ from British politics in the 1960s and early 1970s in surprising and fundamental ways. We have seen the revival of ideological debate, the weakening of the two-party system; the assertion of strong political control over the machinery of central government ... Partly as a result of these developments, the study of British politics has become more dynamic and diverse. (Drucker et al. 1983: 1)

Table 15.1   *Exceptional outcomes arising from long-term trends, 2010–2015*

'Exceptional' outcome	Long-term processes interacting to produce the outcome
Rise of the SNP – winning 56 out of 59 seats in Scotland in 2015	⌘1; ⌘2; ⌘3; ⌘4; ⌘5; ⌘10
Rise of UKIP – winning 13 per cent of the vote in 2015	⌘1; ⌘2; ⌘3; ⌘5; ⌘6; ⌘9; ⌘10
Demise of the Liberal Democrats – the largest decline in vote share recorded in the post-war period	⌘3; ⌘4; ⌘5; ⌘6
The calling of an 'in–out' EU referendum	⌘7; ⌘8; ⌘9; ⌘10;

Key

⌘1 – Greater regional and geographical differentiation of political culture

⌘2 – Increasing presence of non-majoritarian electoral systems in the British polity and the ability to carry success from one electoral system to another

⌘3 – Declining appeal of Westminster valence politics

⌘4 – Declining partisan alignment and identification

⌘5 – Increasing electoral volatility

⌘6 – The 'taint of office' and growing political disaffection with Westminster politics

⌘7 – Growing divisions within the Conservative Party over Europe

⌘8 – Increasing use of referenda to resolve positional issues

⌘9 – Growing anxieties about immigration and competition for jobs associated (rightly or wrongly) with EU enlargement and the free mobility of labour

⌘10 – Growing economic inequality in a context of austerity and low growth

It is the parallels, not the differences, with the present that are here startling.

Ideology, though widely seen as a casualty of the technocratic and depoliticising valence politics of competence, credibility and median voter convergence inaugurated by new Labour, seems to be back. As Michael Kenny's chapter in this volume shows, this takes many guises – Cameron and Osborne's radicalised and austerity-engendered neo-liberal assault on the state, UKIP's nationalist anti-immigration Euroscepticism and, perhaps most clearly, Labour's possibly transitory but distinctly post-Blairite flirtations with unilateralist socialism under Jeremy Corbyn. Similarly, if 2010 and 2015 are anything to go by, the two-party politics that characterised the entire post-war period is at an end. Between them, the Conservatives and Labour scarcely managed to secure two-thirds of the votes cast and the support of not even 45 per cent of eligible voters in either election. And, with the gradual blurring of the boundaries between political and civil service appointments, the growing influence of ministers on the latter, and civil service–directed state retrenchment in the name of austerity (as described in Catherine Haddon's chapter in this volume), the centralised control over the machinery of government in some ways would appear to characterise today's politics rather well. Indeed, it might well be argued that Thatcher's period in office marked a change towards a more presidential style of British politics, continued by Blair and of which Cameron is the latest exponent (Norton 2003; Heffernan 2005).

Plus ca change, plus c'est la même chose? Perhaps. But there is a need for a certain degree of caution here too. Superficial similarities can be misleading – and here they may well serve to mask some significant and important differences. Take first the return of ideology. It may well be that, particularly now that they are able to govern alone unencumbered by an ostensibly moderate coalition partner, the Conservatives' motives for austerity are clear, at least to seasoned political analysts. And it is certainly credible to label these motives ideological. Deborah Mabbett is surely right to suggest that if Osborne and Cameron had, as they claimed, been motivated genuinely to reduce the deficit as quickly as possible and less motivated by the (ideological) conviction that Britain would be better governed if it simply had less state and less state intervention, then the burden of budget consolidation would not have fallen so exclusively on cuts in public expenditure. But the point is that it takes a seasoned political analyst to decipher this – sifting genuine motives from declared motives in the process.

If this is ideology, it is well hidden. It is certainly not ideology in the Thatcherite sense – a clearly enunciated moral/normative conviction that one is right consistently guiding political action. Indeed, couched in such terms, what strikes one about Osborne and Cameron's approach to austerity is that it is distinctly non-ideological. For state retrenchment is presented not as a normative preference in a context of political choice but as the single rational course of action in a context of economic necessity. It is, in other words, *normalised* not *normative* (Hay 2004). Indeed, herein lies an important distinction between the politics of the 1980s and that of the present decade. For today, the traditional political parties (the Conservatives, Labour and the Liberal Democrats) arguably conspire, most of the time, to present economic policy choices, such as austerity and even the form it should take, as valence issues. The question is not whether austerity or competitiveness or state retrenchment are normatively desirable things in and of themselves; they are simply presented as non-negotiable imperatives. The only relevant question, it would seem, is who is deemed more competent to implement them. One might even argue that in today's politics the only way for traditional parties to deal with non-valence issues (Britain's place in Europe, Scotland's place in Britain) is through referenda!

But there is a second point here. For even were one to accept that austerity is a valence issue, by entertaining the suggestion (at least for the benefit of the argument) that there is no credible alternative to it, the form that such austerity might take remains a profoundly non-valence or *positional* question. For whether austerity is achieved through cuts in public spending, increases in rates of taxation or some combination of the two is likely to have major redistributive consequences. As this suggests, to present austerity and a package of reforms designed to achieve deficit reduction to the electorate as a technocratic solution to a technical problem is to choose to turn a positional issue into a valence issue – it is, in short, to depoliticise it (Green 2007; Hay 2007). This sounds more like the masking of ideology than the return to ideology. And it is in the political space vacated by the traditional parties through the re-construal (one might even suggest, mis-construal) of positional issues as valence issues that non-traditional parties like UKIP, the Green Party and, in its own slightly different way, the SNP have flourished. Their politics might be regarded as more genuinely ideological – though in the case of the SNP, perhaps only up to a point. For, while the SNP's success has undoubtedly been achieved in a context shaped decisively by the Scottish electorate's growing contempt for what is often seen as the Westminster-centred valence politics of austerity, there was in fact little substantive policy difference between Labour and the SNP in the 2015 election. The perception, however, was very different – not least because the SNP was able to adopt a rhetoric on a British stage (particularly in the context of a *British* general election) that was positional in the sense of speaking to distinctly (and hence, positionally) 'Scottish' interests while having the luxury of seeking only Scottish votes. That it would seem also to have appealed to so many voters *south* of the border is perhaps an index of the attractiveness of an approach at least ostensibly hostile to austerity.

A similar qualification may be in order when it comes to the weakening of the two-party system. In a sense, the case for such a claim looks stronger today than it was in 1983 when Labour and the Conservatives together polled 70 per cent of the votes cast, achieving the support of just over 50 per cent of eligible voters. As we have seen, today's figures are significantly lower – and the time-series data map out a well-documented long-term secular decline (despite a modest recovery between 2010 and 2015). But, as Paul Webb points out in this volume, if the implication of this is taken to be the increased likelihood of coalition government, we need to proceed with considerable caution. For the prospect of indeterminate elections leading to a proliferation of coalition administrations is significantly attenuated by two factors – the demise (which may or may not prove temporary) of the Liberal Democrats as the centrist third party and the contribution of coalition membership to that demise (through the 'taint' of holding office for the first time and the sense that it was associated with a certain betrayal of principle). The devastating consequences for the Liberal Democrats' electoral prospects of coalition cohabitation with the Conservatives serves as a clear warning to other potential minor coalition partners incapable of governing on their own (UKIP and the Greens especially). Indeed, the very anticipation of such an effect undoubtedly contributed to both parties' refusal, during the 2015 campaign, to contemplate entering into a coalition with any party after the election. And there is a further factor here too. For the single thing that would most increase the probability of coalition government in Britain is electoral reform. With the comfortable defeat of the AV referendum in 2011 and the demise of the Liberal Democrats as the principal carriers of the electoral reform banner, this looks less likely than ever – except perhaps in the context of the kind of wholesale constitutional renewal that any break-up of Britain would surely entail.

The changing context of British politics

Of course, that one can talk without any hint of irony of the potential break-up of Britain in a *Developments in British Politics* chapter is an index of how much British politics has changed in a third of a century. It is important to establish briefly some of the most significant of these contextual changes. Here what we have to attempt is time travel in the opposite direction – asking, in effect, what the time-travelling political scientist, having temporarily misplaced their memory of the 1980s, would find surprising and perplexing about the contents of *Developments 1*.

That is no easy task and there is, of course, no single answer to the question – political scientists, then as now, see different things in the political practices they analyse. As Dunleavy himself suggests, political science debate involves 'rival interpretations, framed from different perspectives ... appealing to different kinds of evidence' (1983: 253). What we see in the present and what we are likely to find different about the past when compared to the present are both likely to be shaped by such perspectives. That said, it is I think credible to suggest that most of today's time-travelling political scientists stepping out of the Tardis in Britain in 1983 to read *Developments 1* would be struck by a number of absences – things integral to the analysis of British politics today yet almost totally absent from the discussion then.

Among these, the following four stand out for me:

- globalisation and Britain's place in the world;
- Britain's changing place in Europe and the rise of Euroscepticism;
- Britain's integrated yet arguably disintegrating polity; and
- the rise of political disaffection.

Each might be seen as a contextual factor. The reason for seeking to identify them quite explicitly now is to suggest that we need, in effect, to recalibrate the discussion of the theoretical controversies Dunleavy identified in the analysis of British politics in the 1980s in the light of these more recent contextual changes.

The first is globalisation and the interdependence between nations and, indeed, policy areas with which it is associated. As already noted, it is hardly surprising that *Developments 1* makes no reference to globalisation, since the term had scarcely entered academic debate in 1983. But what is nonetheless interesting about *Developments 1* is that most chapters proceed as if the boundaries of Britain specified the limits of the processes under consideration – as if, in short, Britain were an island and the determinants of British political processes were all exclusively to be found on its shores.

The second and third points have also already been alluded to and are perhaps better seen less as contexts themselves than as questions the posing of which have changed profoundly the content and hence the context in which British politics now takes place. They are, or have become, integrally interrelated. That said, and with the benefit of a third of century of hindsight, it is easy to see that both of these were emergent issues at the time. Britain's place in Europe was scarcely discussed at all in *Developments 1* as it was then seen (quite rightly) as a settled issue. Where it is discussed, it is looked at almost exclusively in economic terms, very much in keeping with the political discourse of the day. Indeed, that it was discussed in such predominantly economic terms might well have contributed to it being regarded as a settled issue. Certainly the idea that Britain benefitted economically from its EEC membership was the product of a Conservative and Treasury orthodoxy. Labour, of course, would only come to accept that orthodoxy under Neil Kinnock in the early 1990s. Indeed, there is a certain irony here. For it was the Labour Party, not the Conservative Party, that was divided on Europe – divided to such an extent that this was perhaps the single most significant factor precipitating the splitting off of the Social Democratic Party in 1981 (Crewe and King 1995). That, in turn, contributed to the electoral ascendancy of the Conservatives – and hence to the settled character of the issue.

Arguably what has changed today is less the economic calculus under-pinning the Conservative–Treasury orthodoxy than the political salience of such economic considerations in a context in which, for very many British citizens, the free mobility of goods is taken for granted and the free mobility of labour is seen as a major source of labour-market inse-curity and is associated (rightly or wrongly) with the intensification of low-wage competition at a time of wage stagnation. The valencepolitics of the former has been increasingly displaced by thepositional politics of the latter. It is this positional politics, it would seem, that ultimately determined the outcome of Britain's 'in/out referendum' on EU member-ship in 2016.

'Euroscepticism' is another term absent from *Developments 1* (it had not yet been coined). It is one half of the new positional politics of Britain's place in Europe. Its uneven geographical distribution has contributed to the growing significance of a further question – that of Britain's future as an integrated polity. Again, it is hardly remark-able that there is no discussion of British politics qua British politics in *Developments 1*. The question that forms the title of Andrew Gamble's chapter in *Developments 10* – 'What's British about British politics?' – would have seemed a strange question to pose in 1983. The 1979 referendum on Scottish devolution, though it saw a narrow majority in favour of devolution (37 per cent of those eligible to vote opted for 'yes', 32.5 per cent for 'no'; the rest abstained), failed to achieve the 40 per cent which was written into the legislation as a minimum threshold for constitutional change. Indeed, it was more significant politically for serving as the immediate precursor to the 1979 general election (as the SNP withdrew its support from Callaghan's by then minority Labour administration, prompting the vote of no confidence which led ultimately to Thatcher's election). Things look very different 33 years on. With a narrow victory for 'Brexit' in the 2016 referendum on EU membership, with the pro-independence and pro-EU SNP hav-ing secured just over 50 per cent of the vote in Scotland (and all but three of the seats) in the 2015 general election and with public opinion north and south of the border on the question of Europe (and many other issues besides) moving in opposite directions, the future of Britain is very much an open question. It is no longer difficult to imagine a *Developments in British Politics 11* describing the break-up of Britain. As Andrew Gamble puts it, 'British politics may not be British for much longer' (19).

In sum, then, neither Britain's relationship with Europe nor its territorial future were as resolved as was typically assumed at the time, and both were the source of significant political conflict (of an intra- as well as inter-party kind). But it would have been difficult to see the role both issues might come to play in British politics three decades later.

A final contextual change is potentially no less significant. Though politicians have never been universally admired, even in a polity famously described by Gabriel Almond and Sidney Verba as 'deferential' (1963), they have arguably never been held in so much contempt as they are today (Hay 2007; Stoker, Hay and Barr 2015). Distrust, disaffection and disengagement characterise the present, and crucially are *seen* to characterise the present, in a way that they did not in 1983. This shapes profoundly the context in which contemporary politics is conducted. Indeed, the perception is perhaps the crucial issue here. For, as Maria Grasso's chapter shows, it is at least credible to argue that what has changed is not so much levels of political disaffection and disengagement as our awareness of them. It is that awareness, and the preoccupation with political distrust to which it has led, that arguably defines British politics today.

Analysing British politics today: The difference 33 years makes

Dunleavy's aim in what was, in effect, a slightly unconventional though extraordinarily valuable conclusion to the first edition of *Developments*, was to take stock of the political science of British politics by examining a series of (at the time) existing theoretical controversies as they relate to a number of substantive issues in the analysis of British political debate and practice. Almost all of these issues remain current today. Limits of space prevent a detailed discussion of each. Accordingly, and in what follows, I take just two of the issues he discusses, seeking to relate his original account of the controversy to contemporary developments in the light, where relevant, of the four contextual factors identified above. My hope in so doing is to gauge, in effect, the historical specificity of the present British political conjuncture. In conclusion I return to the question posed at the outset, namely whether British politics today has entered some kind of exceptional period and/or whether we can make sense of some of its seemingly exceptional characteristics through appeal to familiar long-term trends and tendencies.

Issue 1: Voting behaviour – why do people vote the way they do?

The first issue Dunleavy discusses, and the first I will consider here, is electoral behaviour – then, as now, the core of the political science of British politics. Yet the central question around which he seeks to organise his discussion, 'why do people vote the way they do?' now seems a little dated. There are two rather different reasons for this – one theoretical, the other more substantive.

The theoretical reason is that much of the debate that Dunleavy describes has now been resolved, at least to a significant extent. It is not that political scientists no longer disagree over the motives informing political choice, including electoral behaviour (far from it). But it is more that they typically see such motives, certainly at the level of the individual, as variable – changing in response to the options with which citizens are presented (for excellent accounts see, for instance, Clarke et al. 2004 and Sanders et al. 2011b). Voters, on such an understanding, are more likely to be motivated by instrumental (or interest-based) considerations when issues are presented to them in positional terms (where they are likely to perceive themselves to have a particular stake in this or that outcome) than when they are presented to them in valence terms (where the stake in the preferred outcome is one they share potentially with all other citizens).

The more substantive development is that the debate has, quite simply, moved on. For it is no longer possible to assume that citizens *do* vote in the way Dunleavy's question seems to imply. At minimum, then, a couple of prior questions need to be asked today before we even get on to the question of why do citizens vote the way they do – 'to what extent do citizens vote?' and 'what motivates their decision to vote or to abstain?'

There is a certain irony here. For in the early 1980s just about the only occasion when the decision to vote or not was discussed at all in academic political science was in the context of the so-called rational voter paradox (Ferejohn and Fiorina 1974; Blais 2000). The paradox was that the expectation of rational choice theory – namely, that rational voters motivated exclusively by self-interest would not turn out to vote since the chances of their vote proving decisive were vanishingly small and voting came at some personal cost to them – was not borne out by the evidence (since, for the most part, they *did* vote). The irony, of course, is that the political science of the 1980s seemed to have trouble explaining why people voted when turnout was comparatively high, while today, with turnout levels demonstrating a long-term secular decline, political science has much more trouble agreeing on why people don't vote and, hence, what might credibly be done to reverse the trend.

One of the most interesting (of many possible) 'solutions' to the rational voter paradox is offered by Mark Franklin. In his provocative book *Voter Turnout and the Dynamics of Electoral Competition* (2004), he suggests that it might be rational for citizens to vote, even in situations in which they know that the casting of their vote will make not an iota of difference to the outcome, if they are capable of taking greater pleasure (and hence a greater hedonistic utility) from the potential success of the party for which they would vote if, and only if, they go to the effort of voting for it (in the same way that one might take more pleasure from the success of one's 'team' if one goes to the trouble of watching it play). There are, of course, some fairly obvious objections to such a thesis – not least its incapacity to explain votes cast for parties which stand absolutely no chance of victory. But it is suggestive of a credible explanation for declining electoral participation in countries like Britain today (though it is not in fact the explanation offered by Franklin himself). For it suggests that declining identification with traditional political parties (for which there is very considerable evidence) might have much to do with it (see, for instance, Grasso 2016; Whiteley 2011). If citizens identify less with the mainstream political parties (as all the evidence suggests they do), then they are likely to take less pleasure from the success of the party they would be most likely to vote for and less likely, in turn, to go to the trouble of voting for it.

This is interesting in a second sense. It takes us straight back to Dunleavy's discussion of voting behaviour. For, in it, he counterposed the traditional 'party-identification' model of electoral behaviour with the (then) recently developed 'issue-voting' model. In the former, citizens' voting behaviour was quite predictable – they voted, typically out of habit and almost out of a sense of obligation for the party they took to approximate most closely their interests, often without much detailed consideration of the policies on offer but through a rather more amorphous sense of some natural affinity between it (*their* party) and people (family, friends, neighbours, co-workers) like them. In the latter, by contrast, in much more narrowly rational choice theoretic terms, citizens applied, in effect, a cost–benefit analysis to the package of political goods offered to them by each party, choosing the party that would best maximise (in their judgement) their own personal utility.

At the time, and as described by Dunleavy, these were contending explanations of the same phenomena. But, with the benefit of over three decades of hindsight, it is now much easier to see these as accounts of very different types of electoral appeal which coexisted to some extent in the 1980s but which do so far less today. As Alan Renwick's chapter in this volume shows so well, voters are much, much less attached to political parties – particularly the traditional political parties – than they were in the 1980s. This is in part because of the decline of class-based identification – the class dealignment famously described by Crewe and Sarlvik (1977; Sarlvik and Crewe 1983). But it is also because political parties started assuming that voters behaved more like the subjects of rational choice theory than the creatures of class-based habit described in the party-identification model. In other words, they started appealing to them in rather different ways. The irony, of course, is that the resulting valence politics of median voter convergence which has since come to characterise contemporary British electoral competition has not proved very attractive to citizens. It is, as it remains, very capable of winning elections – but elections, it seems, in which fewer people vote and in which a seemingly ever smaller share of those who do vote select one of the traditional parties.

Issue 2: Party competition – does the competition between political parties ensure voters' effective representation?

The second issue on which Dunleavy focuses his account of the political science of British politics in the early 1980s is the nature of party competition. This is scarcely less significant a topic and remains as central to the analysis of British politics today as it did in 1983. It is also intimately connected, perhaps even more so now, to assumptions about electoral behaviour. For, as the preceding discussion already indicates, the form that party competition takes and the consequences of such party competition for the representation of the views and preferences of the electorate both crucially depend on the assumptions that political parties make about citizens – that is, their preferences, their propensity to vote, their receptiveness to different types of political appeal and so forth. This is an issue to which we shall return presently. But in *Developments 1*, in keeping with the political science of the time, Dunleavy keeps the two sets of issues quite separate from one another.

As with the issue of voting behaviour, the central organising question that Dunleavy uses to focus his discussion, namely the extent to which party competition secures the effective representation of the electorate, betrays much of the context in which it was posed. British political science much more so then than now, and very much like its US counterpart of the time (from which, in a sense, it took its lead), was preoccupied with the democratic quality of the polity. Once again, there is a certain irony here. For all the available evidence suggests that citizens in the 1980s were far less concerned than they are today with the democratic quality of their own polity. Yet three decades later, at a time of considerable citizen discontent with the political system, academic political scientists appear rather less concerned to consider the character and quality of democratic representation in any holistic way. Dunleavy's question, the question in effect of whether British democracy works, is one that few if any analysts of British politics ask today (though for rare and partial exceptions see Stoker 2006; Webb 2009). That is something of a shame. For it is surely difficult to argue with the claim that the question has become more, not less, pertinent in the ensuing decades. This immediately suggests the value of revisiting Dunleavy's discussion of these themes in *Developments 1*.

That discussion again counterposes rival accounts of the workings of British democracy informed by very different theoretical perspectives. The 'responsible party' model, though something of an orthodoxy in the 1950s, was already being discredited as a rather naïve and convenient fiction by the 1980s. It saw the two-party system as a stable guarantor of transparent outcomes, with the changing balance of public opinion relatively well reflected in the swing between Labour and the Conservatives from one election to the next and with citizens able to ascribe changes in political outcomes to changes in government. British democracy, in short, was working well – and, for as long as the two-party system was in place, it was likely to continue to work well.

If the 'responsible party' model was already well on the wane by 1983, then the most credible candidate to replace it was Anthony Downs's increasingly influential *Economic Theory of Democracy* (1957) and the broader 'economic democracy' model that it inspired. Here, crisply stated in classic rational choice theoretic terms, parties were depicted as vote-maximising rational calculating machines anxious to mould their policy offerings to the preferences of the voter most likely to secure their election. In Britain's first-past-the-post two-party electoral system, this was typically anticipated to produce not clear and clearly attributable policy differences between the parties, but bipartisan convergence on the preferences of the median voter. Or, at least, this is what it was typically assumed to imply. Here too, though for very different reasons, an almost perfectly representative democratic outcome was predicted. For the expectation was that the parties would come to hover over the preferences of the median voter (which were, accordingly, assumed to determine the content of government policy). This was not because parties were assumed virtuous or responsible (as in the previous model) but in spite of the fact that they were not! The (benign) outcome was entirely serendipitous in the sense that parties were assumed not to care at all about the democratic character of the electoral process in which they participated, but to be motivated solely by their own chances of election or re-election. They were (as they remain, in accounts of this kind) cold, calculating, rational vote maximisers.

A final perspective, the 'adversarial party' model, approaches the question in a rather different way. For it looks less at the behaviour of the parties within the system than at the character of the system of representation itself. The result is a kind of critical corrective to the responsible party model. Succinctly stated, the argument is that Britain's first-past-the-post plurality rules essentially insulate and protect the two main parties from genuine third-party competition. The result is an unnecessary and unrepresentative polarisation in which, in effect, the preferences of the median voter are ignored as citizens are presented with a 'Hobson's choice between two equally polarised and unattractive manifestos' (Dunleavy 1983: 258). In 1983 the thesis was naturally applied to the newly formed Social Democratic Party (SDP) which, given the high thresholds inherent in the electoral system, failed to make a decisive electoral breakthrough despite its wide appeal. The thesis has lived on (until at least the rejection of electoral system change at the 2011 AV referendum) in the Liberal Democrats' arguments for electoral reform.

Though it is perhaps an unusual and unconventional thing to do, it is potentially very instructive to revisit these arguments and the debate they generated at the time in the light of more recent developments. A number of points seem worth reflecting upon. First, although it was already discredited in the early 1980s, there is an argument to be made for a suitably revised, duly retitled and rather less naively stated version of the responsible party model. With the demise of the Liberal Democrats, and for as long as Jeremy Corbyn (or someone equivalent) remains Labour Party leader, British party competition (particularly in England) resembles the assumptions of that model quite closely, and certainly rather more so that IT did in 1983. Though it may well not endure for long, and is highly susceptible to a change in the Labour leadership, for the first time in a long time British politics looks just a little like that of the 1960s (or perhaps even the 1920s) – with a two-party core and relatively clear policy differences between the two principal parties. This is, of course, now embedded within a much more complex multiparty system. But the biggest difference is that, unlike the 1960s, it is not at all clear that Labour can win in such an electoral context today. And if that proves correct, the politics of bipartisan convergence and 'catch-up' may well return and we may witness yet another bout of party 'modernisation' (on earlier bouts of which, see Denham and O'Hara 2007; Hay 1999; Heffernan 2001).

But it is by reflecting on the economic theory of democracy in the light of more recent developments that we arguably achieve the greatest analytic purchase on the present. Here there is a new and crucial effect that we need to take account of, that Downs did not begin to envisage at the time. That is, the influence of his own ideas (and those of others inspired by his broad approach to electoral conduct) on the behaviour of the political parties. The issue is not really whether Downs's account is right or wrong, but more the consequences of it having proved so influential. It is undoubtedly the case that the major British political parties (Labour and the Conservatives in particular) in the 1990s, 2000s and 2010s have come to behave in a manner more consistent with Downsian assumptions than they did in preceding decades. This has had major implications for the form and consequences of electoral competition in Britain. Thus, whether they were right to do so or not, the period since the mid-1990s has seen the two big parties (especially Labour under Blair) effectively conspire in a process of bipartisan convergence on economic policy above all, such that the electorate typically sees less and less difference between their policy positions. The process is depoliticising in the sense that what the electorate is increasingly asked to adjudicate is not the content of policy so much as the personnel deemed most competent to administer it. This is not to argue that perceived economic competence is the sole determinant of electoral outcomes, nor that the electorate perceives no difference between the principal parties on matters of economic policy. But it is to suggest that the relative salience of perceived competence is, and has been, rising, in the calculus of voters.

But this is not the only depoliticising dynamic at work in contemporary British politics. For there are two further forms of depoliticisation which arguably characterise the competition between Britain's traditional parties (the Conservatives, Labour and the Liberal Democrats) today. The first exhibits a very clear Downsian logic, though it is not in fact anticipated by Downs himself. It is something discussed already – the construal (even the mis-construal) of positional issues as valence issues. As Alan Renwick's chapter in this volume demonstrates in some detail, Britain's mainstream political parties tend to compete today less and less over positional issues – typically presenting themselves to the electorate not on the basis of sectional appeals (to this or that group which might be advantaged by a particular policy) but on the basis of the claim that they are the most competent to achieve a good valued by all (security, growth, financial stability, competitiveness and so forth).

Deficit reduction is a very good example. Between 2010 and 2015 there was, in effect, a consensus between the Conservatives, Labour and the Liberal Democrats that deficit reduction, if not perhaps desirable in and of itself, was necessary and good for the economy. But deficit reduction can be achieved in a variety of different ways: at one end of the spectrum exclusively through cuts in public spending; at the other end of the spectrum, exclusively though increases in taxation. And *that* choice is positional. Those who do not earn enough to pay income tax and who rely on public services have a clear (or positional) interest in deficit reduction through tax increases, just as top-rate tax payers making relatively little use of public services have a clear (or positional) interest in deficit reduction through cuts in public spending. But the Downsian logic is not to focus upon the sectional interests of those who might benefit from your party's deficit reduction strategy when you can appeal (in valence terms) to the entire electorate. To do so, all that is required is to concentrate on your competence to achieve a more widely desired end – a balanced budget. The strategy is disingenuous, for the issue remains positional; nonetheless, presenting it as a valence issue when it is in fact a positional issue makes good electoral sense. But every time a party does this, the quality of our democracy suffers. What makes for good electoral strategy does not necessarily make for good democratic outcomes.

A final form of depoliticisation also characterises electoral competition between traditional parties today. It arises in a context of globalisation and heightened economic (and even political) interdependence, but has been reinforced by the global financial crisis and its legacy of public debt. It was scarcely a factor in the politics of 1983. Here, in a manner almost directly analogous to the (mis-)construal of positional issues as valence issues, traditional political parties invoke external (typically, but not exclusively, economic) imperatives to override the preferences of the electorate. Among the many examples we might identify are the following: (i) the refusal to impose swingeing tax penalties on banks following the global financial crisis to compensate the tax-payer for the costs of the public bailing out of the banking sector – on the basis that this would encourage banks (in a context of globalisation) to leave Britain for other less-regulated, less-punitive and more-tax-friendly jurisdictions; (ii) the need to reduce, rapidly and decisively, the budget deficit in order to appease Britain's creditors (financial institutions holding British government debt) in a context in which any failure to 'keep the creditors sweet' might result in higher borrowing costs; and (iii) the imperative to maintain a comparatively lightly regulated labour market and weaker workers' rights, at least by comparative European standards, in order to ensure that Britain might retain its attractiveness to mobile inward foreign direct investment.

In each of these examples, and plenty of others besides, citizens' preferences are forsaken and discounted in favour of some overriding external imperative (such as the need to keep creditors sweet). The implicit logic goes something like this: you, the citizens, may well prefer X over Y, but, in a context of globalisation, say, Y is necessary for some reason of which you are scarcely aware and which only we can appreciate in full. So, despite a majority preference for X over Y, the policy will be Y.

Put these three logics of depoliticisation together (only one of which, of course, was even envisionable to Downs) and we have the makings of a powerful account of the origins of contemporary political disaffection. For the brutal reality is that the conventional and habitual practices of mainstream electoral competition in Britain today (at least pre-Corbyn) conspire to make politics a rather tedious, unedifying and even at times duplicitous spectacle. Politics becomes an encounter between traditional parties reluctant to reveal to us their motives, and keen to hide from us the likely distributional consequences of the policy proposals they would have us endorse. In addition, that competition is increasingly personalised and takes place in a highly mediatised environment, where it is the personalities of the principal protagonists rather than their policies that seem to be pitted against one another. Is it any wonder that a growing proportion of the electorate is turning its back on such mainstream valance politics in favour of the new positional politics of opposition?

The post-traditional, more ideological, parties may never be rewarded with the keys to Downing Street. But for as long as valence politics is seen as the condition of electoral success by the traditional parties, these newcomers will surely pose ever more of a challenge to their mainstream adversaries in a context of mounting political disaffection and declining electoral turnout. And voters now have a range of opportunities, including via bodies elected by PR, to register dissatisfaction with conventional politics.

Conclusion

British politics today gives every impression of being in the midst of a period of unprecedented flux. *Developments in British Politics* has never been more challenging to write, because it is so difficult to discern the direction – indeed, the directions – in which those developments are now leading. Writing today, with the dust still settling on Britain's momentous choice for 'Brexit' in the 2016 EU referendum, it is less possible than ever to see into the future. That brings with it a certain frustration. It is now quite possible to imagine that Britain might not exist as an integrated polity when the editors of *Developments of British Politics* sit down to consider an eleventh edition in 2020 or so.

But the frustration that comes with acknowledging our incapacity to discern the future trajectory, while chastening, is no manifesto of despair for the analysis of British politics. Prediction is a dark art – a terrain onto which political scientists and political analysts more broadly should venture only ever rarely, if at all. For, if there is one thing that all political scientists should know, it is that political outcomes – the kind of things that one would want to be able to predict – are politically contingent.

Put slightly differently, if the future is, indeed, genuinely political, it is still to be made – by us. And, if it is made in real time by political actors and thus not given by fate or some divine ordinance, then, strictly speaking, it does not yet exist to be predicted. It is politically contingent or open-ended and, as such, not amenable to the predictive powers of any science.

At times British politics has been quite predictable; at other times less so. Today it would appear the latter. Yet this is not because it is, in some fundamental way, more profoundly contingent than it has ever been. Rather, and more simply, it is that a variety of long-term processes and trends that we have sought to describe in this volume and which political scientists would claim to understand quite well come together and interact to produce a conjuncture in which a great many major issues will be resolved together in an unusually short space of time. In this conjuncture, British politics will not just develop but potentially change decisively and with enduring consequences. But, in the absence of a time travel machine, what those changes will be and how enduring they prove will have to await for the next and subsequent instalment of *Developments in British Politics*.

Guide to Further Reading

Chapter 1: What's British about British Politics?

The multinational character of the UK and the way this has given rise to a new politics of identity is explored by Kenny (2014). For the rise of radical right populism see Ford and Goodwin (2014). Historical treatments of the formation of British identity can be found in Colley (1992) and Davies (1999). A framework for comparing British and other democracies can be found in Lijphart (1999). The idiosyncrasies of Britain's constitution and the inconclusive attempts to reform it are well covered in Bogdanor (2009), Johnson (2004) and King (2015). For the House of Lords, Russell (2013) is indispensable. Devolution is discussed by Mitchell (2009) and Jones et al. (2013). Ideas of empire which shaped British political discourse in the twentieth century are analysed by Bell (2007). The intimate relationship with the United States which set Britain apart from Europe, is examined by Dumbrell (2001), Dimbleby and Reynolds (1989), Hitchens (2004) and Gamble (2003). For the peculiarities of the Anglo-liberal political economy see Hay (2013), Hall and Soskice (2013), Bennett (2004). Bell and Hindmoor (2015) dissect the nature of the Anglo-liberal financial system, while Esping-Andersen (1990) and Hay and Wincott (2012) provide comparative assessments of the British welfare state. For British political culture a very good starting point is Beer (1965). Veliz (1994) and Bennett (2004) celebrate the inventiveness and dynamism of British civic culture, while Whyte (2015) explores some of its more problematic aspects.

Chapter 2: Britain's Experience of Coalition Government: Continuity and Change

For the formation of the Conservative–Liberal Democrat coalition see Adonis (2013) and for its workings see Hazell and Yong (2012) and the collections edited by Seldon and Finn (2015) and Beech and Lee (2011) and (2015). David Laws provides a view from inside the coalition from the perspective of a leading Liberal Democrat and Clegg confidant (2016). For Cameron's role as Prime Minister leading a coalition see Bennister and Heffernan (2012) and (2014) and the study of Cameron by Seldon and Snowden (2015). For a recent discussion on the core executive see Elgie (2011) and on the role of the Prime Minister, see the debate between Dowding (2013), Foley

(2013), Poguntke and Webb (2013) and Heffernan (2013) published in *Parliamentary Affairs*. Bogdanor (2011) explores the impact the coalition had on the British constitution; the House of Commons library has produced a good note on the coalition at Westminster (2015); and the Institute of Government has published several useful reports, especially 2015.

Chapter 3: Voting Behaviour and Electoral Outcomes

Denver, Carman and Johns (2012) give an excellent introduction to elections and voting in the UK. For short, pithy introductions to a wide range of voting-related issues, see Cowley and Ford (2014) – the chapters are aimed at the general reader, but they contain suggestions for further reading that allow deeper digging. The largest study of electoral behaviour in the UK is the British Election Study (BES); the latest analysis from the BES team is Whiteley et al. (2013). Studies of the 2015 election include Cowley and Kavanagh (2015) and Geddes and Tonge (2015). For introductions to electoral systems, see Farrell (2011) and Renwick (2011). On the AV referendum of 2011, see Laycock et al. (2013) and the other articles in the same journal special issue.

Chapter 4: The Party System: Turbulent Multipartyism or Duopolistic Competition?

Clark (2012) and Driver (2011) are two recent undergraduate textbooks on British political parties, and Heffernan (2009) provides an broad overview of their changing structure. There are a number of books on parties at the 2015 general election, among them Cowley and Kavanagh (2015) and Geddes and Tonge (2015). For the Conservatives see the recent work by Bale (2016), Snowdon (2010) and Heppell (2013) and for Labour, Bale (2015) and Goes (2016). For other parties see Laws (2016) and Evans and Sanderson-Nash (2011) on the Liberal Democrats; Ford and Goodwin (2014) on UKIP; and Jackson (2014) and Mitchell, Bennie and Johns (2011) on the SNP. Good sources on electoral behaviour and party support include Denver, Carman and Johns (2012); Evans and Tilley (2012a); and Whiteley et al. (2013) and (2015).

Chapter 5: Ideological Politics and the Party System

For a conceptually sophisticated introduction to ideologies, and debates about their analysis, see Freeden (1998). For an overview of the coalition see Seldon and Snowdon (2015), and on Labour in these years see Bale

(2015). Important statements about contemporary Conservative thought and politics can be found in Kwarteng et al. (2012) and Norman (2014). Mudde (2007) and Taggart (2000) offer accessible and wide-ranging accounts of populist thinking. In relation to the centre-left, a discussion of 'predistribution' can be found in Chwalisz and Diamond (2015), of Blue Labour in Geary and Pabst (2015) and the existential crisis facing social democratic politics in Pearce (2015). The ideological dimensions of Scottish nationalism are discussed in Jackson (2011) and of political Englishness in Kenny (2014). Important statements about feminism were produced by Moran (2012), and environmentalism by Jackson (2011).

Chapter 6: Parliament: A Significant Constraint on Government

For good-quality general introductions to parliament see Norton (2013) and Rogers and Walters (2015). For a book-length account of the House of Lords see Russell (2013). Accounts of recent changes in the Commons can be found in Kelso (2009) and Russell (2011). For a fuller discussion of events in parliament under the coalition see Cowley (2015). Schleiter (2016) has edited a small collection of articles which will be useful for those interested in the impact of the Fixed-Term Parliaments Act on British politics. For more detailed discussion of the power of the Westminster parliament see Russell and Cowley (2015) and Russell et al. (2015). In general, much excellent material can be found on parliament's own website (www.parliament.uk), particularly including the briefing papers from the House of Commons and House of Lords libraries. Blogs such as the Constitution Unit (constitution-unit.com) and the Political Studies Association Specialist Group on Parliament and Legislatures (parliamentsandlegislatures.wordpress.com) include regular updates.

Chapter 7: Political Recruitment and the Political Class

Anne Phillips *The Politics of Presence* (1995) has been extraordinarily influential in how this subject is discussed – and is still a great read more than two decades after first being published. Data on the composition of the House of Commons after each election have been analysed in chapters in the 'Nuffield' election books, of which the most recent chapter is Criddle (2015), and there is an excellent overview in Audickas (2016). Of more detailed work, the nature of the political class is well discussed in Allen and Cairney (2015); the public's attitudes are analysed in Cowley (2013); and one of the few pieces of research on LGB politicians worldwide is

Reynolds (2013). The IPU data on women in parliaments is regularly updated at http://www.ipu.org/wmn-e/classif.htm.

Chapter 8: Political Participation

On political participation in Britain, the seminal study is that by Pattie, Seyd and Whiteley (2004). For an interesting take on definitions of participation see Fox (2014). On the processes of political disengagement, see Hay (2007) and Stoker (2006). For an attempt to map and understand the generational bases for the process of political disengagement from both conventional and unconventional politics and to place Britain in a comparative perspective see Grasso (2016) and Grasso et al. (2016). For focused studies on turnout and party activism see Franklin (2004), Whiteley and Seyd (2002) and Dalton and Wattenberg (2000), and for a more general introduction to citizen politics in advanced democracies Dalton (2008). On social movements and protest politics, the key text is Della Porta and Diani (2006). For a recent paper examining the relationship between protest participation and economic crisis, see Grasso and Giugni (2016).

Chapter 9: Developments in the Civil Service

For accounts of where Whitehall has come from, it is necessary to look at both historical and political science literature and Hennessy (2001), Lowe (2011) and Burnham and Pyper (2008) provide useful insights, as does Diamond (2014). There is a great deal of literature which analyses changing patterns of governance in the United Kingdom including Dunleavy (1991), Bevir and Rhodes (2003) and Richards (2008), and a recent study by Hood and Dixon (2015) explores Whitehall reform. For more recent accounts of what has happened since 2010, it is necessary to look at government and civil service documents including parliamentary reports, particularly the House of Commons (2011) and the House of Lords (2012). National Audit Office reports can be accessed online, as can useful reports from the Institute for Government (www.institute forgovernment.org.uk).

Chapter 10: Politics and the News Media: Messages and Messengers

New overviews of the changing relationship between media and politics are found in Robertson (2015), Perloff (2014) and Ridout (2013). Recent developments in the coverage of politics are covered nicely by Craig (2014); the role of the media in the last election by Jackson and Thorsen (2015); and the ever-important phenomenon of political personalisation is variously explored by Langer (2012) and Stanyer (2013). Useful insights into the politics–media nexus are provided by many past insiders, especially McBride (2013) and the Campbell diaries (2010, 2010a, 2011 and 2012). Both examine past Labour governments; more recent insiders have yet to spill the beans on recent Conservative-led governments; Seldon and Snowdon (2015) is helpful in the interim. Tony Blair's informed, if self-serving, criticisms of media methods (2007) remains well worth consulting – so, too, those of Lloyd (2004). On the role advertising plays in politics see the fun, very informative book by Delaney (2015) and the memoir of the Thatcher confidant Tim Bell (2014). The Reuters Institute for the Study of Journalism at Oxford provides a wealth of statistical information about the modern online media. It is found at http://reutersinstitute.politics.ox.ac.uk

Chapter 11: Governing in Times of Austerity

The Office for Budget Responsibility (OBR) produces regular reports on the government's fiscal plans, as well as assessments of welfare trends. These reports are a good deal more informative than the Treasury's budget documents, but they tend to avoid direct criticism of the government. The Institute for Fiscal Studies (IFS) produces budget analyses that are somewhat more forthcoming in pointing out winners and losers, but they are still rather technical. The Joseph Rowntree Foundation has sponsored a programme of research on the impact of austerity, including both statistical analyses and qualitative studies. There is an abundant literature in economics on the pros and cons (mainly cons) of austerity, to which Blyth (2013) provides a readable introduction. Streeck (2014) has also provided a trenchant analysis of austerity in a number of developed countries, as part of a special issue which also includes several articles on fiscal rules. Gamble (2014) provides an extended account of post-crisis austerity, while Stanley (2014) complements and extends Gamble's arguments about political acceptance of, or acquiescence to, the government's policies.

Chapter 12: The Politics of Immigration: Old and New

One of the best outlines of how immigration policy is shaped in Western liberal democracies, including Britain, is Hampshire (2013). For more specific details about British immigration policy and the factors shaping it see Ford, Jennings and Somerville (2015). For overviews of public opinion on immigration see Duffy (2014) and Ford, Morrell and Heath (2012). Ford (2008) suggests that racial prejudice in Britain is falling. Immigration and party politics is variously explored by Blinder, Ford and Ivarsflaten (2013), Evans and Chzhen (2013) and Biggs and Knauss (2012). An analysis of UKIP support is to be found in Ford and Goodwin (2014). For the economic costs of immigration see Dustmann and Frattini (2013), Rowthorn (2014) and Bloch (2008).

Chapter 13: The United Kingdom after the Scottish Referendum

The best overall account of devolution in the UK is Mitchell (2009) which explores the distinctive trajectories of each part of the UK. Jeffery (2009) gives an account of the absence of overarching purpose and coordination on the part of UK central government, with this prefigured in the analysis in Hazell (1999) which anticipated many more recent challenges. There is as yet no full, published scholarly analysis of the Scottish referendum, though journalistic accounts by McWhirter (2014) and Pike (2015) are useful. Hazell (2006) sets out the parameters of the 'English question' while the McKay Commission (2013) analyses the grounds for introducing English votes on English laws and Jeffery et al. (2014) report on the latest in a series of surveys on English political attitudes.

Chapter 14: Britain and the European Union

For general historical overviews of the relationship between Britain and the EU see Young (1999), Wall (2008) and Geddes (2013). On the dynamics of Euroscepticism in Britain see Spiering (2014) and Gifford (2014), and on the wider European picture see Leconte (2010). For a good analysis of the effects of crises on the EU see Baker and Schnapper (2015). For guides from a variety of perspectives to the key issues in the referendum see Hannan (2012), Dixon (2014) and Bootle (2015). The Conservative–Liberal Democrat coalition government conducted an audit of what the EU does and how it affects the UK called the 'Balance of Competences'. These reviews of EU laws and policies and their implications for the UK can be found here: https://www.gov.uk/guidance/review-of-the-balance-of-competences.

Chapter 15: Developments in (33 years of) British Politics

Patrick Dunleavy's excellent final chapter of *Developments in British Politics 1* (Dunleavy 1983) is the obvious place to start in looking for further readings for this chapter. The introduction to that book is also well worth reading and gives an excellent sense of the state of British politics in 1983 (Drucker et al. 1983). Downs's seminal work (1957) is the key introduction to the economic theory of democracy; Clarke et al. (2004) provide an excellent sense of how the debate has moved on since then. Hay (2007) makes the case for the link between depoliticisation and political disaffection while Grasso (2016) sets British trends on political participation in their comparative context.

Bibliography

Adams, R. (2015) 'DfE lacks effective procedures and insight into schools, watchdog claims', *The Guardian*, 30 January.

Adonis, A. (2013) *Five Days in May: The Coalition and Beyond*, London: Biteback.

Alexander, D. (2014) 'Liberal Democrats have no part in Tory plans for harsh cuts and empty tax promises', *Daily Telegraph*, 8 December.

Allen, P. (2013) 'Linking the pre-parliamentary political experience and political careers of the 1997 general election cohort', *Parliamentary Affairs*, 66(4): 685–707.

Allen, P. (forthcoming) 'Achieving sex equality in executive appointments', *Party Politics*.

Allen, P. and Cairney, P. (2015) 'What do we mean when we talk about the "political class"?', *Political Studies Review* (Early View).

Allen, P., Cutts, D. and Campbell, R. (2014) 'Measuring the quality of politicians elected by gender quotas – are they any different?', *Political Studies* (Early View).

All-Party Parliamentary Inquiry into Hunger in the United Kingdom (2014) *Feeding Britain: A Strategy for Zero Hunger in England, Wales, Scotland and Northern Ireland*, London: The Children's Society (https://foodpoverty inquiry.files.wordpress.com/2014/12/food-poverty-feeding-britain-final.pdf).

Almond, G. and Verba, S. (1963) *The Civic Culture: Political Attitudes and Democracy in Five Nations*, London: Sage Publications.

Alwin, D. and Krosnick, J. (1991) 'Aging, cohorts and the stability of socio-political orientations over the life span', *American Journal of Sociology*, 97: 169–195.

Anthony, A. (2016) 'Is free speech in British universities under threat?, *The Observer*, 24 January (http://www.theguardian.com/world/2016/jan/24/safe-spaces-universities-no-platform-free-speech-rhodes).

Audickas, L. (2016) *Social background of MPs 1979–2015*, Briefing Paper CBP 7483, London: House of Commons Library.

Baker, D. and Schnapper, P. (2015) *Britain and the Crisis of the European Union*, London: Palgrave.

Baker, K. (2015) 'Miliband's Moses moment is ridiculed on a biblical scale', *MailOnline*, 3 May (http://www.dailymail.co.uk/news/article-3066509/Mili-band-s-Moses-moment-gets-internet-treatment.html).

Bale, T. (2011) *The Conservative Party from Thatcher to Cameron*, Cambridge: Polity.

Bale, T. (2012) 'The black widow effect: Why Britain's Conservative–Liberal Democrat coalition might have an unhappy ending', *Parliamentary Affairs*, 65(2): 323–337.

Bale, T. (2015) *Five Year Mission: The Labour Party under Ed Miliband*, Oxford: Oxford University Press.

Bale, T. (2016) *The Conservatives Since 1945: The Drivers of Party Change*, Oxford: Oxford University Press.

Bale, T., Webb, P. and Poletti, M. (2015) 'Ideology is in the eye of the beholder: How British party supporters see themselves, their parties, and their rivals', *LSE British Politics and Policy* (http://blogs.lse.ac.uk/politicsandpolicy/ideology-is-in-the-eye-of-the-beholder/).

Bale, T. and Webb, P. (2015) 'The Conservatives: Their sweetest victory?', in A. Geddes and J. Tonge (eds) *Britain Votes 2015*, Oxford: Oxford University Press.

Bang, H. (2005) 'Among everyday makers and expert citizens' in J. Newman (ed.) *Remaking Governance: Peoples, Politics and the Public Sphere*, Bristol: Policy Press.

Bank of England (2012) 'The distributional effects of asset purchases', *Bank of England Quarterly Bulletin*, Q3: 254–266.

Bartholomew, J. (2015a) 'Hating the Daily Mail is a substitute for doing good', *The Spectator*, 1 April (http://www.spectator.co.uk/2015/04/hating-the-daily-mail-is-a-substitute-for-doing-good/) .

Bartholomew, J. (2015b) 'I invented "virtue signalling". Now it's taking over the world', *The Spectator*, 10 October (http://www.spectator.co.uk/2015/10/i-invented-virtue-signalling-now-its-taking-over-the-world/).

Bates, L. (2014) *Everyday Sexism*, London: Simon & Schuster.

Baxendale, H. and Wellings, B. (2014) 'Euroscepticism and the Anglosphere: Traditions and dilemmas in contemporary English nationalism', *Journal of Common Market Studies*, 53(1): 123–139.

BBC News (2006) 'UKIP demands apology from Cameron', 4 April (http://news.bbc.co.uk/1/hi/4875026.stm).

BBC News (2010) 'Election 2010: National Results', *BBC News Online*.

BBC News (2014) 'Vote 2014: UK European election results' *BBC News Online*.

BBC News (2015a) 'Cameron: "Britain and Twitter are not the same thing"', 7 October (http://www.bbc.co.uk/news/uk-politics-34462075)

BBC News (2015b) 'Election 2015: Results', *BBC News Online*.

BBC News (2015c) 'Tories' £100,000 a month Facebook bill', 5 February (http://www.bbc.co.uk/news/uk-politics-31141547).

BBC News (2016). Election 2016. *BBC News Online*, last accessed 9 May 2016.

Beech, M. and Lee, S. (eds) (2011) *The Cameron-Clegg Government: Coalition Politics in an Age of Austerity*, London: Palgrave.

Beech, M. and Lee, S. (eds) (2015) *The Conservative-Liberal Coalition: Examining the Cameron-Clegg Government*, London: Palgrave.

Beer, S. (1965) *Modern British Politics*, London: Faber.

Bell, D. (2007) *The Idea of Greater Britain: Empire and the Future of World Order, 1860–1900*, Princeton: Princeton University Press.

Bell, S. and Hindmoor, A. (2015) *Masters of the Universe, Slaves of the Market*, Cambridge: Harvard University Press.

Bell, T. (2014) *Right or Wrong: The Memoirs of Lord Bell*, London: Bloomsbury.

Bennister, M. and Heffernan, R. (2012) 'Cameron as prime minister: The intra-executive politics of Britain's coalition government', *Parliamentary Affairs*, 65(4): 778–801.

Bennister, M. and Heffernan, R. (2015) 'The limits to prime ministerial autonomy: Cameron and the constraints of coalition', *Parliamentary Affairs*, 68(1): 25–41.

Bennett, J. (2004) *The Anglosphere Challenge: Why the English-Speaking Countries Will Lead the Way in the Twenty-First Century*, Lanham, MD: Rowman & Littlefield.

Benton, M. and Russell, M. (2012) 'Assessing the impact of parliamentary oversight committees: The select committees in the British House of Commons', *Parliamentary Affairs*, 66(4): 772–797.

Berry, C. (2013) 'Labour and the politics of budget responsibility', *speri.comment*, 15 October (http://speri.dept.shef.ac.uk/2013/10/15/labour-politics-budget-responsibility/).

Bertram, T. (2015a), Tweet (https://twitter.com/theobertram/status/6752882 27360575488).

Bertram, T. (2015b), Tweet (https://twitter.com/theobertram/status/67528504 0876523520).

Bevir, M. and Rhodes, R. A. W. (2003) *Interpreting British Governance*, London: Routledge.

Biggs, M. and Knauss, K. (2012) 'Explaining membership in the British National Party: A multilevel analysis of contact and threat.', *European Sociological Review*, 28(5): 633–646.

Blair, T. (2007) 'Blair speech on the media', *BBC News*, 21 June (http://news.bbc.co.uk/1/hi/uk_politics/6744581.stm).

Blais, A. (2000) *To Vote or Not to Vote? The Merits and Limits of Rational Choice Theory*, Pittsburgh, PA: University of Pittsburgh Press.

Blick, A. (2016) 'Constitutional implications of the Fixed-term Parliaments Act 2011' *Parliamentary Affairs*, 69(1): 19–35.

Blinder, S., Ford, R. and Ivarsflaten, E. (2013) 'The better angels of our nature: How the antiprejudice norm affects policy and party preferences in Great Britain and Germany', *American Journal of Political Science*, 57(4): 841–857.

Bloch, A. (2008) 'Refugees in the UK labour market: The conflict between economic integration and policy-led labour market restriction', *Journal of Social Policy*, 37: 21–36.

Bloch, M. (2015) *Closet Queens: Some 20th Century British Politicians*, London: Little, Brown.

Blyth, M. (2013) *Austerity: The History of a Dangerous Idea*, Oxford: Oxford University Press.

Bogdanor, V. (2009) *The New British Constitution*, Oxford: Hart.

Bogdanor, V. (2011) *The Coalition and the Constitution*, Oxford: Hart.

Bootle, R. (2015) *The Trouble with Europe: Why the EU isn't Working, How It Can Be Reformed, What Could Take its Place*, London: Nicholas Brealey Publishing.

Brand, R. (2014) *Revolution*, London: Century.

British Election Study 2015 (2015) (http://www.britishelectionstudy.com/).

Brown, G. (2014) *My Scotland, Our Britain. A Future Worth Sharing*, London: Simon & Schuster.

Bruni, F. (2015) 'The exploitation of Paris', *New York Times*, 11 November (http://www.nytimes.com/2015/11/14/opinion/the-exploitation-of-paris.html).

Bulpitt, J. (1983) *Territory and Power in the United Kingdom*, Manchester: Manchester University Press.

Burnham, J. and Pyper, R. (2008) *Britain's Modernised Civil Service*, Basingstoke: Palgrave Macmillan.

Burnham, W. D. (1970) *Critical Elections and the Mainsprings of American Politics*, New York: W.W. Norton.

Butler, D. and Stokes, D. (1974) *Political Change in Britain: Forces Shaping Electoral Choice*, New York: St Martin's Press.

Cabinet Office (2012) *Civil Service Reform Plan*, June (http://www.civilservice.gov.uk/wp-content/uploads/2012/06/Civil-Service-Reform-Plan-acc-final.pdf).

Cabinet Office (2013) *Accountability and Responsiveness in the Senior Civil Service: Lessons from Overseas. Report by IPPR*, June (https://www.gov.uk/government/publications/accountability-and-responsiveness-in-the-senior-civil-service).

Cairney, P. (2007) 'The professionalisation of MPs: Refining the 'politics-facilitating' explanation', *Parliamentary Affairs*, 60: 212–233.

Cairney, P. (2011) 'Coalition and minority government in Scotland: Lessons for the United Kingdom?', *Political Quarterly*, 82: 261–269.

Cage, J. (2016) *Saving the Media: Capitalism, Crowdfunding and Democracy*, Cambridge: Harvard University Press.

Cameron, D. (2010) 'Big Society Speech', Liverpool, 19 July (http://www.number10.gov.uk/news/speeches-and-transcripts/2010/07/big-society-speech-53572)

Cameron, D. (2013) EU speech at Bloomberg, 23 January (https://www.gov.uk/government/speeches/eu-speech-at-bloomberg).

Campbell, A. (2010) *Prelude to Power, The Alastair Campbell Diaries Volume One, 1994–1997*, London: Hutchinson.

Campbell, A. (2010a) *Power and the People, The Alastair Campbell Diaries Volume Two, 1997–1999*, London: Hutchinson.

Campbell, A. (2011) *Power and Responsibility, The Alastair Campbell Diaries Volume Three, 1999–2001*, London: Hutchinson.

Campbell, A. (2012) *Burden of Power, The Alastair Campbell Diaries Volume Four, 2001–2003*, London: Hutchinson.

Campbell, A. (2016) 'Alistair's blog: There will always be a need for good journalism, and BBC is an important part of that', 2 January (http://www.alastaircampbell.org/blog/2016/01/21/there-will-always-be-a-need-for-good-journalism-and-bbc-is-an-important-part-of-that/).

Campbell, R. and Childs, S. (2014) 'Parents in parliament: "Where's Mum?"', *Political Quarterly*, 85(4): 487–492.

Castells, M. (2000) *The Rise of the Network Society*, Oxford, UK: Blackwell.

Chadwick, A. and Vaccari, C. (2015) 'Citizen engagement in the dual-screened election campaign', in D. Jackson and E. Thorsen (eds) *UK Election Analysis 2015: Media, Voters and the Campaign*, Bournemouth: Centre for the Study of Journalism, Culture and Community (http://www.electionanalysis.uk/uk-election-analysis-2015/section-6-social-media/citizen-engagement-in-the-dual-screened-election-campaign/).

Chan, G. (2015) 'Tony Abbott delivers his final barbs as he steps into the wilderness', *The Guardian*, 15 September (http://www.theguardian.com/australia-news/2015/sep/15/tony-abbott-delivers-his-final-barbs-as-he-steps-into-the-wilderness).

Chapman, R. A. (1997) 'The end of the civil service', in P. Barberis (ed.) *The Civil Service in an Era of Change*, Aldershot: Dartmouth, 23–37.

Childs, S. and Webb, P. (2011) *Sex, Gender and the Conservative Party. From Iron Lady to Kitten Heels*, London: Palgrave.

Chu, B. (2012) 'Bank's stimulus plan 'has lined pockets of the rich'', *The Independent*, 24 August (http://www.independent.co.uk/news/business/news/banks-stimulus-plan-has-lined-pockets-of-the-rich-8076938.html)

Chwalisz, C. and Diamond, P. (2015) *The Predistribution Agenda: Tackling Inequality and Supporting Sustainable Growth*, London: IB Taurus.

Civil Service Commission (2012) 'Press notice: Civil Service Commission responds to government's reform plan proposals on permanent secretary appointments', Civil Service Commission website, 10 December (http://civilservicecommission.independent.gov.uk/wp-content/uploads/2012/12/PRESS-NOTICE-10-Dec-2012.pdf).

Clark, A. (2012) *Political Parties in the UK*, London: Palgrave.

Clark, T., with Heath, A. (2014) *Hard Times: The Divisive Toll of the Economic Slump*: New Haven and London: Yale University Press.

Clarke H. D., Sanders, D., Stewart, M. C. and Whiteley, P. (2004) *Political Choice in Britain*, Oxford: Oxford University Press.

Cogbill et al., (2016) Challenge and opportunity: The draft Wales Bill 2015, London: The Constitution Unit, (https://www.ucl.ac.uk/constitution-unit/publications/tabs/reports/edit/unit-publications/167.pdf).

Colley, L. (1992) *Britons: Forging the Nation 1707–1837*, New Haven: Yale University Press.

Conservative Party (2015) *The Conservative Party Manifesto 2015*, London: Conservative Party.

Copsey, N., and Haughton, T. (2014) 'Farewell Britannia? "Issue capture" and the politics of David Cameron's 2013 EU referendum pledge', *Journal of Common Market Studies*, 52(S1): 74–89.

Cowley, P. (2002) *Revolts and Rebellions: Parliamentary Voting Under Blair*, London: Politico's.

Cowley, P. (2005) *The Rebels: How Blair Mislaid His Majority*, London: Politico's.

Cowley, P. (2006) 'Making parliament matter?', in P. Dunleavy, R. Heffernan, P. and C. Hay (eds) *Developments in British Politics 8*, London: Palgrave.

Cowley, P. (2012) 'Arise, novice leader! The continuing rise of the career politician in Britain', *Politics*, 32(1): 31–38.

Cowley, P. (2013) 'Why not ask the audience? Understanding the public's representational priorities', *British Politics*, 8: 138–163.

Cowley, P. (2015) 'The coalition and parliament', in A. Seldon and M. Finn (eds) *The Coalition Effect, 2010–2015*, Cambridge: Cambridge University Press.

Cowley, P. and Ford, R. (eds) (2014) *Sex, Lies, and the Ballot Box*, London: Biteback.

Cowley, P. and Kavanagh, D. (2015) *The British General Election of 2015*, Basingstoke: Palgrave Macmillan.

Craig, G. (2014) *Performing Politics: Media Interviews, Debates and Press Conferences*, Cambridge: Polity Press.

Crawford, R. (2010) 'Where did the axe fall?', *Institute for Fiscal Studies* (http://www.ifs.org.uk/publications/5311).

Crewe, I. and King, A. S. (1995) *SDP: The Birth, Life and Death of the Social Democratic Party*, Oxford: Oxford University Press.

Crewe, I. and Sarlvik, B. (1977) 'Partisan dealignment in Britain', *British Journal of Political Science*, 7(2): 129–190.

Criddle, B. (2015) 'Variable diversity: MPs and Candidates', in P. Cowley and D. Kavanagh (eds) *The British General Election of 2015*, London: Palgrave.

Curtice, J. (2013a) 'Politicians, voters, and democracy: The 2011 AV referendum on the alternative vote', *Electoral Studies*, 32(2): 215–223.

Curtice, J. (2013b) *The Score At Half Time: Trends in Support for Independence* (https://www.natcen.ac.uk/media/265693/ssa_the-score-at-half-time.pdf) .

Curtice, J. (2015) 'A return to normality? How the electoral system operated', in A. Geddes and J. Tonge (eds) *Britain Votes 2015*, Oxford: Oxford University Press.

Curtice, J. and Evans, G. (2015) 'Britain and Europe: Are we all Eurosceptics now?', National Centre for Social Research: British Social Attitudes 32.

Curtice, J., Fisher, S. D. and Ford, R. (2015) 'Appendix 1: The results analysed', in P. Cowley and D. Kavanagh (eds) *The British General Election of 2015*, London: Palgrave.

Dalton, R. (2008) *Citizen Politics: Public Opinion and Political Parties in Advanced Industrial Democracies*, Washington, DC: CQ Press.

Dalton, R. (2009) *The Good Citizen: How a Younger Generation is Reshaping American Politics*, Washington, DC: CQ Press.

Dalton, R. and Wattenberg, M. (2000) *Parties Without Partisans: Political Change in Advanced Industrial Democracies*, Oxford: Oxford University Press.

D'Ancona, M. (2014) *In It Together: The Inside Story of the Coalition Government*, London: Penguin.

Dassonneville, R. (2015) *Net Volatility in Western Europe: 1950–2014*, Dataset, Leuven: KU Leuven Centre for Citizenship and Democracy (http://soc.kuleuven.be/web/staticpage/11/95/eng/1197).

Davies, N. (1999) *The Isles: A History*, London: Macmillan.

De Agostini, P., Hills, J. and Sutherland, H. (2014) 'Were we really all in it together? The distributional effects of the UK Coalition government's tax-benefit policy changes', *CASE Working Paper* No SPCCWP10, LSE.

Deacon, D., Downey, J., Stanyer, J. and Wring D. (2015) 'News media performance in the 2015 general election campaign', in D. Jackson and E. Thorsen (eds) *UK Election Analysis 2015: Media, Voters and the Campaign*, Bournemouth: Centre for the Study of Journalism, Culture and Community (http://www.electionanalysis.uk/uk-election-analysis-2015/section-1-media-reporting/news-media-performance-in-the-2015-general-election-campaign/).

Deegan-Krause, K., with Bågenholm, A. and Weeks, L. (2016) 'Where the boys are (and aren't): Analyzing twenty years of political data yearbook statistics on women in government and parliament' (http://www.wileyiwdresearch.com/gender-equality-blog/where-the-boys-are-and-arent-analyzing-twenty-years-of-political-data-yearbook-statistics-on-women-in-government-and-parliament).

Delaney, S. (2015) *Mad Men and Bad Men: What Happened When British Politics Met Advertising?*, London: Faber and Faber.

Della Porta, D. and Diani, M. (2006) *Social Movements: An Introduction*, 2nd Edition, Oxford: Blackwell.

Denham, A. and O'Hara, K. (2007) 'The three "mantras": "Modernization" and the Conservative party', *British Politics*, 2(2): 167–190.

Dennison, J. and Goodwin, M. (2015) 'Immigration, issue ownership and the rise of UKIP', *Parliamentary Affairs*, 68(S1): 168–187.

Denver, D. (2015) 'The results: How Britain voted', in A. Geddes and J. Tonge (eds) *Britain Votes 2015*, Oxford: Oxford University Press,

Denver, D., Carman, C. and Johns, R. (2012) *Elections and Voters in Britain*, 3rd edition, Basingstoke: Palgrave Macmillan.

Diamond, P. (2014) *Governing Britain: Power, Politics and the Prime Minister*, London: I.B. Tauris.

Diamond, P. and C. Chwalisz (eds) (2015) *The Predistribution Agenda: Tackling Inequality and Supporting Sustainable Growth*, London: I.B. Tauris.

Dimbleby, D. and Reynolds, C. (1989) *An Ocean Apart: The Relationship Between Britain and America in the Twentieth Century*, New York: Vintage Books.

Dixon, H. (2014) *The In/Out Question: Why Britain Should Stay in the EU and Fight to Make it Better*, London: CreateSpace Independent Publishing Platform.

Dowding, K. (2013) 'The prime ministerialisation of the British prime minister', *Parliamentary Affairs*, 66(3): 617–635.

Downs, A. (1957) *An Economic Theory of Democracy*, New York: Harper Collins.

Driver, S. (2011) *Understanding British Party Politics*, Cambridge: Polity Press.

Drucker, H., Dunleavy, P., Gamble, A. and Peele, G. (1983) 'Introduction', in H. Drucker et al. (eds) *Developments in British Politics*, Basingstoke: Macmillan.

Duffy B. (2014) 'Perceptions and reality: Ten things we should know about attitudes to immigration in the UK', *The Political Quarterly*, 85(3): 259–266.

Dumbrell, J. (2001) *A Special Relationship: Anglo-American Relations in the Cold War and After*, London: Palgrave Macmillan.

Dunleavy, P. (1983) 'Analysing British politics', in Drucker et al. (eds.) *Developments in British Politics*, Basingstoke: Macmillan.

Dunleavy, P. (1991) *Democracy, Bureaucracy and Public Choice*, Hemel Hempstead: Harvester Wheatsheaf.

Dunleavy, P. and Rhodes, R. (1990) 'Core executive studies in Britain', *Public Administration*, 68(1): 3–28.

Dustmann, C. and Frattini, T. (2013) 'The fiscal effects of immigration to the UK', Discussion Paper Series, CDP No 22/13, Centre for Research and Analysis of Migration, Department of Economics, University College London.

Dustmann, C. and Frattini, T. (2014) 'The fiscal and welfare effects of immigration to the UK', *The Economic Journal*, 124(580): F565–F568.

Duverger, M. (1954) *Political Parties: Their Organization and Activity in the Modern State*, London: Methuen.

Eichhorn, J. and Paterson, P. (2014), *Who is Still Wavering. Turnout and the Undecided*   (http://www.scotcen.org.uk/media/563073/ssa-2014-turnout-and-education.pdf) .

Elgie, R. (2011) 'Core executive studies two decades on', *Public Administration*, 89(1): 64–77.

Esping-Andersen, G. (1990) *The Three Worlds of Welfare Capitalism*, Cambridge: Polity.

Evans, E. and Sanderson-Nash, E. (2011) 'From sandals to suits: Professionalisation, coalition and the Liberal Democrats', *The British Journal of Politics & International Relations*, 13(4): 459–473.

Evans, G. and Chzhen, K. (2013) 'Explaining voters' defection from Labour over the 2005–10 electoral cycle: Leadership, economics and the rising importance of immigration', *Political Studies*, 61(1): 138–157.

Evans, G. and Tilley, J. (2012a) 'How parties shape class politics: Explaining the decline of the class basis of party support', *British Journal of Political Science*, 42(1): 137–161.

Evans, G. and Tilley, J. (2012b) 'The depoliticization of inequality and redistribution: Explaining the decline of class voting', *The Journal of Politics*, 74: 963–976.

Farrell, D. (2011) *Electoral Systems: A Comparative Introduction*, Basingstoke: Palgrave Macmillan.

Fawkes, G. (2016) 'Job culls coming at Indy, Guardian and Telegraph', *Order-Order*, 12 February (http://order-order.com/2016/02/12/job-cull-coming-at-indy-guardian-telegraph/).

Fenno, R. (1978) *Home Style: House Members in Their Districts*, New York: Little, Brown.

Ferejohn, J. A. and Fiorina, M. P. (1974) 'The paradox of not voting: A decision theoretic analysis', *American Political Science Review*, 68(2): 525–536.

Fielding, S. (2015) 'Hell no! Labour's campaign: The correct diagnosis but the wrong doctor', in A. Geddes and J. Tonge (eds) *Britain Votes 2015*, Oxford: Oxford University Press.

Flinders, M. and Kelso, A. (2011) 'Mind the gap: Political analysis, public expectations and the parliamentary decline thesis', *British Journal of Politics and International Relations*, 13(2): 249–268.

Foley, M. (2000) *The British Presidency*, Manchester: Manchester University Press.

Foley, M. (2013) 'Prime ministerialisation and presidential analogies: A certain difference in interpretive evolution', *Parliamentary Affairs*, 66(3): 655–662.

Ford, R. (2008) 'Is racial prejudice declining in Britain?', *The British Journal of Sociology*, 59(4): 609–636.

Ford, R. and Goodwin, M. (2010) 'Angry white men: Individual and contextual predictors of support for the British National Party', *Political Studies*, 58(1): 1–25.

Ford, R. and Goodwin, M. (2014) *Revolt on the Right: Explaining Support for the Radical Right in Britain*, London: Routledge.

Ford, R., Janta-Lipinski, L. and Sobolewska, M. (2015) 'Are the Conservatives really breaking through with ethnic minority voters?', *YouGov*, 12 June (https://yougov.co.uk/news/2015/06/12/are-conservatives-really-breaking-through-ethnic-m/) .

Ford, R., Jennings, W. and Somerville, W. (2015) 'Public opinion, responsiveness and constraint: Britain's three immigration policy regimes', 41(9): 1391–1411.

Ford, R., Morrell, G. and Heath, A. (2012) '"Fewer but better?" British attitudes to immigration', *British Social Attitudes: The 29th Report* (http://www.bsa.natcen.ac.uk/latest-report/british-social-attitudes-29/key-findings/introduction.aspx).

Fox, S. (2014) 'Is it time to update the definition of political participation?', *Parliamentary Affairs*, 67: 495–505.

Franco, A., Malhotra, N. and Simonovits, G. (2014) 'Publication bias in the social sciences: Unlocking the file drawer', *Science, 345(6203):* 1502–1505.

Franklin, M. N. (2004) *Voter Turnout and the Dynamics of Electoral Competition in Established Democracies since 1945*, Cambridge: Cambridge University Press.

Franklin, M., Marsh, M. and McLaren, L. (1994) 'Uncorking the bottle: Popular opposition to European unification in the wake of Maastricht', *Journal of Common Market Studie*s, 32(4): 455–472.

Freeden, M. (1998) *Ideologies and Political Theory: A Conceptual Approach*, Oxford: Oxford University Press.

Freeguard, G., Andrews, A., Devine, D., Munro, R. and Randall, J. (2015) *Whitehall Monitor 2015: The coalition in 163 charts*, London: Institute for Government.

Fresh Start Group (2013) *Manifesto for Change: A New Vision for the UK in Europe*, (http://www.eufreshstart.org/downloads/manifestoforchange.pdf).

Furlong, A. (ed.) (2009) *Handbook of Youth and Young Adulthood*, London: Routledge.

Gallagher, M. (2015) 'Election indices' (www.tcd.ie).

Gallagher, M. and Mitchell P. (eds) (2005) *The Politics of Electoral Systems*, Oxford: Oxford University Press.

Gamble, A. (2000) *Politics and Fate*, London: Palgrave Macmillan.

Gamble, A. (2003) *Between Europe and America: The Future of British Politics*, London: Palgrave Macmillan.

Gamble, A. (2014) *Crisis Without End?: The Unravelling of Western Prosperity*, Basingstoke: Palgrave Macmillan.

Gamble, A. (2015) 'Austerity as statecraft', *Parliamentary Affairs*, 68: 42–57.

Gandy, R. (2014), 'An investigation of politician mobility in the United Kingdom', *British Politics*, 9: 182–209.

Garland, J. and Terry, T. (2015) *The 2015 General Election: A Voting System in Crisis*, London: Electoral Reform Society.

Garton Ash, T. (2001) 'Is Britain European?', *International Affairs*, 77(1): 1–13.

Garton Ash, T (2016) Here's how to argue with a Brexiter – and win, *The Guardian*, 20 February (http://www.theguardian.com/commentisfree/2016/feb/20/how-to-argue-against-brexit-eu-fate-europe-uk-at-stake).

Gash, T., Panchamia, N., Sims, S. and Hotson, L. (2013) *Making Public Service Markets Work: Professionalising Government's Approach to Commissioning and Market Stewardship*, London: Institute for Government.

Geary, I. and Pabst, A. (eds) (2015) *Blue Labour: Forging a New Politics*, London: I.B. Tauris.

Geddes, A. (2011) *The European Union and British Politics*, London: Palgrave Macmillan.

Geddes, A. (2013) *Britain and the European Union*, London: Palgrave.

Geddes, A. and Tonge, J. (2015) *Britain Votes 2015*, Oxford: Oxford University Press; also published as a special issue of *Parliamentary Affairs*, 68, supplement 1 (September).

Gifford, C. (2014) *The Making of Eurosceptic Britain*, Farnham: Ashgate.

Giugni, M., Anduiza, E., Bosi, L., Cinalli, M., Grasso, M. T., Kousis, M., Lahusen, C., Theiss, M. and Uba, K. (2013), European Commission 7th Framework Programme, 'Living with hard times: How citizens react to economic crises and their social and political consequences' (LIVEWHAT) research project running December 2013–December 2016 [grant agreement number 613237].

Glennister, H. (2015) 'The coalition and society (III): Health and long-term care', in A. Seldon. and M. Finn (eds) *The Coalition Effect, 2010–2015*, Oxford: Oxford University Press, 290–316.

Goes, E. (2014) 'The coalition and Europe: A tale of reckless drivers, steady navigators and imperfect roadmaps', *Parliamentary Affairs*, 67(1): 45–63.

Goes, E. (2016) *The Labour Party under Ed Miliband: Trying but Failing to Renew Social Democracy*, Manchester: Manchester University Press.

Goodhart D. (2014) 'The big divide that politicians ignore', *Independent on Sunday*, 9 February.

Goodwin, M., and Milazzo, C. (2015) *UKIP: Inside the Campaign to Redraw the Map of British Politics*, Oxford: Oxford University Press.

Grasso, M. (2011) [with the assistance of J. Rose and the Committee's Research Advisory Board] *Survey of Public Attitudes Towards Conduct in Public Life 2010. Surveys of Public Attitudes Towards Conduct in Public Life*, London: Committee on Standards in Public Life.

Grasso, M. (2013) 'The differential impact of education on young people's political activism: Comparing Italy and the United Kingdom', *Comparative Sociology*, 12: 1–30.

Grasso, M. (2014) 'Age-period-cohort analysis in a comparative context: Political generations and political participation repertoires', *Electoral Studies*, 33: 63–76.

Grasso, M. (2016) *Generations, Political Participation and Social Change in Western Europe*, London: Routledge.

Grasso, M. and Giugni, M. (2016) "Protest participation and economic crisis: The conditioning role of political opportunities." *European Journal of Political Research* Forthcoming

Grasso, M., Farrall, S., Gray, E., Hay, C. and Jennings, W. (2016) "Thatcher's Children, Blair's Babies, political socialisation and trickle-down value-change: An age, period and cohort analysis." *British Journal of Political Science* Forthcoming.

Green, J. (2007) 'When voters and parties agree: Valence issues and party competition', *Political Studies*, 55(3): 629–655.

Greenslade, R. (2015) 'Are national newspaper sales heading for a cliff? Not quite yet...', *The Guardian*, 9 October (http://www.theguardian.com/media/greenslade/2015/oct/09/are-national-newspaper-sales-heading-for-a-cliff-not-quite-yet).

Guttsman, W. L. (1965) *The British Political Elite*, London: MacGibbon and Kee.

Haffert, L. and Mehrtens, P. (2015) 'From austerity to expansion? Consolidation, budget surpluses, and the decline of fiscal capacity', *Politics & Society*, 43(1): 119–148.

Hall, P. and Soskice, D. (2013) *Varieties of Capitalism: The Institutional Foundations of Comparative Advantage*, Oxford: Oxford University Press.

Hampshire, J. (2013) *The Politics of Immigration: Contradictions of the Liberal State*, London: Polity.

Hannan, D. (2012) *A Doomed Marriage: Britain and Europe*, London: Notting Hill Editions.

Hannan, D. (2013) *How We Invented Freedom and Why It Matters*, London: Head of Zeus.

Hannan, D. (2016) *Why Vote Leave*, London: Head of Zeus.

Hansen, R. (2002) *Citizens and Immigration in Postwar Britain*, Oxford: Oxford University Press.

Hanretty, C. (2015) 'Would the Conservatives have been better off under AV?' *LSE British Politics and Policy* blog, 6 May (http://blogs.lse.ac.uk/politicsandpolicy/).

Harrabin, R. (2015) 'CBI warning over renewables subsidies'. *BBC News – Science and Environment*, 22 September (http://www.bbc.co.uk/news/science-environment-34319458).

Hatton, T. J. and Wheatley Price, S. (2005) '5. Migration, migrants, and policy in the United Kingdom', in K. F. Zimmerman (ed.) *European Migration: What Do We Know?*, Oxford: Oxford University Press, 113.

Hay, C. (1999) *The Political Economy of New Labour*, Manchester: Manchester University Press.

Hay, C. (2004) 'The normalizing role of rationalist assumptions in the institutional embedding of neoliberalism', *Economy and Society*, 33(4): 500–527.

Hay, C. (2007) *Why We Hate Politics*, Cambridge: Polity.

Hay, C. (2011) 'Pathology without crisis? The strange demise of the Anglo-Liberal growth model', *Government and Opposition*, 46(1); 1–31.

Hay, C. (2013) *The Failure of Anglo-Liberal Capitalism*, London: Palgrave Macmillan.

Hay, C. and Wincott, D. (2012) *The Political Economy of European Welfare Capitalism*, London: Palgrave Macmillan.

Hawkins, O., Keen, R. and Nakatudde, N. (2015) *General Election 2015*, House of Commons Library Briefing Paper no. CBP7186, 28 July.

Hazell, R. (1999) 'The shape of things to come: What will the UK constitution look like in the early 21st century?', in R. Hazell (ed.) *Constitutional Futures. A History of the Next Ten Years*, Oxford: Oxford University Press,.

Hazell, R. (2000) 'Conclusion: The state and the nations one year after devolution', in R. Hazell (ed.) *The State and the Nations. The First Year of Devolution in the United Kingdom*, Thorverton: Imprint Academic.

Hazell, R. (2001) 'Conclusion: The state of the nations after two years of devolution', in R. Hazell (ed.) *The State of the Nations 2001. The Second Year of Devolution in the United Kingdom*, Thorverton: Imprint Academic.

Hazell, R. (2003) 'Conclusion: The devolution scorecard as the devolved assemblies head for the polls', in R. Hazell (ed.) *The State of the Nations 2003. The Third Year of Devolution in the United Kingdom*, Thorverton: Imprint Academic.

Hazell, R. (2006), 'The English question', *Publius. The Journal of Federalism*, 36(1): 37–56.

Hazell, R. and O'Leary, B. (1999) 'A rolling programme of devolution: Slippery slope of safeguard of the union', in R. Hazell (ed.) *Constitutional Futures. A History of the Next Ten Years*, Oxford: Oxford University Press.

Hazell, R. and Paun, A. (2009) *Making Minority Government Work*, London: Constitution Unit (http://www.ucl.ac.uk/constitution-unit/publications/tabs/unit-publications/147.pdf).

Hazell, R. and Yong, B. (2012) *The Politics of Coalition: How the Conservative-Liberal Democrat Coalition Works*, Oxford: Hart Publishing.

Heath, A., Fisher, S., Rosenblatt, G., Sanders, D. and Sobolewska, M. (2013) *Political Integration of British Ethnic Minorities*, New York: Oxford University Press.

Heath, A., Fisher, S., Sanders, D. and Sobolewska, M. (2011) 'Ethnic heterogeneity in the social bases of voting at the 2010 British general election.' *Journal of Elections, Public Opinion, and Parties* 21 (2) 255–77.

Heath, A., Jowell, R., Curtice, J. and Evans, G. (1990) 'The rise of the new political agenda?', *European Sociological Review*, 6: 31–48.

Heffernan, R. (2001) *New Labour and Thatcherism: Political Change in Britain*, Basingstoke: Palgrave Macmillan.

Heffernan, R. (2005) 'Exploring (and explaining) the British prime minister', *The British Journal of Politics and International Relations*, 7(4): 605–620.

Heffernan, R. (2009) 'British political parties', in C. Hay et al. (eds) *The Oxford Handbook of British Politics*, Oxford: Oxford University Press.

Heffernan, R. (2013) 'There's no need for the "-ization": The prime minister is merely prime ministerial', *Parliamentary Affairs*, 66(3): 636–645.

Heffernan, R. and Webb, P. (2007) 'The British prime minister: More than first among equals', in T. Poguntke and P. Webb (eds.) *The Presidentialisation of Politics: A Comparative Study of Modern Democracies*, Oxford: Oxford University Press.

Henderson, A. and Mitchell, J. (2015) *The Scottish Question, Six Months On* (http://centreonconstitutionalchange.ac.uk/sites/default/files/Scottish%20Referendum%20Study%2027%20March%202015.pdf).

Henderson, A. et al. (2016, forthcoming) *The 2015 Future of England Survey*.

Hennessy, P. (2001) *Whitehall*, London: Pimlico.

Heppell, T. (2014) *The Tories*, London: Bloomsbury.

Hindmoor, A. (2004) *New Labour at the Centre: Constructing Political Space*, Oxford: Oxford University Press.

Hitchens, C. (2004) *Blood, Class, and Empire: The Enduring Anglo-American Relationship*, New York: Nation Books.

Hix, S. and Høyland, B. (2011) *The Political System of the European Union*, London: Palgrave Macmillan.

HM Government (2010a) *Our Programme for Government*, London: Cabinet Office (https://www.gov.uk/government/uploads/system/uploads/attachment_data/file/78977/coalition_programme_for_government.pdf).

HM Government (2010b) *Coalition Agreement for Stability and Reform*, London: Cabinet Office (https://www.gov.uk/government/uploads/system/uploads/attachment_data/file/78978/coalition-agreement-may-2010_0.pdf).

HM Government (2014) *Scotland Analysis. Assessment of a Sterling Currency Union* Cm 8815 (https://www.gov.uk/government/uploads/system/uploads/attachment_data/file/279454/CM8815_2901849_SA_SterlingUnion_acc.pdf).

HM Treasury, Budget 2011 (http://webarchive.nationalarchives.gov.uk/20130129110402/http:/cdn.hm-treasury.gov.uk/2011budget_complete.pdf).

Hobolt, S. B. (2009) *Europe in Question: Referendums on European Integration*, Oxford: Oxford University Press.

Hood, C. and Dixon, R. (2015) *A Government that Worked Better and Cost Less? Evaluating Three Decades of Reform and Change in UK Central Government*, Oxford: Oxford University Press.

Hooghe, L. and Marks, G. (2009) 'A postfunctionalist theory of European integration: From permissive consensus to constraining dissensus', *British Journal of Political Science*, 39(1): 1–23.

House of Commons (2010) *Speaker's Conference (on Parliamentary Representation), Final Report*, HC 239-I.

House of Commons (2011) *House of Commons Public Administration Committee: Change in Government: the agenda for leadership, Thirteenth report of Session 2010–12*, London: TSO (http://www.publications.parliament.uk/pa/cm201012/cmselect/cmpubadm/714/714.pdf).

House of Commons Library (2015) *The 2010 Coalition Government at Westminster* (http://researchbriefings.parliament.uk/ResearchBriefing/Summary/SN06404#fullrepor).

House of Lords (2012), *House of Lords Constitution Committee: The Accountability of Civil Servants, Sixth Report of Session 2012–13*, London: TSO (http://www.publications.parliament.uk/pa/ld201213/ldselect/ldconst/61/61.pdf)

Hume, M. (2015) *Trigger Warning: Is The Fear of Being Offensive Killing Free Speech?*, London: William Collins.

Hunt, T. (2015) 'Welcome to the era of emoji politics, where debate and rationality are suffocated', *Spectator*, 4 September (http://blogs.spectator.co.uk/2015/09/welcome-to-the-era-of-emoji-politics-where-debate-and-rationality-are-suffocated/).

Hurst, G. and Sherman, J. (2012) 'Michael Gove plans big job cuts at Education', *The Times*, 14 November.

IDEA (2015). *Voter Turnout.* Dataset. Available at http://www.idea.int/vt/index.cfm; last accessed 15 January 2015.

Inglehart, R. and Welzel, C. (2005) *Modernization, Cultural Change and Democracy: The Human Development Sequence*, Cambridge, UK: Cambridge University Press.

Institute of Government (2015), *Westminster in an Age of Minorities: How to Form and Sustain a Government after Another Hung Parliament* (http://www.instituteforgovernment.org.uk/sites/default/files/publications/Westminster-in-an-age-of-minorities-FINAL.pdf).

Ipsos MORI (2015a) *Best Party on Key Issues: Asylum and Immigration*, 20 April (https://www.ipsos-mori.com/researchpublications/researcharchive/poll.aspx?oItemID=19&view=wide).

Ipsos MORI (2015b) *EU referendum: Controls on movement of EU citizens key issue for majority of Britons*, London: Ipsos MORI (https://www.ipsos-mori.com/researchpublications/researcharchive/3631/EU-Referendum-Controls-on-movement-of-EU-citizens-key-issue-for-majority-of-Britons.aspx).

Ipsos MORI (n.d.a) *Best Party On Key Issues: Managing the Economy* (https://www.ipsos-mori.com/researchpublications/researcharchive/22/Best-Party-On-Key-Issues-Managing-the-Economy.aspx).

Ipsos MORI (n.d.b) *Government Record: Good Job or Bad Job on Managing the Economy? Trends* (https://www.ipsos-mori.com/researchpublications/researcharchive/2433/Government-Record-Good-Job-or-Bad-Job-on-Managing-the-Economy-Trends.aspx).

Iversen, T. and Soskice, D. (2006) 'Electoral institutions and the politics of coalitions: Why some democracies redistribute more than others', *American Political Science Review*, 100(2): 165–181.

Jackson, B. (2014) 'The political thought of Scottish nationalism', *Political Quarterly*, 85(1): 50–56.

Jackson, D. and Thorsen, E. (eds) (2015) *UK Election Analysis 2015: Media, Voters and the Campaign*, Bournemouth: Centre for the Study of Journalism, Culture and Community (http://www.electionanalysis.uk/).

Jackson, T. (2011) *Prosperity without Growth: Economics for a Finite Planet*, London: Routledge.

Jarman, H. and Greer, S. (2015) 'The big bang: Health and social care reform under the coalition', in M. Beech and S. Lee (eds) *The Conservative-Liberal Coalition Evaluated: Examining the Legacy of the Cameron-Clegg Government*, Basingstoke: Palgrave Macmillan, 50–68.

Jeffery, C. (2008) 'Devolution in the United Kingdom: Problems of a piecemeal approach to constitutional change', *Publius*, 39(2): 289–313.

Jeffery, C. (2009) 'Devolution in the United Kingdom: Problems of a piecemeal approach to constitutional change', *Publius*, 39(2): 289–313.

Jeffery, C. and Hough, D. (2009) 'Understanding post-devolution elections in Scotland and Wales in comparative perspective', *Party Politics*, 152): 219–240.

Jeffery, C. et al. (2014) *Taking England Seriously: The New English Politics* (http://www.centreonconstitutionalchange.ac.uk/sites/default/files/news/Taking%20England%20Seriously_The%20New%20English%20Politics.pdf).

Jensen, M. J. (2016) 'In the 2015 general election campaign, politicians used social media to broadcast to voters rather than converse with them', *Democratic Audit*, February (http://www.democraticaudit.com/?p=19266).

Johnson, N. (2004) *Reshaping the British Constitution: Essays in Interpretation*, London: Palgrave Macmillan.

Jones, O. (2015a) 'Russell Brand has endorsed Labour – and the Tories should be worried', *The Guardian*, 4 May (http://www.theguardian.com/commentisfree/2015/may/04/russell-brand-endorsed-labour-tories-should-be-worried?CMP=fb_gu).

Jones, O. (2015b) *The Establishment: And How They Get Away With It*, London: Penguin.

Jones, R., Lodge, G., Jeffery, C., Gottfried, G., Scully R., Henderson, A. and Wincott, D. (2013) *England and Its Two Unions: The Anatomy of a Nation and Its Discontents*, London: IPPR.

Kavanagh, D. (2007) 'The Blair premiership', in A. Seldon (ed.) *Blair's Britain, 1997–2007*, Cambridge: Cambridge University Press, 3–15.

Kavanagh, D. and Cowley, P. (2010) *The British General Election of 2010*, Basingstoke: Palgrave Macmillan.

Keen, R. (2014) *Membership of UK Political Parties: Standard Note SN/SG/5125*, London: House of Commons Library.

Kellner, P. (2013) 'UKIP support less right wing than Tories', *The Guardian*, 5 March.

Kellner, P. (2014) 'Where UKIP gets its support', *YouGov*, 24 February (https://yougov.co.uk/news/2014/02/24/where-ukip-gets-its-support/).

Kelso, A. (2009) *Parliamentary Reform at Westminster*, Manchester: Manchester University Press.

Kenny, M. (2014) *The Politics of English Nationhood*, Oxford: Oxford University Press.

Kenny, M. (2015) 'The return of "Englishness" in British political culture: The end of the unions?', *Journal of Common Market Studies*, 53(1): 35–51.

Kenny, M. and Pearce, N. (2015) 'The rise of the Anglosphere: How the right dreamed up a new conservative world order', *New Statesman*, 10 February (http://www.newstatesman.com/politics/2015/02/rise-anglosphere-how-right-dreamed-new-conservative-world-order).

Key, V. O. (1955) 'A theory of critical elections', *Journal of Politics*, 17: 3–18.

King, A. (1981) 'The rise of the career politician in Britain – and its consequences', *British Journal of Political Science*, 11: 249–285.

King, A. (2015) *Who Governs Britain?*, London, Pelican.

Kirby, P. (2016) *Leading People 2016: The Educational Backgrounds of the UK Professional Elite*, London: Sutton Trust.

Kubala, M. (2011) 'Select committees in the House of Commons and the media', *Parliamentary Affairs*, 64(2): 694–713.

Kwarteng, K., Patel, P., Raab, D., Skidmore, C. and Truss, E. (2012) *Britannia Unchained: Global Lessons for Growth and Prosperity*, Basingstoke: Palgrave.

Kymlicka, W. (1996) *Multicultural Citizenship: A Liberal Theory of Minority Rights*, Oxford: Oxford University Press.

Laakso, M. and Taagepera, R. (1979) 'Effective number of parties: A measure with application to Western Europe', *Comparative Political Studies*, 12: 3–27.

Langer, A. (2012) *The Personalisation of Politics in the UK: Mediated Leadership from Attlee to Cameron*, Manchester: Manchester University Press.

Laurence, J. (2011) 'The effect of ethnic diversity and community disadvantage on social cohesion: A multi-level analysis of social capital and interethnic relations in UK communities', *European Sociological Review*, 27(1): 70–89.

Laurence, J. (2014) 'Reconciling the contact and threat hypotheses: Does ethnic diversity strengthen or weaken community inter-ethnic relations?', *Ethnic and Racial Studies*, 37(8): 1328–1349.

Laws, D. (2016) *Coalition: The Inside Story of the Conservative-Liberal Democrat Coalition Government*, London: Biteback.

Laycock, S., Renwick, A., Stevens, D. and Vowles, J. (2013) 'The UK's electoral reform referendum of May 2011', *Electoral Studies*, 32(2): 211–214.

Leconte, C. (2010) *Understanding Euroscepticism*, London: Palgrave.

Lee, S. (2015) 'The political economy of the coalition: Indebted and unbalanced', in M. Beech and S. Lee (eds) *The Conservative-Liberal Coalition Examining the Cameron-Clegg Government*, Basingstoke: Palgrave Macmillan.

Lent, A. (2014) 'Britain is facing a crisis of democracy but the main parties cannot respond', *Democratic Audit UK Blog*, 25 October (www.democraticaudit.com/?p=8803).

Liddle, R. (2015) 'The green ink brigade is now running the show', *Spectator*, 5 September (http://www.spectator.co.uk/columnists/rod-liddle/9621922/pig-ignorant-click-activists-are-in-charge-now-jeremy-corbyns-success-proves-it/).

Lijphart, A. (1999) *Patterns of Democracy: Government Forms and Performance in Thirty-Six Countries*, New Haven: Yale University Press.

Lloyd, J. (2004) *What Are the Media Doing to Our Politics?*, London: Constable.

Lohmann, S. (2003) 'Why do institutions matter? An audience-cost theory of institutional commitment', *Governance*, 16(1): 95–110.

Lowe, R. (2011) *The Official History of the British Civil Service: Reforming the Civil Service, Volume I: The Fulton Years, 1966–81*, London: Routledge.

LSE Growth Commission (2013) *Investing for Prosperity: Skills, Infrastructure and Innovation* (http://www.lse.ac.uk/researchAndExpertise/units/growth Commission/home.aspx).

Lynch, P. (2015) 'Conservative modernisation and European integration: From silence to salience and schism', *British Politics*, 10(2): 185–203.

Lynch, P., and Whitaker, R. (2013) 'Rivalry on the right: The Conservatives, the UK Independence Party (UKIP) and the EU issue', *British Politics*, 8(3): 285–312.

Macedo, S., Alex-Assensoh, Y. and Berry, J. (2005) *Democracy at Risk: How Political Choices Undermine Citizen Participation, and What We Can Do about It*, Washington, DC: Brookings.

Mackie, T. and Rose, R. (1991) *The International Almanac of Electoral History*, 3rd edition, Basingstoke: Macmillan.

Macwhirter, I. (2014) *Disunited Kingdom. How Westminster Won a Referendum but Lost Scotland*, Glasgow: Cargo Publishing.

Mair, P. (2006) 'Ruling the void? The hollowing of Western democracy', *New Left Review*, 42: 25–51.

Manjoo, F. (2015) 'The Internet's loop of action and reaction is worsening', *New York Times*, 9 December (http://www.nytimes.com/2015/12/10/technology/shut-down-internet-donald-trump-hillary-clinton.html?_r=0).

Mannheim, K. (1928) *The Problem of Generations Essays on the Sociology of Knowledge*, London: Routledge.

Marsh, D., O'Toole, T. and Jones, S. (2007) *Young People and Politics in the UK. Apathy or Alienation?*, Basingstoke: Palgrave.

Martin, L. W. and Vanberg, G. (2011) *Parliaments and Coalitions: The Role of Legislative Institutions in Multiparty Governance*, Oxford: Oxford University Press.

Mason, P. (2013) 'Why it's still kicking off everywhere: Are we witnessing a global revolt against neoliberalism?', *New Left Project*, 26 April (http://www.newleftproject.org/index.php/site/article_comments/why_its_still_kicking_off_everywhere).

Mason, R. (2012) 'No, minister! Senior civil servants deliberately block policy, says Francis Maude', *The Telegraph*, 1 October.

Maude, F. (2011) *Oral evidence to the Public Administration Select Committee*, 3 March (http://www.publications.parliament.uk/pa/cm201012/cmselect/cmpubadm/714/714.pdf).

Maude, F. (2013) 'Ministers and mandarins: Speaking truth unto power', Speech to Policy Exchange, 5 June.

McBride, D. (2013) *Power Trip: A Decade of Policy, Plots and Spin*, London: Biteback.

McKay Commission (2013), *Report of the Commission on the Consequences of Devolution for the House of Commons* (http://webarchive.nationalarchives.gov.uk/20130403030652/http://tmc.independent.gov.uk/wp-content/uploads/2013/03/The-McKay-Commission_Main-Report_25-March-20131.pdf).

Mezey, M. L. (1979) *Comparative Legislatures*, Durham, NC: Duke University Press.

Migration Advisory Committee (MAC) (2012) *Analysis of the Impacts of Migration*, (https://www.gov.uk/government/uploads/system/uploads/attachment_data/file/257235/analysis-of-the-impacts.pdf).

Milne, S. (2015) 'Cameron isn't colonising the centre: That's fraudulent spin', *The Guardian*, 7 October.

Mitchell, J. (2009) *Devolution in the UK*, Manchester: Manchester University Press.

Mitchell, J., Bennie, L. and Johns, R. (2011) *The Scottish National Party: Transition to Power*, Oxford: Oxford University Press.

Mitchell, J. and van der Zwet, A. (2010) 'A catenaccio game: The 2010 election in Scotland', *Parliamentary Affairs*, 63(4) (October): 708–725.

Moran, C. (2012) *How To Be a Woman*, London: Ebury Press.

Moran, M. (2006) 'Gender, identity and the teaching of British politics: A comment', *Politics*, 26(3): 200–202.

Mouffe, C. (2005) *On the Political*, New York: Routledge.

Mount, H. (2015) 'On the road with my cousin, the prime minister', *Sunday Times*, 5 April (http://www.thesundaytimes.co.uk/sto/Magazine/article1536390.ece).

Mudde, C. (2007) *Populist Radical Right Parties in Europe*, Cambridge: Cambridge University Press.

Mulgan, G. (2015) 'Trotsky, Blair and the new politics', *New Statesman*, 19 October (http://www.newstatesman.com/politics/uk/2015/10/trotsky-blair-and-new-politics).

Murray, R. (2014) 'Quotas for men: Reframing gender quotas as a means of improving representation for all', *American Political Science Review*, 108(3): 520–532.

Nardelli, A. (2014) 'Party membership in the UK is tiny', *The Guardian*, 29 September.

Nohlen, D. and Stöver, P. (eds) (2010) *Elections in Europe: A Data Handbook*, Baden-Baden: Nomos.

Norman, J. (2014) *Edmund Burke: The Visionary Who Invented Modern Politics*, London: Collins.

Norris, P. (2011) *Democratic Deficit: Critical Citizens Revisited*, Cambridge: Cambridge University Press.

Norton, P. (2003) 'The presidentialization of British politics', *Government and Opposition*, 38(2): 274–278.

Norton, P. (2013) *Parliament in British Politics*, London: Palgrave.

Nugent, M. K. and Krook, M. L. (2016), 'All-women shortlists: Myths and realities', *Parliamentary Affairs*, 69(1): 115–135.

O'Connor, S. (2012) 'OBR denies making life easy for Osborne', *Financial Times*, 11 December.

Oborne, P. (2008) *The Triumph of the Political Class*, London: Pocket Books.

OBR (2011) *Economic and Fiscal Outlook* Cm 8036, March.

OBR (2014a) *Economic and Fiscal Outlook* Cm 8966, December.

OBR (2014b) *Welfare Trends Report,* October.

OBR (2015) *Economic and Fiscal Outlook* Cm 9088, July.

Ofcom (2015) *Adults Media Use and Attitudes: Report 2015* (http://stakeholders. ofcom.org.uk/binaries/research/media-literacy/media-lit-10years/2015_ Adults_media_use_and_attitudes_report.pdf).

Office for National Statistics (2015) 'Population and migration' (http://www. ons.gov.uk/ons/taxonomy/index.html?nscl=Migration).

O'Neill, B. (2015) 'Call me Caitlyn or else: The rise of authoritarian transgender politics', *Spectator Coffee House*, 2 June (http://blogs.spectator. co.uk/2015/06/call-me-caitlyn-or-else-the-rise-of-authoritarian-transgender-politics/).

O'Neill, B. (2016) 'Twitter's new "Safety Council" makes a mockery of free speech', *Spectator Coffee House*, 11 February (http://blogs.spectator.co.uk/2016/02/ twitters-new-safety-council-makes-a-mockery-of-free-speech/).

Open Europe (2015) *What If...? The Consequences, Challenges and Opportunities Facing Britain Outside the EU*, London: Open Europe.

Page, J., Pearson, J., Jurgeit, B. and Kidson, M., (2013) *Transforming Whitehall Departments*, London: Institute for Government.

Pattie, C. and Johnston, R. (2001) 'A low turnout landslide: Abstention in the general election of 1997', *Political Studies*, 49: 286–305.

Pattie, C. J., Johnston, R. J. and Stuart, M. (1998) 'Voting without party?' in P. Cowley (ed.) *Conscience and Parliament*, Frank Cass: London.

Pattie, C., Seyd, P. and Whiteley, P. (2004) *Citizenship in Britain: Values, Participation and Democracy*, Cambridge: Cambridge University Press.

Paun, A., Harris, J. and Magee, I. (2013) *Permanent Secretary Appointments and the Role of Ministers*, London: Institute for Government.

Pearce, N. (2015) 'In the valley of death: Labour and the disintegration of social democracy', *New Statesman*, 27 September (http://www.newstatesman.com/ politics/uk/2015/09/valley-death).

Pedersen, M. N. (1979) 'The dynamics of European party systems: Changing patterns of electoral volatility', *European Journal of Political Research*, 7: 1–26.

Penman, D. (2013) 'Ministers hand picking civil servants will create political "firewall"', *The Guardian*, 10 July.

Perloff, R. M. (2014) *The Dynamics of Political Communication. Media and Politics in a Digital Age,* London: Routledge.

Pharr, S. and Putnam, R. (eds) (2000) *Disaffected Democracies: What's Troubling the Trilateral Countries?,* Princeton, NJ: Princeton University Press.

Phillips, A. (1995) *The Politics of Presence*, Oxford: Oxford University Press.

Phillips, A. (2012) 'Representation and inclusion', *Politics and Gender*, 8(4): 512–518.

Pickles, N. (2016) 'Safer Internet Day: Protecting the global town square of Twitter', *The Guardian*, 10 February (http://www.theguardian.com/technology/2016/feb/08/twitter-safer-internet-day-nick-pickles-online-diversity).

Pike, J. (2015) *Project Fear*, London: Biteback Publishing.

Piketty, T. (2014) *Capital in the Twenty-First Century*, Cambridge, MA: Harvard University Press.

Pitkin, H. (2004) 'Representation and democracy: Uneasy alliance', *Scandinavian Political Studies*, 27: 335–342.

Poguntke, T. and Webb. P. (2013) 'The presidentialisation of politics thesis defended', *Parliamentary Affairs*, 66(3): 646–654.

Polsby, N. W. (1975) 'Legislatures' in F. Greenstein and N. Polsby (eds) *Handbook of Political Science*, Vol. 5, Reading, MA: Addison-Wesley, 251–319.

Public Administration Select Committee (2011) 'Change in government: the agenda for leadership' (http://www.publications.parliament.uk/pa/cm201012/cmselect/cmpubadm/714/714.pdf).

Pulzer, P. (1967) *Political Representation and Elections in Britain*, London: Allen & Unwin.

Putnam, R. (2000) *Bowling Alone: The Collapse and Revival of American Community*, New York: Simon & Schuster.

Ramsay, A. (2015) *Another Note on Party Memberships in the UK* (https://www.opendemocracy.net/ourkingdom/adam-ramsay/another-note-on-party-memberships-in-uk).

Rawnsley, A. (2016) 'Now if only I had followed my own advice about opinion polls....', *The Observer*, 17 January (http://www.theguardian.com/commentisfree/2016/jan/17/opinion-polls-matter-despite-wrong-predictions-general-election).

Reif, K. and Schmitt, H. (1980) 'Nine second-order national elections – A conceptual framework for the analysis of European election results', *European Journal for Political Research*, 8:1, 3–44.

Renwick, A. (2011) *A Citizen's Guide to Electoral Reform*, London: Biteback.

Reuters Institute (2015) *Reuters Institute Digital News Report, 2015: Supplementary Report* (http://reutersinstitute.politics.ox.ac.uk/sites/default/files/Supplementary%20Digital%20News%20Report%202015.pdf).

Reynolds, A. (2013) 'Representation and rights: The impact of LGBT legislators in comparative perspective', *American Journal of Political Science*, 107(2): 259–274.

Reynolds, A. (2015) 'The UK broke its own record for LGBT representation last week', *New Statesman*, 13 May (http://www.newstatesman.com/politics/2015/05/uk-broke-its-own-record-lgbt-representation-last-week).

Rhodes, R. A. W. (1997) *Understanding Governance: Policy Networks, Governance, Reflexivity and Accountability*, Buckingham: Open University.

Richards, D. (2008) *New Labour and the Civil Service: Reconstituting the Westminster Model*, Basingstoke: Palgrave Macmillan.

Richardson, J. J. and Jordan, A. G. (1979) *Governing Under Pressure: The Policy Process in a Post-Parliamentary Democracy*, Oxford: Martin Robertson.

Riddell, P. (2015) 'The coalition and the executive', in A. Seldon and M. Finn (eds) *The Coalition Effect, 2010–2015*, Oxford: Oxford University Press, 113–135.

Riddell, P. and Haddon, C. (2011) *Transitions: Lessons Learned – Reflections on the 2010 UK General Election – and Looking Forward to 2015*, London: Institute for Government.

Ridout, T. N. (ed.) (2013) *New Directions in Media and Politics*, London: Routledge.

Robertson, A. (2015) *Media and Politics in a Globalizing World*, Cambridge: Polity Press.

Robinson, N. (2015) *Election Notebook*, London: Bantam Press.

Rogers, B. (2005) 'From membership to management? The future of political parties as democratic organisations', *Parliamentary Affairs* 58: 600–610.

Rogers, R. and Walters, R. (2015) *How Parliament Works*, London: Routledge.

Rokkan, R. and Urwin, D. (1983) 'Introduction: Centres and peripheries in Western Europe', in S. Rokkan and D. Urwin (eds) *The Politics of Territorial Identity*, London: Sage.

Roper Center (2012) 'How groups voted in 2012' (http://ropercenter.cornell.edu/polls/us-elections/how-groups-voted/how-groups-voted-2012/).

Rosenthal, R. (1979) 'The "file drawer problem" and the tolerance for null results', *Psychological Bulletin*, 86(3): 638–641.

Rowthorn, R. (2014) *Large-Scale Immigration: Its Economic and Demographic Consequences for the UK*, London: Civitas.

Rusbridger, A. (2015) '"Farewell, readers": Alan Rusbridger on leaving The Guardian after two decades at the helm', *The Guardian*, 29 May (http://www.theguardian.com/media/2015/may/29/farewell-readers-alan-rusbridger-on-leaving-the-guardian).

Russell, A. T., Johnston, R. J. and Pattie, C. J. (1992) 'Thatcher's children: Exploring the links between age and political attitudes', *Political Studies*, 40: 742–756.

Russell, M. (2010) 'A stronger second chamber? Assessing the impact of House of Lords reform in 1999, and the lessons for bicameralism', *Political Studies*, 58(5): 866–885.

Russell, M. (2011) '"Never allow a crisis to go to waste": The Wright committee reforms to strengthen the House of Commons', *Parliamentary Affairs*, 64(4): 612–633.

Russell, M. (2013) *The Contemporary House of Lords: Western Bicameralism Revived*, Oxford: Oxford University Press.

Russell, M. and Cowley, P. (2015) 'The policy power of the Westminster parliament: The "parliamentary state" and the empirical evidence', *Governance*, 29(1): 121–137.

Russell, M., Gover, D. and Wollter, K. (2015) 'Does the executive dominate the Westminster legislative process? Six reasons for doubt', *Parliamentary Affairs*, 69(2): 286–308.

Sanders, D., Clarke, H. D., Stewart, M. C. and Whiteley, P. (2011a). 'Simulating the effects of the alternative vote in the 2010 UK general election', *Parliamentary Affairs*, 64(1) (January): 5–23.

Sanders, D., Clarke, H.D., Stewart, M.C. and Whiteley, P. (2011b) 'Downs, Stokes and the dynamics of electoral choice', *British Journal of Political Science*, 41(2): 287–314.

Sarlvik, B. and Crewe, I. (1983) *Decade of Dealignment: The Conservative Victory of 1979 and Electoral Trends in the 1970s*, Cambridge: Cambridge University Press.

Schattschneider, E. (1942) *Party Government*, New York: Greenwood Press.

Schleiter, P. (2016) Special edition on the Fixed Term Parliament Act, *Parliamentary Affairs*, 69(1).

Schofield, C. (2013) *Enoch Powell and the Making of Postcolonial Britain*, Cambridge: Cambridge University Press.

Scottish Government (2013) *Scotland's Future. Your Guide to an Independent Scotland*, Edinburgh: Scottish Government.

Scruton, R. (2014) *How To Be a Conservative*, London: Bloomsbury.

Seldon, A. and Finn, M. (eds) (2015) *The Coalition Effect, 2010–2015*, Oxford: Oxford University Press.

Seldon, A. and Snowdon, P. (2015) *Cameron at 10: The Inside Story, 2010–2015*, London: William Collins.

Sloam, J. (2007) 'Rebooting democracy: Youth participation in politics in the UK', *Parliamentary Affairs*, 60(4): 548–567.

Smith Commission (2014) *Report of the Smith Commission for Further Devolution of Powers to the Scottish Parliament* (https://www.smith-commission.scot/wp-content/uploads/2014/11/The_Smith_Commission_Report-1.pdf).

Snowdon, P. (2010) *Back from the Brink: The Extraordinary Fall and Rise of the Conservative Party*, London: HarperPress.

Sobolewska, M. (2014) 'The British Obamas: Ethnic minority MPs', in P. Cowley and R. Ford (eds) *Sex, Lies and the Ballot Box*, London: Biteback.

Sobolewska, M. (2016) 'Representation of citizens of immigrant origin in Britain', presentation to the Pathways Project Media Briefing, 15 February.

Social Mobility and Child Poverty Commission (2014) *Elitist Britain?*, Report of the Social Mobility and Child Poverty Commission, London.

Sparrow, A. (2015a) Guardian Politics Live, 8 December (http://www.theguardian.com/politics/blog/live/2015/dec/08/tom-watson-says-momentum-entryists-could-damage-labour-politics-live).

Sparrow, A. (2015b) 'Jeremy Corbyn wins Labour leadership race in stunning victory – as it happened', *The Guardian*, 14 September (http://www.theguardian.com/politics/blog/live/2015/sep/12/labour-announces-leadership-election-result-with-corbyn-tipped-to-win-politics-live).

Spiering, M. (2014) *A Cultural History of British Euroscepticism*, London: Palgrave.

Stanley, L. (2014) '"We're reaping what we sowed": Everyday crisis narratives and acquiescence to the age of austerity', *New Political Economy*, 19(6): 895–917.

Stanyer, J. (2013) *Intimate Politics: Publicity, Privacy and Personal Lives of Politicians in Media Saturated Democracies*, Cambridge: Polity Press.

Steve Richards (2016), Leadership, Loyalty and the Rise of Jeremy Corbyn. The Political Quarterly, 87: 12–17.

Stoker, G. (2006) *Why Politics Matters. Making Democracy Work*, Basingstoke: Palgrave Macmillan.

Stoker, G. (2011) 'Anti-politics in Britain' in Heffernan, R., Cowley, P. and Hay, C. (eds) *Developments in British Politics 9*, Basingstoke, Palgrave.

Stoker, G., Hay. C. and Barr, M. (2015) 'Fast thinking: Implications for democratic politics', *European Journal of Political Research*, 55(1): 3–21.

Stone, J. 'More people have joined Labour since the election than are in the entire Conservative Party', *The Independent*, 8 October 2015.

Streeck, W. (2014) 'The politics of public debt: Neoliberalism, capitalist development and the restructuring of the state', *German Economic Review*, Special Issue: Special Issue on Government Debt in Democracies: Causes, Effects, and Limits, 15(1): 143–165.

Strom, K., Muller, W. and Bergman, T. (eds) (2010) *Cabinets and Coalition Bargaining: The Democratic Life Cycle in Western Europe*, Oxford: Oxford University Press.

Taggart, P. (2000) *Populism*, Milton Keynes: Open University.

Taggart, P. (2004) 'Populism and representative politics in contemporary Europe', *Journal of Political ideologies*, 9(3): 269–288.

theMediabriefing (2015) 'Digital habits in the UK: Social media, mobile apps, and online news' (http://www.themediabriefing.com/article/digital-habits-in-the-uk-social-media-mobile-apps-and-online-news)

Thornton, D., Pearson, J. and Andrews, E. (2015) *Managing with Less: The 2015 Spending Review*, London: Institute for Government.

Timmins, N. (2012) *Never Again? The Story of the Health and Social Care Act 2012*, London: The King's Fund (http://www.kingsfund.org.uk/sites/files/kf/field/field_publication_file/never-again-story-health-social-care-nicholas-timmins-jul12.pdf).

Trench, A. (2004) 'The more things change the more they stay the same. Intergovernmental Relations Four Years on', in A. Trench (ed.) *The State of the Nations 2003. The Third Year of Devolution in the United Kingdom*, Thorverton: Imprint Academic, 165–192.

UK Government (2013–2014) *Scotland Analysis* (https://www.gov.uk/government/collections/scotland-analysis).

Van Biezen, I., Mair, P. and Poguntke, T. (2012) 'Going, going, ... gone? The decline of party membership in contemporary Europe', *European Journal of Political Research*, 51: 24–56.

Van Heerde-Hudson, J. (ed.) (2014) *The Political Costs of the 2009 British MPs' Expenses Scandal*, Basingstoke: Palgrave.

Veliz, C. (1994) *The New World of the Gothic Fox: Culture and Economy in English and Spanish America*, Berkeley, CA: University of California Press.

Verba, S., Nie, N. H. and Kim, J. (1978) *Participation and Political Equality*, Cambridge: Cambridge University Press.

Verba, S., Schlozman, K. and Brady, H. (1995) *Voice and Equality: Civic Voluntarism in American Politics*, Cambridge, MA: Harvard University Press.

Vollmer, P. M. (2012) *Work of the House of Lords: Statistics (LLN 2012/009)*, London: House of Lords Library (http://www.parliament.uk/briefing-papers/LLN-2012-009.pdf).

Walker, P. (2015) 'No more coalitions: Two-thirds of voters want one party in power', *The Guardian*, 26 March.

Wall, S. (2008) *A Stranger in Europe: Britain and the EU from Thatcher to Blair*, Oxford: Oxford University Press.

Watson, R., Sylvester, R. and Thomson, A. (2013) 'No, Minister: Whitehall in "worst" crisis', *The Times*, 14 January.

Webb, P. (2000) *The Modern British Party System*, London: Sage Publications.

Webb, P. (2009) 'The failings of political parties: Reality or perception?', *Representation*, 45(3): 265–275.

Webb, P. and Bale, T. (2014) 'Why do Tories defect to UKIP?', *Political Studies*, 62(4): 961–970.

Wellings, B. and Vines, E. (2015) 'Populism and sovereignty: The EU Act and the in-out referendum, 2010–2015', *Parliamentary Affairs*, 69(2): 309–326.

Wells, A. (2012), 'Polling on abortion', *UK Polling Report* (http://ukpollingreport.co.uk/blog/archives/6253).

Whiteley, P. F. (2011) 'Is the party over? The decline of party activism and membership across the democratic world', *Party Politics*, 17(1): 21–44.

Whiteley, P., Clarke, H. D., Sanders, S. and Stewart, M. C. (2013) *Affluence, Austerity, and Electoral Change in Britain*, Cambridge: Cambridge University Press.

Whiteley, P., Clarke, H. D., Sanders, D. and Stewart, M. C. (2015) 'The economic and electoral consequences of austerity policies in Britain', *Parliamentary Affairs* 68(1): 4–24.

Whiteley, P., Seyd, P. and Richardson, J. (1994) *True Blues*, Oxford: Clarendon Press.

Whiteley, P. and Seyd, P. (2002) *High-Intensity Participation: The Dynamics of Party Activism in Britain*, Ann Arbor: University of Michigan Press.

Whyte, D. (ed.) (2015) *How corrupt is Britain?*, London, Pluto.

Wintour, P. (2012) 'Ministers to be given say in civil service appraisals', *The Guardian*, 5 August.

Wintour, P. (2014) 'Ed Miliband: If you want a PM who looks good in a photo, don't vote for me', *The Guardian*, 25 July (http://www.theguardian.com/politics/2014/jul/25/ed-miliband-leadership-principle-not-personality).

Wintour, P. (2015) 'Social media disconnecting Labour from wider public, says Tristram Hunt', *The Guardian*, 8 October (http://www.theguardian.com/politics/2015/oct/08/social-media-disconnecting-labour-from-wider-public-says-tristram-hunt?CMP=Share_iOSApp_Other).

Wren-Lewis, S. and Portes, J. (2014) 'Issues in the design of fiscal policy rules', *Economics Series Working Papers* 704, University of Oxford, Department of Economics.

Wring, D. and Ward, S. (2015) 'Exit velocity: The media election', *Parliamentary Affairs*, 68 (suppl 1) (September): 224–240.

Yong, B. (2012) 'The coalition in parliament', in R. Hazell and B. Yong (eds) *The Politics of Coalition: How the Conservative–Liberal Democrat Government Works*, Oxford: Hart.

Young, H. (2003) *This Blessed Plot: Britain and Europe from Churchill to Blair*, London: Macmillan.

YouGov (2015) *YouGov/The Times Survey Results*, 19–23 November (https:// d25d2506sfb94s.cloudfront.net/cumulus_uploads/document/h15sm4vwaa/ TimesResults_151123_LabourMembers.pdf).

Index